Financial Econometrics Modeling: Market Microstructure, Factor Models and Financial Risk Measures

Also by Greg N. Gregoriou and Razvan Pascalau

FINANCIAL ECONOMETRICS MODELING: Derivatives Pricing, Hedge Funds and Term Structure Models

NONLINEAR FINANCIAL ECONOMETRICS: Markov Switching Models, Persistence and Nonlinear Cointegration

NONLINEAR FINANCIAL ECONOMETRICS: Forecasting Models, Computational and Bayesian Models

Contents

Tables

Figures

Acknowledgments

We thank Lisa von Fircks and Renee Takken at Palgrave and the team at Newgen Imaging Systems. We also thank a handful of anonymous referees for the selection of papers for this book. Neither the contributors nor the publisher is held responsible for the contents of each chapter. The contents of each chapter remain the sole responsibility of each author.

About the Editors

Greg N. Gregoriou has published 40 books, over 55 refereed publications in peer-reviewed journals and 20 book chapters since his arrival at SUNY (Plattsburgh) in August 2003. Professor Gregoriou's books have been published by John Wiley & Sons, McGraw-Hill, Elsevier-Butterworth/Heinemann, Taylor and Francis/CRC Press, Palgrave-MacMillan and Risk books. His articles have appeared in the *Journal of Portfolio Management, Journal of Futures Markets, European Journal of Operational Research, Annals of Operations Research, Computers and Operations Research* etc. Professor Gregoriou is hedge fund editor and editorial board member for the *Journal of Derivatives and Hedge Funds*, as well as editorial board member for the *Journal of Wealth Management, Journal of Risk Management in Financial Institutions, The IEB International Journal of Finance* and the *Brazilian Business Review*. A native of Montreal, Professor Gregoriou obtained his joint PhD at the University of Quebec at Montreal in Finance, which merges the resources of Montreal's four major universities (University of Quebec at Montreal, McGill University, Concordia University and HEC–Montreal). Professor Gregoriou's interests focus on hedge funds, funds of hedge funds and managed futures. He is also a member of the Curriculum Committee of the Chartered Alternative Investment Analyst Association (CAIA). He is also Research Associate at the EDHEC Business School in Nice, France.

Razvan Pascalau joined the School of Business and Economics at SUNY Plattsburgh in Fall 2008. He graduated with a PhD in Economics and MSc in Finance from the University of Alabama. He also holds an MSc in Financial and Foreign Exchange Markets from the Doctoral School of Finance and Banking in Bucharest, Romania. In 2004, he worked full-time for the Ministry of Finance in Romania as Counselor of European Integration. His primary field of interest is (applied) time-series econometrics with an emphasis on modeling nonlinear structures in macro and financial data. His research interests also include topics related to financial risk management, international finance and managerial finance/economics. He has published in *Applied Economic Letters* and the *Journal of Wealth Management*.

Notes on Contributors

David E. Allen is Professor of Finance at Edith Cowan University, Perth, Western Australia. He is the author of three books and monographs and over 70 refereed publications on a diverse range of topics covering corporate financial policy decisions, asset pricing, business economics, funds management and performance bench-marking, volatility modeling and hedging and market microstructure and liquidity.

Robert D. Brooks is Professor in the Department of Econometrics and Business Statistics at Monash University. He has published a number of papers on empirical finance including papers in the *Journal of Banking and Finance, Journal of International Money Finance* and *Emerging Markets Review*.

Bidisha Chakrabarty is Associate Professor of Finance at the John Cook Business School, Saint Louis University. She has a Ph.D. from SUNY, Buffalo, and her research interests include market microstructure, the design on trading platforms and high-frequency data modeling. She is also a faculty member at the Boeing Institute of International Business.

Lurion Demello is currently a Ph.D. student in economics at Macquarie University in Sydney, NSW. He has been a tutor in finance and economics at Curtin and Edith Cowan Universities. He has also worked as a research assistant at Edith Cowan University and at King Fahd University of Petroleum and Minerals in Saudi Arabia.

Dean Fantazzini is Associate Professor in Econometrics and Finance at the Moscow School of Economics, Moscow State University. He graduated with honours from the Department of Economics at the University of Bologna (Italy) in 1999. He obtained a Master's in Financial and Insurance Investments at the Department of Statistics, University of Bologna (Italy) in 2000 and a Ph.D. in Economics in 2006 at the Department of Economics and Quantitative Methods, University of Pavia (Italy). Before joining the Moscow School of Economics, he was Research Fellow at the Chair for Economics and Econometrics, University of Konstanz (Germany) and at the Department of Statistics and Applied Economics,

University of Pavia (Italy). He is a specialist in time-series analysis, financial econometrics and multivariate dependence in finance and economics. The author has to his credit more than 20 publications, including three monographs.

Don U.A. Galagedera is Senior Lecturer in the Department of Econometrics and Business Statistics at Monash University. He has published a number of papers on empirical finance including in the *Emerging Market Review, Journal of Multinational Financial Management* and *Quantitative Finance.*

Yuko Hashimoto is Associate Professor of Economics at Tokyo University. She was Special Appointee at the Research Department and Asia and Pacific Department of the International Monetary Fund from October 2007 to September 2008. She worked as a visiting scholar/research associate at Hong Kong Institute for Monetary Research, Japan Bank for International Cooperation and Bank of Japan. Her academic research covers international finance and exchange rate systems. She has written extensively on Asian currency-crisis contagions (co-authored with Takatoshi Ito), market microstructure of foreign exchange rates and foreign reserve accumulations in Asia. She has a PhD in Economics from the University of Tokyo.

Javed Iqbal is Lecturer in the Department of Statistics at Karachi University. He has published a number of papers on empirical finance including papers in the *Journal of Multinational Financial Management* and *International Journal of Business.*

Takatoshi Ito is Professor at the Graduate School of Economics, University of Tokyo and has taught extensively both in the United States and Japan, including at the University of Minnesota, Hitotsubashi University and Harvard University. Professor Ito also served as Senior Advisor in the Research Department, IMF (1994–1997) and as Deputy Vice-Minister for International Affairs at the Ministry of Finance, Japan (1999–2001). He is the author of many books including *The Japanese Economy, The Political Economy of the Japanese Monetary Policy* and *Financial Policy and Central Banking in Japan*, and of more than 50 academic journal articles on international finance and the Japanese economy. He was President of the Japanese Economic Association in 2004. He was a member of the Prime Minister's Council of Economic and Fiscal Policy from October 2006 to October 2008.

Maria Elvira Mancino is Full Professor of Mathematical Finance and Actuarial Sciences at the Faculty of Economics, University of Firenze (since November 2006). She has a Ph.D. in Mathematics. Her main research interests are in financial econometrics and stochastic analysis methods for finance, in particular, nonparametric volatility estimation with high-frequency data and option pricing–hedging strategies through stochastic calculus of variations.

Robert Powell has 20 years banking experience in South Africa, New Zealand and Australia. He has been involved in the development and implementation of several credit and financial analysis models in banks. He has a Ph.D. from Edith Cowan University, where he currently works as a Researcher and Senior Lecturer in banking and finance.

Erick W. Rengifo gained his Ph.D. in Economics from CORE (Université Catholique de Louvain, Belgium). His fields of research include financial econometrics, market microstructure, portfolio optimization and behavioral finance. He is Assistant Professor at the Department of Economics at Fordham University, New York. He teaches graduate courses in financial economics and financial econometrics. His recent publications are in the *Journal of Empirical Finance and Computational Statistics and Data Analysis*.

Jeroen V.K. Rombouts obtained his Ph.D. in Economics in 2004 at the Catholic University of Louvain. He is now Assistant Professor at the Institute of Applied Economics at HEC–Montreal. With respect to research, Jeroen concentrates on time-series econometrics from a parametric, non parametric, Bayesian and classical-inference point of view. All his applications focus on financial topics such as risk management and option pricing. His results are published in international journals that focus on econometrics, finance and statistics.

Antonio Rubia holds a Ph.D. in Finance from the University of Alicante, Spain. He was Visiting Scholar at the Anderson School of Management, University of California, Los Angeles. Currently, he is Associate Professor at the University of Alicante. His major research interests are in the field of financial econometrics, including volatility forecasting, nonstationary analysis and predictive regressions. Recent work in these areas has been published in the *Journal of Forecasting and Econometric Theory*.

Lidia Sanchis-Marco holds an M.S. in Quantitative Finance and Banking from the University Complutense of Madrid, Spain. Currently, she is working at the Department of Quantitative Modelling in the Caja de Ahorros del Mediterraneo (CAM), the sixth Spanish bank by size, developing and implementing credit-risk models according to the Basel 2 requirements.

Simona Sanfelici is Associate Professor of Mathematical Methods for Economics, Actuarial Sciences and Finance at the Faculty of Economics, University of Parma (since December 2005). Her background is in numerical analysis and her main research interests are volatility estimation for high-frequency financial data under market microstructure effects, option pricing, asset allocation, stochastic processes and stochastic differential equations, variational methods, numerical solutions to degenerate nonlinear PDEs and to problems in unbounded domains, the Galerkin finite element method, finite difference method and the Monte Carlo method.

Abhay Kumar Singh is a B.Tech. graduate with an MBA in Finance from the Indian Institute of Information Technology and Management Gwalior, India. He currently works as a Research Associate in the School of Accounting, Finance and Economics at Edith Cowan University.

Konstantin Tyurin is Vice-President of Financial Engineering at the Investment Technology Group (ITG). He has a Ph.D. from Yale University and worked, prior to joining ITG, as an assistant professor of Economics at Indiana University. His research interests include financial econometrics, empirical market microstructure and transaction cost analysis.

Abstracts

1. Covariance Estimation and Dynamic Asset-Allocation under Microstructure Effects via Fourier Methodology

Maria Elvira Mancino and Simona Sanfelici

We analyze the properties of different estimators of multivariate volatilities in the presence of microstructure noise, with particular focus on the Fourier estimator. This estimator is consistent in the case of asynchronous data and is robust to microstructure effects; further, we prove the positive semi-definiteness of the estimated covariance matrix. The in-sample and forecasting properties of the Fourier method are analyzed through Monte Carlo simulations. We study the economic benefit of applying the Fourier covariance estimation methodology over other estimators in the presence of market microstructure noise from the perspective of an asset-allocation decision problem. We find that using Fourier methodology yields statistically significant economic gains under strong microstructure effects.

2. Market Liquidity, Stock Characteristics and Order Cancellations: The Case of Fleeting Orders

Bidisha Chakrabarty and Konstantin Tyurin

We document stylized facts about very short-lived – fleeting – orders submitted to a limit order trading platform, and study the dynamics of fleeting order activity. Principal component analysis for the probabilities of limit order cancellation shows that most of the cross-sectional variation in limit order cancellation probabilities can be explained by the inverse of the relative tick size of the stock, which can be interpreted as the limit order book granularity for this stock. We model the nonmarketable limit order flow as a mixture of two order types; one for very short duration orders and the other for longer duration orders. By allowing the mixing probability to depend on time of the day, stock characteristics and market conditions, we find that fleeting orders are more likely to be observed at more aggressive prices and in markets characterized by higher volatility, wider bid–ask spreads and higher volumes of hidden transactions inside the spread.

3. Market Microstructure of the Foreign Exchange Markets: Evidence from the Electronic Broking System

Yuko Hashimoto and Takatoshi Ito

Availability of high-frequency exchange rate data for researchers has improved technical details and statistical accuracy of exchange rate research in recent years. Based on an event-study analysis and time series methodology, this chapter shows the intraday pattern of dollar/yen transaction activities, predictability of exchange rate movements and impact of macroeconomic news announcements on returns in minute(s) after the announcement.

4. The Intraday Analysis of Volatility, Volume and Spreads: A Review with Applications to Futures' Markets

Dean Fantazzini

The growing interest in financial markets' microstructure and the fact that financial professionals have access to huge intraday databases have made high-frequency data modeling a hot issue in recent empirical finance literature. We analyze the 12 main issues that are at stake when analyzing intraday financial time series, with particular emphasis on the joint dynamics of volatility, volume and spreads. We review the main econometric models used for volatility analysis in an intraday environment that works with non-equally spaced data and considers the whole information set provided by the market. Given the growing importance of tick-by-tick data analysis, we present an empirical application of ACD and ordered probit models to the Standard & Poor 500 and Nasdaq100 index futures' data, and we point out the advantages and disadvantages of both approaches.

5. The Consumption-Based Capital Asset-Pricing Model (CCAPM), Habit-Based Consumption and the Equity Premium in an Australian Context

David E. Allen and Lurion Demello

We adopt the habit utility specification of Campbell and Cochrane (1995) to estimate the Australian equity premium: the return on a market portfolio of equities in excess of the risk-free rate. We use Australian quarterly data for private household consumption, population, equity returns, risk-free asset returns, dividend yields and price dividend ratios taken from Datastream International™ over a 28-year period from January 1973 to June 2002 providing 118 observations. A habit utility specification is able to reproduce an equity premium that is comparable to the actual equity premium. A variance ratio test rejected the hypothesis that the variance of estimates of the habit-based Arrow–Debreu equity asset prices were the same as those based on estimates using CRRA to assess volatility or on the Hansen–Jagannathan lower bound. The habit model is able to account for more of the variability in equity prices than the CRRA model. The smooth consumption puzzle is not as severe in the Australian context when the habit model is applied to this data set. However, the habit model still does not completely resolve the equity premium puzzle in an Australian context – stock volatility is still too high compared to consumption volatility and the coefficient of risk aversion is unreasonable.

6. Testing the Lower Partial Moment Asset-Pricing Models in Emerging Markets

Javed Iqbal, Robert D. Brooks and Don U.A. Galagedera

In the literature, the multivariate tests of asset-pricing models are developed focusing on the characteristics of developed markets. For example, the pioneering Gibbons' (1982) test of the "capital asset-pricing model" (CAPM) and Harlow and Rao's (1989) test of the "mean lower partial moment" (MLPM) model both employ a "likelihood ratio test" that assumes multivariate normality of monthly asset returns. Emerging market returns are known to be non-normal and have greater predictability than those of developed markets. Considering these stylized facts, the paper extends Harlow–Rao's likelihood ratio test to develop multivariate tests robust to these features. In a sample of portfolio data from an emerging market, namely Pakistan, it is shown that multivariate tests of both CAPM and MLPM individually do not reject the restriction of the two financial models, respectively. However, a more powerful nested test of CAPM against MLPM with bootstrap p-values rejects the CAPM in favor of MLPM.

7. Asset Pricing, the Fama–French Factor Model and the Implications of Quantile-Regression Analysis

David E. Allen, Abhay Kumar Singh and Robert Powell

This chapter empirically examines the behavior of the three risk factors from the Fama–French factor model of stock returns using quantile regressions and a US data set. It draws on the work of Koenker and Basset (1982) and Koenker (2005), who developed quantile regression which features inference concerning conditional quantile functions. The study shows that the factor models do not necessarily have consistent linear relationships across the quantiles.

8. The Value of Liquidity and Trading Activity in Forecasting Downside Risk

Lidia Sanchis-Marco and Antonio Rubia

In this paper, we analyze the role played by market liquidity and trading-related variables in forecasting one-day-ahead "value-at-risk" (VaR). We use the quantile-regression methodology, as this allows us to directly study the effects of the predictive variables on the tail distribution of returns. Our empirical setting builds on the so-called CAViaR model put forward by Engle and Manganelli (2004) and extends it empirically by incorporating further information beyond volatility. The backtesting VaR analysis, based on unconditional and conditional coverage tests, reveals that liquidity and trading variables considerably enhance the VaR performance.

9. Portfolio Selection with Time-Varying Value-at-Risk

Erick W. Rengifo and Jeroen V.K. Rombouts

We propose a portfolio-selection model that maximizes expected returns subject to a time-varying value-at-risk constraint. The model allows for time-varying skewness and kurtosis of portfolio distributions estimating the model parameters by weighted maximum likelihood in an increasing-window setup. We determine the best daily investment recommendations in terms of percentage to borrow or lend and the optimal weights of the assets in a risky portfolio. An empirical application illustrates in an out-of-sample context which models are preferred from a statistical and economic point of view.

10. A Risk and Forecasting Analysis of West Texas Intermediate Prices

David E. Allen and Abhay Kumar Singh

In this chapter, we perform a two-step analysis that involves a sample of logarithmic returns formed from the daily closing prices of WTI oil prices.

In the first step we employ CAViaR, a modeling approach formulated by Engle and Manganelli in 2004 which is a "value-at-risk" (VaR) modeling technique that uses quantile regression, to forecast WTI value-at-risk. In the second step we show the applicability of "support-vector regression" for oil-price prediction and compare it with more standard time-series ARIMA modeling.

Part I

Market Microstructure Dynamics

1

Covariance Estimation and Dynamic Asset-Allocation under Microstructure Effects via Fourier Methodology

Maria Elvira Mancino and Simona Sanfelici

1.1 Introduction

The recent availability of large, high-frequency financial data sets potentially provides a rich source of information about asset-price dynamics. Specifically, nonparametric variance/covariance measures constructed by summing intra-daily return data (i.e. realized variances and covariances) have the potential to provide very accurate estimates of the underlying quadratic variation and covariation and, as a consequence, accurate estimation of betas for asset pricing, index autocorrelation and lead–lag patterns. These measures, however, have been shown to be sensitive to market microstructure noise inherent in the observed asset prices. Moreover, it is well known from Epps (1979) that the nonsynchronicity of observed data leads to a bias towards zero in correlations among stocks as the sampling frequency increases. Motivated by these difficulties, some modifications of realized covariance-type estimators have been proposed in the literature (Martens, 2004; Hayashi and Yoshida, 2005; Large, 2007; Voev and Lunde, 2007; Barndorff-Nielsen et al., 2008a; Kinnebrock and Podolskij, 2008).

A different methodology has been proposed in Malliavin and Mancino (2002), which is explicitly conceived for multivariate analysis. This method is based on Fourier analysis and does not rely on any data-synchronization procedure but employs all the available data. Therefore, from the practitioner's point of view the Fourier estimator is easy to implement as it does not require any choice of synchronization method or sampling scheme.

Most of the work concerning the comparison of the efficiency of different variance/covariance estimators considers only simple statistics such as "bias" and "mean squared error" (MSE). In this regard, some of the most recent papers (Voev and Lunde, 2007; Griffin and Oomen, 2010) investigate the properties of three covariance estimators, namely "realized covariance," "realized covariance plus lead- and lag-adjustments" and the "covariance estimator" by Hayashi and Yoshida (2005), for price observations that are subject to nonsynchronicity and contaminated by i.i.d. microstructure noise. They conclude that the ranking of the covariance estimators in terms of efficiency depends crucially on the level of microstructure noise. Gatheral and Oomen (2010) compare 20 realized variance estimators using simulated data and find that the best variance estimator is not always the one suggested by theory. The bias and MSE of the Fourier estimator of integrated volatility are computed in Mancino and Sanfelici (2008a). The authors show through an analytical and an empirical study that the Fourier estimator is nearly unaffected by market microstructure effects. The analysis is extended to the multivariate case in Mancino and Sanfelici (2008b), where both the nonsynchronicity issue and the effect of (dependent) microstructure noise are taken into account.

In this chapter, we consider a different approach to the comparison of covariance estimators in the context of a relevant economic criterion. We consider the gains offered by the Fourier estimator over other covariance measures from the perspective of an asset-allocation decision problem, following the approach of Fleming et al. (2001, 2003), Engle and Colacito (2006), Bandi et al. (2008) and De Pooter at al. (2008), who study the impact of volatility timing versus unconditional, mean-variance, efficient static asset-allocation strategies and of selecting the appropriate sampling frequency or choosing between different bias and variance reduction techniques for the realized covariance matrices. A different issue is considered by Kyj et al. (2009), who analyze the effect of conditioning techniques applied to large-dimension realized covariance matrices in the context of mean-variance portfolio optimization. A preliminary result we prove here concerns the positive semi-definiteness of the estimated covariance matrix using Fourier methodology when the "Fejer kernel" is used. This property has important consequences in the asset-allocation framework. An investor is assumed to choose his/her portfolio to minimize variance subject to required return constraints. Investors with different covariance forecasts will hold different portfolios. Correct covariance information will allow the investor to achieve lower portfolio volatility. Therefore we study the forecasting power of the Fourier estimator and of other alternative realized variance measures in the context of an important economic metric, namely the "long-run utility" of a conditional mean-variance investor rebalancing his/her portfolio each period. We show that the Fourier estimator carefully extracts information from noisy high-frequency asset-price data for the purpose of realized variance/covariance estimation and allows for nonnegligible utility gains in portfolio management.

Inspired by Fleming et al. (2001) and Bandi et al. (2008), we construct daily variance/covariance estimates using the Fourier method, the method proposed by Hayashi and Yoshida (2005), its subsampled version proposed by Voev and Lunde (2007) and the multivariate realized kernel by Barndorff-Nielsen et al. (2008a), as well as estimates obtained by using conventional (in the existing literature) 1-, 5- and 10-minute intervals and MSE-based optimally sampled continuously compounded returns for the realized measures. From each of these series we derive one-day-ahead forecasts of the variance/covariance matrix. A conditional mean-variance investor can use these forecasts to optimally rebalance his/her portfolio each period. We compare the investor's long-run utility for optimal portfolio weights constructed from each forecast. Our simulations show that the gains yielded by the Fourier methodology are statistically significant and can be economically large, although the subsampled Hayashi–Yoshida estimator and the realized covariance with one lead–lag bias correction and suitable sampling frequency can be competitive. The analysis is conducted through Monte Carlo simulations using the programming language Matlab.

The chapter is organized as follows. In Section 1.2 we describe the Fourier estimation methodology and we prove the positive semi-definiteness of the Fourier covariance matrix. In Section 1.3 we explain the asset-allocation framework and metric to evaluate the economic benefit of different covariance forecasts. Section 1.4 presents several numerical experiments to value the gains offered by Fourier estimator methodology in this context and to analyze its in-sample and forecasting properties. Section 1.5 concludes.

1.2 Some properties of the Fourier estimator

The Fourier method for estimating co-volatilities was proposed in Malliavin and Mancino (2002) considering the difficulties arising in the multivariate setting when applying the quadratic covariation theorem to the true returns data, given the nonsynchronicity of observed prices for different assets. In fact, the quadratic covariation formula is unfeasible when applied to estimate cross-volatilities because it requires synchronous observations which are not available in real situations. Being based on the integration of "all" data, the Fourier estimator does not need any adjustment to fit nonsynchronous data. We briefly recall the methodology below (see also Malliavin and Mancino, 2009).

Assume that $p(t) = (p^1(t),\ldots,p^k(t))$ are Brownian semi-martingales satisfying the following Itô stochastic differential equations

$$dp^j(t) = \sum_{i=1}^{d} \sigma_i^j(t)dW^i(t) + b^j(t)dt \quad j=1,\ldots,k, \tag{1.1}$$

where $W = (W^1,\ldots,W^d)$ are independent Brownian motions. The price process $p(t)$ is observed on a fixed time window, which can always be reduced to $[0, 2\pi]$ by a change of the origin and rescaling, and σ_*^* and b^* are adapted random processes satisfying the hypothesis

$$E\left[\int_0^{2\pi} (b^i(t))^2 dt\right] < \infty,\ E\left[\int_0^{2\pi} (\sigma_i^j(t))^4 dt\right] < \infty \quad i=1,\ldots,d,\ j=1,\ldots,k. \tag{H}$$

From the representation (1.1) we define the "volatility matrix," which in our hypothesis *depends upon time*

$$\Sigma^{ij}(t) = \sum_{r=1}^{d} \sigma_r^i(t)\sigma_r^j(t).$$

The Fourier method reconstructs $\Sigma^{**}(t)$ on $[0, 2\pi]$ using the Fourier transform of $dp^*(t)$.

The main result in Malliavin and Mancino (2009) relates the Fourier transform of Σ^{**} to the Fourier transform of the log-returns dp^*. More precisely, the following result is proved: compute the Fourier transform of dp^j for $j=1,\ldots,k$, defined for any integer z by

$$F(dp^j)(z) = \frac{1}{2\pi}\int_0^{2\pi} e^{-izt}dp^j(t)$$

and consider the Fourier transform of the cross-volatility function defined for any integer z by

$$F(\Sigma^{ij})(z) = \frac{1}{2\pi}\int_0^{2\pi} e^{-izt}\Sigma^{ij}(t)dt,$$

then the following convergence in probability holds

$$F(\Sigma^{ij})(z) = \lim_{N\to\infty} \frac{2\pi}{2N+1} \sum_{|s|\leq N} F(dp^i)(s)F(dp^j)(z-s). \tag{1.2}$$

By formula (1.2) we gather all the Fourier coefficients of the volatility matrix by means of the Fourier transform of the log-returns. Then it is possible to obtain the reconstruction of the cross-volatility functions $\Sigma^{ij}(t)$ ("instantaneous cross-volatility") from their Fourier coefficients as follows: define for $i,j = 1,2$

$\Phi^i_N(z) := F(dp^i)(z)$ for $|z| \leq 2N$ and 0 otherwise

and, for any $|z| \leq N$,

$$\Psi^{ij}_N(z) := \frac{2\pi}{2N+1} \sum_{s\in Z} \Phi^i_N(s)\Phi^j_N(z-s).$$

Finally, the Fourier–Fejer summation gives

$$\Sigma^{ij}(t) = \lim_{N\to\infty} \sum_{|z|<N} \left(1 - \tfrac{|z|}{N}\right) \Psi^{ij}_N(z) \exp(izt) \quad \text{for all } t \in (0,2\pi). \tag{1.3}$$

In Malliavin and Mancino (2009) it is proved that in the absence of microstructure noise the Fourier estimator of instantaneous cross-volatility is consistent in probability uniformly in time and converges in law to a mixture of Gaussian distributions.

As a particular case (by choosing $z = 0$ in [1.2]) we can compute the "integrated covariance," given the log-returns of stocks, as the following limit in probability

$$\int_{]0,2\pi[} \Sigma^{ij}(t)dt = \lim_{N\to\infty} \frac{(2\pi)^2}{2N+1} \sum_{|z|<N} F(dp^i)(s)F(dp^j)(-s). \tag{1.4}$$

From this convergence result we can derive a suitable estimator for the integrated covariance matrix. We assume that the price process for asset $j (j = 1,\ldots,k)$ is observed at high-frequency intra-daily times $\left\{t^j_l,\ l = 1,\ldots,n_j\right\}$, which may be different on each daily trading period normalized to length 2π. Let $\rho(n_j) := \max_{1\leq l\leq n_j-1} |t^j_l - t^j_{l+1}|$ and for any i,j let $\rho(n) := \rho(n_i) \vee \rho(n_j)$. Set

$$F(dp^j_{n_j})(s) := \frac{1}{2\pi} \sum_{l=1}^{n_j-1} \exp(-ist^j_l)\delta_{I^j_l}(p^j),$$

where $\delta_{I^j_l}(p^j) := p^j(t^j_{l+1}) - p^j(t^j_l)$. The "Fourier estimator" of the integrated covariance $\int_0^{2\pi} \Sigma^{ij}(t)dt$ is then

$$\widehat{\Sigma}^{ij}_{N,n_i,n_j} := \frac{(2\pi)^2}{2N+1} \sum_{|s|\leq N} F(dp^i_{n_i})(s)F(dp^j_{n_j})(-s)$$

$$= \sum_{u=1}^{n_i-1} \sum_{l=1}^{n_j-1} D_N(t^i_u - t^j_l)\delta_{I^i_u}(p^i)\delta_{I^j_l}(p^j), \tag{1.5}$$

where $D_N(x) = \frac{1}{2N+1} \frac{\sin[(N+1/2)x]}{\sin(x/2)}$ is the rescaled "Dirichlet kernel."

In Mancino and Sanfelici (2008b) it is proved that the Fourier covariance estimator is consistent under asynchronous observations; more precisely, we have

Theorem 1.1 *Let $\widehat{\Sigma}^{ij}_{N,n_i,n_j}$ be defined in (1.5). If $\rho(n)N \to 0$, the following convergence in probability holds*

$$\lim_{n_i,n_j,N\to\infty} \widehat{\Sigma}^{ij}_{N,n_i,n_j} = \int_0^{2\pi} \Sigma^{ij}(t)dt. \tag{1.6}$$

The construction of the estimator (1.5) can be modified by considering the Fejer summation, therefore, in the sequel we will consider the variant obtained through the "Fejer kernel"

$$\tilde{\Sigma}^{ij}_{N,n_i,n_j} := \sum_{u=1}^{n_i-1} \sum_{l=1}^{n_j-1} F_N(t^i_u - t^j_l)\delta_{I^i_u}(p^i)\delta_{I^j_l}(p^j), \tag{1.7}$$

where $F_N(x) = \left(\frac{\sin Nx}{Nx}\right)^2$. This estimator has the advantage of preserving the positivity of the covariance matrix, as it is stated by the following:

Proposition 1.2 *The Fourier estimator $\widetilde{\Sigma}_N$ is positive semi-definite.*

Proof. Using Bochner theorem (see Malliavin, 1995: 255) it suffices to prove that

$$\int_0^{\infty} \frac{\sin^2 t}{t^2} e^{itx} dt \geq 0 \quad \forall x \in \Re.$$

As the Fourier transform of $\pi\chi_{[-\frac{1}{2\pi},\frac{1}{2\pi}]}(t)$ is the function $\frac{\sin x}{x}$,

$$\int_0^{\infty} \frac{\sin^2 t}{t^2} e^{itx} dt = \pi^2 \int_0^{\infty} \chi_{[-\frac{1}{2\pi},\frac{1}{2\pi}]}(x-t)\, \chi_{[-\frac{1}{2\pi},\frac{1}{2\pi}]}(t) dt \geq 0 \quad \forall x \in \Re.$$

In the sequel we assume that the observed prices are affected by "microstructure noise" in the form

$$\tilde{p}^i(t) = p^i(t) + \eta^i(t) \quad i = 1, \ldots, k \tag{1.8}$$

where $p^i(t)$ is the efficient log-price process and $\eta^i(t)$ is the microstructure noise. We can think of $p^i(t)$ as the log-price in equilibrium, that is, the price that would prevail in the absence of market microstructure frictions. The econometrician does not observe the returns of the true return series, but the returns contaminated by market microstructure effects. Therefore, an estimator of the integrated covariance should be constructed using the contaminated returns.

We assume that the noise process is i.i.d. and the following assumptions hold:

M1. p and η are independent processes, moreover $\eta(t)$ and $\eta(s)$ are independent for $s \neq t$ and $E[\eta(t)] = 0$ for any t.
M2. $E[\eta^i(t)\eta^j(t)] = \omega_{ij} < \infty$ for any t and $i, j = 1, \ldots, k$.

A structural model like (1.8) has been proposed in Aït-Sahalia et al. (2005) and Bandi and Russell (2008). It is coherent with the model free-volatility estimation method introduced in Malliavin and Mancino (2002), but here we *explicitly* introduce microstructure effects. The instantaneous volatility process is allowed to display jumps, diurnal effects, high persistence, nonstationarities and leverage effects.

Remark 1.3 *In general the noise return moments may depend on the sampling frequency. Here we consider the simplified case where the microstructure noise displays an MA(1) structure. The MA(1) model is typically justified by bid–ask bounce effects (Roll, 1984). It is known to be a realistic approximation in decentralized markets where trades arrive in a random fashion with idiosyncratic price-setting behavior – the foreign exchange market being a valid example (see Zhang et al., 2005, Bandi and Russell, 2006 and Hansen and Lunde, 2006 for additional discussions on this point).*

The statistical properties of the Fourier estimator are studied by Mancino and Sanfelici (2008a, 2008b), who show that the bias of the covariance estimator is not affected by the presence of i.i.d. noise and the MSE does not diverge as the number of observations increases under a suitable growth condition for the number of frequencies N and the number of data n. This result is due to the following property of the Fourier estimator: the high-frequency noise is ignored by the Fourier estimator by cutting the highest frequencies. More precisely, the following result holds (see Mancino and Sanfelici, 2008b for the proof and the exact specification of the sampling considered):

Theorem 1.4 *Consider the model (1.8). Suppose that the observations of the asset prices are asynchronous and the noise process satisfies assumptions* **M1** *and* **M2**, *then if $\rho(n)N \to 0$ as $n, N \to \infty$, it holds that*

$$E\left[\left(\widehat{\sum}^{ij}_{N,n_i,n_j} - \int_0^{2\pi} \sum\nolimits^{ij}(t)dt\right)^2\right] = o(1)$$

$$+2\omega_{jj}\sum_{l=1}^{n_i-1} D_N^2\left(t_l^i - t^j_{n_j/2-1}\right)E\left[\int_{t_l^i}^{t_{l+1}^i}\sum\nolimits^{ii}(t)dt\right] + 2\omega_{ii}$$

$$\times\sum_{l=1}^{n_j/2-1} D_N^2(t^i_{n_i-1} - t_l^j)E\left[\int_{t_l^j}^{t_{l+1}^j}\sum\nolimits^{jj}(t)dt\right] + 4\omega_{jj}\omega_{ii}D_N^2\left(t^i_{n_i-1} - t^j_{n_j/2-1}\right), \quad (1.9)$$

where $o(1)$ is a term which goes to zero in probability.

We note that the term $4\omega_{jj}\omega_{ii}D_N^2(t^i_{n_i-1} - t^j_{n_j/2-1})$ converges to the constant $4\omega_{jj}\omega_{ii}$ as n, N increase at the proper rate $\rho(n)N \to 0$. In conclusion, the Fourier estimator of multivariate volatility is consistent under asynchronous observations and it is robust in the presence of i.i.d. microstructure noise. Mancino and Sanfelici (2008b) also investigate the behavior of the estimator in the presence of noise correlated with the efficient price process and show that the properties of the estimator are not substantially affected.

In the final part of this section we recall, for completeness, the definition of the other estimators of covariance which will be considered in our analysis.

The realized covariance-type estimators are based on the choice of a synchronization procedure, which gives the observation times $\{0 = \tau_1 \leq \tau_2 \leq \cdots \leq \tau_n = 2\pi\}$ for both assets. The quadratic covariation-realized covariance estimator is defined by

$$RC^{ij} := \sum_{u=1}^{n-1} \delta_u(p^i)\delta_u(p^j),$$

where $\delta_u(p^*) = p^*(\tau_{u+1}) - p^*(\tau_u)$. It is known that the realized covariance estimator is not consistent under asynchronous trading (Hayashi and Yoshida, 2005).

The realized covariance plus leads and lags estimator is defined by

$$RCLL^{ij} := \sum_{u} \sum_{h=-l}^{L} \delta_{u+h}(p^i)\delta_u(p^j). \tag{1.10}$$

The estimator (1.10) has good properties under microstructure noise contamination of the prices, but it is still not consistent for asynchronous observations. This is due to the fact that all the realized covariance-type estimators need a data-synchronization procedure, because of the definition of the quadratic covariation process. Nevertheless, the inclusion of one lead and one lag appears to provide a correction for the downward bias by nonsynchronous trading.

The estimator proposed by Hayashi and Yoshida (2005) is

$$AO^{ij}_{n_i,n_j} := \sum_{l,u} \delta_{I^i_l}(p^i)\delta_{I^j_u}(p^j)I_{(I^i_l \cap I^j_u \neq \varnothing)}, \tag{1.11}$$

where $I_{(P)} = 1$ if proposition P is true and $I_{(P)} = 0$ if proposition P is false. We will refer to this estimator as the "all-overlapping" (AO) estimator. It is unbiased in the absence of noise. However, in Griffin and Oomen (2010) and Voev and Lunde (2007) the AO estimator is proved to be inconsistent in the presence of microstructure noise, because the MSE diverges as the number of observations increases. The same happens for the realized covariance estimator.

A modification of the AO estimator which can lead to consistency is the subsampled version proposed by Voev and Lunde (2007), where the returns of the base asset span several ticks. While less efficient in the absence of noise, it reduces the variance due to noise and has a bias-reducing effect. This estimator can be written as

$$AO^{ij}_{sub} := \frac{1}{S}\sum_{s=1}^{S} AO^{ij}(s), \tag{1.12}$$

where the $AO^{ij}(s)$'s are computed on different nonoverlapping subgrids using only the skip-S returns for the base asset.

Finally, we will consider the multivariate realized kernel of Barndorff-Nielsen et al. (2008a):

$$K^{ij} := \sum_{h=-H}^{H} k\left(\frac{h}{H+1}\right)\Gamma^{ij}_h,$$

where Γ^{ij}_h is the h-th realized autocovariance of assets i and j and $k(\cdot)$ is a weight function. The synchronization procedure uses the "refresh time," that is, the first time when both posted prices are updated, setting the price of the quicker asset to its most recent value ("last-tick interpolation"). In order to reduce end effects, the asymptotic theory dictates we need to average m prices at the very beginning and end of each day. Barndorff-Nielsen et al. (2008a) prove that the estimator is consistent also in the case of covariance stationary endogenous noise, that is, dependent on the efficient price, if the realized kernel applied to the noise process converges to zero as $n \to \infty$.

1.3 Forecasting and asset allocation

We use the methodology suggested by Fleming et al. (2001) and Bandi et al. (2008) to evaluate the economic benefit of the Fourier estimator of integrated covariance in the context of an asset-allocation strategy. Specifically, we compare the utility obtained by virtue of covariance forecasts based on the Fourier estimator to the utility obtained through covariance forecasts constructed using the more familiar realized covariance and other recently proposed estimators. In the following, we adopt a notation which is common in the literature about portfolio management. It will not be difficult for the reader to match it with the one in the previous section.

Let R^f and R_{t+1} be the risk-free return and the return vector on k risky assets over a day $[t,t+1]$, respectively. Define $\mu_t = E_t[R_{t+1}]$ and $\Phi_t = E_t[(R_{t+1} - \mu_t)(R_{t+1} - \mu_t)']$ as the conditional expected value and the conditional covariance matrix of R_{t+1}. We consider a mean-variance investor who solves the problem

$$\min_{\omega_t} \omega_t' \Phi_t \omega_t,$$

subject to

$$\omega_t' \mu_t + (1 - \omega_t' \mathbf{1}_k) R^f = \mu_p,$$

where ω_t is a k-vector of portfolio weights, μ_p is a target expected return on the portfolio and $\mathbf{1}_k$ is a $k \times 1$ vector of ones. The solution to this program is

$$\omega_t = \frac{(\mu_p - R^f)\Phi_t^{-1}(\mu_t - R^f \mathbf{1}_k)}{(\mu_t - R^f \mathbf{1}_k)' \Phi_t^{-1} (\mu_t - R^f \mathbf{1}_k)}. \quad (1.13)$$

We estimate Φ_t using one-day-ahead forecasts $\hat{C}_t$ given a time series of daily covariance estimates obtained using the Fourier estimator, the realized covariance estimator, the realized covariance plus leads and lags estimator, the AO estimator, its subsampled version and the kernel estimator. The out-of-sample forecast is based on a univariate ARMA model.

Given sensible choices of R^f, μ_p and μ_t, each one-day-ahead forecast leads to the determination of a daily portfolio weight ω_t. The time series of daily portfolio weights then leads to daily portfolio returns. In order to concentrate on volatility approximation and to abstract from the issues that would be posed by expected stock-return predictability, for all times t we set the components of the vector $\mu_t = E_t[R_{t+1}]$ equal to the sample means of the returns on the risky assets over the forecasting horizon. Finally, we employ the investor's long-run mean-variance utility as a metric to evaluate the economic benefit of alternative covariance forecasts $\hat{C}_t$, that is,

$$U^* = \overline{R}^p - \frac{\lambda}{2}\frac{1}{m}\sum_{t=1}^{m}(R^p_{t+1} - \overline{R}^p)^2,$$

where $R^p_{t+1} = R^f + \omega_t'(R_{t+1} - R^f\mathbf{1}_k)$ is the return on the portfolio with estimated weights ω_t, $\overline{R}^p = \frac{1}{m}\sum_{t=1}^{m} R^p_{t+1}$ is the sample mean of the portfolio returns across $m \leq n$ days and λ is a coefficient of risk aversion.

Following Bandi et al. (2008), in order to avoid contamination induced by noisy first-moment estimation, we simply look at the variance component of $U*$, namely

$$U = \frac{\lambda}{2}\frac{1}{m}\sum_{t=1}^{m}(R^p_{t+1} - \overline{R}^p)^2, \tag{1.14}$$

(see Engle and Colacito, 2006 for further justifications of this approach). The difference between two utility estimations, say $U^A - U^B$, can be interpreted as the fee that the investor would be willing to pay to switch from covariance forecasts based on estimator A to covariance forecasts based on estimator B. In other words, $U^A - U^B$ is the utility gain that can be obtained by investing in portfolio B with the lowest variance for a given target return μ_p.

1.4 Valuing the economic benefit by simulations

In the following sections we show several numerical experiments to assess the gains offered by the Fourier estimator over other estimators in terms of in-sample and out-of-sample properties and from the perspective of an asset-allocation decision problem. In Section 1.4.1 our attention is focused mainly on covariance estimation, since in this respect effects due to both nonsynchronicity and microstructure noise become effective. As for the finite sample variance analysis of the Fourier method, we refer the reader to Mancino and Sanfelici (2008a) for in-sample statistics and to Barucci et al. (2008) for the forecasting performance. Nevertheless, the results in Sections 1.4.2, 1.4.3 and 1.4.4 can be fully justified only by considering the properties of the different estimators for both the variance and the covariance measures. Following a large literature, we simulate discrete data from the continuous time bivariate Heston model

$$
\begin{aligned}
dp^1(t) &= (\mu_1 - \sigma_1^2(t)/2)dt + \sigma_1(t)dW_1,\\
dp^2(t) &= (\mu_2 - \sigma_2^2(t)/2)dt + \sigma_2(t)dW_2\\
d\sigma_1^2(t) &= k_1(\alpha_1 - \sigma_1^2(t))dt + \gamma_1\sigma_1(t)dW_3,\\
d\sigma_2^2(t) &= k_2(\alpha_2 - \sigma_2^2(t))dt + \gamma_2\sigma_2(t)dW_4
\end{aligned}
$$

where $corr(W_1, W_2) = 0.35$, $corr(W_1, W_3) = -0.5$ and $corr(W_2, W_4) = -0.55$. The other parameters of the model are as in Zhang et al. (2005): $\mu_1 = 0.05$, $\mu_2 = 0.055$, $k_1 = 5$, $k_2 = 5.5$, $\alpha_1 = 0.05$, $\alpha_2 = 0.045$, $\gamma_1 = 0.5$, $\gamma_2 = 0.5$. The volatility parameters satisfy Feller's condition $2k\alpha \geq \gamma^2$, which makes the zero boundary unattainable by the volatility process. Moreover, we assume that the additive logarithmic noises $\eta_l^1 = \eta^1(t_l^1)$, $\eta_l^2 = \eta^2(t_l^2)$ are i.i.d. Gaussian, contemporaneously correlated and independent from p. The correlation is set to 0.5 and we assume $\omega_{ii}^{1/2} = (E[(\eta^i)^2])^{1/2} = 0, 0.002, 0.004$, that is, we consider the case of no contamination and two different levels for the standard deviation of the noise. We also consider the case of dependent noise, assuming for simplicity $\eta_l^i = \alpha[p^i(t_l^i) - p^i(t_{l-1}^i)] + \overline{\eta}_l^i$, for $i = 1, 2$ and $\overline{\eta}_l^i$ i.i.d. Gaussian. We set $\alpha = 0.1$. From the simulated data, integrated covariance estimates can be compared to the value of the true covariance quantities.

We generate (through simple Euler–Monte Carlo discretization) high-frequency, evenly sampled efficient and observed returns by simulating second-by-second return and variance paths over a daily trading period of $h = 6$ hours, for a total of 21600 observations per day. In order to simulate high-frequency unevenly sampled data we extract the observation times in such a way that the durations between observations are drawn from an exponential distribution with means $\lambda_1 = 6$ sec and $\lambda_2 = 8$ sec for the two assets, respectively. Therefore, on each trading day the processes are observed at a different, discrete unevenly spaced grid $\left\{0 = t_1^i \leq t_2^i \leq \cdots \leq t_{n_i}^i \leq 2\pi\right\}$ for any $i = 1, 2$.

For the realized covariance-type estimators we generate equally spaced continuously compounded returns using the previous tick method. We consider 1-, 5- and 10-min sampling intervals or optimally sampled realized covariances. Bandi et al. (2008) provide an approximate formula for optimal sampling, which holds for uniform synchronous data. Given our general data setting, the optimal sampling frequency can be obtained by direct minimization of the true mean squared error. In order to preserve the positive definiteness of the covariance matrices, in the asset-allocation application we use a unique sampling frequency for realized variances and covariances, given by the maximum among the three optimal sampling intervals. For the Fourier and AO estimators we employ all the available data set. In implementing the Fourier estimator $\tilde{\Sigma}^{12}_{N,n_1,n_2}$, the smallest wavelength that can be evaluated in order to avoid aliasing effects is twice the smallest distance between two consecutive prices (the "Nyquist frequency"). Nevertheless, as pointed out in the univariate case by Mancino and Sanfelici (2008a) and confirmed in the bivariate case in Mancino and Sanfelici (2008b), smaller values of N may provide better variance/covariance measures. More specifically, the optimal cutting frequencies for the various volatility measures can be obtained independently by minimizing the true MSE. Although the positivity result of Proposition 1.2 is ensured only when the same N is used for all the entries of the covariance matrix, numerical experiments show that the use of different optimal cutting frequencies N for variances and covariances still preserves positive definiteness of the covariance matrix both in the sample and in the forecasting horizon. In the same vein, with regard to the kernel estimator, a single-bandwidth parameter H should be considered for both variances and covariances. Possible choices are the minimum, the maximum or the average bandwidth. Nevertheless, in our simulations, the use of separate parameters does not spoil the positive-definiteness property of the estimator.

We employ the "flat-top Tukey–Hanning$_2$" weight function. In particular, the diagonal elements are estimated by the flat-top realized kernel of Barndorff-Nielsen et al. (2008b), which converges at a faster rate but is less robust to endogeneity and serial dependence in noise – and in rare cases it can go negative. Nevertheless, in our simulations this possibility never occurs. The jittering parameter is set to $m = 2$. Finally, in the case of the subsampled all-overlapping estimator, the diagonal elements of the covariance matrix are estimated by the "two-scale estimator" of Zhang et al. (2005), while the off-diagonal entries are given by (1.12); the optimal number of subgrids S is obtained by minimizing the MSE for the variances and the covariances separately.

1.4.1 Covariance estimation and forecast

As a first application we perform an in-sample analysis in order to shed light on the properties of the different estimators in terms of different statistics of the covariance estimates, such as bias, MSE and others. More precisely, we consider the following relative error statistics:

$$\mu = E\left[\frac{\hat{C}^{12} - \int_0^{2\pi} \Sigma^{12}(t)dt}{\int_0^{2\pi} \Sigma^{12}(t)dt}\right], \quad \text{std} = \left\{Var\left[\frac{\hat{C}^{12} - \int_0^{2\pi} \Sigma^{12}(t)dt}{\int_0^{2\pi} \Sigma^{12}(t)dt}\right]\right\}^{1/2}$$

which can be interpreted as relative bias and standard deviation of an estimator $\hat{C}^{12}$ for the covariance. The estimators have been optimized by choosing the cutting frequency N of the Fourier expansion, the parameters H and S and the sampling interval for RC^{opt} on the basis of their MSE. The results are reported in Tables 1.1 and 1.2. Within each table, entries are the values of μ, *std*, MSE and bias, using 750 Monte Carlo replications, which roughly correspond to three years. Rows correspond to the different estimators. The sampling interval for the realized covariance-type estimators is indicated as a superscript. The optimal sampling frequency for RC^{opt} is obtained by direct minimization of the true MSE of the covariance estimates and corresponds to 1 min in the absence of noise, to 1.33 min when $\omega_{ii}^{1/2} = 0.002$, to 1.67 min when $\omega_{ii}^{1/2} = 0.004$ and to 1.5 min when $\omega_{ii}^{1/2} = 0.004$ and the noise is dependent on the price. The other optimal MSE-based parameter values are listed in the tables.

When we consider covariance estimates, the most important effect to deal with is the "Epps effect." The presence of other microstructure effects represents a minor aspect in this respect. On the contrary, it may in some sense even compensate the effects due to nonsynchronicity, as we can see from the smaller MSE of the 1-min realized covariance estimator with respect to the 5-min estimator in the cases with noise. We remark that the corresponding 1-min estimator for variances is more affected by the presence of noise, since it is not compensated for by nonsynchronicity. Moreover, in the absence of noise the Epps effect hampers consistency of the realized covariance estimates, yielding an optimal MSE-based frequency of 1 min.

In fact, as with any estimator based on interpolated prices, the realized covariance-type estimators suffer from the Epps effect when trading is

Table 1.1 Relative and absolute error statistics for the in-sample covariance estimates for different estimators and no noise

Method	μ	*std*	$MSE \cdot 10^6$	$bias \cdot 10^4$	**Optimal Parameters**
$\omega_{ii} = 0$					
RC^{1min}	−0.1222	0.1659	0.6740	−4.4364	–
RC^{5min}	−0.0168	0.3855	2.4043	−0.6813	–
RC^{10min}	−0.0119	0.5451	4.7389	−0.5420	–
$RCLL^{1min}$	−0.0006	0.2898	1.3100	0.1398	–
$RCLL^{5min}$	−0.0089	0.6400	6.4182	−0.3968	–
$RCLL^{10min}$	−0.0074	0.9118	13.6689	−0.9159	–
RC^{opt}	−0.1222	0.1659	0.6740	−4.4364	1
AO	−0.0054	0.1095	0.2091	−0.1887	–
K	−0.0878	0.1471	0.4837	−3.2381	4
AO_{sub}	−0.0054	0.1095	0.2091	−0.1887	1
Fourier	−0.0864	0.1435	0.4504	−3.1598	258

Note: The optimal parameter values correspond to the sampling interval (in minutes), to the number of autocovariances H, to the number of subgrids S and to the cutting frequency N. The values of MSE and bias are multiplied by 10^6 and 10^4, respectively.

nonsynchronous. The lead–lag correction reduces such an effect, at least in terms of bias, to the disadvantage of a slightly larger MSE. Note that the lead–lag correction contrasts with the Epps effect, thus producing occasionally positive biases. In the absence of noise the best performance is achieved by the unbiased AO estimator and this justifies the optimal S value for its subsampled version which is set to 1, that is, no subsampling is needed. We remark that the optimal H value for the kernel estimator (K) is set to 4, that is, the use of some weighted autocovariance is needed to contrast with the Epps effect, differently from the variance estimation, where the optimal MSE-based H value is equal to 0, which corresponds to the realized variance. On the other hand, the presence of noise strongly affects the AO estimator. This is due to the "Poisson trading scheme" with correlated noise. In fact, the AO remains unbiased under independent noise whenever the probability of trades occurring at the same time is zero, which is not the case for Poisson arrivals. In the same fashion, the Kernel estimator provides an acceptable estimate in the absence of noise but is rapidly swamped by the presence of noise. This is quite striking, because the corresponding variance estimator provides the best estimates at the highest frequencies in the presence of noise, as already discussed in Mancino and Sanfelici (2008a). Nevertheless, Barndorff-Nielsen et al.

Table 1.2 Relative and absolute error statistics for the in-sample covariance estimates for different estimators and different noise levels

Method	μ	***std***	***MSE*** · **106**	***bias*** · **104**	**Optimal parameters**
$\omega_{ii} = 0.002$					
RC^{1min}	−0.0943	0.2196	0.8764	−3.7488	–
RC^{5min}	−0.0196	0.3982	2.7114	−0.6585	–
RC^{10min}	−0.0197	0.5433	5.3391	−0.7647	–
$RCLL^{1min}$	0.0219	0.3285	1.7748	1.0255	–
$RCLL^{5min}$	−0.0283	0.6531	7.8200	−0.7391	–
$RCLL^{10min}$	0.0010	0.9532	16.3032	0.4461	–
RC^{opt}	−0.0667	0.2399	0.9451	−2.7689	1.33
AO	0.5739	0.3560	3.6314	17.6157	–
K	0.2567	0.3148	1.0142	6.0711	1
AO_{sub}	0.0914	0.1801	0.5535	2.7958	6
Fourier	−0.0662	0.1682	0.5268	−2.5972	264
$\omega_{ii} = 0.004$					
RC^{1min}	0.0371	0.4202	1.7864	0.3246	–
RC^{5min}	0.0201	0.4737	2.7938	0.3650	–
RC^{10min}	−0.0234	0.6046	5.1154	−0.8832	–
$RCLL^{1min}$	0.0043	0.4639	2.3407	0.2869	–
$RCLL^{5min}$	−0.0265	0.7025	7.3021	−0.8156	–
$RCLL^{10min}$	0.0044	0.9278	14.0091	−0.0225	–
RC^{opt}	0.0434	0.4061	1.6860	0.8409	1.67
AO	2.3729	1.3924	52.2654	70.0999	–
K	0.1548	0.5854	3.7007	4.7011	14
AO_{sub}	0.1532	0.2338	0.9723	4.7858	16
Fourier	0.0215	0.2683	0.7881	0.4342	208
$\omega_{ii} = 0.004$ Dependent noise					
RC^{1min}	−0.0827	0.4124	1.9353	−3.2344	–
RC^{5min}	−0.0181	0.4905	3.6050	−0.9942	–
RC^{10min}	0.0211	0.6069	6.1241	0.5165	–
$RCLL^{1min}$	0.0044	0.4561	2.8256	0.3324	–
$RCLL^{5min}$	0.0353	0.7101	8.8449	1.5281	–
$RCLL^{10min}$	0.0775	0.9594	16.6870	3.2548	–
RC^{opt}	−0.0407	0.3827	1.6816	−1.4413	1.5
AO	0.1189	0.5973	3.3385	4.6671	–
K	0.0257	0.6103	3.5066	1.3703	13
AO_{sub}	0.0279	0.2247	0.6756	1.0456	9
Fourier	−0.0276	0.2549	0.8358	−1.0891	190

Note: The optimal parameter values correspond to the sampling interval (in minutes), to the number of autocovariances H, to the number of subgrids S and to the cutting frequency N. The values of MSE and bias are multiplied by 10^6 and 10^4, respectively.

(2008a) themselves, in their simulations, find out that there is not a great deal of difference between the multivariate realized (Parzen) kernel and the sparse-sampled realized covariance. Maybe this could be related to the synchronization procedure, which may result in excessive data reduction. On the contrary, both the Fourier and the subsampled AO estimator enable estimation without data loss in situations where asset prices are observed at very different frequencies. The Fourier estimator provides good covariance measures, both in terms of bias and MSE, in all the cases considered. Mancino and Sanfelici (2008b) show that this covariance estimator is asymptotically unbiased under the condition $N/n \to 0$, as $n, N \to \infty$. Its biasedness in finite samples is evident in the no-noise case. Nevertheless, the choice of a suitable MSE minimizing cutting frequency makes this estimator invariant to the inclusion of microstructure noise and it may have a bias-reduction effect as well. A good alternative is provided by the subsampled Hayashi–Yoshida estimator, which slightly outperforms Fourier in the absence of noise and becomes comparable or is sometimes overcome by the Fourier estimator for increasing noise. Therefore, we can conclude that contrary to the other estimators the Fourier covariance estimator is not much affected by the presence of noise, so that it becomes a very interesting alternative, especially when microstructure effects are particularly relevant in the available data.

Before turning to asset allocation, we evaluate the forecasting power of the different estimators. In the tradition of Mincer and Zarnowitz (1969), we regress the real daily integrated covariance over the forecasting period on one-step-ahead forecasts obtained by means of each covariance measure. More precisely, following Andersen and Bollerslev (1998), we split our samples into two parts: the first one containing 30 percent of total estimates is used as a "burn-in" period to fit a univariate AR(1) model for the estimated covariance time series and then the fitted model is used to forecast integrated covariance on the next day. The choice of the AR(1) model comes from Aït-Sahalia and Mancini (2008), who consider the univariate Heston data-generating process. The total number of out-of-sample forecasts m is equal to 525. Each time a new forecast is performed, the corresponding actual covariance measure is moved from the forecasting horizon to the first sample and the AR(1) parameters are reestimated in real time. For each time series of covariance forecasts, we project the real daily integrated covariance on day $[t, t+1]$ on a constant and the corresponding one-step-ahead forecasts $\hat{C}_t^{Fourier}$ obtained from the series of Fourier estimates and from each of the other covariance measures $\hat{C}_t$.

The regression takes the form

$$\int_t^{t+1} \Sigma^{12}(s)ds = \phi_0 + \phi_1 \hat{C}_t^{Fourier} + \phi_2 \hat{C}_t + error_t,$$

where $t = 1,2,\ldots,m$. The R^2 from these regressions provides a direct assessment of the variability in the integrated covariance that is explained by the particular estimates in the regressions. The R^2 can therefore be interpreted as a simple gauge of the degree of predictability in the volatility process and hence of the potential economic significance of the volatility forecasts. The results are reported in Tables 1.3, 1.4, 1.5 and 1.6 for different shapes and extents of noise, using a Newey–West covariance matrix. Let us start with Table 1.3 – the case with no noise. In this case, the optimally sampled realized covariance and the subsampled AO estimator reduce to the 1-min realized covariance and to the AO estimator, respectively, and hence they are omitted. When we consider a single regressor, the R^2 is the highest for the AO estimator, immediately followed by the Fourier and the kernel estimator, while $RCLL^{10min}$ explains less than five percent of the time-series variability. For none of the estimators can we reject the hypothesis that $\phi_0 = 0$ and $\phi_1 = 1$ (or $\phi_0 = 0$ and $\phi_2 = 1$) using the corresponding t tests. When we include alternative forecasts besides the Fourier estimator in the regression, the R^2 improves very little relative to the R^2 based solely on Fourier. Moreover, the coefficient estimates for ϕ_1 are generally close to unity, while for the other estimators the coefficients are not significantly different from zero at the 5 percent level. The only exceptions are given by the multiple regression on Fourier and AO forecasts, as a consequence of the higher accuracy and lower variability of AO covariance estimates, and by the multiple regression on Fourier and kernel forecasts, which has no statistically significant coefficients at the 5 percent level, although the F-statistic is 64.57. In the latter case, the explanatory powers of the explanatory variables overlap and the marginal contribution of each explanatory variable is quite small. Table 1.4 refers to the case of simultaneously correlated noise with $\omega_{ii}^{1/2} = 0.002$. In the upper panel, the highest R^2 is achieved by the Fourier estimator. For none of the estimators can we reject the hypothesis that $\phi_0 = 0$ and $\phi_1 = 1$ (or $\phi_0 = 0$ and $\phi_2 = 1$) using the corresponding t tests, except for $RCLL^{10min}$, AO and K. When we include alternative forecasts besides the Fourier estimator in the regression, the R^2 does not change much relative to the R^2 based solely on Fourier. Moreover, the coefficient estimates for ϕ_1 are generally close to unity, while for the other estimators the coefficients are not significantly different from zero at the 5 percent level. These results are in agreement with the ones of Table 1.2,

Table 1.3 OLS estimates from regressions of real integrated covariance on a constant and each covariance forecast over the forecasting horizon for $\omega_{ii} = 0$

Method	ϕ_0	ϕ_1	ϕ_2	R^2
Fourier	−0.000357	1.189359	–	0.193886
	(0.000344)	(0.102915)		
RC^{1min}	−0.000160	–	1.175931	0.189368
	(0.000326)		(0.101524)	
RC^{5min}	−0.000875	–	1.253498	0.131912
	(0.000559)		(0.155701)	
RC^{10min}	−0.000633	–	1.180675	0.095597
	(0.000718)		(0.199363)	
$RCLL^{1min}$	−0.000431	–	1.101692	0.156135
	(0.000429)		(0.115191)	
$RCLL^{5min}$	0.000481	–	0.872040	0.095959
	(0.000467)		(0.129550)	
$RCLL^{10min}$	0.000494	–	0.878594	0.042197
	(0.000693)		(0.193523)	
AO	−0.000432	–	1.115636	0.208508
	(0.000326)		(0.090716)	
K	−0.000345	–	1.189693	0.193926
	(0.000351)		(0.106857)	
$F+RC^{1min}$	−0.000367	0.763583	0.445468	0.196213
	(0.000342)	(0.388643)	(0.380325)	
$F+RC^{5min}$	−0.000523	1.120893	0.109524	0.194250
	(0.000547)	(0.205312)	(0.282750)	
$F+RC^{10min}$	−0.000494	1.156734	0.067775	0.194055
	(0.000655)	(0.141495)	(0.247474)	
$F+RCLL^{1min}$	−0.000411	1.132873	0.065820	0.194006
	(0.000422)	(0.273765)	(0.294081)	
$F+RCLL^{5min}$	−0.000536	1.117881	0.114582	0.194842
	(0.000436)	(0.142965)	(0.168453)	
$F+RCLL^{10min}$	−0.000274	1.199005	−0.031849	0.193928
	(0.000674)	(0.125196)	(0.224384)	
F + AO	−0.000407	−0.156772	1.253392	0.208696
	(0.000337)	(0.499995)	(0.449527)	
F + K	−0.000443	0.606863	0.609752	0.198321
	(0.000345)	(0.411885)	(0.409939)	

Note: Heteroskedasticity robust standard errors are listed in parenthesis.

upper panel, where the Fourier estimator provides the best covariance measures. In Table 1.5, upper panel, the highest R^2 is now achieved by the subsampled AO estimator, immediately followed by the Fourier estimator. Here $\omega_{ii}^{1/2} = 0.004$. For none of the estimators can we reject

Table 1.4 OLS estimates from regressions of real integrated covariance on a constant and each covariance forecast over the forecasting horizon for $\omega_{ii}^{1/2} = 0.002$

Method	ϕ_0	ϕ_1	ϕ_2	R^2
Fourier	−0.000332 (0.000480)	1.157481 (0.140910)	–	0.205784
RC^{1min}	−0.000289 (0.000451)	–	1.181207 (0.136302)	0.184666
RC^{5min}	−0.001000 (0.000742)	–	1.268707 (0.203271)	0.146490
RC^{10min}	−0.001001 (0.000962)	–	1.287550 (0.265957)	0.081930
$RCLL^{1min}$	−0.000318 (0.000641)	–	1.042285 (0.168353)	0.143733
$RCLL^{5min}$	0.000950 (0.000772)	–	0.760240 (0.212317)	0.050982
$RCLL^{10min}$	0.001794 (0.000502)	–	0.509909 (0.132649)	0.045674
RC^{opt}	−0.000264 (0.000511)	–	1.143849 (0.150600)	0.167163
AO	−0.002548 (0.000787)	–	1.134663 (0.145365)	0.186150
K	−0.002641 (0.000787)	–	1.451911 (0.184398)	0.178058
AO_{sub}	−0.000532 (0.000497)	–	1.051885 (0.126151)	0.200171
$F + RC^{1min}$	−0.000428 (0.000472)	0.961752 (0.296739)	0.229556 (0.285214)	0.206874
$F + RC^{5min}$	−0.000625 (0.000708)	1.043689 (0.178552)	0.184948 (0.259055)	0.206908
$F + RC^{10min}$	−0.000040 (0.000822)	1.204018 (0.172272)	−0.123419 (0.273671)	0.206204
$F + RCLL^{1min}$	−0.000168 (0.000578)	1.280343 (0.224206)	−0.152806 (0.239584)	0.206554
$F + RCLL^{5min}$	0.000073 (0.000729)	1.240015 (0.153765)	−0.187946 (0.209257)	0.207853
$F + RCLL^{10min}$	−0.000356 (0.000546)	1.152115 (0.151030)	0.010830 (0.115970)	0.205800
$F + RC^{opt}$	−0.000327 (0.000494)	1.164856 (0.251018)	−0.008959 (0.240091)	0.205786
F + AO	−0.000773 (0.000854)	0.989668 (0.284309)	0.185971 (0.284508)	0.206459
F + K	−0.000844 (0.000674)	0.991119 (0.272156)	0.249324 (0.296789)	0.206783
$F + AO_{sub}$	−0.000427 (0.000502)	0.871595 (0.416460)	0.270876 (0.381009)	0.206504

Note: Heteroskedasticity robust standard errors are listed in parenthesis.

Table 1.5 OLS estimates from regressions of real integrated covariance on a constant and each covariance forecast over the forecasting horizon for $\omega_{ii}^{1/2} = 0.004$

Method	ϕ_0	ϕ_1	ϕ_2	R^2
Fourier	0.000289	0.934596	–	0.159878
	(0.000447)	(0.127683)		
RC1min	0.000238	–	0.958151	0.097955
	(0.000594)		(0.171193)	
RC^{5min}	0.001138	–	0.708021	0.106261
	(0.000365)		(0.106029)	
RC^{10min}	0.000822	–	0.821870	0.089039
	(0.000476)		(0.138801)	
$RCLL^{1min}$	0.000152	–	0.981620	0.124185
	(0.000493)		(0.141241)	
$RCLL^{5min}$	0.000602	–	0.871933	0.068160
	(0.000617)		(0.174710)	
$RCLL^{10min}$	0.000421	–	0.899933	0.047621
	(0.000808)		(0.223244)	
RC^{opt}	0.000094	–	1.032842	0.153681
	(0.000511)		(0.142621)	
AO	−0.006479	–	0.960790	0.120925
	(0.001467)		(0.141400)	
K	0.000697	–	0.744498	0.078797
	(0.000472)		(0.120660)	
AO_{sub}	0.000027	–	0.900493	0.163476
	(0.000472)		(0.119631)	
$F+RC^{1min}$	0.000290	0.934879	−0.000472	0.159878
	(0.000584)	(0.160315)	(0.209145)	
$F+RC^{5min}$	0.000156	0.804672	0.166798	0.162685
	(0.000456)	(0.162177)	(0.125648)	
$F+RC^{10min}$	−0.000005	0.829524	0.192210	0.162727
	(0.000529)	(0.143006)	(0.148598)	
$F+RCLL^{1min}$	−0.000147	0.725966	0.330217	0.165964
	(0.000507)	(0.180395)	(0.201237)	
$F+RCLL^{5min}$	−0.000122	0.860920	0.189859	0.162116
	(0.000632)	(0.143192)	(0.188459)	
$F+RCLL^{10min}$	-0.000534	0.869414	0.288530	0.163995
	(0.000770)	(0.134253)	(0.216120)	
$F+RC^{opt}$	−0.000302	0.560295	0.531720	0.174964
	(0.000530)	(0.154433)	(0.201200)	
F+AO	−0.002963	0.712225	0.383016	0.170044
	(0.001259)	(0.142840)	(0.136055)	
F+K	0.000325	0.947413	−0.020439	0.159907
	(0.000486)	(0.166833)	(0.142337)	
$F+AO_{sub}$	−0.000017	0.430555	0.525662	0.169082
	(0.000482)	(0.231898)	(0.234024)	

Note: Heteroskedasticity robust standard errors are listed in parenthesis.

Table 1.6 OLS estimates from regressions of real integrated covariance on a constant and each covariance forecast over the forecasting horizon for $\omega_{ii}^{1/2} = 0.004$ and dependent noise

Method	ϕ_0	ϕ_1	ϕ_2	R^2
Fourier	−0.000553 (0.000360)	1.206333 (0.101268)	–	0.228107
RC^{1min}	−0.000092 (0.000433)	–	1.156458 (0.130600)	0.133428
RC^{5min}	−0.000428 (0.000619)	–	1.175871 (0.168303)	0.077988
RC^{10min}	−0.001231 (0.001051)	–	1.337231 (0.274826)	0.057487
$RCLL^{1min}$	0.000376 (0.000429)	–	0.916729 (0.112831)	0.108334
$RCLL^{5min}$	−0.000642 (0.000861)	–	1.144396 (0.219782)	0.065329
$RCLL^{10min}$	0.000993 (0.000656)	–	0.700703 (0.158462)	0.055697
RC^{opt}	−0.000223 (0.000438)	–	1.133138 (0.125219)	0.155574
AO	−0.000139 (0.000423)	–	0.950547 (0.103165)	0.132463
K	−0.000353 (0.000460)	–	1.088604 (0.122791)	0.162078
AO_{sub}	−0.000498 (0.000325)	–	1.128151 (0.084872)	0.229336
$F+RC^{1min}$	−0.000565 (0.000421)	1.200380 (0.152692)	0.009791 (0.184195)	0.228111
$F+RC^{5min}$	0.000013 (0.000556)	1.307011 (0.138977)	−0.255483 (0.208519)	0.230200
$F+RC^{10min}$	0.000415 (0.000998)	1.296528 (0.121808)	−0.339960 (0.312605)	0.230547
$F+RCLL^{1min}$	−0.000405 (0.000405)	1.275637 (0.160140)	−0.105193 (0.169297)	0.228781
$F+RCLL^{5min}$	−0.000477 (0.000769)	1.214562 (0.119038)	−0.026815 (0.231508)	0.228132
$F+RCLL^{10min}$	−0.000942 (0.000627)	1.157871 (0.123250)	0.137724 (0.187821)	0.229891
$F+RC^{opt}$	−0.000611 (0.000411)	1.164916 (0.173187)	0.058059 (0.198324)	0.228247
F + AO	−0.000712 (0.000412)	1.138820 (0.151219)	0.096222 (0.145790)	0.228750
F + K	−0.001014 (0.000446)	0.985978 (0.126263)	0.326911 (0.143702)	0.235112
$F+AO_{sub}$	−0.000689 (0.000349)	0.603879 (0.265580)	0.605376 (0.230310)	0.237252

Note: Heteroskedasticity robust standard errors are listed in parenthesis.

the hypothesis that $\phi_0 = 0$ and $\phi_1 = 1$ (or $\phi_0 = 0$ and $\phi_2 = 1$), except for RC^{5min}, AO and K. When we include alternative forecasts besides the Fourier estimator in the regression, the R^2 are generally slightly increased relative to the R^2 based solely on Fourier, but in general the coefficient ϕ_2 does not significantly differ from zero. Exceptions are given by RC^{opt}, AO and AO_{sub}. In particular, in both the regressions involving the AO estimator, the intercept ϕ_0 differs significantly from zero and, in particular, in the multiple regression it represents a large part of the true integrated volatility and in some sense it compensates for the large bias of the AO estimates. Finally, let us consider the case with noise dependent on the efficient price. In Table 1.6, upper panel, the highest R^2 is achieved by the subsampled AO estimator and by the Fourier estimator. When we include alternative forecasts besides the Fourier estimator in the regression, the R^2 slightly increases, but the coefficients ϕ_2 remain not significantly different from zero, while the coefficient estimates for ϕ_1 are generally close to unity and significant at the 5 percent level. The last two regressions in the table provide coefficients which all significantly differ from zero and the highest R^2.

Therefore, we can conclude that the above results confirm the ranking between different covariance estimators obtained in the in-sample analysis, because the higher accuracy and lower variability of Fourier and subsampled-AO covariance estimates translate into superior forecasts of future covariances.

1.4.2 Dynamic portfolio choice and economic gains

In this section, we consider the benefit of using the Fourier estimator with respect to others from the perspective of the asset-allocation problem of Section 1.3. Given any time series of daily variance/covariance estimates we split our samples of 750 days into two parts: the first one containing 30 percent of total estimates is used as a "burn-in" period, while the second one is saved for out-of-sample purposes. The out-of-sample forecast is based on univariate ARMA models, as in the previous section. More precisely, following Aït-Sahalia and Mancini (2008), the estimated series of 225 in-sample covariance matrices is used to fit univariate AR(1) models for each variance/covariance estimate separately.

The total number of out-of-sample forecasts m for each series is equal to 525. Each time a new forecast is performed, the corresponding actual variance/covariance measure is moved from the forecasting horizon to the first sample and the AR(1) parameters are reestimated in real time. Given sensible choices of R^f, μ_p and μ_t, each one-day-ahead variance/covariance forecast leads to the determination of a daily portfolio weight ω_t. The time series of daily portfolio weights then leads to daily portfolio returns and utility estimation.

We implement the criterion in (1.14) by setting R^f equal to 0.03 and considering three target μ_p values, namely 0.09, 0.12 and 0.15. In order to concentrate on volatility timing and abstract from issues related to expected stock-return predictability, for all times t we set the components of the vector $\mu_t = E_t[R_{t+1}]$ equal to the sample means of the returns on the risky assets over the forecasting horizon. For all times t, the conditional covariance matrix is computed as an out-of-sample forecast based on the different variance/covariance estimates.

We interpret the difference $U^{\hat{C}} - U^{Fourier}$ between the average utility computed on the basis of the Fourier estimator and that based on alternative estimators $\hat{C}$, as the fee that the investor would be willing to pay to switch from covariance forecasts based on estimator $\hat{C}$ to covariance forecasts based on the Fourier estimator. Tables 1.7, 1.8 and 1.9 contain the results for three levels of risk aversion and three target expected returns in the different noise scenarios considered in our analysis. We remark that, in general, the optimal sampling frequencies for the realized variances and covariances are different within each scenario, due to the different effects of microstructure noise and nonsynchronicity on the volatility measures. Therefore, in the asset-allocation application we chose to use a unique sampling frequency for realized variances and covariances, given by the maximum among the optimal sampling intervals corresponding to variances and covariances. These sampling intervals

Table 1.7 Annualized fees $U^{\hat{C}} - U^{Fourier}$ (in basis points) that a mean-variance investor would be willing to pay to switch from $\hat{C}$ to fourier estimates

Method	$\mu_p = 0.09$			$\mu_p = 0.12$			$\mu_p = 0.15$		
λ	2	7	10	2	7	10	2	7	10
RC^{1min}	1.907	6.675	9.536	4.291	15.019	21.456	7.629	26.701	38.144
RC^{5min}	0.361	1.262	1.803	0.811	2.839	4.056	1.442	5.048	7.211
RC^{10min}	1.801	6.303	9.004	4.052	14.181	20.258	7.203	25.210	36.014
$RCLL^{1min}$	−1.817	−6.359	−9.084	−4.088	−14.308	−20.439	−7.267	−25.436	−36.337
$RCLL^{5min}$	3.245	11.359	16.227	7.302	25.557	36.510	12.981	45.435	64.906
$RCLL^{10min}$	8.587	30.056	42.937	19.321	67.625	96.607	34.349	120.222	171.746
RC^{opt}	0.110	0.385	0.551	0.248	0.867	1.239	0.441	1.542	2.203
AO	5.236	18.326	26.180	11.781	41.133	58.905	20.944	73.304	104.720
K	−1.169	−4.090	−5.844	−2.630	−9.204	−13.148	−4.675	−16.362	−23.374
AO_{sub}	−0.980	−3.429	−4.898	−2.204	−7.714	−11.020	−3.918	−13.714	−19.592

Note: Case $\omega_{ii}^{1/2} = 0.002$.

Table 1.8 Annualized fees $U^{\hat{C}} - U^{Fourier}$ (in basis points) that a mean-variance investor would be willing to pay to switch from $\hat{C}$ to fourier estimates

Method	$\mu_p = 0.09$			$\mu_p = 0.12$			$\mu_p = 0.15$		
λ	2	7	10	2	7	10	2	7	10
RC^{1min}	4.673	16.355	23.364	10.514	36.799	52.570	18.691	65.420	93.457
RC^{5min}	2.803	9.811	14.015	6.307	22.074	31.535	11.212	39.243	56.061
RC^{10min}	3.505	12.268	17.526	7.887	27.603	39.433	14.020	49.072	70.103
$RCLL^{1min}$	0.747	2.613	3.733	1.680	5.880	8.399	2.986	10.452	14.932
$RCLL^{5min}$	5.145	18.009	25.727	11.577	40.520	57.886	20.582	72.036	102.909
$RCLL^{10min}$	5.247	18.363	26233	11.805	41.317	59.024	20.986	73.452	104.931
RC^{opt}	2.168	7.588	10.840	4.878	17.073	24.390	8.672	30.352	43.360
AO	4.206	14.722	21.032	9.464	33.125	47.322	16.826	58.889	84.128
K	3.088	10.808	15.440	6.948	24.318	34.740	12.352	43.232	61.760
AO_{sub}	1.644	5.755	8.221	3.700	12.948	18.497	6.577	23.018	32.883

Note: Dependent Noise, with $\omega_{ii}^{1/2} = 0.004$.

Table 1.9 Annualized fees $U^{\hat{C}} - U^{Fourier}$ (in basis points) that a mean-variance investor would be willing to pay to switch from $\hat{C}$ to fourier estimates

Method	$\mu_p = 0.09$			$\mu_p = 0.12$			$\mu_p = 0.15$		
λ	2	7	10	2	7	10	2	7	10
RC^{1min}	4.944	17.305	24.722	11.125	38.937	55.624	19.778	69.221	98.887
RC^{5min}	1.805	6.316	9.023	4.060	14.211	20.301	7.218	25.264	36.091
RC^{10min}	2.311	8.090	11.557	5.201	18.202	26.002	9.245	32.359	46.227
$RCLL^{1min}$	−0.066	−0.232	−0.332	−0.149	−0.522	−0.746	−0.265	−0.929	−1.327
$RCLL^{5min}$	2.823	9.880	14.115	6.352	22.231	31.758	11.292	39.521	56.458
$RCLL^{10min}$	4.689	16.412	23.446	10.551	36.927	52.753	18.757	65.649	93.784
RC^{opt}	1.555	5.442	7.774	3.498	12.243	17.491	6.219	21.766	31.094
AO	8.509	29.782	42.546	19.146	67.010	95.728	34.037	119.128	170.183
K	0.918	3.213	4.590	2.066	7.229	10.328	3.672	12.852	18.360
AO_{sub}	−0.417	−1.461	−2.087	−0.939	−3.287	−4.695	−1.669	−5.843	−8.347

Note: Dependent Noise, with $\omega_{ii}^{1/2} = 0.004$.

are 2.67 min when $\omega_{ii}^{1/2} = 0.002$ and 4.5 min when $\omega_{ii}^{1/2} = 0.004$. We omit the case with no noise to keep the discussion shorter.

Consider Table 1.7, corresponding to $\omega_{ii}^{1/2} = 0.002$. The entries represent the difference $U^{\hat{C}} - U^{Fourier}$ for three levels of risk aversion and three target expected returns; therefore, a positive number is evidence in favor of better performance of the Fourier estimator over $\hat{C}$. For instance, when

$\hat{C} = RC^{1min}$ and the target is 0.09, the investor would pay between 1.9 basis points (when $\lambda = 2$) and 9.5 basis points (when $\lambda = 10$) per year to use the Fourier estimator versus the RC^{1min} estimator. When the target is 0.12, the investor would pay between 4.3 basis points (when $\lambda = 2$) and 21.5 basis points (when $\lambda = 10$). Finally, when the target is 0.15, the investor would pay between 7.6 basis points (when $\lambda = 2$) and 38.1 (when $\lambda = 10$). The same investor would pay marginally less to abandon RC^{5min}. The remaining part of the table can be read similarly.[1] In the last two lines, the negative values imply a better performance of the kernel and subsampled AO estimators.

Unexpectedly, a minor but statistically significant utility loss is encountered when considering the $RCLL^{1min}$ estimator. Notice that the optimally sampled realized covariance estimator cannot achieve the same performance. In particular, this evidence partially contradicts the conclusions of De Pooter at al. (2008) about the greater effects obtainable by a careful choice of the sampling interval rather than by bias-correction procedures. When we consider the case $\omega_{ii}^{1/2} = 0.004$ of Table 1.8, all the entries are positive and we do not dwell on discussion. Finally, when we allow for dependency between noise and price (cfr. Table 1.9) we get a modest utility loss moving from the subsampled AO estimator to the Fourier estimator, according to the good in-sample properties of the former estimator for the whole covariance matrix, which translate into precise forecasts. Unexpectedly, a modest utility loss is encountered when considering the $RCLL^{1min}$ estimator as well. In all the other cases there are nonnegligible utility gains to the investor associated with the Fourier method.

1.4.3 The statistical significance of the economic gains

One way to assess the statistical significance of the economic gains resulting from Tables 1.7–1.9 is to perform the following joint statistical test. For any target $\mu_p$and any estimator, one can define alternative covariance forecasts $\hat{C}_t$ and portfolio returns $R_{t+1}^{p(\hat{C})}$. Define

$$a_{t+1}^{\hat{C}} = \left(R_{t+1}^{p(Fourier)} - \overline{R}^{p(Fourier)}\right)^2 - \left(R_{t+1}^{p(\hat{C})} - \overline{R}^{p(\hat{C})}\right)^2.$$

Assessing the statistical significance of the economic gains of the Fourier estimate over alternative forecasts can be conducted by testing whether the mean of $a_{t+1}^{\hat{C}}$ is larger than (or equal to) zero against the alternative that the mean is smaller than zero. Following Bandi et al.

(2006), for any target return $d = 0.09$, 0.12, 0.15, we define the vector

$$A^d_{t+1} = (a^{\hat{C}_1}_{t+1}, a^{\hat{C}_2}_{t+1}, \ldots, a^{\hat{C}_r}_{t+1})',$$

where the r-uple of estimators $(\hat{C}_1, \hat{C}_2, \ldots, \hat{C}_r)$ is given by $(RC^{1min}, RC^{5min}, RC^{10min})$, $(RCLL^{1min}, RCLL^{5min}, RCLL^{10min})$ and $(RC^{opt}, AO, K, AO_{sub})$ or any other combination of methods we want to test. We also stack all the methods simultaneously and check the overall ability of the Fourier method to yield a significant economic gain over the others. We write the regression model

$$A^d_{t+1} = \delta^d \mathbf{1}_r + \varepsilon_{t+1},$$

where δ^d is a scalar parameter. Series $a^{\hat{C}}_{t+1}$ associated to losses (i.e. negative values in Tables 1.7–1.9) are multiplied by -1 before regression. We perform the one-sided test H_0: $\delta^d \geq 0$, against H_A: $\delta^d < 0$. The parameter δ^d is estimated by GMM using a Bartlett HAC covariance matrix. A similar approach is used by Engle and Colacito (2006). The t-statistics of all the tests imply rejection of the null hypothesis, and hence statistical significance of the economic gains/losses at the 5 percent level. In particular, we remark that when testing the different methods altogether ($r = 10$) we get rejection of the null hypothesis even if we do not change the sign of the series $a^{\hat{C}}_{t+1}$ associated to losses. Indeed, in this case the corresponding t-statistics are -5.69, -4.44 and -7.30, respectively, revealing that on average the Fourier methodology yields a statistically significant economic gain at the 1 percent level.

1.5 Conclusion

We have analyzed the gains offered by the Fourier estimator from the perspective of an asset-allocation decision problem. The comparison is extended to realized covariance-type estimators, to lead–lag bias corrections, to the all-overlapping estimator, to its subsampled version and to the realized kernel estimator.

We show that the Fourier estimator carefully extracts information from noisy high-frequency asset-price data and allows for nonnegligible utility gains in portfolio management. Specifically, our simulations show that the gains yielded by the Fourier methodology are statistically significant and can be economically large, while only the subsampled all-overlapping estimator and, for low levels of market microstructure noise, the realized covariance with one lead–lag bias correction and suitable sampling frequency can be competitive.

Analyzing the in-sample and out-of-sample properties of different covariance measures, we find that for increasing values of microstructure noise the Fourier estimator continues to provide precise variance/covariance estimates which translate into more precise forecasts with respect to the other estimators under consideration, AO_{sub} being the only competitive method.

Note

1. As already noted by Bandi et al. (2008), the risk-aversion coefficient simply rescales the portfolio variances but does not affect the portfolio holding directly. Hence the gains/losses are monotonic in the value of this coefficient.

References

Aït-Sahalia, Y. and Mancini, L. (2008) "Out of Sample Forecasts of Quadratic Variations," *Journal of Econometrics*, 147 (1): 17–33.

Aït-t-Sahalia, Y., Mykland, P. and Zhang, L. (2005) "How Often to Sample a Continuous-Time Process in the Presence of Market Microstructure Noise," *Review of Financial Studies*, 18 (2): 351–416.

Andersen, T. and Bollerslev, T. (1998) "Answering the Skeptics: Yes, Standard Volatility Models do Provide Accurate Forecasts," *International Economic Review*, 39 (4): 885–905.

Bandi, F.M. and Russell, J.R. (2006) "Separating Market Microstructure Noise from Volatility," *Journal of Financial Economics*, 79 (3): 655–692.

Bandi, F.M. and Russell, J.R. (2008) "Microstructure Noise, Realized Variance and Optimal Sampling," *Review of Economic Studies*, 75 (2): 339–369.

Bandi, F.M., Russel, J.R. and Zhu, Y. (2008) "Using High-frequency Data in Dynamic Portfolio Choice," *Econometric Reviews*, 27 (1–3): 163–198.

Barndorff-Nielsen, O.E., Hansen, P.R., Lunde, A. and Shephard, N. (2008a) "Multivariate Realised Kernels: Consistent Positive Semi-Definite Estimators of the Covariation of Equity Prices with Noise and Non-synchronous Trading," Economics Series Working Paper No 397, University of Oxford, Oxford, United Kingdom.

Barndorff-Nielsen, O.E., Hansen, P.R., Lunde, A. and Shephard, N. (2008b) "Designing Realized Kernels to Measure the Ex-Post Variation of Equity Prices in the Presence of Noise," *Econometrica*, 76 (6): 1481–1536.

Barucci, E., Magno, D. and Mancino, M.E. (2008) "Forecasting Volatility with High Frequency Data in the Presence of Microstructure Noise," Working paper, University of Firenze, Firenze, Italy.

De Pooter, M., Martens, M. and van Dijk, D. (2008) "Predicting the Daily Covariance Matrix for S&P100 Stocks Using Intraday Data: But Which Frequency to Use?" *Econometric Reviews*, 27 (1): 199–229.

Engle, R. and Colacito, R. (2006) "Testing and Valuing Dynamic Correlations for Asset Allocation," *Journal of Business & Economic Statistics*, 24 (2): 238–253.

Epps, T. (1979) "Comovements in Stock Prices in the Very Short Run," *Journal of the American Statistical Association,* 74 (366): 291–298.

Fleming, J., Kirby, C. and Ostdiek, B. (2001) "The Economic Value of Volatility Timing," *The Journal of Finance,* LVI (1): 329–352.

Fleming, J., Kirby, C. and Ostdiek, B. (2003) "The Economic Value of Volatility Timing Using 'Realized' Volatility," *The Journal of Financial Economics,* 67 (3): 473–509.

Gatheral, J. and Oomen, R.C.A. (2010) "Zero-intelligence Realized Variance Estimation," *Finance and Stochastics,* 14 (2): 249–283.

Griffin, J.E. and Oomen, R.C.A. (2010) "Covariance Measurement in the Presence of Non-Synchronous Trading and Market Microstructure Noise," *Journal of Econometrics,* forthcoming.

Hansen, P.R. and Lunde, A. (2006) "Realized Variance and Market Microstructure Noise (with discussions)," *Journal of Business and Economic Statistics,* 24 (2): 127–218.

Hayashi, T. and Yoshida, N. (2005) "On Covariance Estimation of Nonsynchronously Observed Diffusion Processes," *Bernoulli,* 11 (2): 359–379.

Kinnebrock, S. and Podolskij, M. (2008) "An Econometric Analysis of Modulated Realized Covariance, Regression and Correlation in Noisy Diffusion Models," Unpublished paper, Oxford Financial Research Centre, Oxford, United Kingdom.

Kyj, L., Ostdiek, B. and Ensor, K. (2009) "Realized Covariance Estimation in Dynamic Portfolio Optimization," Working Paper, Quantitative Products Laboratory, Berlin, Germany.

Large, J. (2007) "Accounting for the Epps Effect: Realized Covariation, Cointegration and Common Factors," Working Paper, University of Oxford, Oxford, United Kingdom.

Malliavin, P. (1995) *Integration and Probability,* Graduate Texts in Mathematics, Springer Verlag, New York.

Malliavin, P. and Mancino, M.E. (2002) "Fourier Series Method for Measurement of Multivariate Volatilities," *Finance and Stochastics,* 6 (1): 49–61.

Malliavin, P. and Mancino, M.E. (2009) "A Fourier Transform Method for Nonparametric Estimation of Multivariate Volatility," *Annals of Statistics,* 37 (4): 1983–2010.

Mancino, M.E. and Sanfelici, S. (2008a) "Robustness of Fourier Estimator of Integrated Volatility in the Presence of Microstructure Noise," *Computational Statistics and Data Analysis,* 52 (6): 2966–2989.

Mancino, M.E. and Sanfelici, S. (2008b) "Estimating Covariance via Fourier Method in the Presence of Asynchronous Trading and Microstructure Noise," Working Paper, University of Parma, Parma, Italy.

Martens, M. (2004) "Estimating Unbiased and Precise Realized Covariances," *EFA 2004 Maastricht Meetings Paper* No. 4299, Holland.

Mincer, J. and Zarnowitz, V. (1969) "The Evaluation of Economic Forecasts," in J. Mincer (ed.), *Economic Forecasts and Expectations,* National Bureau of Economic Research, New York.

Roll, R. (1984) "A Simple Measure of the Bid-Ask Spread in an Efficient Market," *Journal of Finance,* 39 (4): 1127–1139.

Voev, V. and Lunde, A. (2007) "Integrated Covariance Estimation Using High-Frequency Data in the Presence of Noise," *Journal of Financial Econometrics,* 5 (1): 68–104.

Zhang, L., Mykland, P. and Aït-Sahalia, Y. (2005) "A Tale of Two Time Scales: Determining Integrated Volatility with Noisy High Frequency Data," *Journal of the American Statistical Association,* 100 (1): 1394–1411.

2
Market Liquidity, Stock Characteristics and Order Cancellations: The Case of Fleeting Orders

Bidisha Chakrabarty and Konstantin Tyurin

2.1 Introduction

Estimates vary by the trading platform, sample period and sample stocks, but the range of limit order "cancellations" documented in the literature is generally between one-tenth and two-thirds of all order submissions for US-based equities.[1] While this is a significant proportion of total orders submitted, the focus of both theoretical and empirical finance has been on limit order "executions." In studies that do model limit order cancellations, all cancellations are usually treated as homogenous or are characterized by a homogeneous index, which is the same for all limit orders. Such characterization often leads to misspecified distributions relative to the empirical properties exhibited by order cancellations.

Empirical observation of limit order termination shows that most of the nonmarketable limit orders submitted to the order book end up being cancelled without execution and the majority of cancelled orders get cancelled within a very short time. Figure 2.1 presents the Weibull probability plot for the survival to cancellation probability $S(t)$ as a function of limit order duration t for ask limit orders for one stock, Comcast Corporation (ticker: CMCSA), submitted via the INET ECN during regular trading hours on September 20, 2006. The limit order durations are marked on the logarithmic scale on the horizontal axis, while the monotonic double-negative logarithmic transformations $^{\sim}\ln(^{\sim}\ln(S(t)))$ of the order survival-to-cancellation function are reported on the vertical axis. The six equidistant dashed vertical lines on the graph mark the duration times (0.01, 0.1, 1, 10, 100 and 1000 seconds) since the limit order submission.[2] Between 50 and 90 percent of limit orders in each order

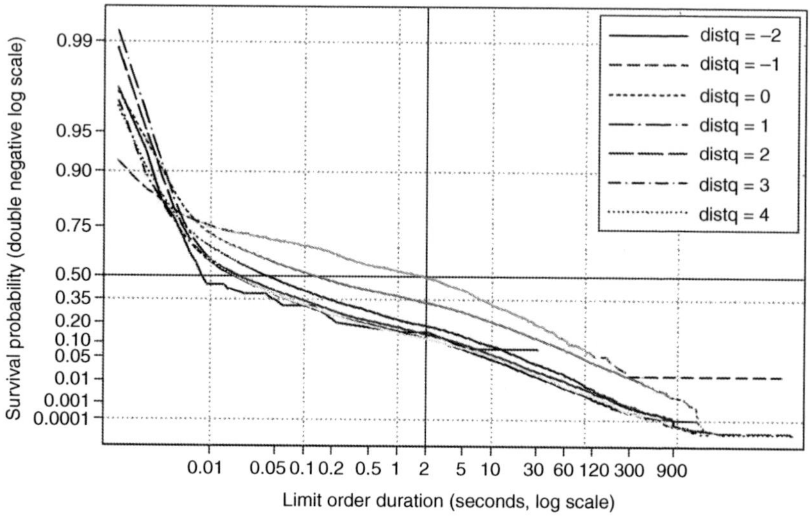

Figure 2.1 Survival to cancellation for ask limit orders on CMCSA
Note: Limit orders arriving on September 20, 2006, between 9.30 am and 4.00 pm.

aggressiveness strata (where aggressiveness is measured by the tick distance from the best same-side quote) are cancelled within two seconds after the order submission.

The four equidistant dashed horizontal lines are drawn at the levels corresponding to the survival rates 99 percent, 90 percent, 35 percent and 0.0001 percent. Those values are chosen so that the incremental distances between the horizontal lines on the double-negative logarithmic scale $\ln(\ln(0.90)/\ln(0.99)) \approx \ln(\ln(0.35)/\ln(0.90)) \approx \ln(\ln(0.0001)/\ln(0.35)) \approx \ln(10)$ are approximately equal to the incremental distances ln(10) between the consecutive vertical lines on the log-duration scale. Note that if order cancellations in any order aggressiveness category occurred according to the Weibull distribution, which is a popular choice of the survival function literature, then the survival-to-cancellation function $S(t) = \exp\tilde{(}At\beta)$ in the transformed scales would be plotted as a straight line with slope $^{\sim}\beta$. While the constancy of the Weibull parameter $0 < \beta < 1$ can be accepted if our focus is exclusively on relatively large times to cancellation, approaching the fleeting orders with the constant Weibull parameter assumption is clearly inappropriate.

While this is an illustration for one stock-day, our empirical analysis finds that this pattern is robust. Yet, apart from a recent paper by Hasbrouck and Saar (2007), these fleeting orders have not been the focus of any study. There must be reasons why traders or algorithms submit limit orders and subsequently cancel their orders within such a short period of time.

What explains such a large number of cancellations, often within milliseconds of placement? Under what market conditions do we expect this type of order to be more prevalent? For what type of stocks are fleeting orders likely to be observed more often? What types of orders are more likely to be fleeting orders? How may the prevalence of fleeting orders affect the shape and dynamics of the limit order book and the process of price discovery? These are some of the questions we answer in this study.

We find that the median time to cancellation is much shorter than the median time to execution for a given limit order. For our sample of Nasdaq 100 stocks the median ask (bid) order placed at the best quotes gets cancelled within 2.41 (2.68) seconds while the comparable time to execution is 11.33 (10.29) seconds. The highest priced stocks have a much shorter time to cancellation. Fifty per cent of limit orders placed at the best quotes for the 25 highest priced stocks are cancelled within 1.14 (1.15) seconds for ask (bid) orders. Interestingly, the time to cancellation for high priced stocks is even lower for orders placed one tick away from the best quotes on the same side, but increases once the quotes move further away (deeper inside the book). We find a nonlinear relationship between order aggressiveness and times to cancellation.

This difference in order cancellations at various price increments leads us to the next step in our analysis. Here we model order cancellations at various levels of quote aggressiveness and relate that to market conditions and stock characteristics. For this, we draw upon the literature on modeling the limit order book. For example, Lo et al. (2002) provide a set of covariates that relate the limit order book characteristics to stock characteristics. However, we find that some covariates are correlated and perform a dimension reduction to extract the principal components and find significant factor loadings for the first five components. Tick size, volatility and quote aggressiveness emerge as the main drivers of order cancellation.

The intuition we derive from the results so far is that order cancellations at various price increments in the order book are not driven linearly by the same factors. There are considerable variations in order cancellation dynamics depending on the duration of the order and the relative location of the quote vis-à-vis the best quote on the same side of the book. Any modeling attempt should reflect this important dimension of the data. We address this issue by employing a "mixture of distributions" model that specifies two distribution functions; one for cancellations at very short durations and another for the longer duration cancellations. We estimate this mixture of distributions model separately for each level of quote aggressiveness and for each stock.

The results are consistent across stocks and days. For any observed limit order submitted at the best quote, the probability that the order being classified as "fleeting" is:

- increasing with the size of the bid–ask spread;
- decreasing with the depth on the same side of the limit order book (and is most sensitive to the depth near the best quote);
- increasing with the depth on the opposite side of the book (and is generally equally sensitive to the depth near and depth further away from the best quote).

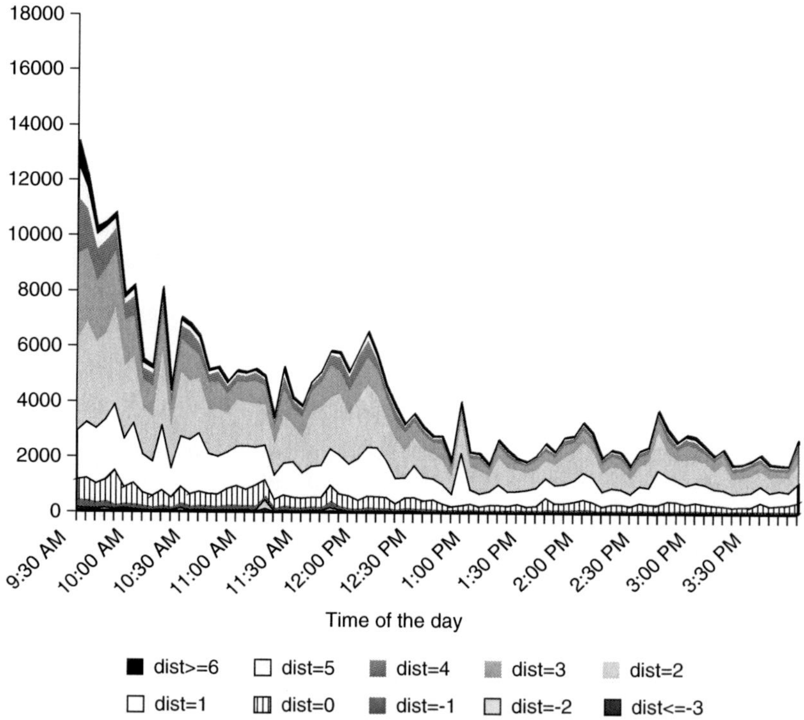

Figure 2.2 Diurnal patterns of bid limit order cancellations for CMCSA **(by tick distance from last-seller-initiated transaction price)**

Also, the estimated expected durations of "fleeting" orders (for the orders submitted at the best quotes) are relatively stable[3] across trading days, even though there is some variation day-by-day and stock-by-stock, centering around 0.1–0.2 sec. This is in contrast with the traditional two-second definition for fleeting order cut-off durations. Finally, the intensity of limit order cancellations for Comcast Corporation (ticker: CMCSA) at all-limit price levels is sensitive to time-of-the-day (Figure 2.2), attaining its highest level in the morning hours and gradually falling through the rest of the trading day. This distinct intra-day pattern of cancellation intensities appears to be robust over time and across liquid securities.

2.2 Literature review

A trader submitting an order to a limit order platform can choose between placing a marketable limit order (which gets immediate execution at the best prevailing price) or a limit order that enters the book and awaits execution. Once the order is in the book, it "risks" termination either by execution or by cancellation. Liu (2009) analyses the relation between limit order submission risk and monitoring costs borne by the trader. Limit order traders face two types of risk – first, they may be picked off due to expected price changes and second, they face the possibility of nonexecution. To mitigate these risks traders monitor the market and cancel or revise their orders as needed. But monitoring is costly, resulting in a trade-off between the cost of monitoring and the risks of limit order submission. The theoretical model predicts that if the stock is actively traded, limit order submission risks and order cancellations/revisions are positively related. Stocks with wide bid–ask spreads have lower rates of order cancellations and large capitalization stocks have lower costs of gathering information (and hence more intense monitoring of limit orders) and therefore more order revisions and cancellations. However, the empirical evidence from our study suggests that this is not the case.

Apart from stock characteristics, order characteristics are also related to the rates of cancellation. Menkhoff and Schmeling (2005) separate limit orders into those that are aggressively priced – "screen orders" – and ordinary ones that wait in the book. They find that screen orders have a much lower cancellation rate than ordinary limit orders. In a study that focuses on time to cancellation of limit orders, Eisler et al. (2007) show that to correctly model the empirical properties of a limit order book and price formation therein, it is essential to specify a correct functional form for the cancellation process. They find that the transaction time, the first passage time, the time to (first) fill and time to cancel are best described as asymptotically power-law distributed. In contrast, Challet and Stinchcombe (2003) show that for four highly liquid stocks on the Island ECN's order book,[4] the distribution for cancelled orders seems to have an algebraic decay with particular numerical values of the exponent.[5] Rosu (2009) proposes a continuous time model of price formation and shows that to generate results that are close to those observed in the actual data, incorporating order cancellations is important.

While all the above studies tangentially focus on order cancellation, to our knowledge the first paper to actually make the distinction between order cancellations at longer durations and "fleeting order" cancellations is Hasbrouck and Saar (2002). In that version of their paper they use order data from the Island ECN and find that close to 28 percent of all visible submitted orders are cancelled within two seconds. They coin the term "fleeting orders" to describe these very short-lived orders. Although it is the first to describe fleeting orders, the 2002 study does not focus on these orders (in fact, these are eliminated from the sample in their subsequent analysis).

Hasbrouck and Saar (2007) present a contemporaneous working paper that is most closely related to ours. They offer three hypotheses to explain the prevalence of fleeting orders. The "chasing hypothesis" argues that fleeting orders arise as traders chase prices that are moving away by cancelling the existing orders and repricing their orders. The "search hypothesis" argues that fleeting orders are used to probe for hidden liquidity in the book. The "cost of immediacy hypothesis" states that fleeting orders arise when existing limit orders are cancelled, to be resubmitted as marketable orders.

While Hasbrouck and Saar (2007) document interesting results at the aggregate level, we show that at the disaggregate level the dynamics are not a linear decomposition of the aggregate statistics. For example, we show that for most stocks the probability of cancellation of orders submitted at best quotes is lower than the probability of cancellation of orders at the nearest ticks above and below the best quotes, and that this is true for both bid and ask sides. In other words, a limit order submitted at the best quotes is less likely to be fleeting than limit orders submitted at the neighboring ticks. However, for some stocks this trough in the probability of cancellation is observed for orders submitted one tick within the bid–ask spread. This is usually the case when stocks have a wider bid–ask spread and higher price.

The probabilities of cancellation within two seconds tend to be almost uniformly higher than those reported by Hasbrouck and Saar (2007). This is not surprising since their sample period of October 2004 is two years older than ours. We document systematic differences in the shapes of cancellation probabilities across alternative levels of order aggressiveness and across stocks. These and other results discussed in the rest of the chapter show that there are various facets of these fleeting orders that could warrant further investigation.

2.3 Data sample characteristics

Our sample comprises of the Nasdaq 100 stocks and the sample period is July–December 2006. We use the first three months (63 trading days) for estimation purposes and the next three for out-of-sample robustness checks. Our data comes from several sources. We use limit order placement and cancellation data from the INET ECN. The ITCH® data feed from INET provides anonymous histories for all limit orders – when the orders were placed, modified, cancelled and executed – for all stocks that are traded on that platform. We use CRSP data for our firm-specific covariates and TAQ data from the NYSE to build the "National Best Bid and Offer" (NBBO) series of spreads and depths for our sample stocks. Additionally, we use earnings announcements data from I/B/E/S to partition our sample days into anticipated news days versus nonnews days in order to check the robustness of our estimates.

2.3.1 Firm-specific summary statistics

Table 2.1 shows some basic characteristics of our sample firms by price deciles. Close to half of the 100 stocks (48 stocks) have INET spread between one and two cents. The spread is even tighter when we look at the NBBO spreads for the sample stocks, as shown in Table 2.2. With close to ten million dollars, Google Inc. has the highest five-minute dollar trading volume, while the vast majority of the sample (80 percent) has under one-million-dollar's worth of trading volume in the average five minutes.

Table 2.2 shows some summary statistics of the sample, aggregated by stock-days. The value weighted average share price is $39.37, which is much higher than the average share price for the Nasdaq universe of stocks. The lowest priced share in our sample is JDS Uniphase, whose average price over the sample period is $2.23 (Table 2.1) but because of its relatively higher market value, the value weighted minimum price in our sample is about $4. Google Inc. is the highest priced share in our sample. As expected, the Nasdaq 100 firms are all high market-capitalization firms, so the mean market value of equity is 18.1 billion,

Table 2.1 Price deciles of NASDAQ 100 stocks

	Ticker	JDSU	SUNW	SIRI	JNPR	FLEX	TLAB	BEAS	XMSR	ATVI	DISCA
Decile	Price ($)	2.23	4.53	4.02	14.42	11.34	10.39	12.78	12.45	12.74	13.88
1	INET sprd. ¢	1.01	1.01	1.01	1.10	1.11	1.11	1.12	1.16	1.26	1.46
	5′ range ¢	1.2	1.6	1.3	3.8	2.7	3.7	3.7	4.3	3.7	2.5
	5′ INET $ vol.	0.29	0.85	0.49	0.55	0.23	0.40	0.45	0.42	0.24	0.06
	Ticker	INTC	ORCL	AMAT	SYMC	ALTR	CDNS	CHKP	APCC	EXPE	URBN
Decile 2	Price ($)	18.57	15.52	16.23	17.71	17.98	16.30	17.73	17.96	14.78	15.83
2	INET sprd. ¢	1.02	1.02	1.02	1.09	1.10	1.43	1.48	1.51	1.51	1.57
	5′ range ¢	4.4	3.5	4.1	3.9	5.0	3.7	4.0	4.2	3.3	5.2
	5′ INET $ vol.	5.49	3.26	1.78	1.01	0.40	0.15	0.16	0.17	0.13	0.23
	Ticker	CSCO	DELL	ATYT	XLNX	VRSN	SPLS	LBTYA	MRVL	CMVT	RHAT
Decile 3	Price ($)	20.06	22.02	19.24	21.38	19.75	23.17	23.27	22.07	20.02	23.25
3	INET sprd. ¢	1.02	1.07	1.07	1.12	1.34	1.35	1.47	1.63	1.63	1.81
	5′ range ¢	4.4	5.7	3.1	6.8	4.8	5.1	3.4	10.0	5.5	7.5
	5′ INET $ vol.	4.65	2.27	0.96	0.73	0.31	0.45	0.15	0.95	0.24	0.43
	Ticker	MSFT	EBAY	BRCM	NVDA	IACI	MEDI	PTEN	ROST	PETM	NTLI
Decile 4	Price ($)	25.05	26.20	26.95	24.27	26.68	26.98	25.90	24.79	24.71	24.40
4	INET sprd. ¢	1.02	1.12	1.23	1.41	1.93	1.97	2.06	2.27	2.29	2.85
	5′ range ¢	3.9	8.1	11.1	9.7	5.1	6.2	8.7	5.1	5.0	6.5
	5′ INET $ vol.	6.14	2.24	2.02	1.04	0.23	0.27	0.36	0.14	0.13	0.22
	Ticker	YHOO	SBUX	LLTC	AMZN	MXIM	ADBE	DISH	NTAP	ERIC	INTU
Decile 5	Price ($)	28.50	32.18	32.28	30.26	29.22	31.72	32.31	32.07	31.98	31.93
5	INET sprd. ¢	1.10	1.30	1.41	1.43	1.48	1.62	2.01	2.05	2.06	2.29
	5′ range ¢	6.9	7.4	8.7	8.5	9.0	9.2	6.2	9.6	4.7	7.8
	5′ INET $ vol.	2.41	1.09	0.60	0.97	0.69	0.68	0.32	0.56	0.17	0.35
	Ticker	CMCSA	BBBY	TEVA	MCHP	PAYX	CTXS	BMET	PDCO	ADSK	XRAY
Decile 6	Price ($)	34.03	34.29	33.76	32.92	35.86	32.67	32.54	32.80	33.33	36.18
6	INET sprd. ¢	1.05	1.41	1.69	2.04	2.21	2.52	2.52	2.54	2.85	2.86
	5′ range ¢	5.7	6.2	7.2	8.3	6.3	10.1	6.9	5.4	9.4	5.2
	5′ INET $ vol.	1.64	0.54	0.54	0.31	0.30	0.43	0.24	0.11	0.38	0.10
	Ticker	QCOM	CTAS	LNCR	LRCX	FAST	AKAM	CKFR	MNST	JOYG	MICC
Decile 7	Price ($)	36.37	37.09	36.36	41.43	36.53	38.21	40.98	38.67	39.26	37.08
7	INET sprd. ¢	1.32	2.75	2.80	3.59	3.68	3.97	4.06	4.24	4.91	5.02
	5′ range ¢	11.2	6.8	5.4	14.6	9.1	15.6	10.2	11.6	18.0	6.6
	5′ INET $ vol.	2.58	0.15	0.12	0.57	0.17	0.70	0.26	0.28	0.49	0.08
	Ticker	KLAC	BIIB	FISV	ERTS	APOL	CELG	AMLN	SEPR	EXPD	CHRW
Decile 8	Price ($)	42.34	42.73	44.52	48.62	47.85	43.98	46.00	47.97	44.63	46.27
8	INET sprd. ¢	1.70	2.41	2.54	2.91	3.59	3.92	4.06	4.42	4.45	5.02
	5′ range ¢	13.3	11.1	7.3	12.6	9.9	14.4	13.5	13.9	14.5	14.4
	5′ INET $ vol.	0.90	0.51	0.23	0.64	0.25	0.62	0.34	0.40	0.36	0.26
	Ticker	AAPL	AMGN	SNDK	COST	GILD	GENZ	WFMI	LAMR	CDWC	NIHD
Decile 9	Price ($)	66.41	67.38	49.27	50.97	61.59	65.82	56.54	51.25	57.42	53.44
9	INET sprd. ¢	1.37	1.87	2.07	2.26	2.76	3.86	4.01	4.29	4.70	6.01
	5′ range ¢	18.9	13.6	17.7	10.5	14.8	14.6	13.1	8.6	11.3	15.3
	5′ INET $ vol.	8.43	2.03	2.18	0.92	0.93	0.58	0.45	0.16	0.22	0.31

Continued

Table 2.1 Continued

	Ticker	RIMM	PCAR	SIAL	ESRX	CTSH	WYNN	GRMN	SHLD	GOOG	ISRG
Decile 10	Price ($)	74.74	67.41	71.63	78.16	68.01	71.08	74.22	148.00	382.92	103.21
10	INET sprd. ¢	4.04	5.11	5.46	5.76	6.34	7.41	9.04	10.76	12.84	14.27
	5′ range ¢	20.9	14.2	10.2	16.0	17.6	19.7	25.6	34.2	78.0	32.3
	5′ INET $ vol.	1.61	0.34	0.13	0.50	0.39	0.43	0.64	1.15	9.97	0.45

Note: This table presents some disaggregated stock-specific summary measures for the Nasdaq 100 stocks trading on the INET ECN between July and September, 2006. We restrict the trading time to the exchange open hours (9.30–16.00 EST). Stocks are sorted by INET transaction price and placed into ten deciles, with Decile 1 being the lowest priced and Decile 10 being the highest priced. INET spd. is the spread on the INET trading platform, which is usually a little higher than NBBO spreads since INET does not route orders away to markets displaying better prices. 5′ range is the difference between the highest and lowest INET trade price in five-minute increments, aggregated over the 84 five-minute intervals in each trading day, over the 63 trading days. 5′ INET $ vol. is INET trading volume, in millions of US dollars over each such five-minute interval.

with the lowest and highest being 2.8 and 234.4 billion, respectively, for JDSU and GOOG. Since our sample is a group of high-volume stocks, we expected that the spreads for these stocks would be very tight – and that is also what our data show. The average NBBO spread is just over two cents, which is about 0.06 percent of price. INET spread is slightly higher – close to 3 cents – which is 0.07 percent of price.

2.3.2 Times to order executions and cancellations

We approach the issue of characterizing fleeting orders in two alternative ways. First we fix the probability of cancellation or execution (to one) and examine, respectively, the time it takes for a given fraction of our sample stocks (25 percent, 50 percent etc.) to be executed or cancelled. Alternatively, we fix the time to cancellation for fractions of sample stocks (grouped by price deciles) and estimate the probabilities of cancellation at various levels of quote aggressiveness within the fixed time. Below we describe the first approach to calculate the times to execution and cancellation.

We stratify limit orders by their quote aggressiveness and define quote aggressiveness as in the previous literature, according to the position of the limit order price on the pricing grid relative to the best quote available on the same side of the book at the limit order arrival time.

Table 2.3 shows the median times to execution (Panel A) and cancellation (Panel B). Pa_i (Pb_i) denotes the category of ask (bid) limit orders priced one tick better than the current best ask (bid) price. Pa_0 (Pb_0) denotes the category of ask (bid) orders with a limit price equal to the

Table 2.2 Cross-sectional summary statistics of daily averages

			Distribution				
	Mean	**St Dev**	**Min**	**25th %**	**Median**	**75th %**	**Max**
Value weighted average share price ($)	39.37	41.40	4.03	21.23	32.60	44.98	391.82
Market value of equity ('000,000 $)	18151	30837	2888	4895	7954	14956	234445
Average daily volume ('000 shares)	8171	12616	368	1749	3307	7889	64343
Average daily INET volume ('000 shares)	2639	4224	136	572	1052	2619	22846
$ Quoted spread (NBBO)	0.022	0.018	0.010	0.011	0.015	0.029	0.124
% Quoted spread (NBBO)	0.06	0.03	0.02	0.04	0.05	0.07	0.23
$ Quoted spread (INET)	0.028	0.024	0.010	0.013	0.020	0.037	0.143
% Quoted spread (INET)	0.07	0.05	0.02	0.05	0.06	0.08	0.45
Average depth at NBO ('00 shares)	82	289	2.78	5.51	9.50	25.1	1957
Average depth at NBB ('00 shares)	83	292	2.87	5.66	9.02	24.7	1955
Average depth at Best Ask (INET)	74	278	2.07	4.40	7.25	17.8	1984
Average depth at Best Bid (INET)	73	278	2.14	4.58	6.89	17.3	1983
Average depth at best ask to best ask+4 (INET)	359	1355	5.07	14.3	31.7	86.7	9511
Average depth at best bid to best bid-4 (INET)	357	1351	5.36	16.0	29.7	88.0	9445

Note: This table presents the cross-sectional summary statistics of our sample stocks at the daily level. Measures of interest are first averaged over the 63 trading days for each stock and then averaged across stocks. Value weighted share price in the NBBO trade price is weighted by the market value of equity. Both NBBO and INET spreads and depths for the same stocks are shown for comparison purposes. Additionally, we also report cumulative depth on the INET limit order book up to four ticks away from the best quote at any given time.

Table 2.3 Times to execution and cancellation for limit orders

	Sample median	Standard deviation	Grouping by price: 1st Quartile	2nd Quartile	3rd Quartile	4th Quartile
Panel A: Times to execution						
medtime(Pai)	2.26	5.19	4.30	1.62	2.07	2.16
medtime(Pa0)	11.33	36.81	25.81	11.49	8.34	6.70
medtime(Pa1)	25.29	207.12	74.46	29.96	18.12	14.16
medtime(Pbi)	2.18	4.16	3.68	1.28	2.09	2.00
medtime(Pb0)	10.29	30.02	25.13	10.13	7.83	6.24
medtime(Pb1)	25.71	217.99	76.23	30.29	19.47	13.49
Panel B: Times to cancellation						
medtime(Pai)	1.11	96.13	6.02	1.11	0.81	0.41
medtime(Pa0)	2.41	3.73	7.49	2.71	2.13	1.14
medtime(Pa1)	2.19	21.26	7.57	2.34	1.71	0.91
medtime(Pa2)	4.72	47.79	21.52	4.88	3.56	1.85
medtime(Pa3)	10.42	57.05	24.88	12.98	8.29	4.01
medtime(Pa4)	10.73	21.73	30.89	12.34	6.79	3.57
medtime(Pbi)	1.01	60.14	5.50	1.14	0.78	0.40
medtime(Pb0)	2.68	3.83	8.26	2.82	1.94	1.15
medtime(Pb1)	2.25	28.25	10.87	2.91	1.71	0.89
medtime(Pb2)	4.62	46.58	24.44	5.02	3.65	1.65
medtime(Pb3)	10.61	43.34	28.57	14.03	8.22	3.99
medtime(Pb4)	10.22	24.00	32.92	13.42	7.04	4.12
Panel C: Sample characteristics						
Price	44.19	50.73	22.19	38.49	53.01	78.27
Day range	0.97	1.18	0.47	0.80	1.21	1.86
Percentage daily range	2.22	0.44	2.23	2.17	2.36	2.20

Note: This table presents the times to execution and the times to cancellation for orders at various levels of quote aggressiveness. Median times to execution are shown in Panel A and cancellation in Panel B. Panel C presents some summary characteristics of the stocks to facilitate comparison of executions and cancellations across stock-specific characteristics. Pa_i (Pb_i) denotes an ask (bid) limit order arriving with a limit price which is one tick better than the current best ask (bid) price. Pa_0 (Pb_0) is an ask (bid) limit order priced the same as the existing best quote, Pa_1 (Pb_1) is placed one tick away from the prevailing best quote and so on. Apart from sample medians, stocks are also grouped by price quartiles, where quartile 1 represents the lowest priced 25 stocks and quartile 4 represents the highest priced 25 stocks.

existing best ask (bid) quote, Pa_1 (Pb_1) denotes the category of limit orders placed one tick away from the prevailing best quote and so on.

Comparing Panels A and B immediately makes it apparent that the times to execution are much larger than times to cancellation for *all* levels of quote aggressiveness. The median price-improving order tends to be cancelled (1.11 seconds for ask and 1.01 seconds for bid orders) twice as fast as it is executed (2.26 seconds for ask and 2.18 seconds for bid orders). This symmetry across ask and bid sides of the order book persists for all levels of quote aggressiveness. Focusing on times to cancellation, we note that price-improving limit orders are cancelled twice as fast as orders placed at the existing best quotes. As we move deeper into the limit order book, away from the best quotes, the speed of cancellation decreases significantly.

2.3.3 Probabilities of order cancellations by quote aggressiveness

Our second approach to examining the characteristics of fleeting orders involves estimating the probability of cancellation given a fixed time since order placement. We assume that for each order there are two competing risks – execution and cancellation. If there is zero risk of cancellation, the probability of execution by a given time, say X seconds after submission, would be given by the Kaplan–Meier estimate of the survival function to execution at X seconds. One way to interpret this is as the fraction of all executed orders that were executed within X seconds, but adjusted for cancellations, which are treated as independent censoring events. Similarly, assuming there is zero risk of execution, the probability of cancellation by X seconds after submission would be given by the Kaplan–Meier estimate of the survival function to cancellation at X seconds (the fraction of all cancelled orders that happened to be cancelled within X seconds, adjusted for executions, which are now treated as independent censoring events). So the probability of cancellation (or execution) would be estimated as one minus the Kaplan–Meier estimator of the survival function to cancellations (or to executions, respectively) evaluated at the duration of interest, in our case two seconds, half a second and 100 milliseconds.

Table 2.4 shows the probabilities of order cancellation at various aggressiveness levels. It is clear that the probability of order cancellation at all levels of quote aggressiveness is higher for higher priced stocks. For example, for orders placed at any level of aggressiveness there is more than a 60 percent chance of cancellation within two seconds of order placement for stocks that are in the highest price decile. However, the probability of cancellation within two seconds varies between 24 percent and 47 percent for the lowest price decile stocks, depending on where the limit order arrived on the pricing grid. Similarly, the probability of cancellation varies with the position of the limit order for other cut-off

Table 2.4 Probability of order cancellations at various levels of quote aggressiveness

		$P_{lim}=P_{ii}$	$P_{lim}=P_i$	$P_{lim}=P_0$	$P_{lim}=P_1$	$P_{lim}=P_2$	$P_{lim}=P_3$	$P_{lim}=P_4$	$P_{lim}=P_5$
		Probability of cancellation in less than 2 seconds							
	Decile 1	0.47[a]	0.24	0.24	0.35	0.26	0.26	0.28	0.28
	Decile 3	0.57[b]	0.41	0.41	0.47	0.44	0.41	0.41	0.40
Ask	Decile 5	0.59	0.56	0.48	0.52	0.52	0.45	0.46	0.43
Side	Decile 7	0.55	0.58	0.46	0.55	0.54	0.45	0.48	0.46
	Decile 9	0.60	0.60	0.54	0.59	0.58	0.52	0.53	0.53
	Decile 10	0.68	0.70	0.61	0.68	0.67	0.63	0.62	0.60
	Decile 1	0.47[a]	0.27	0.23	0.28	0.24	0.25	0.27	0.27
	Decile 3	0.55[b]	0.42	0.40	0.45	0.43	0.41	0.41	0.40
Bid	Decile 5	0.59	0.57	0.47	0.51	0.50	0.45	0.45	0.44
Side	Decile 7	0.55	0.59	0.46	0.55	0.53	0.45	0.48	0.45
	Decile 9	0.61	0.62	0.54	0.59	0.57	0.52	0.53	0.52
	Decile 10	0.69	0.70	0.62	0.69	0.68	0.63	0.63	0.61
		Probability of cancellation in less than 0.5 seconds							
	Decile 1	0.36[a]	0.19	0.16	0.25	0.18	0.19	0.21	0.22
	Decile 3	0.44[b]	0.33	0.29	0.33	0.33	0.30	0.30	0.31
Ask	Decile 5	0.47	0.45	0.35	0.37	0.39	0.33	0.34	0.33
Side	Decile 7	0.41	0.46	0.32	0.39	0.40	0.33	0.36	0.35
	Decile 9	0.47	0.47	0.38	0.41	0.42	0.38	0.39	0.40
	Decile 10	0.55	0.58	0.47	0.52	0.53	0.49	0.49	0.48
	Decile 1	0.37[a]	0.22	0.15	0.20	0.17	0.18	0.21	0.21
	Decile 3	0.44[b]	0.34	0.29	0.33	0.32	0.30	0.31	0.31
Bid	Decile 5	0.48	0.46	0.34	0.36	0.38	0.33	0.34	0.34
Side	Decile 7	0.42	0.47	0.32	0.40	0.39	0.33	0.36	0.35
	Decile 9	0.48	0.49	0.38	0.42	0.41	0.38	0.39	0.39
	Decile 10	0.56	0.58	0.47	0.53	0.54	0.49	0.50	0.48
		Probability of cancellation in less than 100 milliseconds							
	Decile 1	0.24[a]	0.15	0.10	0.13	0.12	0.13	0.16	0.17
	Decile 3	0.30[b]	0.24	0.19	0.20	0.22	0.20	0.21	0.23
Ask	Decile 5	0.33	0.35	0.23	0.23	0.27	0.23	0.23	0.24
Side	Decile 7	0.26	0.32	0.19	0.25	0.25	0.22	0.25	0.25
	Decile 9	0.31	0.33	0.25	0.26	0.27	0.25	0.26	0.28
	Decile 10	0.38	0.41	0.32	0.36	0.37	0.33	0.35	0.34
	Decile 1	0.25[a]	0.16	0.10	0.12	0.11	0.12	0.15	0.16
	Decile 3	0.31[b]	0.25	0.19	0.21	0.21	0.20	0.21	0.22

Continued

Table 2.4 Continued

		$P_{lim} = P_{ii}$	$P_{lim} = P_i$	$P_{lim} = P_0$	$P_{lim} = P_1$	$P_{lim} = P_2$	$P_{lim} = P_3$	$P_{lim} = P_4$	$P_{lim} = P_5$
Bid	Decile 5	0.35	0.36	0.23	0.23	0.26	0.23	0.24	0.25
Side	Decile 7	0.27	0.33	0.19	0.24	0.25	0.22	0.25	0.25
	Decile 9	0.32	0.35	0.24	0.26	0.27	0.25	0.26	0.27
	Decile 10	0.39	0.41	0.31	0.36	0.38	0.34	0.35	0.35

Notes: This table presents the probabilities of cancellation for orders at various levels of aggressiveness. Assuming there is zero risk of execution, the probability of order cancellation within time T after the order arrival is given by the Kaplan–Meier estimate of the survival function to cancellation at duration T. Then the probability of cancellation within time T since the order submission is estimated as 1 minus the Kaplan–Meier estimate of the survival function to cancellation (execution) evaluated at duration T, where $T = 2$ sec, 0.5 sec or 100 milliseconds. P_{ii} (P_i) denotes the limit order aggressiveness category that includes all arriving orders with the limit price two (one) tick better than the concurrent best quote on the same side. P_0 is the limit order price equal to the existing best quote on the same side, while P_k is the limit order price that is k ticks inside the limit order book, away from the prevailing same-side best quote. To conserve space, we report the probability of cancellation summaries for stocks in six of the ten price deciles.

[a] Due to insufficient # of observations for 6 stocks in decile 1, this probability is based on data for 4 decile 1 stocks.

[b] Due to insufficient # of observations for 3 stocks in decile 3, this probability is based on data for 7 decile 3 stocks.

duration levels. For example, the probability to cancellation within half a second varies between 47 percent and 58 percent for highest decile stocks and between 15 percent and 37 percent for the lowest decile stocks.

When we reduce the order duration to truly *fleeting* level – 100 milliseconds – the results are more interesting. There is a better than 30 percent chance that orders placed at the best quotes will get cancelled within 100 milliseconds for the stocks in the highest price decile. When we look at orders that improve price by one tick the probability of cancellation increases to over 40 percent. At all levels of quote aggressiveness the probability that an order will be cancelled within 100 milliseconds is more than twice for the highest decile stocks, compared to the lowest decile ones.

Figures 2.3 and 2.4 show the limit order cancellation dynamics at other time increments for various levels of quote aggressiveness. While the probability of limit order execution increases monotonically with order aggressiveness across price deciles and cut-off duration levels (Figure 2.3), the probability of cancellation exhibits a non-monotone and potentially complicated relationship (Figure 2.4). Overall, our results so far make it clear that order cancellation times depend on stock-specific characteristics such as its price and market capitalization, as well as the market

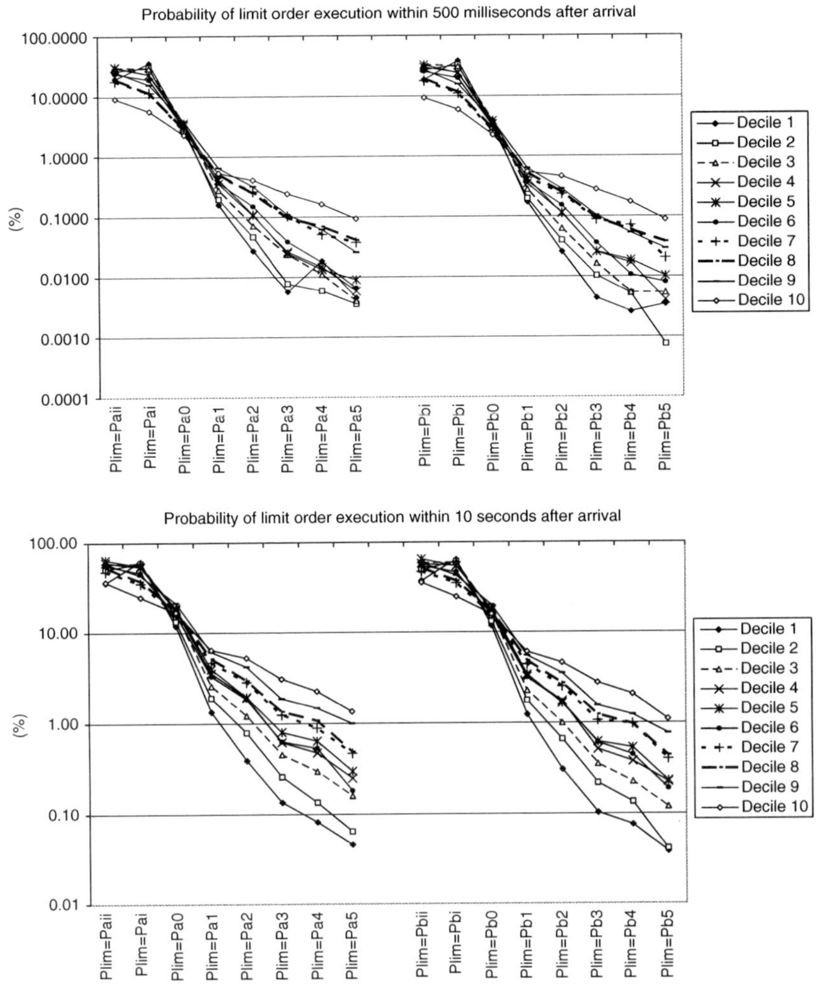

Figure 2.3 Probability of limit order executions
Limit order execution probabilities within half a second and 10 seconds after arrival by share price deciles. Decile 1 includes the least expensive shares; decile 10 includes the most expensive shares. Limit orders are stratified by side of the limit order book (ask versus bid) and aggressiveness. Similar to Hasbrouck and Saar (2007), the probabilities are calculated under the hypothetical scenario that the limit orders are not cancelled within half a second after their arrival. The actual execution probabilities will be smaller due to the censoring of executions by cancellation events (i.e. by fleeting order activity).

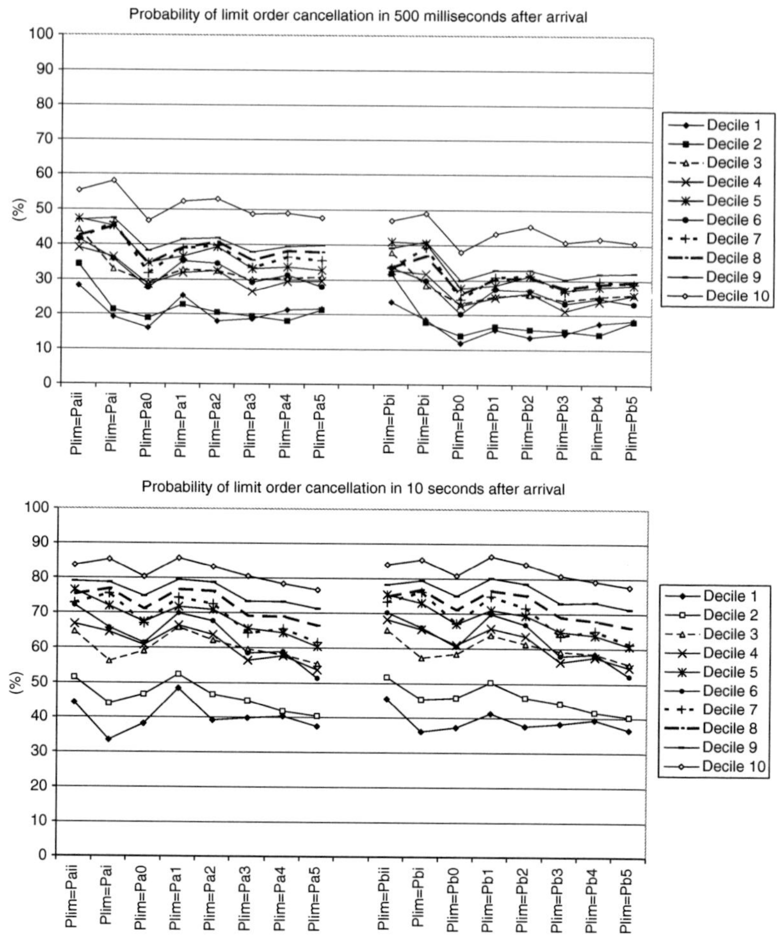

Figure 2.4 Probability of limit order executions
Limit order cancellation probabilities within half a second and 10 seconds after arrival by share price deciles. Decile 1 (10) includes the least (highest) priced shares. Limit orders are stratified by side of the limit order book (ask versus bid) and aggressiveness. Similar to Hasbrouck and Saar (2007), the probabilities of limit order cancellation within half a second are calculated under the hypothetical scenario that the limit orders are not executed within half a second upon arrival. The empirically observed cancellation probabilities will be smaller due to the censoring of cancellations by execution events (mostly for the aggressively priced limit order categories, $P_{\text{lim}} = P_{\text{aii}}$, P_{ai} or P_{a0} on the ask side and $P_{\text{lim}} = P_{\text{bii}}$, P_{bi} or P_{b0} on the bid side). The graph illustrates clearly that orders on the ask side of the limit order book are more likely to be cancelled within half a second than their bid side counterparts. Note also the nonlinear dependence of the cancellation probability on the limit price aggressiveness.

conditions such the bid–ask spread, depth of the limit order book and the relative position of the limit order on the pricing grid.

2.4 Principal components of execution and cancellation probabilities

We use the following covariates for our principal components analysis:

- *Price* = the INET average transaction price per share,
- *Sprd* = the INET inside spread,
- *Range* = the five-minute INET price range,
- *Disvol* = the INET share volume from executions against displayed limit orders,
- *Hinvol* = the INET volume of executions against hidden orders inside the INET spread,
- *Houtvol* = the five-minute INET volume from executions against hidden orders on the edges of the INET bid–ask spread,
- *Dep1* = the average displayed depth of the INET book at the best bid and ask prices,
- *Dep5* = the average displayed depth of the INET order book at the top five ticks on bid and ask sides of the book, and
- *Shrs* = the number of outstanding common shares for each stock on June 30, 2006.

Panel A of Table 2.5 shows the correlation matrix for the above covariates. The majority of these variables have a coefficient of correlation of greater than 50 percent with at least one of the other variables. Given this, we apply principal component analysis to effect a dimension reduction. We extract the first five principal components for the stock-specific averages of our covariates *Logprice* = ln(*Price*), *Logsprd* = ln(*Sprd*–1), *Logrange* = ln(*Range*), *Logdisvol* = ln(*Disvol*), *Loghinvol* = ln(*Hinvol*), *Loghoutvol* = ln(*Houtvol*), *Logdep1* = ln(*Dep1*), *Logdep5* = ln(*Dep5*) and *Logshrs* = ln(*Shrs*). The five principal components *PC*1,..., *PC*5 are constructed as linear combinations of the above covariates so that they have orthonormal loading coefficients and *PC*1 is chosen to explain the largest proportion of variation in the covariates, *PC*2 explains the largest proportion of the variation that is left unexplained by the first component, *PC*3 explains the largest proportion of variance unexplained by the first two components and so forth. The linear combination coefficients for each principal component are reported in Panel C of Table 2.5. The first five factors *PC*1, ..., *PC*5 are related to our covariates by the

Table 2.5 Correlation matrix and principal components of covariates

	Covariates (log transformed)								
	log(Price)	**log(Sprd)**	**log(Range)**	**log(Disvol)**	**log(Hinvol)**	**log(Houtvol)**	**log(Dep1)**	**log(Dep5)**	**log(Shrs)**
Panel A: Correlation matrix									
log(Price)	1	–	–	–	–	–	–	–	–
log(Sprd)	0.79	1	–	–	–	–	–	–	–
log(Range)	0.92	0.77	1	–	–	–	–	–	–
log(Disvol)	−0.47	−0.84	−0.34	1	–	–	–	–	–
log(Hinvol)	−0.15	−0.54	0.03	0.85	1	–	–	–	–
log(Houtvol)	−0.36	−0.65	−0.17	0.90	0.83	1	–	–	–
log(Dep1)	−0.79	−0.96	−0.74	0.84	0.62	0.63	1	–	–
log(Dep5)	−0.78	−0.98	−0.72	0.87	0.62	0.67	0.99	1	–
log(Shrs)	−0.48	−0.83	−0.44	0.89	0.69	0.77	0.81	0.84	1
Panel B: Variations explained by the eigenvalues									
Components	**Eigenvalue**	**Difference**	**Proportion**	**Cumulative**					
PC1	6.572	4.761	0.730	0.730					
PC2	1.811	1.554	0.201	0.932					
PC3	0.257	0.038	0.029	0.960					
PC4	0.219	0.143	0.024	0.985					
PC5	0.076	0.033	0.008	0.993					
PC6	0.043	0.029	0.005	0.998					
PC7	0.014	0.009	0.002	0.999					
PC8	0.005	0.002	0.001	1.000					
PC9	0.002	–	0.000	1.000					

	log(Price)	log(Sprd)	log(Range)	log(Disvol)	log(Hinvol)	log(Houtvol)	log(Dep1)	log(Dep5)	log(Shrs)
Panel C: Factor loadings of the five principal components									
PC1	0.29	0.38	0.26	−0.36	−0.27	−0.31	−0.38	−0.38	−0.35
PC2	0.46	0.15	0.56	0.25	0.47	0.35	−0.13	−0.10	0.14
PC3	−0.60	0.10	−0.11	0.00	0.11	0.54	−0.06	−0.06	−0.59
PC4	0.07	0.04	0.16	−0.07	0.53	−0.53	0.32	0.18	−0.52
PC5	0.51	−0.42	0.19	0.41	−0.32	0.01	−0.15	−0.10	−0.53

Note: This table presents the correlation coefficients of the possible covariates that explain order cancellations, and the subsequent principal component analysis to effect a dimension reduction. Panel A reports the matrix of correlation coefficients for the nine covariates. Panel B shows the eigenvalues of the 9×9 variance matrix of the covariates and the proportions of the total variation in the covariates explained by their k principal components ($k = 1,\ldots,9$). Panel C shows the contributions (loadings) of the covariates to their first five principal components. Price is the INET transaction price per share, Sprd is the INET inside spread, Range is the five-minute INET price range, Disvol is the INET share volume from executions against displayed limit orders, Hinvol is the INET share volume from executions against hidden orders inside the bid–ask spread, Houtvol is the five-minute INET share volume from executions against hidden orders on the boundaries of the bid–ask spread, Dep1 is the geometric average displayed depth of the INET order book at the best bid and ask prices and Dep5 is the geometric average displayed depth of the INET order book at the top five ticks on bid and ask sides of the book. Finally, Shrs is the number of outstanding common shares for each stock on June 30, 2006. The covariance matrix and principal components are calculated for the logarithmically transformed covariates.

following equations:

$$PC1 = 0.29Logprice + 0.38Logsprd + 0.26Logrange - 0.36Logdisvol - 0.27Loghinvol - 0.31Loghoutvol - 0.38Logdep1 - 0.38Logdep5 - 0.35Logshrs,$$

$$PC2 = 0.46Logprice + 0.15Logsprd + 0.56Logrange + 0.25Logdisvol + 0.47Loghinvol + 0.35Loghoutvol - 0.13Logdep1 - 0.10Logdep5 + 0.14Logshrs,$$

$$PC3 = -0.60Logprice + 0.10Logsprd - 0.11Logrange + 0.00Logdisvol + 0.11Loghinvol + 0.54Loghoutvol - 0.06Logdep1 - 0.06Logdep5 - 0.59Logshrs,$$

$$PC4 = 0.07Logprice + 0.04Logsprd + 0.16Logrange - 0.07Logdisvol + 0.53Loghinvol - 0.53Loghoutvol + 0.32Logdep1 + 0.18Logdep5 - 0.52Logshrs,$$

$$PC5 = 0.51Logprice - 0.42Logsprd + 0.19Logrange + 0.41Logdisvol - 0.32Loghinvol + 0.01Loghoutvol - 0.15Logdep1 + 0.10Logdep5 - 0.53Logshrs.$$

The contributions to the first principal component *PC*1 are positive (and have roughly equal size) for the nominal covariates *Logrange, Logprice* and *Logspread,* and are negative (and have roughly equal size) for all covariates measured as the number of shares traded or available to trade. Therefore, we can interpret *PC*1 as the "granularity" of the limit order book.

The contributions to *PC*2 are positive for all variables other than the limit order book depth; the contributions of *Logdep1* and *Logdep5* are both negative and equal to each other. Among the covariates, *Logrange, Logprice, Loghinvol, Loghoutvol* and *Logdisvol* have the largest coefficients, suggesting a natural interpretation for the second component as stock volume-driven "liquidity." Indeed, *PC*2 tends to be high for large dollar volume stocks, which are also more volatile (due to a large amount of trading) and have a large amount of hidden liquidity within and near the current inside spread.

The contributions to the *PC*3 are negative (and approximately equal) for share price and the number of outstanding shares, and positive for the number of hidden shares executed at the edges of the bid–ask spread.

Therefore, the third principal component can be interpreted as a measure of "hidden liquidity"*available behind* the displayed depth of the INET limit order book.

A tentative interpretation of the fourth principal component *PC*4 is the amount of hidden liquidity supplied inside the INET bid–ask spread relative to the hidden liquidity supplied outside of the bid–ask spread. Finally, *PC*5 might be interpreted as the amount of liquidity available away from the bid–ask spread, since the sensitivity of PC5 tends to be positive for more expensive and more volatile stocks with large depth available away from the current spread.

Table 2.6 presents the results of regression analysis for the times to execution (Panel A) and cancellation (Panel B) on the five principal components. The results can be qualitatively interpreted as follows:

(1) The times to cancellation tend to be uniformly smaller for stocks with high values of the first two principal components, which confirms our original observation that fleeting activity is more prevalent for larger more liquid and more expensive stocks. Similarly, the times to execution tend to be smaller for stocks with large values of the first two principal components, with one exception. The times to execution for orders submitted inside the bid–ask spread tend to be unrelated to the value of *PC*1, which is closely associated with share price and granularity of the tick grid of the order book.
(2) The sensitivity of time to cancellation to the third principal component is significantly negative only for orders submitted inside the bid–ask spread; the sensitivities to *PC*3 for less aggressively priced limit orders are also negative but insignificant. The time to execution for displayed limit orders is also negatively related to the third principal component, but only for the orders submitted sufficiently close to the current market price. These two observations suggest that stocks with greater hidden liquidity behind the best quotes also tend to be the ones with more extensive limit order cancellation activity, especially for the orders submitted inside the bid–ask spread.
(3) The sensitivity of times to order cancellation to the fourth principal component is negative for the limit orders submitted far away from the current best quotes and positive for the limit orders submitted inside the bid–ask spread. In contrast, the sensitivities of times to order execution are positive and statistically significant for all limit orders. Therefore, less aggressively priced limit orders, especially submitted three to five ticks away from the concurrent best quotes, are

Table 2.6 Cross-sectional regression analysis for median times to execution and median times to cancellation

Panel A: Regressions of $\log(TTE_s)$ at different levels of order aggressiveness on five principal components									
Regressor	$\log(TTE_{ii})$	$\log(TTE_i)$	$\log(TTE_0)$	$\log(TTE_1)$	$\log(TTE_2)$	$\log(TTE_3)$	$\log(TTE_4)$	$\log(TTE_5)$	$\log(TTE_{6:7})$
PC1	0.06	0.00	**−0.11**	**−0.22**	**−0.24**	**−0.25**	**−0.26**	**−0.25**	**−0.27**
PC2	**−0.65**	**−0.42**	**−0.55**	**−0.55**	**−0.59**	**−0.57**	**−0.55**	**−0.50**	**−0.50**
PC3	0.23	**−0.55**	**−0.22**	**−0.12**	0.04	−0.08	−0.09	**−0.19**	−0.14
PC4	**1.65**	**0.72**	**0.41**	**0.35**	**0.26**	**0.25**	**0.27**	**0.25**	**0.25**
PC5	**−3.21**	**−1.50**	**−1.00**	**−0.75**	**−0.71**	**−0.59**	**−0.58**	**−0.59**	**−0.50**
R-squared	0.67	0.72	0.91	0.95	0.95	0.95	0.94	0.87	0.89
Panel B: Regressions of $\log(TTC_s)$ at different levels of order aggressiveness on five principal components									
Regressor		$\log(TTC_i)$	$\log(TTC_0)$	$\log(TTC_1)$	$\log(TTC_2)$	$\log(TTC_3)$	$\log(TTC_4)$	$\log(TTC_5)$	$\log(TTC_{6:7})$
PC1		**−0.25**	**−0.18**	**−0.24**	**−0.30**	**−0.23**	**−0.22**	**−0.21**	**−0.36**
PC2		**−0.58**	**−0.70**	**−0.55**	**−0.69**	**−0.81**	**−0.82**	**−1.02**	**−1.02**
PC3		**−0.61**	−0.15	−0.05	−0.07	−0.23	−0.24	−0.32	−0.37
PC4		0.53	−0.19	−0.21	−0.24	**−0.42**	**−0.35**	**−0.60**	−0.48
PC5		**−1.72**	**−1.16**	**−0.70**	**−0.79**	**−1.03**	−0.34	0.22	−0.17
R-squared		0.43	0.73	0.73	0.67	0.74	0.70	0.68	0.64

Note: This table presents the results of cross-sectional regressions of median times to execution (TTE_s) and median times to cancellation (TTC_s) for limit orders submitted at different aggressiveness levels. TTE_s and TTC_s are calculated as average daily median times to execution and daily median times to cancellation, respectively, for orders of alternative aggressiveness levels *s*, where the averages of the median times are taken over 63 trading days from July–September 2006. The number of observations in each regression equation equals 100 and the regressors include five principal components PC1, …, PC5 extracted from the nine covariates as shown in Table 2.5. The subscript *s* denotes the level of limit order aggressiveness, where subscript ii (i) pertains to the price-improving limit orders arriving at prices that are two (one) ticks better than the concurrent best quote on the same side of the book. Subscripts 0, 1, 2… pertain to the limit orders placed arriving inside the limit order at the best quotes, one tick away from the best quote, two ticks away from the best quote and so on, on the same side of the INET limit order book. Boldfaced entries highlight the regression coefficients significant at the 95 percent confidence level.

more likely to be fleeting for stocks with higher amounts of hidden execution inside the bid–ask spread.

(4) Finally, the times to cancellation for relatively aggressive limit orders and the times to order execution for all limit orders tend to be negatively related to the fifth principal component, which is related to the amount of liquidity provided further away from the current market price of the stock.

2.5 The mixture of distributions model

We began our analysis by illustrating order cancellation rates for one stock, Comcast (CMCSA) – showing the high rates of cancellation at very short durations, which then taper off as time increases. We then showed that this pattern is robust across stocks. The dynamics of order cancellation at very short durations differ from those at longer time intervals. We use these observations to posit that instead of specifying one distribution to model order cancellations, a better approach would be to formulate a mixture of distributions – one that draws the fleeting orders from one distribution and longer duration orders from another.

2.5.1 Assumptions and notation

Assume we have access to the complete history of a limit order k, which was entered into the limit order book at time T_0. Prior to the limit order entering the book, the observed covariates capturing the market conditions were at the level $\boldsymbol{x}_{k0}$. Assume that the first change of the covariates to the new level $\boldsymbol{x}_{k1}$ occurs at time T_1, within t_{k1} seconds since the order arrival; the second change of the covariates to the new level $\boldsymbol{x}_{k2}$ occurs at time T_2, within t_{k2} seconds since this limit order arrival; and so on, until termination of the limit order at time $T_{i(k)}$, within $t_{ki(k)}$ seconds after the order arrival and the covariates prior to the limit order termination stayed at the level $\boldsymbol{x}_{ki(k)}$. Assume there are three possible causes for limit order termination: (1) cancellation, (2) full execution, and (3) censoring. In addition, we may allow for the possibility of partial executions during the lifetime of the limit order.

Upon arrival, the limit order assumes one of the two types: (1) fleeting or (2) regular (non-fleeting). The newly arrived order is fleeting with probability $\pi(\boldsymbol{x}_{k0}) = \exp(-\boldsymbol{\pi}'\boldsymbol{x}_{k0})/(1+\exp(-\boldsymbol{\pi}'\boldsymbol{x}_{k0}))$ and non-fleeting with the complementary probability $1/(1+\exp(-\boldsymbol{\pi}'\boldsymbol{x}_{k0}))$. If the order is fleeting then the risk of its cancellation depends on the level of covariates just prior to (or, alternatively, immediately after) this limit order arrival, with the hazard rate of the cancellation given by the index function

$\nu(\boldsymbol{x}_{k0}) = \exp(\boldsymbol{\nu}' x_{k0})$ (or, alternatively, by $\nu(\boldsymbol{x}_{k1}) = \exp(\boldsymbol{\nu}' x_{k1})$). If the order is non-fleeting then the instantaneous risk of its cancellation depends on the contemporaneous level of covariates; therefore, for a non-fleeting limit order observed within the duration episode Δt_{ki}, the hazard rate of its cancellation is given by the index function $\xi(\boldsymbol{x}_{ki}) = \exp(\xi' x_{ki})$. Conditional on the limit order being "at risk" of execution within the episode Δt_{ki} both fleeting and non-fleeting orders are subject to execution risk, which is characterized by its hazard rate $\mu(\boldsymbol{x}_{ki}) = \exp(\boldsymbol{\mu}' x_{ki})$. The indicator of being "at risk" of being executed within the duration episode Δt_{ki} is given by $R_{ki} = R(\boldsymbol{x}_{ki})$, which is a zero-one switch function of covariates $\boldsymbol{x}_{ki}$. In addition, the limit order history may also be censored at time $T_{i(k)}$ without execution or cancellation, in which case it will be assumed that the censoring occurs independently of the execution and cancellation events.

2.5.2 The timeline of a limit order history

A stylized timeline of the limit order history is shown on the next page. The first row marks the clock time T_i (measured in seconds since start of the trading day), the second row marks the time t_{ki} since the moment t_{k0} of kth limit order arrival, the third row marks $i(k)$ duration episodes Δt_{ki} between consecutive changes of covariates $\boldsymbol{x}_{ki}$ and the fourth row shows the values of time-varying covariates immediately before the beginning of each new episode of the limit order history. Row five shows the hazard rate $\boldsymbol{\nu}(\boldsymbol{x}_{k0})$ of cancellation for fleeting orders, row six shows the hazard rate $\xi(\boldsymbol{x}_{ki})$ of cancellation for regular (non-fleeting) limit orders and row seven shows the hazard rate $\mu(\boldsymbol{x}_{ki})R(\boldsymbol{x}_{ki})$ of order execution in each of the durations prior to the kth limit order termination.

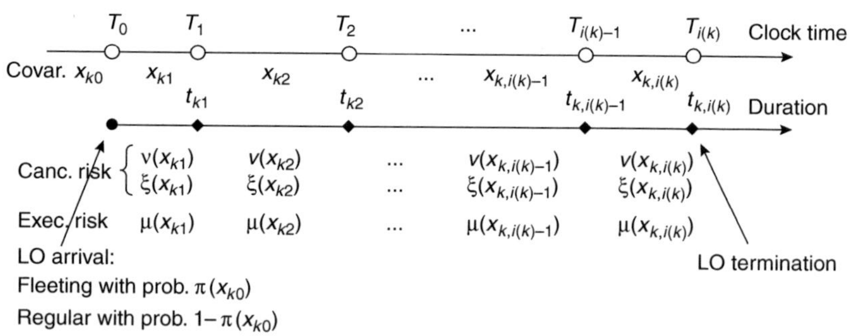

2.5.3 The likelihood function

To derive the expression for the likelihood function L_k of kth limit order, we start with the model where the risks of execution and cancellation are conditionally independent given the values of covariates. Then we show how the derived log-likelihood function can be maximized by standard methods of survival analysis, since the likelihood function L_k can be decomposed into the product of two terms, L_{ck} and L_{ek}, corresponding to the likelihood terms of cancellation and execution risks. The likelihood function of cancellation can be written as follows:

$$L_{ck}(\pi,\nu,\xi) = \frac{e^{-\pi' x_{k0}}}{1+e^{-\pi' x_{k0}}} \exp\left[\sum_{i=1}^{i(k)} (\delta_{ki} \ln \nu(x_{k0}) - \nu(x_{k0})\Delta t_{ki})\right] + \frac{1}{1+e^{-\pi' x_{k0}}} \exp\left[\sum_{i=1}^{i(k)} (\delta_{ki} \ln \xi(x_{ki}) - \xi(x_{ki})\Delta t_{ki})\right],$$

where δ_{ki} is the indicator of the event that ith duration episode is terminated by cancellation. The likelihood function of execution is written similarly as:

$$L_{ek}(\mu) = \exp\left[\sum_{i=1}^{i(k)} (d_{ki} \ln \mu(x_{ki}) - R(x_{ki})\mu(x_{ki})\Delta t_{ki})\right],$$

where d_{ki} is the indicator of the event that ith duration episode is terminated by execution.

The log-likelihood function corresponding to the cancellation risk can be written in the additive form as follows:

$$\ln L_{ck}(\pi,\nu,\xi) = -(\pi' x_{k0} + \ln(1+e^{-\pi' x_{k0}}) + \ln(1+Z_{ck}(\pi,\nu,\xi))) + \sum_{i=1}^{i(k)} (\delta_{ki} \ln \nu(x_{k0}) - \nu(x_{k0})\Delta t_{ki}),$$

where

$$Z_{ck}(\pi,\nu,\xi) = \pi' x_{k0} + \sum_{i=1}^{i(k)} (\delta_{ki} y_{ki} - \nu(x_{k0})(1 - e^{y_{ki}})),$$

and

$$y_{ki} = \ln \xi(x_{ki}) - \ln \nu(x_{k0}).$$

The log-likelihood function corresponding to execution risk is written similarly as follows:

$$\ln L_{ek}(\mu) = \sum_{i=1}^{i(k)} (d_{ki} \ln \mu(x_{ki}) - R(x_{ki})\mu(x_{ki})\Delta t_{ki}).$$

The log-likelihood function corresponding to the entire data set capturing the records of complete histories of K limit orders is given by

$$\ln L(\pi, \nu, \xi) = \sum_{k=1}^{K} (\ln L_{ck}(\pi, \nu, \xi) + \ln L_{ek}(\mu)).$$

2.5.4 Estimation results

Panel A of Table 2.7 shows the results for the model of intensity of limit order arrival at best quotes for ask orders for 13 randomly chosen stocks and Panel B shows the same for the mixture model for cancellation of limit orders arriving at best quotes. Estimates that have the same sign at least 90 percent of the days are boldfaced.

Panel B shows that the probability of a fleeting order at best ask quotes depends:

- positively on bid–ask spread,
- positively on recent buyer-initiated trading volume (in the last 5 seconds),
- positively (but not as strongly) on recent (last 5 seconds) executions of hidden bid orders,
- negatively on LOB depth at and near the best quote on the same side,
- negatively (except for ISRG) on LOB depth at best quote on the opposite side,
- negatively for small relative spread stocks (AAPL, CMCSA) and positively for larger relative spread stocks (AKAM, GOOG, ISRG) on recent (in the last five seconds) seller-initiated trading volume.

The intensity of limit order arrival at best ask quotes (shown in Panel A)

- depends positively on bid–ask spread,
- depends positively on recent (in the last five seconds) buyer- and seller-initiated trading volume, although more strongly on seller-initiated trading volume,
- depends negatively on LOB depth at and near the best quote on the opposite side,
- exhibits positive dependence on LOB depth near the same side best quote for AMGN and ISRG and negative dependence on LOB depth near the same side best quote for CMCSA.

In Table 2.8 we provide results from the mixture of distributions model for orders placed with limit price that is one tick away from the best

Table 2.7 Hazard rates of arrival and cancellation for limit orders at the best ask quotes

Panel A: Log intensity of ask limit order arrival at the best ask quote													
Ticker	**AAPL**	**ADBE**	**ADSK**	**AKAM**	**ALTR**	**AMGN**	**AMZN**	**CMCSA**	**GOOG**	**ISRG**	**ORCL**	**SBUX**	**YHOO**
Log hazard of arrival at Pask0	Median	Median	Median	Median	Median	Median	Median	Median	Median	Median	Median	Median	Median
log(1+0.01Disvolask)	**0.02**	**0.12**	**0.18**	**0.11**	**0.05**	**0.06**	**0.09**	**0.11**	**0.06**	**0.26**	**0.02**	**0.07**	**0.06**
log(1+0.01Hidvolask)	0.02	0.05	0.03	0.09	0.03	0.03	0.02	0.03	0.08	0.05	0.04	0.05	0.05
log(1+0.01Disvolbid)	**0.26**	**0.40**	**0.50**	**0.44**	**0.36**	**0.43**	**0.35**	**0.32**	**0.42**	**0.55**	**0.17**	**0.40**	**0.29**
log(1+0.01Hidvolbid)	−0.02	−0.03	0.01	0.08	−0.03	−0.01	−0.03	−0.03	0.09	0.29	−0.03	−0.02	−0.03
log(RelSprd)	**0.79**	**0.72**	**0.67**	**1.15**	**0.57**	**0.78**	**0.83**	0.53	**1.73**	**1.39**	**−0.91**	**0.90**	**0.68**
log(Dask0)	−0.05	0.00	**0.14**	−0.09	**0.15**	**0.18**	−0.04	**−0.56**	−0.19	0.03	**−0.17**	**0.07**	0.03
log(Dask1/Dask0)	−0.04	**0.05**	**0.25**	**0.09**	**0.17**	**0.27**	−0.02	**−0.65**	**0.06**	**0.17**	−0.17	**0.14**	−0.01
log(Dask2/Dask1)	0.05	**0.17**	**0.18**	**0.07**	**0.07**	**0.24**	0.02	**−1.05**	**−0.26**	**0.32**	0.01	0.07	−0.08
log(Dask3/Dask2)	**−0.20**	0.05	0.05	−0.04	0.01	**0.08**	−0.05	**−0.88**	−0.22	**0.25**	0.03	−0.03	−0.15
log(Dask4/Dask3)	−0.06	**0.05**	0.23	0.07	0.15	**0.03**	−0.01	**−0.97**	**−0.30**	**0.18**	−0.12	**0.13**	0.02
log(Dask9/Dask4)	−0.02	**0.17**	0.22	0.04	**0.18**	**0.11**	0.10	**−0.73**	−0.19	**0.16**	−0.32	**0.13**	0.00
log(Dbid0)	**−0.47**	**−0.40**	**−0.28**	**−0.26**	**−0.54**	**−0.47**	**−0.42**	**−0.69**	**−0.42**	−0.18	−0.22	**−0.45**	**−0.39**
log(Dbid1/Dbid0)	**−0.41**	**−0.31**	**−0.19**	**−0.25**	**−0.47**	**−0.44**	**−0.30**	**−0.69**	**−0.41**	−0.17	−0.34	**−0.44**	**−0.33**
log(Dbid2/Dbid1)	**−0.24**	−0.15	−0.10	**−0.19**	−0.15	**−0.22**	−0.15	−0.46	**−0.33**	−0.13	−0.19	**−0.31**	−0.13
log(Dbid3/Dbid2)	−0.09	−0.12	−0.09	−0.13	−0.13	−0.11	−0.07	−0.18	**−0.30**	−0.07	−0.27	**−0.21**	−0.16
log(Dbid4/Dbid3)	−0.05	−0.11	−0.11	−0.12	−0.22	−0.19	−0.13	0.20	**−0.35**	−0.04	−0.83	−0.19	−0.15
log(Dbid9/Dbid4)	−0.01	−0.05	−0.03	−0.05	−0.17	−0.10	0.02	0.14	**−0.18**	−0.01	−0.06	−0.08	−0.03

Continued

Panel B: Logit transformed probability of fleeting order for limit orders submitted at the best ask quote													
Ticker	**AAPL**	**ADBE**	**ADSK**	**AKAM**	**ALTR**	**AMGN**	**AMZN**	**CMCSA**	**GOOG**	**ISRG**	**ORCL**	**SBUX**	**YHOO**
Logit transform of fleeting prob. at Pask0	Median	Median	Median	Median	Median	Median	Median	Median	Median	Median	Median	Median	Median
log(1 + 0.01Disvolask)	**0.12**	**0.12**	**0.30**	**0.22**	**0.13**	**0.20**	**0.08**	**0.22**	**0.13**	**0.33**	**0.11**	**0.25**	**0.20**
log(1 + 0.01Hidvolask)	0.02	0.03	−0.01	0.06	**0.08**	0.02	0.00	−0.04	0.01	0.01	0.04	0.01	−0.01
log(1 + 0.01Disvolbid)	**−0.11**	−0.02	**0.17**	**0.22**	**−0.14**	0.03	−0.02	**−0.09**	**0.20**	**0.25**	**−0.14**	**−0.06**	**−0.09**
log(1 + 0.01Hidvolbid)	**0.07**	**0.11**	**0.15**	0.12	**0.09**	**0.16**	**0.10**	0.09	0.00	**0.08**	**0.05**	**0.14**	**0.08**
log(RelSprd)	**0.95**	**1.12**	**0.74**	**1.15**	**1.59**	**0.84**	**0.99**	**0.67**	**1.27**	1.30	**−0.38**	**1.53**	**1.21**
log(Dask0)	**−0.32**	**−0.28**	**−0.29**	**−0.38**	**−0.14**	−0.12	**−0.24**	**−1.02**	**−0.71**	**−0.52**	−0.63	−0.04	**−0.20**
log(Dask1/Dask0)	**−0.33**	**−0.27**	**−0.27**	**−0.27**	**−0.17**	−0.17	**−0.28**	**−1.24**	**−0.57**	**−0.44**	**−0.76**	−0.02	**−0.15**
log(Dask2/Dask1)	**−0.49**	−0.14	**−0.25**	**−0.30**	**−0.20**	**−0.23**	**−0.30**	**−1.40**	**−0.59**	**−0.30**	**−0.70**	−0.12	**−0.26**
log(Dask3/Dask2)	**−0.22**	−0.07	**−0.24**	**−0.20**	−0.10	**−0.14**	−0.08	**−1.16**	**−0.66**	**−0.28**	**−0.79**	−0.08	**−0.21**
log(Dask4/Dask3)	**−0.20**	−0.15	**−0.24**	**−0.17**	**−0.33**	**−0.12**	−0.05	**−1.48**	**−0.67**	**−0.25**	−1.40	−0.13	**−0.18**
log(Dask9/Dask4)	**−0.09**	0.04	−0.07	**−0.10**	−0.11	0.02	0.05	**−1.02**	**−0.41**	**−0.19**	**−0.78**	0.00	**−0.09**
log(Dbid0)	**−0.38**	**−0.36**	**−0.14**	**−0.21**	**−0.27**	**−0.30**	**−0.31**	**−0.40**	**−0.28**	−0.02	−0.09	**−0.39**	**−0.20**
log(Dbid1/Dbid0)	**−0.27**	−0.11	**−0.06**	**−0.21**	0.02	**−0.29**	**−0.15**	**−0.25**	**−0.24**	−0.04	0.10	**−0.20**	**0.09**
log(Dbid2/Dbid1)	**−0.08**	−0.02	−0.07	**−0.19**	**0.34**	**−0.08**	−0.06	**−0.21**	**−0.35**	0.04	0.07	**−0.13**	**0.10**
log(Dbid3/Dbid2)	0.00	−0.02	−0.10	−0.16	**0.34**	**−0.02**	−0.01	0.17	**−0.33**	−0.02	**0.46**	**−0.08**	**0.14**
log(Dbid4/Dbid3)	0.02	0.02	−0.04	−0.12	**0.21**	**−0.03**	0.05	**0.48**	**−0.38**	0.04	**0.30**	**−0.01**	**0.30**
log(Dbid9/Dbid4)	0.03	−0.01	0.02	−0.03	**0.19**	**−0.01**	0.07	**0.45**	−0.24	0.03	0.40	0.00	0.07

Note: This table reports the estimates of covariate sensitivities for the intensity of limit order arrival for ask quotes, and the probability that the arriving order is fleeting for 13 randomly selected Nasdaq 100 stocks. The intensity of limit order arrival reported in Panel A is estimated as an exponential function of a linear covariate index, diurnally adjusted for time-of-the-day effect using linear splines. The probability of fleeting order reported in Panel B is estimated as a logit transformation of a linear covariate index. Disvolask (Disvolbid) is the number of shares displayed as part of the ask-side (bid-side) depth of the INET order book that was executed on INET within the last 5 seconds prior to the limit order arrival. Hidvolask (Hidvolbid) is the amount of hidden depth on the ask (bid) side of the INET order book that was executed on INET within the last 5 seconds prior to the limit order arrival. RelSprd denotes the relative INET inside spread. $Dask_k$ ($Dbid_k$) denotes the cumulative displayed depth of the ask (bid) side of the INET limit order book within k ticks of the best ask (bid) quote, where $k = 0, 1, 2, 3, 4, 9$. Estimates that have the same sign at least 90 percent of the days are boldfaced.

Table 2.8 Hazard rates of arrival and cancellation for limit orders at one tick away from the best ask quotes

Panel A: Log intensity of ask limit order arrival at one tick away from the best ask quote										
Ticker	**AAPL**	**ADBE**	**AKAM**	**AMGN**	**AMZN**	**CMCSA**	**GOOG**	**ISRG**	**SBUX**	**YHOO**
Log hazard of arrival at Pbid0	Median	Median	Median	Median	Median	Median	Median	Median	Median	Median
log(1 + Disvolbid)	**0.11**	**0.30**	**0.21**	**0.21**	**0.20**	**0.15**	0.06	**0.14**	**0.24**	**0.14**
log(1 + Hidvolbid)	**0.03**	**0.13**	0.10	0.06	0.08	0.01	**0.08**	**0.19**	**0.06**	**0.08**
log(1 + Disvolask)	**0.20**	**0.36**	**0.29**	**0.31**	**0.31**	**0.20**	**0.28**	**0.30**	**0.27**	**0.27**
log(1 + Hidvolask)	−0.01	−0.03	0.11	−0.06	−0.01	0.02	**0.11**	**0.31**	0.03	−0.03
log(RelSprd)	**0.70**	**0.72**	**1.49**	**0.92**	**0.94**	0.31	**2.18**	**1.70**	**1.38**	**0.74**
Log(Dbid0)	**−0.47**	**−0.42**	−0.10	**−0.34**	**−0.57**	**−0.96**	0.00	0.08	**−0.44**	**−0.50**
log(Dbid1/Dbid0)	**−0.28**	−0.17	0.05	**−0.23**	**−0.32**	**−0.91**	0.00	0.09	**−0.22**	**−0.14**
log(Dbid2/Dbid1)	0.01	**0.13**	**0.25**	**0.18**	−0.02	**−1.48**	**0.49**	**0.44**	0.03	−0.03
log(Dbid3/Dbid2)	0.04	0.03	0.01	0.00	−0.11	**−0.86**	−0.24	**0.30**	**−0.16**	**−0.17**
log(Dbid4/Dbid3)	−0.08	−0.01	0.03	−0.11	0.00	**−0.98**	−0.22	**0.26**	**−0.07**	0.07
log(Dbid9/Dbid4)	−0.07	0.10	0.05	0.00	0.06	**−0.82**	−0.21	**0.16**	0.03	0.07
Log(Dask0)	**−0.30**	**−0.24**	**−0.26**	−0.26	−0.19	−0.31	**−0.43**	−0.14	**−0.27**	**−0.27**
log(Dask1/Dask0)	**−0.36**	**−0.14**	**−0.21**	**−0.17**	**−0.15**	−0.15	**−0.35**	−0.17	**−0.19**	**−0.24**
log(Dask2/Dbid1)	**−0.34**	**−0.15**	**−0.25**	**−0.18**	**−0.15**	−0.02	**−0.53**	−0.15	**−0.27**	**−0.17**
log(Dask3/Dask2)	**−0.23**	**−0.16**	**−0.07**	**−0.13**	**−0.17**	**0.17**	**−0.36**	0.02	**−0.23**	**−0.23**
log(Dask4/Dask3)	−0.04	0.00	**−0.08**	**−0.19**	**−0.07**	**0.27**	**−0.31**	−0.05	**−0.16**	**−0.13**
log(Dask9/Dask4)	−0.01	0.03	−0.03	**−0.02**	0.01	0.12	**−0.20**	0.04	0.02	−0.02

Continued

Table 2.8 Continued

Panel B: Logit transformed probability of fleeting order for limit orders submitted one tick away from the best ask quote										
Ticker	**AAPL**	**ADBE**	**AKAM**	**AMGN**	**AMZN**	**CMCSA**	**GOOG**	**ISRG**	**SBUX**	**YHOO**
Log hazard of arrival at Pbid0	Median	Median	Median	Median	Median	Median	Median	Median	Median	Median
log(1 + Disvolbid)	**0.12**	**0.14**	**0.25**	**0.29**	**0.08**	**0.13**	**0.25**	**0.24**	**0.10**	**0.05**
log(1 + Hidvolbid)	**0.05**	**0.09**	0.08	0.07	0.05	−0.02	0.00	0.07	**0.07**	0.04
log(1 + Disvolask)	**−0.04**	0.05	**0.17**	0.03	0.05	**−0.05**	**0.10**	0.02	**0.03**	**0.04**
log(1 + Hidvolask)	**0.05**	0.04	0.11	0.05	0.07	0.04	−0.01	0.00	**0.08**	0.01
log(RelSprd)	**0.62**	**0.45**	**0.76**	**0.58**	**0.65**	0.49	**1.15**	**0.54**	**1.02**	**0.79**
Log(Dbid0)	**−0.49**	**−0.36**	**−0.18**	**−0.40**	**−0.42**	**−0.81**	**−0.45**	**−0.21**	**−0.24**	**−0.24**
log(Dbid1/Dbid0)	**−0.34**	**−0.11**	**−0.12**	**−0.21**	**−0.14**	**−0.88**	**−0.48**	**−0.23**	0.03	0.12
log(Dbid2/Dbid1)	**−0.39**	**−0.17**	**−0.16**	**−0.26**	**−0.25**	**−1.10**	−0.22	**−0.22**	**−0.19**	**−0.21**
log(Dbid3/Dbid2)	**−0.22**	**−0.15**	**−0.16**	**−0.24**	**−0.16**	**−0.54**	**−0.48**	**−0.27**	**−0.17**	**−0.15**
log(Dbid4/Dbid3)	**−0.11**	0.02	−0.06	−0.19	0.03	**−0.36**	**−0.55**	**−0.31**	−0.06	0.12
log(Dbid9/Dbid4)	−0.07	0.02	−0.04	−0.03	0.10	**−0.58**	**−0.38**	**−0.19**	0.00	0.06
Log(Dask0)	**−0.35**	**−0.20**	**−0.24**	**−0.34**	**−0.31**	−0.05	**−0.26**	0.03	**−0.29**	**−0.39**
log(Dask1/Dask0)	**−0.37**	**−0.14**	**−0.24**	**−0.35**	**−0.22**	0.03	−0.22	−0.01	**−0.11**	**−0.29**
log(Dask2/Dbid1)	**−0.19**	−0.03	**−0.22**	**−0.13**	−0.06	−0.06	**−0.34**	0.11	**−0.16**	**−0.09**
log(Dask3/Dask2)	**−0.11**	−0.04	**−0.14**	**−0.05**	−0.11	0.12	**−0.34**	0.06	**−0.05**	−0.06
log(Dask4/Dask3)	0.00	0.07	**−0.15**	**−0.09**	−0.05	0.11	**−0.34**	−0.02	**−0.09**	**−0.15**
log(Dask9/Dask4)	0.05	−0.01	−0.02	0.03	0.05	0.09	**−0.26**	0.08	**−0.07**	**−0.19**

Note: This table reports the estimates of covariate sensitivities for the intensity of limit order arrival at one tick away from the best ask quote and the probability that the arriving order is fleeting for 10 randomly selected Nasdaq 100 stocks. The intensity of limit order arrival reported in Panel A is estimated as an exponential function of a linear covariate index, diurnally adjusted for time-of-the-day effect using linear splines. The probability of a fleeting order reported in Panel B is estimated as a logit transformation of a linear covariate index. Disvolask (Disvolbid) is the number of shares displayed as part of the ask-side (bid-side) depth of the INET order book that was executed on INET within the last 5 seconds prior to the limit order arrival. Hidvolask (Hidvolbid) is the amount of hidden depth on the ask (bid) side of the INET order book that was executed on INET within the last 5 seconds prior to the limit order arrival. RelSprd denotes the relative INET inside spread. $Dask_k$ ($Dbid_k$) denotes the cumulative displayed depth of the ask (bid) side of the INET limit order book within k ticks of the best ask (bid) quote, where $k = 0, 1, 2, 3, 4, 9$. Estimates that have the same sign at least 90 percent of the days are boldfaced.

current ask price. The results are shown for 10 of the 13 stocks in the previous Table 2.7, and these results are qualitatively similar.

2.6 Conclusion

Order cancellations are only very recently being recognized as important events in identifying patterns in the limit order book. Prix et al. (2007) use order cancellation patterns to identify traces of algorithmic trading in the Xetra order submissions. Hendershott et al. (2007) show how algorithmic trades improve liquidity, and identification of algorithmic trades relies, in part, on order cancellation messages. We add to this growing literature by showing that the times to cancellation of limit orders depend nonlinearly on both stock-specific factors as well as market conditions, and establishing the specific factors and market conditions that have the highest power to explain order cancellations.

We document stylized facts about very short-lived – fleeting – orders submitted to a limit order trading platform and study the dynamics of fleeting order activity. We show that cancellation times are systematically and jointly dependent upon (1) the degree of quote aggressiveness, and (2) the stock price. In other words, to characterize an order as fleeting, we would have to know where in the pricing grid the quote was placed relative to the existing best quotes, and what is the share price of that stock.

Principal component analysis for the probabilities of limit order cancellation shows that most of the cross-sectional variation in cancellation probabilities can be explained by the stock price, which can be interpreted as the limit order book granularity for this stock. We model the nonmarketable limit order flow as a mixture of two order types and interpret one type in this mixture as fleeting orders. By allowing the mixing probability to depend on stock characteristics and market conditions, we find that fleeting orders are more likely to be observed for aggressive quotes and in market conditions characterized by higher volatility, wider bid–ask spreads and higher volumes of hidden transactions inside the spread.

Notes

1. Biais et al. (1995) find that close to 11 percent of limit orders on the Paris Bourse CAC 40 stocks are cancelled. Using data on 148 NYSE listed stocks' trades for one week in mid-2001, Ellul et al. (2005) find close to 33 percent of orders are cancelled. Fong and Liu (2006) show that in the Australian Stock Exchange, the frequency of order cancellations ranges from 10.1 percent (sell/small cap stocks) to 14.1 percent (buy/large cap stocks). Prix et al. (2007) find that the

percentage of no-fill orders that are terminated amount to close to 70 for the DAX 30 stocks for January 5–12, 2005. The more recent studies indicate that cancellation rates increased to more than 90 percent with proliferation of high-frequency trading.

2. Note that the leftmost dashed line corresponds to cancellation within ten milliseconds of submission. This is close to the technological limit on signal transmission in ECNs (approximately one-third the speed of light in a glass medium).
3. We note here that stability depends on the model specification and our comment on stability is only with respect to the double-exponential mixture of distributions that we have specified. We are currently also trying to use alternative models (Weibull distributions in particular) to examine if that could improve the goodness-of-fit of our model.
4. Challet and Stinchcombe (2003) analyse high frequency data from the Island ECN order book for four stocks – Cisco (CSCO), Dell (DELL), Microsoft (MSFT), and Worldcom (WCOM). However, they use the screen-shots data that was publicly available. This order submission data is truncated at the 15th highest bids and lowest asks orders at a given time. Unlike theirs, our dataset comprises of all orders placed / modified / executed / cancelled at all depths at any given time.
5. Specifically, for time to cancellation, they find that the exponent could be in the range of -2.1 ± 0.1.

References

Biais, B., Hillion, P. and Spatt C. (1995) "An Empirical Analysis of the Limit Order Book and the Order Flow in the Paris Bourse," *Journal of Finance*, 50 (5): 1655–1689.

Challet, D. and Stinchcombe, R. (2003) "Limit Order Market Analysis and Modelling: On an Universal Cause for Over-Diffusive Prices," *Physica A: Statistical Mechanics and Its Applications*, 324 (1–2): 141–145.

Eisler, Z., Kerkesz, J., Lillo, F. and Mantegna, R. N. (2007) "Diffusive Behavior and the Modeling of Characteristic Times in Limit Order Executions," Working Paper, available online at http://ssrn.com/abstract=960521.

Ellul, A., Holden, C. W., Jain, P. and Jennings, R. (2007) "Order Dynamics: Recent Evidence from NYSE," *Journal of Empirical Finance*, 14 (5): 636–661.

Fong, K. and Liu, W.-M. (2006) "Limit Order Revisions," Working Paper, available at http://ssrn.com/abstract=890463.

Hasbrouck, J. and Saar, G. (2002) "Limit Orders and Volatility in a Hybrid Market: The Island ECN," Working Paper, Department of Finance, Stern School of Business, NYU, New York.

Hasbrouck, J. and Saar, G. (2007) "Technology and Liquidity Provision: The Blurring of Traditional Definitions," Working Paper, Department of Finance, Stern School of Business, NYU, New York.

Hendershott, T., Jones, C. M. and Menkveld, A. J. (2008) "Does Algorithmic Trading Improve Liquidity?" Working Paper, available at http://ssrn.com/abstract=1100635.

Liu, W.-M. (2009) "Monitoring and Limit Order Submission Risks," *Journal of Financial Markets*, 12 (1): 107–141.

Lo, A. W., MacKinlay, C. A. and Zhang, J. (2002) "Econometric Models of Limit Order Execution," *Journal of Financial Economics*, 65 (1): 31–71.

Menkhoff, L. and Schmeling, M. (2005) "Informed Trading in Limit Order Markets: Evidence on Trinary Order Choice," Working Paper, University of Hannover, Germany.

Prix, J., Loistl, O. and Huetl, M. (2007) "Algorithmic Trading Patterns in Xetra Orders," *The European Journal of Finance*, 13 (8): 717–739.

Rosu, I. (2009) "A Dynamic Model of the Limit Order Book," *Review of Financial Studies*, 22 (11): 4601–4641.

3

Market Microstructure of the Foreign Exchange Markets: Evidence from the Electronic Broking System

Yuko Hashimoto and Takatoshi Ito

3.1 Introduction

The foreign exchange market remains sleepless. In contrast to stock exchange markets which are subject to strict opening and closing times each day and where transactions are done in a specific space (such as the New York Stock Exchange and Tokyo Stock Exchange), someone is trading somewhere all the time – 24 hours a day, (almost) 7 days a week in foreign exchange markets.

The state of the global foreign exchange market is clarified by a market survey conducted by central banks under coordination of the Bank for International Settlements (BIS) once every three years. The most recent survey was conducted in April 2007 and the BIS report was issued in 2007. According to the survey, as shown in Table 3.1, following a brief decline between 1998 and 2001, the average daily turnover of the foreign exchange steadily increased after 2001 reaching \$1.8trl in 2004 followed by the record high of \$3.1trl in 2007.[1] Of the turnover in 2007, spot transactions accounted for \$1005 billion,[2] outright forward \$361 for billion and swaps \$1714 billion. Decomposing into currencies, approximately 43 percent of transactions are in US dollars, 18 percent are in euros, 8 percent in Japanese yen, 7 percent in pound sterling and 3 percent in Swiss francs. As for the currency pairs, \$/euro accounted for \$840bil, \$/yen for \$397bil and \$/GBP for \$361bil.

Foreign exchange transactions take place between dealers of reporting financial institutions, between a dealer and another financial institution or between a dealer and a nonfinancial customer. One of the remarkable features is a recent sharp increase in transactions between dealers

Table 3.1 Foreign exchange turnover

	Billion of USD			
	1998	**2001**	**2004**	**2007**
Total foreign exchange turnover, daily average	1430	1173.07	1794	3081
Spot	568	387	831	1005
Outright forwards	128	131	209	362
swaps	734	656	954	1714
Between Reporting dealers	908	688	956	1319
(Percentage share to Total turnover)	(64)	(59)	(53)	(43)
Between Dealer and other fin institutions	279	329	585	1235
(Percentage share to Total turnover)	(20)	(28)	(33)	(40)
Between Dealer and non-fin institutions	242	156	252	527
(Percentage share to Total turnover)	(17)	(13)	(14)	(17)
Specified currency against all other currencies*				
USD	1260	1060	1573	2660
Euro	503	442	659	1139
Yen	300	266	359	510
Pound sterling	158	155	299	461
Swiss franc	101	71	108	209
Currency pair (Top 3)				
USD/Euro	348	354	503	840
USD/Yen	267	231	294	397
USD/GBP	118	125	248	361

Note: *Because two currencies are involved in each transaction, the sum of transactions in individual currencies comes to twice the total reported turnover.
Source: Bank for International Settlements, Triennial Central Bank Survey of Foreign Exchange and Derivatives Market Activity in 2007, December 2007 (BIS 2007).

and other financial institutions, whereas the percentage share of transactions between dealers and between dealers and nonfinancial institutions remains almost constant. The declining share of transactions between dealers who report to the BIS surveys can be partly explained by the growing role of electronic brokers in the spot interbank market.[3] This trend means that "hot potatoes" (Lyons, 1997), transmissions of orders by large retail customers to a bank that generate multiplied transactions in the interbank market through a price discovery process, are less important now and a cool supercomputer has become increasingly important.

As electronic broking has become the dominant method of transaction in foreign exchange markets, interbank transaction patterns have also shifted. Until several years ago, bank policy allowed dealers who received customer orders to hold their own proprietary positions for profit-taking. They tended to add their own positions when they executed customers' orders if they felt that these orders contained some valuable information. Receiving customers' orders meant a special information advantage in forecasting the direction of the foreign exchange rate. Dealers in banks now have only very small volumes of their own proprietary positions. Responsibility for proprietary trading has been transferred to an independent department, sometimes characterized as an in-house hedge fund, and this proprietary trading section uses more computer modeling to seek profit opportunities by betting on the direction of the exchange rate within the very short-run; from a few minutes to several hours.

Given the background of the changing structure of the foreign exchange market and the evolving trading behavior, this chapter aims to shed light on the high-frequency foreign exchange market. More precisely, we examine intraday patterns of the market and analyze the reaction of exchange rates to the release of major macroeconomic statistics in Japan using one-second sliced transaction data obtained from the actual trading platform, EBS.

The rest of this chapter is organized as follows. Section 3.2 gives a literature review. Section 3.3 describes data used in the analysis. Section 3.4 summarizes intraday patterns of the foreign exchange market. Section 3.5 shows the exchange rate reactions to macroeconomic statistics' releases. Section 3.6 concludes this chapter.

3.2 Literature review

Conventional wisdom in the academic literature is that the exchange rate follows random walk for frequencies less than annual, for example, daily, weekly or even monthly, whereas it sometimes shows time trends, cyclicality or, in general, history dependence at lower frequencies. While traditional economics textbooks are based on the random-walk hypothesis, financial institutions continue to bet millions of dollars on the predictability of exchange rate movements. The gap between the random walk in academia and the prediction model in the real world is remarkable, but in recent years there has been a growing academic literature on exchange rate forecasting and empirical investigation using high-frequency data – "market microstructure" analysis.[4]

As for predictability and random walk, using high-frequency deal and quote prices of USDJPY and EURUSD exchange rates, Hashimoto et al. (2008) found that deal price movements tend to continue a run once started, whereas quote prices mostly follow a random walk. Ito and Hashimoto (2008) showed by using high-frequency data from the actual trade platform that exchange rates could be predictable at up to five minutes and the predictability disappears after 30 minutes. Evans and Lyons (2005a, 2005b) also examined daily EURUSD exchange rate returns based on the end-user data and found a persistent (days) effect in currency markets.

Some studies focus on whether exchange rates respond to pressures of customers' orders. Evans and Lyons (2002), for example, reported a positive relation between daily exchange rate returns and order flows for Deutsche mark/dollar. Love and Payne (2003) and Berger et al. (2005) studied the contemporaneous relationship between order flow and the exchange rate. Evans and Lyons (2005c) consider heterogeneity of order flow in estimating its price impact. Based on the end-user order flow data, they show that order flow provides information to market makers. Lyons' series of papers (1995, 1996, 1997, 1998, 2001) developed a theoretical model of order flows and information transmission. In line with the information and pricing in markets, Lyons and Moore (2005) found that exchange rate prices are affected by transactions.

Intraday activities such as the number of deals and transaction volume in foreign exchange markets are also of interest in the market microstructure analysis. Admati and Pfleiderer (1988), Brock and Kleidon (1992) and Hsieh and Kleidon (1996) provided theoretical and empirical backgrounds of intraday patterns of the bid–ask spread and volatility. Baillie and Bollerslev (1990) and Andersen and Bollerslev (1997, 1998) were some of the earliest studies that examined intraday volatility of exchange rates using indicative quotes. Finally, Chaboud et al. (2004), Berger et al. (2005) and Ito and Hashimoto (2006, 2008) examine the intraday behavior of exchange rates using up-to-date high-frequency data.

The examination of news impact on exchange rates has evolved with data availability. Intraday exchange rate observations meant five times per day at the time of Ito and Roley (1987). Once an electrically recorded exchange rate database became available, many studies exploited the data. Goodhart and Payne (1996) and Goodhart et al. (1996) were among the first to use the Reuter trading platform data (D-3000). Andersen and Bollerslev (1998) and Andersen et al. (2003) examined the effect of macroeconomic announcements on intra-daily exchange markets using the Reuter indicative quote data. Hashimoto (2005) used the "event-study approach" to examine the foreign exchange transaction patterns during the Japanese banking crisis of 1997. Andersen et al. (2007) and Faust et al. (2003) studied US news releases and their impact on foreign exchange markets and Ehrmann and Fratzscher (2005) examined the impact of US, German and Euro Area news releases on the foreign exchange markets.

In recent years, the EBS has provided researchers with data which are recorded from the actual trading platform. Chaboud et al. (2004) examined the impact of the US macroeconomic statistics' releases on the euro–dollar and dollar–yen exchange rates. Their findings are consistent with those in recent literature in that the conditional mean of exchange rates responds very quickly to an unexpected component of news releases. Hashimoto and Ito (2009) studied the impact of the 12 Japanese macroeconomic statistics' releases on the dollar–yen exchange rates. They found that the exchange rate response to a surprise component of news varies from one statistic release to another. Many of the statistics' announcements before 8.50 am are found to significantly affect the exchange rate but not others, and the impact lasts at least up to 30 minutes. As for the trading volume, both studies found that news releases increase the volume of transactions. Surprisingly, a surge in trading volume is found even if the released news indicators are entirely in line with expectations.

3.3 Data

The spot foreign exchange markets have evolved in recent years and now the overwhelming majority of spot foreign exchange transactions are executed through a global electronic broking systems such as EBS and Reuters D-3000. These electronic broking systems provide trading technology and display quotes and transactions continuously for 24 hours a day. Fifteen years ago brokers in the interbank market were mostly human and direct deals between dealers held a substantial share of the spot market. The foreign exchange market of today is very different. Now, each financial institution that establishes an account with EBS and/or Reuters D-3000 is given a specific computer screen and is able to trade via this screen by putting in and hitting prices. The EBS has a stronger market share in absolute terms than Reuters D-3000 in currencies such as the dollar/yen, euro/dollar, euro/yen, euro/chf etc., and is said to cover more than 90 percent of the dollar/yen and euro/dollar trades. In contrast, Reuters has significant market share in transactions related to the pound sterling, the Canadian dollar and the Australian dollar.

The EBS data set has advantages over the frequently used indicative quotes of exchange rate data such as the FXFX of Reuters in at least two important aspects. First, the quotes in the EBS data set are "firm," in that banks that post quotes are committed to trade at those quoted prices, when they are "hit."[5] In contrast, the indicative quotes of the FXFX screen are those input by dealers for information only, without any commitment for trade. Indicative quotes are much less reliable than firm quotes in capturing the whole picture of a market reality. Second, transactions' data available in the EBS data set is simply not available on the FXFX screen. Although exact trading volume is not disclosed, transaction counts (counts of seconds that had at least one transaction) and trade volume shares (a percentage share of trading volumes in one minute) are available in the EBS data set.

As part of facilitating an orderly market, EBS requires any newly linked institution to secure a sufficient number of other banks that are willing to open credit lines with the newcomer. A smaller or a regional bank may have fewer trading relationships, thus not as many credit relationships. Then the best bid and ask for that institution may be different from the best bid and ask of the market. A smaller or regional bank may post more aggressive prices (higher bids or lower asks) because they will have relatively fewer credit relationships, implying that they will see fewer dealable prices generally.

The EBS global system consists of three regional computer sites based in Tokyo, London and New York, and it matches orders either within the same site or across different sites. Each region covers Europe, North America and Asia, respectively. The three regions are often abbreviated as LN, NY and TY regions in this paper. The intra-regional deal of LN, for example, consists of deals whose makers and takers are both from the London region. And inter-regional deals of LN–NY consist of deals whose makers and takers are from two different regions of London and New York.

The EBS system works as follows.[6] A bank dealer places a "firm" limit order, either ask or bid, with specified price and units that the dealer is ready to trade if hit. The EBS computers collect these orders and show "best ask," "best bid," "best ask for the member" and "best bid for the member" on the screen. The former two do not necessarily agree with the latter two, respectively, because the EBS system controls for the bilateral credit lines and shows the best available quote for each institution. Hence, if the member does not have a credit line with the market maker(s) that is (are) posting the "best" ask/bid in the market, then the individually available best quotes deviate from the market best quotes. The EBS-registered trader's screen shows the best bid and best offer of the market and best bid and best offer for that particular institution. In normal times, the best bid of the market is lower than the best offer of the market, otherwise, an institution that has positive credit lines with both institutions on the bid and ask sides will be able to make profits by arbitrage. The computer continuously clears the order whenever the sell and buy order matches at the same price – this could happen either because a buyer hits the ask quote posted in the system or a seller hits the bid quote posted in the system. The electronic broking system is a centralized network of traders. In a sense, the electronic broking system can be regarded either as a collection of large numbers of market makers or as a continuous (Walrasian) auctioneer.

In recent years, the EBS has made price and trade volume data available to researchers.[7] The EBS price data contains information on, among other things, firm bid (best bid), firm ask (best ask), deal prices done on the bid side (lowest given) and deal prices done on the ask side (highest paid).[8]

The firm bid and firm ask data are the bid and offer that are committed to trade if someone on the other side is willing to trade at that price. A "firm ask" ("firm bid") means that the institution that posts the quote is ready to sell (buy, respectively) the shown currency (e.g. the dollar in exchange for the quoted yen). The ask quote is almost always higher than the bid quote.[9] When the deal is done at the ask side, it means that the firm ask (ready to sell) quote is "hit" by a buyer. When the deal is done at the bid side, the firm bid quote is "hit" by a seller. Therefore the ask deal is a buyer-initiated deal and the bid deal is a seller-initiated deal, according to the description in Berger et al. (2005).[10] If ask (bid) deals are continuously hit, then the ask (bid) deal prices tend to move up (down), because of the buy (sell, respectively) pressure.

The lowest given (bid-side deal) or highest paid (ask-side deal) are recorded for each second when at least one deal on either side was executed during the second.[11] An ask-side deal means that the ready-to-sell quote was hit by a buyer, thus it represents a buyer-initiated deal, that is, a piece of buying pressure. A bid-side deal means that the ready-to-buy quote was hit by a seller, thus it represents a seller-initiated deal, that is, a piece of selling pressure.

Data used in this chapter covers from 1999 to 2005. The data on intraday patterns of foreign exchange market activities In Section 3.4 covers a sample period from 1999 to 2001 for both the dollar/yen and euro/dollar exchange rates, and the data on the effects of Japanese macroeconomic

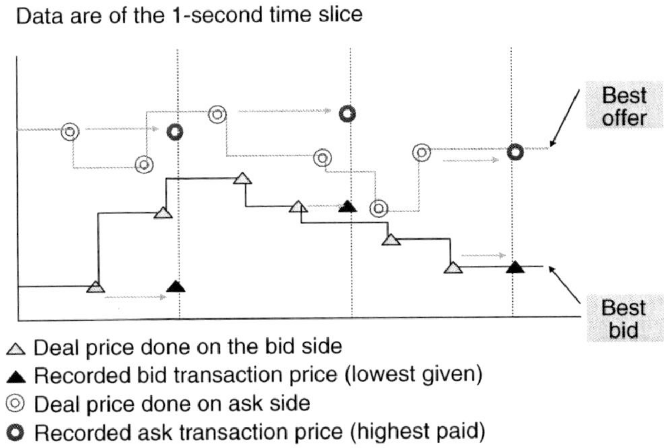

Figure 3.1 EBS data

statistics' releases on the dollar/yen transaction cover from 2001 to 2005. All the data are provided by EBS. Section 3.4 utilizes data on 1-second sliced quote and deal prices and volume shares (the percentage share of transaction volume of one minute relative to the total transaction volume of the day) and in Section 3.5 we use exchange rate data from EBS and Japanese macroeconomic statistics' releases (release timestamp and the actual and predicted values) collected from Bloomberg.

3.4 Intraday patterns

3.4.1 Activities during a day

The intraday patterns of foreign exchange transaction are anecdotally and instinctively known to bank dealers. However, only a few academic papers have statistically examined market activities so far. Ito and Hashimoto (2004, 2006) were one of the first teams to analyze the foreign exchange market using tick-by-tick deal data.

Following Ito and Hashimoto (2006), this section examines high-frequency data on foreign exchange market activities such as the "number of quotes," the "number of deals," "bid–ask spread" and the "relative volume share" in order to show the intraday patterns of the foreign exchange market. The sample period is from 1999 to 2001. The number of quotes is calculated as the number of seconds where quotes are recorded, and the number of deals is the sum of bid-side deals and ask-side deals in each hour of the day.[12] The "relative volume" is defined as

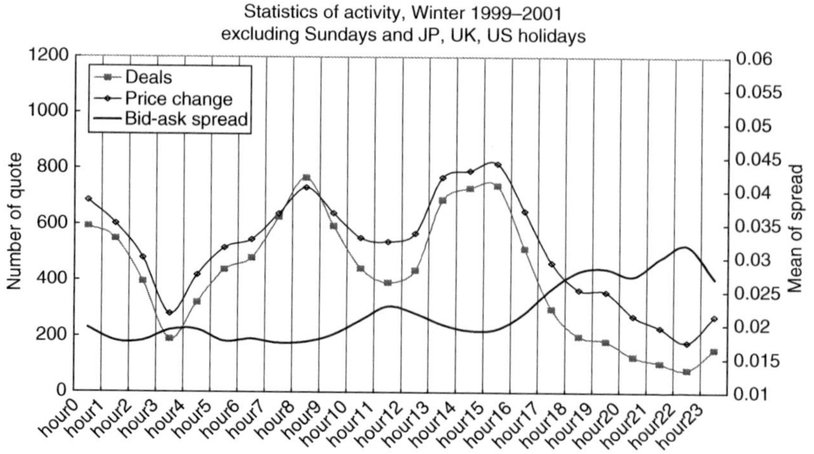

Figure 3.2 Relative volume (USDJPY), winter 1999–2001

hourly aggregated relative volumes: the percentage share of transaction volume in one minute relative to the total transaction volume in one day. The hourly transaction volumes, with each contract (transaction) being one million of the "base currency" (the first currency in the currency pair name), are divided by the total trading volume of the day.[13] These indicators of market activities are calculated for one hour and then averaged over three years with a differentiation of the standard and daylight saving time.[14]

Figure 3.2 shows the intraday (Hour 0–23) patterns of the numbers of deals, quotes and the bid–ask spread of the USDJPY and Figure 3.3 shows those of the EURUSD.[15]

As is clear from these figures, there are several features in the intraday patterns. First, there are three peaks and three troughs in the numbers of deals and quotes in a day. For the dollar/yen exchange transactions, peaks of the market activities are seen at GMT Hour 0, Hours 6–7 and Hours 12–14 in the summer and Hour 0, Hour 8 and Hours 13–15 in the winter. The troughs are at Hour 3, Hours 10–11 and Hour 21 in the summer and at Hour 3, Hour 11 and Hour 22 in the winter. Peaks and troughs also fall on similar hours of the day for euro/dollar exchange rate transactions. That is, the first peak corresponds to the opening of the Tokyo market, the second peak corresponds to the opening of the London and European markets and the third peak corresponds to the opening of the New York market and the afternoon business hours of the London and European markets. Each of the three troughs corresponds to Tokyo lunch time,

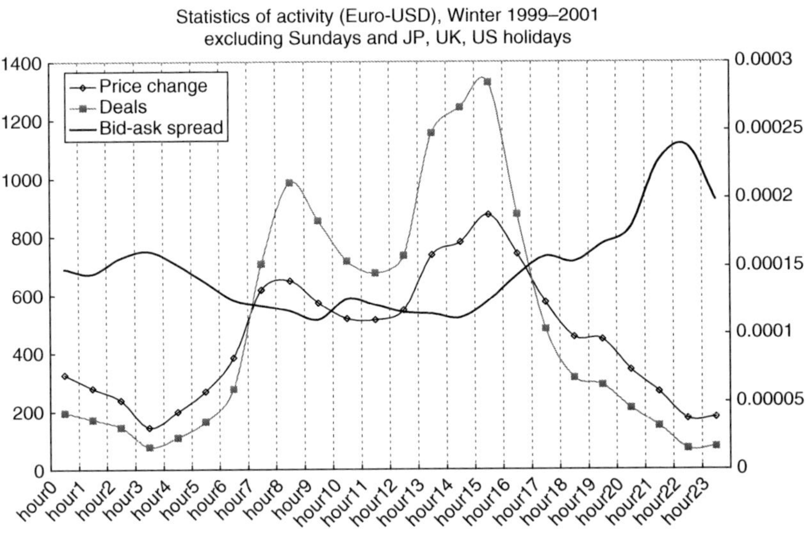

Figure 3.3 Relative volume (EURUSD), winter 1999–2001

London lunch time and the hours just before the Asia and the Pacific markets open, respectively.

The decline in activities during the Tokyo lunch hour is remarkable. There used to be regulations that prohibited interbank foreign exchange trading during the lunch hour in Tokyo. The tradition seems to have lasted even though the regulation was lifted in December 1994 – history seems to matter.[16]

As for the peaks in the activities, the dollar/yen transaction and the euro/dollar transaction have several distinctive features. The height of the first peak at Hour 0 is much lower for the euro/dollar transactions than the dollar/yen transactions. This means that in the Tokyo market the euro/dollar trade is very small compared to the dollar/yen trade. It is also remarkable that during peak London morning hours and the overlapping hours of London afternoon and New York morning, the second and the third daily peaks, respectively, the number of deals becomes quite large and exceeds the number of quotes. This is evidence that the London and New York markets are thick enough for transactions not to result in the change in exchange rate quotes.

Second, for the dollar/yen transactions we detect high correlation between the number of deals and the number of quotes. Third, the bid–ask spread is narrower during the first half of the day, then it becomes wider after GMT Hours 16–17 and peaks at Hours 21–22. More precisely, the bid–ask spread tends to be negatively correlated with the number of deals (or quotes). In the figures, three troughs in the number of deals (quotes) mostly correspond to three peaks in the bid–ask spread. One exception is Hour 0, when the bid–ask spread is higher than during other business hours in the Tokyo market (except the lunch hour at Hour 3) but the numbers of deals and quotes are also at one of the peaks. That is, unlike other times of the day, there seems to be a positive correlation between the bid–ask spread and the number of deals and quotes during the first business hour of the Tokyo market.

In summary, by comparing USDJPY and EURUSD trading, intraday activities are found to have similar patterns, with the following notable exceptions. First, there seems to be a "home-market advantage." That is, activities of the Tokyo market relative to the London market are higher for USDJPY and lower for EURUSD. In fact, the heights of the three peaks for the dollar/yen transactions are roughly equal to each other. On the other hand, the euro/dollar transactions during the Tokyo opening hour have a distinctively lower peak. This means that the Tokyo (and the Asian) market is not significantly active for euro/dollar trading. Second, the EURUSD market is particularly deep in the London morning and even deeper in the London afternoon hours that overlap with the New York morning.

3.4.2 Regional contribution

The above analysis based on counts of deals and quotes reveals that the transaction activities become exceptionally high during the overlapping business hours of the currency pair home markets – the Tokyo afternoon and London morning (the second peak) and the London afternoon and the US morning (the third peak). The next question is on the regional contribution to the surge in activities. For example, whether a surge in activities in the Tokyo mid-afternoon hours and London morning hours can be attributed to the activity of Tokyo participants or London participants. In the following section, we decompose the regional contributions to the activity surge by the relative trading volume shares which have the label of participants (regional names).

The regional contributions to the surge in trades for dollar/yen activities are shown in Figure 3.4 and for euro/dollar in Figure 3.5.[17] The dollar/yen trades during the overlapping hours of the Tokyo afternoon and London morning are done by Tokyo (and Asian) participants (financial institutions in Japan and Asia region) and London (and European) participants (financial institutions in Europe) around GMT Hours 6–8,

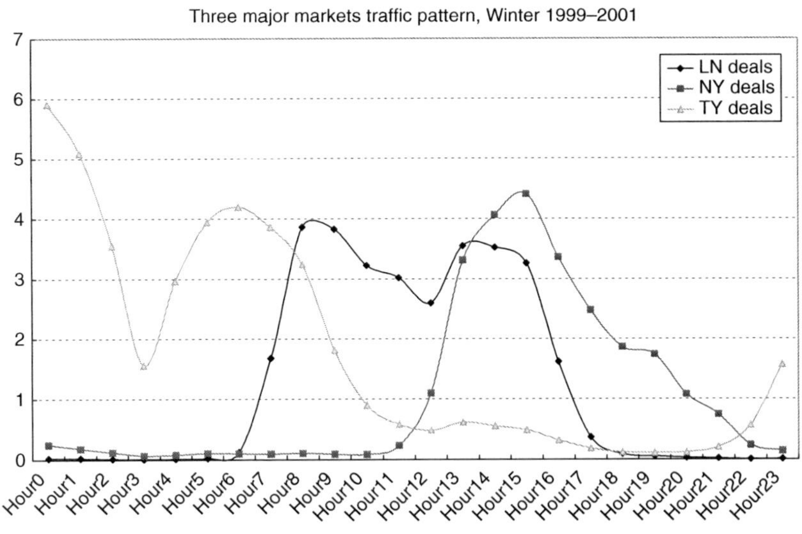

Figure 3.4 Relative volume (USDJPY), winter 1999–2001

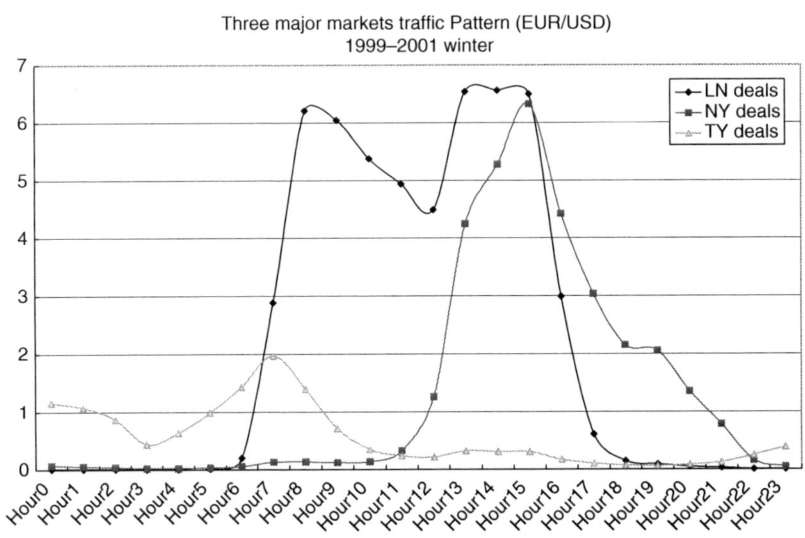

Figure 3.5 Relative volume (EURUSD), winter 1999–2001

with the majority of Tokyo participants at the beginning and then with the increasing share of London participants. During this time period, transactions from New York (the United States) participants (financial institutions in North America) are quite small and almost negligible. On the other hand, the dollar/yen trades during the overlapping hours of the London afternoon and the New York morning are mainly done by London and New York participants with some Tokyo participants.

The figures also reveal that transactions by Tokyo participants and London participants exhibit a U-shape pattern, whereas the transactions by New York participants have a single-peak pattern. The monotonic decline in market activities, the number of deals and quotes, after the New York afternoon may be due to two reasons: there is no pickup effect in the New York afternoon (unlike the Tokyo or London markets) and the transactions after GMT 16 are mainly done by the New York participants (almost no participants from Tokyo and London). The very large trade volume among the Tokyo participants during the Tokyo business hours (except for lunch hours) implies that, for the dollar/yen trade, the Tokyo market has new information, inducing heterogeneous reactions to the news, thereby generating more trade.

As for the euro/dollar transactions, it is immediately clear from Figure 3.2 that the share of Tokyo participants is quite small compared to London and New York participants and also compared to their presence in the dollar/yen trades. It is also interesting to note that even for the euro trading, London and New York participants are almost nonexistent during the Tokyo business hours.

Going back to regional contributions, the share of London participants is particularly high in the euro market during the two peaks in the euro/dollar transactions (Hours 8 and 13–15 in winter; Hours 7 and 12–13 in summer). London participants are also dominant during the overlapping hours of the Tokyo afternoon and London morning, and New York participants share the market as much as London participants do during the London afternoon and New York morning overlapping hours.

Again, a U-shape pattern of transactions is found for Tokyo and London participants, whereas transactions by New York participants have a single-peak pattern. Although there is a U-shape pattern in the euro trading by Tokyo participants, the shape and height of the U-curve is quite different: the U-shape is flatter and the second peak of the U-shape is higher for the euro trading. This implies that, for the euro/dollar trade, Tokyo participants have to wait for London participants to start their transactions in order to find counterparties.

3.4.3 Market opening hours

As seen in the analysis above, each market experiences a surge in transactions during the opening hours. When there are many participants in the market (the market is "deep"), trading volume tends to be higher and spreads tend to be narrower. The opening hour of the Tokyo market appears to have special characteristics because it follows a few hours of extremely low activity after the New York market closes. In particular, the Monday morning of the Tokyo market probably has some specific activity patterns because the Tokyo market is the first to open after a long weekend break, from Friday night to Monday morning. The first hour of Tokyo on Monday (Hour 0 in adjusted GMT) may be different because the volume of orders accumulated during the weekend (about 35 hours) is much larger than those accumulated during the overnight gap (2–3 hours between the New York close and Tokyo opening) resulting in much higher activity compared to the same hour on any other day of the week. Similarly, we expect the opening hours of the London and New York markets to show some special characteristics in trading activity.

Ito and Hashimoto (2006) examined the opening-hour effect of the three markets (Tokyo, London and New York), the Monday morning effect and the (lack of) U-shape pattern by testing the significance of dummy variables that take the value 1 when deals/quotes are recorded in the opening hours (or Monday opening hours). They found that, in general, the negative relationship between the number of deals (quotes) and the spread holds even for these opening hours. That is, when the market is deep (when the number of price [quotes] changes is large) the bid–ask spread tends to be narrower.

The Tokyo opening effect and Tokyo Monday opening effect are tested by examining the relationship between the spread and the number of deals/quotes with opening-hour dummies.[18] For the Tokyo opening effect in 1999, it turns out that the spread becomes narrower as the number of deals/quotes increases during the opening hour, 9 am Tokyo time, for both the dollar/yen trade and the euro/dollar trade. On the other hand, as for the Monday opening effect, it is found that the number of deals significantly increases during the Monday opening hours for the dollar/yen trade in 1999 and 2000, suggesting that the market participants carry out some orders accumulated over the weekend in the first hour of the week, the Monday Tokyo morning at GMT Hour 0, despite the relatively wide bid–ask spread. The Monday Tokyo effect is not found for the euro/dollar trade.

As for the London and New York opening effects, we find that the number of deals becomes significantly larger during the opening hours of London and New York, while the spread during the opening hours is not significantly different from other hours for both the dollar/yen and euro/dollar trades.[19] The effects are (partly) significant during 1999 and 2000, but the effects are mostly insignificant as estimated during 2001.

The disappearance of the opening effect on the spread and the lack of the upswing of the U-shape in the afternoon for the trading activities in the New York market in recent years are probably due to the recent widespread practice of continuous trading and better control of inventory. For the past several years, many financial institutions, from small hedge funds to big banking groups, have invested in computer programs that signal buy and sell orders in an automatic response to the changes in market trends. Electronic broking systems have further facilitated the execution of such trades. The U-shape, in particular the increase in the afternoon, is often regarded as willingness to trade in order to control inventory ahead of a long break (between the days or over the weekend). However, the widespread use of computer trading systems has made it much easier for dealers and proprietary traders to find market rates and counter-parties even in other regions of the world regardless of the local hours and to manage inventories continuously. This may have contributed to the disappearance of the pickup of the activities towards the end of the business hours in New York, and minor changes of the bid–ask spread during the business hours from Tokyo, London and New York.[20] The widespread use of computer trading systems may, in the future, contribute to the elimination of the particular intraday patterns.

3.5 News effects on the exchange rate[21]

As shown in the previous section, transaction volume tends to surge during a particular time of the day. One of the reasons for a surge in transactions is a concentrated arrival of new macro information in the markets. The possible existence of private information may cause a different trading response by dealers, some of them informed and some uninformed, to the arrival of new information. Then the trading may be intensified between these two types of dealers, as described in the "private information model" of Easley and O'Hara (1992).

In this section, the exchange rate reaction to the release of major macroeconomic statistics is examined. In particular, this section examines how the dollar/yen exchange rate market digests information contained in the various macroeconomic statistics' releases – to what extent transactions and prices react to the macroeconomic statistics' news, how long the news effect lasts and which news has the most/least impact on the exchange rate. In the analysis, the unexpected component of macroeconomic announcements, a "surprise," is defined by the difference between the actual indicator announcement and the average of predicted indicators by the market. The sample period is from 2001 to 2005 and we examine the impacts from 12 Japanese macroeconomic statistics' releases on the exchange rate returns, volatility and the transaction volume.

3.5.1 Japanese macroeconomic announcements

Chaboud et al. (2004) study the impact of US macroeconomic announcements on exchange rates using the following US macro variables: payroll, GDP advanced, PPI, retail sales, trade balance and Fed funds rate (target). These authors found a significant impact on exchange rate returns from a surprise component in the announcement. In the European perspective, Ehrmann and Fratzscher (2005) used GDP, Ifo business climate index, business confidence balance, PPI, CPI, retail sales, trade balance, M3, unemployment, industrial production and manufacturing orders as proxies for Germany news releases.[22]

In contrast to US macroeconomic announcements, most of which come out at 8.30 am (EST), the release time of Japanese news announcements varies from news to news. Some of the announcements are released in the morning and others in the afternoon. Most of the major macroeconomic statistics come out at either 8.30 am, 8.50 am, 10.30 am, 2.00 pm or 2.30 pm.

After 2001, the announcement time for Japanese macroeconomic statistics has become fairly standardized. Until 2000, however, a lot of news was released one hour earlier than the current release time, while some news releases were fixed later or went back and forth. For example, the current CPI release time was set at 8.30 only in 2002. Release time of three news announcements (balance of payments [8:50], trade balance [8:50] and retail sales [14:30]) changed once in early 2000 and moved back to the original time about six months later.

Figures 3.6 and 3.7 show the average of number of deals on news-release days and non-announcement days for Tankan (Bank of Japan, business survey) and GDP preliminary (GDPP, at 8.50 am JST). This announcement time is just before the first peak in transactions within the day and, therefore, this surge of activity may likely reflect the impact of news releases.[23] Each figure plots the 15-minute averages in the number

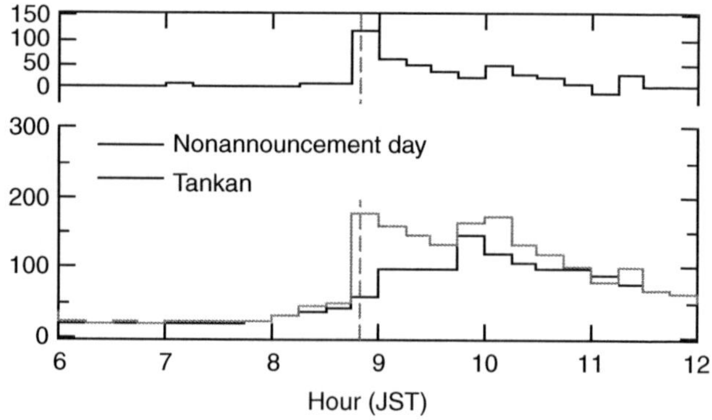

Figure 3.6 Transaction and news release; Tankan (Bank of Japan, Business survey) (JST 8.50 am)

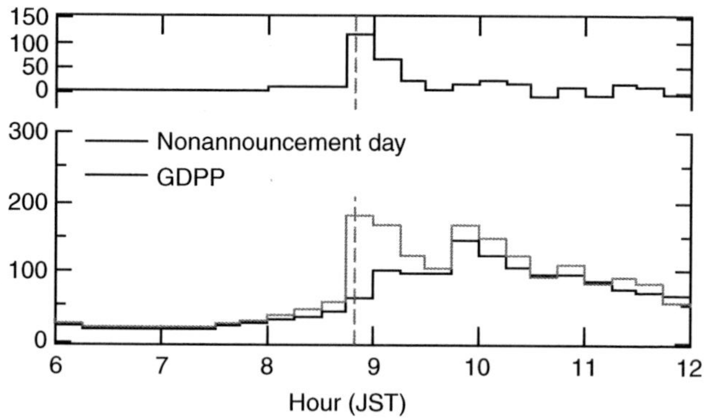

Figure 3.7 Transaction and news release; GDP preliminary (JST 8.50 am)

of transactions from 6 am to 12 noon for 2001–2005. The red line shows the benchmark of no macro announcement, and the black line shows the deal activity on announcement days. The top panel of the figure shows the difference in the number of deals between news-announcement days and non-announcement days.

A look at the graphs reveals that news releases such as Tankan and GDPP result in a huge increase in the number of deals around the news-announcement time. For example, the number of deals jumps more than 3 times when a Tankan indicator is released and the number of deals at the time of GDPP releases is about 2.5 times higher than that of no-news days. Intuitively, the surge in deals around 9.00 am (JST) seems, in part, caused by macro news announcements of Tankan and GDPP.

3.5.2 Impact of surprises on exchange rate activities

When an announcement has unexpected content the announcement is expected to be followed by a change in the exchange rate, because market participants react to this unexpected part by rebalancing their portfolio positions. That is, a surprise would result in changes – positively or negatively – in the exchange rate returns through changes in the number of deals. The release of a news announcement itself, regardless of surprises, may affect price volatility. Suppose that the actual announcement of a macro announcement is exactly the same as the average of market expectations. Then there should not be any positive or negative returns that follow the announcement of no surprise. However, even if the "average" expectation is confirmed by the actual announcement, individuals may be heterogeneous and some are positively surprised and some negatively surprised. Hence, those who were off the average have incentives to trade and price volatility may rise with returns being zero. The total amount of deals may increase at the time of macroeconomic announcement. Unless market participants are homogeneous in expectations on the news – which is very unlikely – some deals are bound to occur right after the announcement. When there is a surprise component in the news, additional deal activities will be stimulated.

Hashimoto and Ito (2009) examined whether and how much an unexpected component of a macroeconomic news announcement, a "surprise," will affect returns, volatility and the number of transactions in the dollar/yen exchange market with the following estimations:[24]
Return regression:

$$\Delta s(t,u) = \sum_{i(u)=1}^{n(u)} \alpha_{i(u)} N_{i(u)}(t,u) + \varepsilon(t,u) \tag{3.1}$$

$$\Delta s(t,u) = \sum_{i(u)=1}^{n(u)} \alpha_{i(u)} N_{i(u)}(t,u) + \delta \Delta s(t,u-k) + \theta ND(t,u-k) + \varepsilon(t,u). \tag{3.2}$$

Volatility regression:

$$V(t,u) = \alpha_0 + \alpha_1 V(t,u-1) + \sum_{i(u)=1}^{n(u)} \beta_i(u) |N_{i(u)}(t,u)| + \sum_{i=1}^{n(u)} \gamma_{i(u)} DUMN_{i(u)}(t,u) + \varepsilon(t,u). \tag{3.3}$$

Transaction regression:

$$TD(t,u) = \alpha_0 + \alpha_1 TD(t,u-k) + \sum_{i(u)=1}^{n(u)} \beta_i(u)|N_i(u)(t,u)|$$
$$+ \sum_{i(u)=1}^{n(u)} \gamma_{i(u)} DUMN_{i(u)}(t,u) + \varepsilon(t,u). \quad (3.4)$$

In the return regressions (3.1) and (3.2), $\Delta s(t,u)$is the exchange rate return measured by log-difference from time u to $u+k$ on da yt,k is the number of minutes and u is the announcement time of the day for news $N_{i(u)}$. $N_{i(u)}(t,u)$ is a surprise of i-th macroeconomic news statistics in a time window of $u$and measured as the difference between actual (announced) values and the market-consensus forecast of macroeconomic statistics' releases. That is, $N_{i(u)}(t,u)$ is defined as "actual" minus "expected" of a macroeconomic statistics' release. In the time window u, there are $n(u)$ variables that are scheduled to be announced. In the volatility regression (3.3), the volatility (V) of time window u on day t is explained by one-lagged volatility ($V(t,u-1)$), the absolute value of surprise components of macroeconomic announcements ($|N|$) and the dummy variable of macroeconomic news release (*DUMN*). In the transaction regression (3.4), *TD(t, u)* is the total number of deals in the time window from announcement time u to $u+k$ minute. In all regressions, a time interval of k is considered for four patterns, $k = 1, 5, 15$ and 30 minutes.

The estimation results show that a surprise in many macroeconomic statistics' releases in the morning, in particular the 8.30 am and 8.50 am announcements, significantly affects returns, increases volatility and stimulates transactions.[25] For returns, the coefficients of surprises are more or less similar for the 1-, 5-, 15- and 30-minute windows – this suggests that most of the exchange rate reaction occurs within one minute after a news release as a onetime sudden jump to a new equilibrium. This is consistent with what has been established in the literature on US macro announcements. As for volatility, the absolute value of surprises in the 8:50 macroeconomic statistics' releases are found to increase volatility for at least 30 minutes after these news releases.

We also find that Tankan and GDPP have a significant impact on the number of deals. In addition, estimated coefficients of surprises become larger for longer time windows. For example, surprise coefficients of Tankan are 23.22 for a 1-min window, 108 for 5-min, 215 for 15-min and 277 for 30-min windows. The deal activity increases by 23 transactions (out of a possible 120 transactions) within the minute. This means that the number of transactions jumps following the Tankan (manufacturing) announcements, regardless of the size of surprise, and continues to increase for up to 30 minutes. Similarly, the impact of GDPP is large, suggesting that the announcement itself stimulates deal activities. The fact that both Tankan and GDPP have a large impact on transactions means that the announcements are subject to heterogeneous interpretations, so that disagreement has to be resolved with deal activities.

3.6 Conclusion

This chapter examined intraday patterns of the foreign exchange market using one-second sliced transaction data derived from the actual trading platform, EBS, against the background of the changing structure of the foreign exchange market and evolving trading behavior.

First, it is empirically observed that the foreign exchange rate activities have a significant intraday pattern: three peaks which correspond to the Tokyo market, London market and New York market opening hours, and three troughs during Tokyo lunch and London lunch hours and after the New York market close. The opening-hour effects are empirically examined to show the negative relationship between the spread and the transaction volume. That is, the spread becomes significantly narrower and the number of deals (quotes) significantly higher during the opening hours of each market. The disappearance of the opening effect on the spread and the lack of the upswing of the U-shape in the afternoon for the trading activities in the New York market in recent years are presumably because of the recent widespread practice of continuous computer trading.

Second, we examine transaction volume on the Japanese news-announcement days on a presumption that the surge in activities during the opening hours may reflect macroeconomic statistics' news releases. We find that some of the Japanese macroeconomic statistics' releases at 8:50 (JST) significantly increase the number of deals. The surge in activity at GMT 0 Hour (9.00 am Japanese Standard Time) may reflect these JST 8:50 news releases. These findings are comparable to the US case in that the US macroeconomic statistic's releases have significant impact on the foreign exchange market during the New York opening hours.

Notes

The following research support by JSPS Grants-in-aid for Scientific Research is gratefully acknowledged: Grant-in-Aid for Young Scientists (B) 21730260 to the first author and Grant-in-Aid for (A) No. 15203008 to the second author.

1. The decline in transactions from 1998 to 2001 was partly attributed to "the introduction of Euro" (BIS, 2002: 6).
2. All figures are shown in net basis: that is, data are adjusted for both local and cross-border double counting.
3. "The use of electronic brokers implies that foreign exchange dealers generally need to trade less actively among themselves" (BIS, 2002: 7).
4. For the general reference on the microstructure of the foreign exchange market, see Goodhart and O'Hara (1997), Lyons (1995) and Lyons (2001).
5. See Goodhart and O'Hara (1997: 78) for general discussions on the difference between indicative and firm quotes.
6. Details of the EBS system and characteristics of the data are explained in Ito and Hashimoto (2004, 2006).
7. At first, the trade volume data was not fully available for most of the researchers. Ito and Hashimoto (2006) used "relative trade volume shares" that are the percentage share of trade volumes at one minute relative to the total trading volumes of that day. Since 2009, more detailed (and voluminous) foreign exchange rate data has become available for a fee from the EBS, now a part of ICAP. As for bid and ask quote prices, they are available from the best to the 10th (maximum) rank for the same timestamp, representing how far the price is from the best price.
8. EBS data Ito and Hashimoto (2004) first used did not contain information on the volume of transactions associated with bid, offer or deal.
9. However, in the EBS data set the reverse (bid higher than ask) can happen, when the two parties do not have credit lines to each other and there is no third party that has credit lines to the two quote-posting parties. The EBS system facilitates, as part of the dealing rules, each institution to control bilateral credit lines. Namely, each EBS-linked institution sets credit lines (including zero) against all other potential counter-parties. Therefore, an institution faces a restriction of bid, offer or deal from other institutions. When bid and offer rates are posted for the system, they are not necessarily available to all participants of the EBS system. The EBS-registered trader's screen shows the best bid and best offer of the market and best bid and best offer for that particular institution. In normal times, the best bid of the market is lower than the best offer of the market. Otherwise, an institution that has positive credit lines with both institutions on the bid and ask sides will be able to make profits by arbitrage.
10. The buyer-initiated trades (the seller-initiated trades) used in Berger et al. (2005) correspond to the number of deals on the ask side (the number of deals on bid side) in our chapter, respectively. The order flow, the net excess of buyer-initiated trades in Berger et al., corresponds to the "netdeal" in our paper. Berger et al. had access to the data of actual transaction volumes – proprietary data of EBS – while we use the number of seconds in which at least one deal was done. The number of deals, rather than the signed (actual)

volume, is a good enough proxy for the volume of transaction. In fact, the actual transaction volume is not revealed to participants other than parties involved so that they are not able to be used in prediction of price movement in real time.

11. The deal (on either side) recorded at zz second includes those that took place between zz-1 second to zz second. When there are multiple trades within one second, "lowest given price" and "highest paid price" will be shown. A highest paid deal means the highest price hit (done) on the ask side within one second and the lowest given deal means the lowest price hit (done) on the bid side within one second.
12. Note that the number of quotes and the number of deals in the data set may not exactly match the "true" total number of quotes and deals recorded in the EBS system, because the data we use are in terms of the one-second slice. Therefore, if there are multiple quotes and deals within one second, the numbers in the data set are less than the true numbers. Accordingly, the maximum number of quotes or deals in one hour is 3600.
13. The difference between the deal count and the trading volume share is twofold. The deal count is the number of seconds in which there is one deal or more. Therefore a second that experienced the deal may contain more than one deal and one deal may mean one million US dollars or several millions of US dollars. The trading volumes are the total amount of deals, but expressed as the share within the day.
14. Daylight saving time in 1999 was from April 4 to October 31 in the United States; from March 28 to October 31 in the United Kingdom; in 2000, from April 2 to October 29 in the United States, and from March 26 to October 29 in the United Kingdom; and in 2001, from April 1 to October 28 in the United States and from March 25 to October 28 in the United Kingdom.
15. Intraday patterns only for winter are shown in this section. For summer figures, please see Ito and Hashimoto (2006). Aggregation for a year is divided into two periods: Daylight Saving (Summer) Time from the first Sunday of April to the last Sunday of October; and Standard (Winter) Time from January to the last Sunday of March and from the last Monday (or the next working day of the last Sunday) of October to the end of December. We eliminate the one-week period in the spring when Europe is in Summer Time but the United States is not. Also excluded from the sample are Saturdays, Sundays and days in which one of the three markets is closed for national holidays.
16. Historically, the interbank foreign exchange transactions had a lunch break (regulatory shutdown) during the lunch hours. When the regulation was removed, the activities during the lunch hour increased at the expense of those before and after; the net effect was higher. See Ito, Lyons and Melvin (1998) and Covrig and Melvin (2005). Then, in the afternoon and market-ending hours of the Tokyo market, activity again increases in terms of relative transaction volume: it peaks around GMT Hours 5–6.
17. Again, only winter patterns are shown in this section. Please see Ito and Hashimoto (2006) for summer intraday patterns.
18. For a description please see Ito and Hashimoto (2006). The estimation models for the Tokyo opening effect and the Monday opening effect are as follows: $Spread_{(t)} = constant + (a_1 + a_2 * HOdum) * number\ of\ deals\ (or\ quotes)_{(t)} + \varepsilon_{(t)}$. In the

model, *H0dum* is an hour 0 dummy for testing the Tokyo opening effect, and Monday hour 0 dummy for the Monday opening effect.

19. The estimation model for London and New York opening effects is: $y_{(t)} = \beta * D1 + \gamma * D2 + \varepsilon_{(t)}$, where y is one of the three variables, number of price changes, the number of deals or the bid–ask spread; and *D*1 and *D*2 are dummy vectors. *D*1 consists of hour dummies to control the hour of the day effects. *D*2 are dummy vectors that examine opening and lunch hours over and above the GMT hour effect. Opening hours of London and New York can be identified separately from the GMT hour dummies because the opening hour shifts by one hour between summer and winter. Since the Tokyo market does not observe daylight saving time, Tokyo local time does not shift against GMT hour, and therefore we use the dummy vector *D*2 that identifies the London opening, London lunch and New York opening over and above k hours after Tokyo opens regardless of the daylight saving time. For more details please see Ito and Hashimoto (2006).
20. We thank Rich Lyons for his suggestion of this interpretation.
21. This section follows Hashimoto and Ito (2009).
22. Chaboud et al. (2004) used the following US macro variables: Payroll, GDP advanced, PPI, Retail sales, Trade Balance, and Fed Funds Rate (Target). Andersen et al. (2003) used GDP (advance, preliminary, final), Nonfarm Payroll, Retail Sales, Industrial Production, Capacity Utilization, Personal Income, Consumer Credit, Personal Consumption Expenditure, New Home Sales, Durable Goods Orders, Construction Spending, Factory Orders, Business Inventories, Government Budget Deficit, Trade Balance, PPI, CPI, Consumer Confidence Index, NAPM Index, Housing Starts, Index of Leading Indicators, Target Federal Funds Rate and Money Supply. The Ifo Business Climate Index is a closely watched indicator of German business conditions, based on a monthly survey of about 7000 companies. It is widely seen as a barometer for economic conditions of the Eurozone.
23. Ito and Hashimoto (2006) show that there are three peaks in a day: about 9–10am (JST), 4–6pm (JST), and 10pm-midnight (JST). They clearly correspond to the Tokyo opening, London opening, and New York opening times, respectively. The last peak corresponds to hours when London and New York business hours overlap. Each of the three troughs, between 2am and 8am (JST), about 12am-1pm (JST), and 8pm (JST), correspond to New York market close, Tokyo lunch time, and London Lunch time, respectively.
24. In Chaboud et al. (2004), the estimation model takes the form of $r = b*s+e$, where r is the return from one minute before the announcement release to h minutes after the release and s is the unexpected surprise component. The model is estimated only on days when there is a news release, not for the whole sample period.
25. Please see Hashimoto and Ito (2009) for detailed descriptions of estimation.

References

Admati, A.R. and Pfleiderer, P. (1988) "A Theory of Intra-Day Patterns: Volume and Price Variability," *Review of Financial Studies*, 1 (1): 3–40.

Andersen, T.G. and Bollerslev, T. (1997) "Intra-Day Periodicity and Volatility Persistence in Financial Markets," *Journal of Empirical Finance*, 4 (2&3): 115–158.

Andersen, T.G. and Bollerslev, T. (1998) "Deutsche Mark-Dollar Volatility: Intra-Day Activity Patterns, Macroeconomic Announcements, and Longer Run Dependencies," *Journal of Finance*, 53 (1): 219–265.

Andersen, T.G., T. Bollerslev, F.X. Diebold and C. Vega. (2003) "Micro Effects of Macro Announcements: Real-Time Price Discovery in Foreign Exchange," *American Economic Review*, 93 (1): 38–62.

Andersen, T.G., T. Bollerslev, F.X. Diebold and C. Vega. (2007) "Real-Time Price Discovery in Stock, Bond and Foreign Exchange Markets," *Journal of International Economics*, Elsevier, 73 (2): 251–277.

Baillie, R.T. and Bollerslev, T. (1990) "Intra-Day and Inter-Market Volatility in Foreign Exchange Rates," *Review of Economic Studies*, 58 (3): 565–585.

Bank of International Settlements (BIS) (2007) *Triennial Central Bank Survey of Foreign Exchange and Derivatives Market Activity*, various issues, Basle, Switzerland: Bank of International Settlements, Available at http://www.bis.org/publ/rpfx02.htm#pgtop

Berger, D., A.P. Chaboud, S.V. Chernenko, E. Howorka, R.S. K. Iyer, D.Liu and J.H. Wright (2005) "Order Flow and Exchange Rate Dynamics in Electronic Brokerage System Data," Board of Governors of the Federal Reserve System, *International Finance Discussion Papers*, 830, April, Washington, D.C., USA.

Brock, W.A. and Kleidon, A. (1992) "Periodic Market Closure and Trading Volume: A Model of Intra-Day Bids and Asks," *Journal of Economic Dynamics and Control*, 16 (3&4): 451–489.

Chaboud, A.P., S.V. Chernenko, E. Howorka; R.S.K. Iyer, D.Liu and J.H. Wright. (2004) "The High-Frequency Effects of U.S. Macroeconomic Data Releases on Prices and Trading Activity in the Global Interdealer Foreign Exchange Market," Board of Governors of the Federal Reserve System, *International Finance Discussion Papers*, 823, November, Washington, D.C., USA.

Covrig, V. and Melvin, M. (2005) "Tokyo Insiders and the Informational Efficiency of the Yen/Dollar Exchange Rate," *International Journal of Finance and Economics*, 10 (2): 185–193.

Easley, D. and O'Hara, M. (1992) "Time and the Process of Security Price Adjustment," *Journal of Finance*, 47 (2): 577–605.

Ehrmann, M. and Fratzscher, M. (2005) "Exchange Rates and Fundamentals New Evidence from Real-Time Data," *Journal of International Money and Finance*, 24 (2): 317–341.

Evans, M. and Lyons, R.K. (2002) "Order Flow and Exchange Rate Dynamics," *Journal of Political Economy*, 110 (1): 170–180.

Evans, M. and Lyons, R.K. (2005a) "Do Currency Markets Absorb News Quickly?" *Journal of International Money and Finance*, 24 (2): 197–217.

Evans, M. and Lyons, R.K. (2005b) "Meese-Rogoff Redux: Micro-Based Exchange Rate Forecasting," *American Economic Review*, 95 (2): 405–414.

Evans, M. and Lyons, R.K. (2005c) "Understanding Order Flow," NBER Working Paper, no.11748, Cambridge, MA.

Faust, J., J.H. Rogers, S.Y.B. Wang and J.H. Wright. (2003) "The High Frequency Response of Exchange Rates and Interest Rates to Macroeconomic

Announcements," Board of Governors of the Federal Reserve System, *International Finance Discussion Papers*, 784, Washington, D.C.

Goodhart, C., T. Ito and R. Payne. (1996) "One Day in June 1993: A Study of the Working of the Reuters 2000–2 Electronic Foreign Exchange Trading System," in J.A. Frankel, G. Galli, and A. Giovannini (eds.), *The Microstructure of Foreign Exchange Markets*, Chicago, IL: The University of Chicago Press: 107–179.

Goodhart, C. and Payne, R. (1996) "Microstructural Dynamics in a Foreign Exchange Electronic Broking System," *Journal of International Money and Finance*, 15 (6): 829–852.

Goodhart, C., A.E. and M. O'Hara. (1997) "High Frequency Data in Financial Markets: Issues and Applications," *Journal of Empirical Finance*, 4 (2&3): 73–114.

Hashimoto, Y. (2005) "The Impact of the Japanese Banking Crisis on the Intra-Day FX Market in Late 1997," *Journal of Asian Economics*, 16 (2): 205–222.

Hashimoto, Y., Ohnishi, T., H. Takayasu, T. Ito, M. Takayasu and T. Watanabe. (2008) "Dynamics of Quote and Deal Prices in the Foreign Exchange Market," *Journal of Economic Interaction and Coordination*, 3 (1): 99–106.

Hashimoto, Y. and Ito, T. (2009) "Effects of Japanese Macroeconomic Announcements on the Dollar/Yen Exchange Rate: High-Resolution Picture," NBER working paper, no. 15020, Cambridge, MA.

Hsieh, D.A. and Kleidon, A.W. (1996) "Bid-Ask Spreads in Foreign Exchange Markets: Implications for Models of Asymmetric Information," in J.A. Frankel, G. Galli, and A. Giovannini (eds.), *The Microstructure of Foreign Exchange Markets*, Chicago: The University of Chicago Press: 41–67.

Ito, T., R.K. Lyons, and M.T. Melvin. (1998) "Is There Private Information in the FX Market? The Tokyo Experiment," *Journal of Finance*, 53 (3): 1111–1130.

Ito, T. and Hashimoto, Y. (2004) "Microstructure of the Yen/Dollar Foreign Exchange Market: Patterns of Intra-day Activity in the Electronic Broking System," NBER working paper, no. 10856, Cambridge, MA.

Ito, T. and Hashimoto, Y. (2006) "Intra-Day Seasonality in Activities of the Foreign Exchange Markets: Evidence from the Electronic Broking System,"*Journal of the Japanese and International Economies*, 20 (4): 637–664.

Ito, T. and Hashimoto, Y. (2008) "Price Impacts of Deals and Predictability of the Exchange Rate Movement," in Takatoshi Ito and Andrew Rose (eds.), *International Financial Issues in the Pacific Rim: Global Imbalances, Financial Liberalization, and Exchange Rate Policy*, NBER-University of Chicago: Chicago, 17: 177–215.

Ito, T. and Roley, V.V.(1987) "News from the U.S. and Japan: Which Moves the Yen/Dollar Exchange Rate?" *Journal of Monetary Economics*, 19 (2): 255–277.

Love, R. and Payne, R. (2003) "Macroeconomic News, Order Flow and Exchange Rates," LSE Financial Markets Group Discussion Paper 475, London, UK.

Lyons, R. (1995) "Tests of Microstructural Hypotheses in the Foreign Exchange Market," *Journal of Financial Economics*, 39 (2–3): 321–351.

Lyons, R. (1996) "Foreign Exchange Volume: Sound and Fury Signifying Nothing?" in J.A. Frankel, G. Galli, and A. Giovannini (eds.), *The Microstructure of Foreign Exchange Markets*, Chicago, IL: The University of Chicago Press: 183–205.

Lyons, R. (1997) "A Simultaneous Trade Model of the Foreign Exchange Hot Potato," *Journal of International Economics*, 42 (3&4): 275–298.

Lyons, R. (1998) "Profits and Position Control: A Week of FX Dealing," *Journal of International Money and Finance*, 17 (1): 97–115.

Lyons, R. (2001) *The Microstructure Approach to Exchange Rates,* MIT Press: Cambridge, UK.

Lyons, R.K. and Moore, M.J. (2005) "An Information Approach to International Currencies," NBER Working Paper, no.11220, Cambridge, MA.

4

The Intraday Analysis of Volatility, Volume and Spreads: A Review with Applications to Futures' Markets

Dean Fantazzini

4.1 Introduction

When an operator starts to analyze financial microdata that is passing from a traditional "low-frequency" data set (usually daily or weekly) to a "high-frequency" one (from hourly data to tick-by-tick data), the volatility analysis tends to become more complex due to the strong relation among volatility, volume and spreads. This intraday relationship presents very special patterns due to market organizations and different kinds of market operators. This particular feature of financial markets must be considered if we want to gain a better understanding of their operation and consistent estimates to use in different financial fields, such as portfolio management, option pricing etc. What we do in this work is to review the main econometric models used for the analysis of volatility in an intraday environment which works with non-equally spaced data and considers the whole information set provided by the market. We then present an empirical application of ACD and ordered probit models to the Standard & Poor 500 (SP500) and Nasdaq100 index futures' data, and we point out the advantages and disadvantages of both approaches.

The rest of the chapter is organized as follows. In Section 4.2 we consider the main issues that arise when jointly modeling volatility, volume and spreads in an intraday environment, while in Section 4.3 we present the econometric models used to test and analyze intraday financial data. In Section 4.4 we apply the most important models with American futures' contracts SP500 and Nasdaq 100, while we conclude in Section 4.5.

4.2 Volatility, volumes and spreads

One of main characteristics of the intraday market process is that traded volumes, price volatilities and bid–ask spreads follow a "*U*-shaped" path (or to be more precise, an inverted *J*): these three variables reach their highest values at the market opening then go down and reach their lower point around the lunch hours. Finally, they rise again at the market closing. A similar pattern is present both in stock markets where there is a separate opening with a single multilateral auction (NYSE, Milan, for example), and in those without such a system, as in the CBOT (Sheikh and Ronn, 1994) or the Toronto Stock Exchange (McInish and Wood, 1990), while it is not present in the FX market. The interesting fact about these empirical regularities is that they are not easy to explain from a theoretical point of view, in the case where we want to use the traditional microstructural models with informed traders, uninformed ones and market makers. For instance, if we use Admati and Pfleiderer's model (1988), you will expect uninformed traders to enter the market when transactions costs are smaller, thus determining the already known "cluster market" effects. Given such a convergence of market orders and the consequent higher depth and market liquidity, the informed traders would also enter the market during these temporal periods to hide their identity. Since more private information is revealed, the asset prices would show a greater volatility. For these reasons, you would expect a strong correlation between volume and volatility, but *not*, at the same time, with spreads (since liquidity traders would enter the market only when transaction costs are smaller).

Similarly, you would expect a positive relationship between spreads and volatility, but a *negative* relationship with depth (Lee et al., 1993): a higher volatility would be associated with the revealing of private information, and this new information would then lead to an increase in market uncertainty and therefore in market spreads. The presence of such a positive correlation is present in all the main microstructural empirical studies, within which the direction of causality goes from volatility to spreads, rather than in the opposite direction (which is quite natural if you think that it is private information that moves spreads, not the opposite!). At this point, the main problem is to understand *why traded volumes are so high at the markets' opening and closing,* despite the high transaction costs that must be paid during these trading periods.

In regard to this problem, it must be said that a similar temporal path for volatility, spread and volume is not generalized to all financial markets: the London Stock Exchange, for instance (which, however, does not have a separated opening and closing like the NYSE and other European stock exchanges), presents a U-shape for spreads and volatility, while for traded volumes it has a double hump-shape path instead (see Fantazzini, 2004 for a review). If we consider the Forex markets and use the frequency of intraday quotes' data as a reasonable proxy for traded volumes, we can note that traded volumes do not show this U-shape path at all during the American trading hours, while the European and Asian markets show a rather weak temporal path (Demos and Goodhart, 1992).

This "strange" volume concentration at the opening and closing of the markets was first modeled by Brock and Kleidon (1992), who extend the Merton model (1971) in order to show how the number of trades is greater and less elastic at the market opening and closing: news coming out during the night and the subsequent necessity to rebalance assets portfolios can explain the high traded volume at the market opening. The fact that you cannot readjust your asset portfolios for more than 17 hours during the night and for 60 hours at the weekends, forces institutional investors and traders to adjust their portfolios just before the closing. The presence of this concentrated trading produces an increase both in volumes and in volatility, while the strong increase of *market* orders reveals the presence of private information and *interpretations* of public news. It is therefore easy to understand why an increase in volatility causes a widening of the spreads, whatever the implemented market microstructure is.

Besides, Brock and Kleidon (1992) underline the monopoly position of NYSE specialists and their ability to maximize profits by exploiting the increasing and inelastic demand of trades at the market opening and closing. This idea is confirmed by Chan et al. (1995), who pointed out that Nasdaq spreads tend to be relatively stable during the day and then narrow at the market closing. Similarly, Chan et al. (1995) showed that stock options' spreads quoted on the CBOE tend to go down after the market opening and then stabilize: both the Nasdaq and the CBOE have many "market makers," while the NYSE has a single specialist.

One of the most interesting studies to analyze this matter is by Gwinlym et al. (1999), who use quotes and transaction prices of futures and options listed on the LIFFE (London International Financial Futures and Options Exchange). In respect to futures, the studies by Gwinlym et al. (1999) highlight that both volumes and volatility respect the traditional U-shape, even though both of these variables are higher at the opening than at the closing. An interesting aspect of their work is the importance of "price reversals." This is a price change that goes in the opposite direction to the previous one, while a price change that goes in the same direction is called a "continuation." Price reversals are generally the result of the casual arrival of bid–ask orders which are executed at *stationary* bid and ask prices, thus causing the known "bounce effect" between bid and ask quotes. Continuations, however, are associated with new information, which has the effect of producing an unbalance between offer and demand and a subsequent modification of bid and ask quotes in order to incorporate the new asset value.

Gwinlym et al. (1999) show that futures' market openings present a smaller number of price reversals than the daily average, so that high volatility and high traded volumes would be the result of informed trading, thus sustaining Admati and Pfleiderer's model (1988). However, a very high percentage of reversals characterizes the high volumes and volatility at the market closing and this fact cannot be explained by the influx of new information. An interesting explanation that these researchers propose is that high volumes and volatility at the market closing are caused by particular operators, the "scalpers," who operate at the end of the trading day in order to close their positions before the night. As for the FTSE100 index options, volatility presents the known U-shape, while bid–ask spreads tend to be wide during the opening and then decrease for the whole trading day until the market closing: this spread decrease cannot be explained by informed trading nor by a greater number of trades due to scalpers. This evidence is instead consistent with Chan et al. (1995), who underline that market makers reduce their spreads at the market closing in order to attract trades and therefore reduce the inventories to maintain overnight. Their results confirm the idea by Brock and Kleidon (1992) that market microstructure influences spreads' behavior: financial markets with many different market makers present narrower spreads at the market closing than centralized markets' spreads, which are instead characterized by a single specialist (like the NYSE).

4.3 Econometric models for intraday volatility analysis

We now consider the main econometric models used for volatility analysis in an intraday environment that make use of non-equally spaced data (also known as "transaction-time" models), thus considering the whole information set provided by the market.

4.3.1 ACD models

Transaction-data models

A particular methodology that makes use of different time samples, but that takes the whole informative set into account thanks to single-transactions analysis, is represented by the ACD models ("autoregressive conditional duration"), initially introduced by Engle and Russell (1995 and 1998) and which are a particular evolution of GARCH models. It is an econometric representation for data *not* equally spaced, whose aim is to forecast the expected duration till the next transaction and use this information in order to determine if informed traders are present in the market, and thus to infer if asset values are far away from their equilibrium values.

Let's call $x_i = t_i - t_{i-1}$ the time interval between two consecutive transactions (the so-called duration) and let ψ_i be the expected value of the *i-th* duration, conditional to the past history of $x_i(x_{i-1}, x_{i-2}, \ldots, x_1)$. The ACD model can then be expressed in the following way,

$$x_i = \psi_i \varepsilon_I \tag{4.1}$$

$$\psi_i = \omega + \sum_{j=1}^{m} \alpha_j x_{i-j} + \sum_{k=1}^{q} \beta_k \psi_{i-k} \tag{4.2}$$

where ε_i represents a sequence of random variables "independent and identically distributed" (i.i.d.), with density function to be specified and mean equal to 1 (it is common practice to use the exponential distribution or the Weibull one). Engle and Russell (1998) assume that expected conditional durations depend on q past expected values and m past durations, plus a constant. If the conditional mean of x_i is ψ_i, the unconditional mean is

$$E(x_i) = \mu = \frac{\omega}{(1 - \sum(\alpha_j + \beta_j)} \tag{4.3}$$

while when $m = q = 1$, the conditional variance of x_i is ψ_i^2, and the unconditional one is,

$$\sigma^2 = \mu^2 \left(\frac{1 - \beta^2 - 2\alpha\beta}{1 - \beta^2 - 2\alpha\beta - 2\alpha^2} \right). \tag{4.4}$$

The ACD model (m, q) can be formulated as an ARMA(m, q) model in the observed duration x_i, using the transformation $\eta_i = x_i - \psi_i$, which is a martingale sequence by construction. In this case we have:

$$x_i = \omega + \sum_{j=0}^{\max(m,q)} (\alpha_j + \beta_j) x_{i-j} - \sum_{j=0}^{q} \beta_j \eta_{i-j} + \eta_i. \tag{4.5}$$

We review here four interesting cases:

(1) **Exponential–ACD (EACD)**: when we use an exponential distribution for the error term ε_i, the maximum likelihood estimation is a pseudo-ML. Engle and Russell (1998) show the consistency and asymptotic normality of the ML estimation, and that the model can be estimated by means of common ARCH software, using $\sqrt{x_i}$ as a dependent variable and setting the mean equal to zero. The EACD log likelihood is the following:

$$\mathrm{Logl}(\theta) = -\sum_{i=1}^{N(t)} \left[\log(\psi_i) + \frac{x_i}{\psi_i} \right] \tag{4.6}$$

where x_i is modeled as in (4.1)–(4.2), with the following constraints on the coefficients: $\omega > 0$, $\alpha_i \geq 0$, $\beta_i \geq 0$ and $\Sigma(\alpha_i + \beta_i) < 1$. The last constraint ensures the existence of the unconditional mean of the durations, while the others ensure the positivity of the conditional durations.

(2) **Weibull–ACD (WACD)**: an alternative to the exponential model is to consider a Weibull conditional distribution, which assumes that $(x_i/\varphi_i)\gamma$ is exponential and where φ_i is a function of past values. If we specify the observed duration as a mixing process:

$$x_i = \varphi_i \varepsilon_i \tag{4.7}$$

where $\varepsilon_i \sim$ i.i.d. and follows a Weibull distribution with parameters $(1, \gamma)$, and φ_i are proportional to the conditional expected durations ψ_i, which is modeled as the autoregressive process (4.2)

$$\psi_i = \omega + \sum_{j=1}^{m} \alpha_j x_{i-j} + \sum_{k=1}^{q} \beta_k \psi_{i-k} \tag{4.8}$$

in this case, the condition that $\psi_i = \mathrm{E}(x_i | \mathrm{I}_{i-1})$ where I_{i-1} is the information set available at time $t_i - 1$, gives us a third equation that allows us to connect (4.7) and (4.8):

$$\psi_i = \Gamma(1 + 1/\gamma)\varphi_i \tag{4.9}$$

where $\Gamma(\cdot)$ is the Gamma function. If $\gamma = 1$, the Weibull distribution becomes an exponential and $\varphi_i = \psi_i$. The simplest WACD model is the one with $m = q = 1$, whose log likelihood is the following

$$\text{Logl}(\theta) = \sum_{i=1}^{N(T)} \ln\left(\frac{\gamma}{x_i}\right) + \gamma \ln\left(\frac{\Gamma(1+1/\gamma)x_i}{\psi_i}\right) - \left(\frac{\Gamma(1+1/\gamma)x_i}{\psi_i}\right)^{\gamma}. \tag{4.10}$$

As before, if $\gamma = 1$ the log likelihood turns into an exponential one. The constraints on the coefficients are the same as the ones for the EACD model.

(3) **Log–EACD:** the logarithmic version of the ACD model modifies equation (4.1) as follows:

$$x_i = e^{\psi_i}\varepsilon_i \tag{4.11}$$

where ε_i are i.i.d. and follow an exponential distribution, while the conditional duration $\psi_i = \ln E(x_i|\mathrm{I}_{i-1})$ is modeled according to an autoregressive form (we consider here the case $m = q = 1$):

$$\psi_i = \omega + \alpha g(x_{i-1}, \epsilon_{i-1}) + \beta\psi_{i-1}. \tag{4.12}$$

Thanks to formula (4.11), we do not need to impose any restrictions on the sign of the parameters ω, $\alpha e \beta$ to guarantee a positive result of x_i. Bauwens and Giot (2000) propose two different possibilities to model the function $g(x_{i-1}, \epsilon_{i-1})$:

(a) $g(x_{i-1}, \epsilon_{i-1}) = \ln x_{i-1}$. In this case, the logarithm of the conditional duration is:

$$\psi_i = \omega + \alpha \ln x_{i-1} + \beta\psi_{i-1}, \tag{4.13}$$

and ψ_i, is covariance stationary if $|\alpha + \beta| < 1$.

(b) $g(x_{i-1}, \epsilon_{i-1}) = \epsilon_{i-1}$. The logarithm of the conditional duration is then given by:

$$\psi_i = \omega + \alpha\epsilon_{i-1} + \beta\psi_{i-1} = \omega + \alpha\frac{x_{i-1}}{e^{\psi_{i-1}}} + \beta\psi_{i-1}, \tag{4.14}$$

With this specification, the logarithm of the conditional duration depends on its lagged value and on the lagged value of the "excess duration." ψ_i, is covariance stationary if $|\beta| < 1$.

Bauwens and Giot (2000) show that the second solution gives the best results. For this reason, we will refer only to equation (4.14) from now on.

(4) **Log–WACD**: in this case we have,

$$x_i = e^{\phi_i} \varepsilon_i \tag{4.15}$$

where ε_i are i.i.d. and follow a Weibull distribution $(1, \gamma)$, while φ_i is proportional to the logarithm of the conditional expectation of x_i, that is ψ_i, which has the following autoregressive form:

$$\beta\psi_i = \omega + \alpha \frac{x_{i-1}\Gamma(1+1/\gamma)}{e^{\psi_{i-1}}} + \beta\psi_{i-1}, \tag{4.16}$$

The condition $\psi_i = \ln E(x_i|I_{i-1})$ or $e^{\Psi_i} = \ln E(x_i|I_{i-1})$ provides us with a third equation, linking (4.15) and (4.16):

$$e^{\phi_i}\Gamma(1+1/\gamma) = e^{\Psi_i}. \tag{4.17}$$

The log likelihood is then given by:

$$\text{Logl}(\theta) = \sum_{i=1}^{N} \ln(\gamma) - \ln(x_i) + \gamma \ln[x_i\Gamma(1+1/\gamma)]$$
$$- \gamma\psi_i - \left(\frac{x_i\Gamma(1+1/\gamma)}{e^{\psi_i}}\right)^{\gamma} \tag{4.18}$$

where $\psi_i =$ is defined as in (4.16). As initial values, Bauwens and Giot (2000) suggest setting x_0 e e^{ψ_0} equal to the unconditional mean of x_i. The expected conditional value of x_i is e^{ψ_i} by definition. The analytical expression for the unconditional moments has been given by Bauwens et al. (2008), to whom we refer for further information.

4.3.2 An extension: Intraday market patterns

The dynamic specification of the conditional durations can be easily generalized by introducing nonlinear functions and including other variables such as past trades and related marks:

$$\psi_i = \psi x_{i-1}, \ldots, x_{i-m}; \psi_{i-1}, \ldots, \psi_{i-p}; z_{i-1}, \ldots, z_{i-m}\theta). \tag{4.19}$$

An important case is represented by the inclusion of intraday market periodicities in (4.19), which are well documented in many empirical papers (Engle, 2000; Bauwens and Giot, 2000, among others). It is a well-known feature that the number of trades is higher at market opening and closing, and thus expected duration must be decomposed in a deterministic and a stochastic component, usually by using a multiplicative function:

$$\tilde{x}_i = x_i / s(t_{i-1}; \theta_s) \tag{4.20}$$

where $s(t_{i-1};\ \theta_s)$ is the intraday pattern, while the expected duration is equal to

$$E_{i-1}(x_i) = s(t_{i-1};\ \theta_s)\psi(\tilde{x}_{i-1},\ \ldots,\tilde{x}_1;\ \theta\psi) \tag{4.21}$$

where the two parameters can be jointly estimated with the previous log likelihoods. Engle and Russell (1998) use a cubic spline with knots at every hour, with a further knot for the last half hour, in order to have more flexibility in modeling the intraday seasonal pattern. The equations to be used within maximum likelihood estimation are thus the following:

$$\text{EACD}(1,1):\ \psi_i = \omega + \alpha_1\tilde{x}_{i-1} + \beta_1\psi_{i-1},\quad \text{where } \tilde{x}_{i-1} = \frac{x_{i-1}}{s(t_{i-1})}$$

$$s(t_{i-1}) = \sum_{j=1}^{K} I_j[c_j + d_{1,j}(t_{i-1} - k_{j-1}) + d_{2,j}(t_{i-1} - k_{j-1})^2 + d_{3,j}(t_{i-1} - k_{j-1})^3] \tag{4.22}$$

where I_j is an indicator variable for the j-segment of the spline, so that $I_j = 1$ if $k_{j-1} \leq t_{i-1} < k_j$, it is zero otherwise. c_{11} is normalized by restricting the unconditional mean of the diurnal factor to equal the observed sample mean.

Andersen–Bollerslev (1998) and Pohlmeier–Gerhard (2001) use instead a Fourier series approximation based on the work of Gallant (1981). If we assume a polynomial of degree q, the deterministic seasonal pattern is of the form:

$$s(\delta, t_i^*, q) = \delta t_i^* + \sum_{q=1}^{Q} \left(\delta_{c,q}\cos(t_i^* \cdot 2\pi q) + \delta_{s,q}\sin(t_i^* \cdot 2\pi q)\right) \tag{4.23}$$

where δ, $\delta_{c,q}, \delta_{s,q}$ are the coefficients to be estimated, while $t_i * \epsilon[0,\ 1]$ is a normalized intraday time trend, which is defined as the number of seconds from market opening until the occurrence of transaction i divided by the length of the trading day.

It must be noted that ACD and spline parameters can be estimated jointly or in a two-step procedure, where the seasonal pattern is accounted for first. The normalized durations $\tilde{x}_{i-1}$ are then used to estimate the ACD model (Engle and Russell, 1998; Engle, 2000).

4.3.3 Models form intraday analysis of volatility, volume and spreads

An interesting evolution of this model that analyses volatility dynamics is the UHF–GARCH proposed by Engle (2000): the aim of this particular model is to measure price volatility by means of transactions' data in order to understand how the timing of the trades influence intraday volatility. The returns and volatility equations of the basic model UHF–GARCH (1,1) are the following ones:

$$\frac{r_i}{\sqrt{x_i}} = \rho \frac{r_{i-1}}{\sqrt{x_{i-1}}} + e_i + \phi e_{i-1} \tag{4.24}$$

$$\sigma_i^2 = \omega + \alpha e_{i-1}^2 + \beta \sigma_{i-1}^2 \tag{4.25}$$

where the observed returns r_i divided by the square root of their durations, follow an ARMA(1,1) with innovations e (equation 4.24), while the conditional variance σ_i^2 follows a GARCH(1,1) model, which is modified in order to account for irregular time samples (equation 4.25). Engle (2000) includes the current duration into (4.24) as well, which can reflect two conflicting effects: the longer the interval over which the return is measured, the higher the expected return because both risk-free and risky returns are measured per unit of time. However, if no trades mean bad news as in Diamond and Verrecchia (1987), longer durations should be associated with declining prices. This model can be estimated as a traditional GARCH(1,1) where the dependent variable is returns divided by the square root of durations, while the conditional mean is modeled as an ARMA, with the addition of the current duration. A wider specification can include both observed durations and expected ones (which are calculated thanks to an ACD(1,1) model of observed durations), a volatility long-memory component, as well as economic variables such as the market spread and volume, so that microstructural models previously discussed can be tested.

A more realistic and interesting specification, where the durations enter the conditional variance equation directly, is given below:

$$\sigma_i^2 = \omega + \alpha e_{i-1}^2 + \beta \sigma_{i-1}^2 + \gamma x_i^{-1}. \tag{4.26}$$

If the Easley and O'Hara (1992) hypothesis is true ("no trades, no news, low volatility"), the parameter γ should be positive, as longer durations imply a market without any news with stable prices and low volatility (Engle's empirical results confirm this theory). A wider specification includes both observed and expected durations as well as a long-run volatility variable:

$$\sigma_i^2 = \omega + \alpha e_{i-1}^2 + \beta \sigma_{i-1}^2 + \gamma_1 x_i^{-1} + \gamma_2 \frac{x_i}{\psi_i} + \gamma_3 \xi_{i-1} + \gamma_4 \psi_i^{-1} \tag{4.27}$$

where ξ_i is the long-run volatility component, which is estimated by exponentially smoothing r^2/x with a parameter equal to 0.995 as proposed by Engle (2000):

$$\xi_i = 0.005(r_{i-1}^2/x_{i-1}) + 0.995\xi_{i-1}. \qquad (4.28)$$

If we estimate the model with equation (4.27), the impact of durations on volatility will be given by three coefficients which measure: (1) reciprocal durations – γ_1 –, (2) surprises in durations – γ_2 –, and (3) expected trade arrival rates – γ_3 – (the reciprocal of expected durations). Expected durations are estimated by an ACD(1,1) model on observed durations. In order to improve the volatility forecasting, Engle also introduces economic variables into this model, such as the spread and the volume: Easley and O'Hara (1992) argue that a greater number of informed traders causes a higher volatility and a widening of spreads. Wider spreads should point out the presence of informed trading and therefore improve the forecast of future volatility. Likewise, a greater number of trades are likely to be indicators of information (private and public) and therefore predictors of the volatility (Engle, 2000).

4.3.4 Ordered probit models

Theoretical background

As the first studies about high-frequency data were unable to consider the three fundamental aspects of (1) asset prices' discrete values, (2) the timing of single transactions, and (3) the distribution of price changes conditionally to traded volumes, durations and the sequence of past prices changes, Hausman et al. (1992) have proposed the "ordered probit model" with conditional variance to account for these important aspects. They applied this model to the discreet movements of stock prices quoted on the NYSE. Bollerslev and Melvin (1994) used the same approach for the analysis of Forex quotes, as well as Hautsch and Pohlmeier (2001) for BUND future data.

The ordered probit model (from now on "OP") can be considered the generalization of the linear regression model to the case where the dependent variable is a discrete one. The basic idea of this model is a "virtual" regression of a set of latent dependent variables Y^*, whose conditional mean is a linear function of some observable explanatory variables. Although Y^* is not observable, however, it is linked to a discreet random variable Y which is instead observable, and whose values are determined by the particular state of Y^*. If the state space of the latent variable Y^* is partitioned into a finite number of separate regions, Y can be considered as an indicator function for Y^* over these regions: for example, a discreet random variable Y with values [−0.01; 0; 0.01] can be modeled as an indicator variable that takes on the value −0.01 whenever $Y^* \leq \alpha_1$, the value 0 whenever $\alpha_1 < Y^* \leq \alpha_2$ and the value +0.01 whenever $Y^* > \alpha_2$. The OP model then estimates α_1, α_2 and the coefficients of the unobserved "virtual" regression which determines the conditional mean and variance of Y^*. Besides, since α_1, α_2 and Y^* can depend on a vector of regressors Z, the OP analysis is more general and complex than its simple structure may suggest, and can analyze the price effects of many economic variables in a way that models of the unconditional distribution of price changes cannot (Hausman et al., 1992).

Let's consider a price sequence $p(t_0), p(t_1), \ldots, p(t_n)$ observed at times $t_0, t_1, \ldots t_n$, and use $y_1, y_2, \ldots, y_n$ as the corresponding price changes, where $y_k = p(t_k) - p(t_{k-1})$ is an integer multiple of some divisor called a "tick" (for example, a Euro cent). Let y_k^* be an unobservable continuous random variable such that

$$y_k^* = z_k' \beta + \varepsilon_k, E[\varepsilon_k | z_k] = 0, \quad \varepsilon_k \sim i.n.i.d.\ N(0, \sigma_k^2) \tag{4.29}$$

$$\sigma_k^2 = \sigma_0^2 \left[\exp(\omega_k' \gamma)\right]^2 \tag{4.30}$$

where z_k is a $(K \times 1)$ vector of observed independent variables that determine the conditional mean of y_k^*, while "i.n.i.d." indicates that ε_k are independently but not identically distributed, because their variance is conditioned by a set of economic variables w_k, through a multiplicative heteroskedasticity form. The main idea of OP modeling is that price changes y_k are linked to the continuous variable y_k^* in the following way:

$$y_k = \begin{cases} s_1 & if \quad y_k^* \in S_1 \\ s_2 & if \quad y_k^* \in S_2 \\ \cdot & \\ \cdot & \\ \cdot & \\ s_m & if \quad y_k^* \in S_m \end{cases} \tag{4.31}$$

where the regions S_j represent a precise partition of the state space Ω^* of y_k^*, that is, $\Omega^* = \bigcup_{j=1}^{m} S_j$ and $S_i \cap S_j = \varnothing$ for $i \neq j$, while the s_j are the discrete values that comprise the state space Ω of y_k.

As for this, it must be noted that even though the number of price changes considered can be as high as needed, all past empirical works assume m to be finite, so that the number of parameters to estimate is finite: for example, in Hausman et al. (1992), the s_j are equal to stock "ticks" 0, −1/8, +1/8, −2/8, +2/8 and so on; in Hautsch and Pohlmeier's model (2001), they are instead equal to −2, −1, 0, +1, +2. Hausman et al.

(1992) point out that the inclusion of further states to improve the estimates does not change the asymptotic estimates of β on condition that the model (4.29–4.30) is correctly specified. Besides, you cannot consider an endless number of states due to the fact that the most extreme ones do not have any observation so that the relative parameters cannot be estimated anyway.

The conditional distribution of price changes Δp, conditionally to z_k e w_k, is determined by the partition of the state space Ω^* and by the distribution of ε_k. If ε_k are Gaussian, the conditional distribution is:

$$P(y_k = s_i|z_k, w_k) = P(z_k'\beta + \varepsilon_k \in S_i|z_k, w_k) \tag{4.32}$$

$$= \begin{cases} P(z_k'\beta + \varepsilon_k \leq \alpha_1|z_k, w_k) & \text{if } i=1 \\ P(\alpha_{i-1} < z_k'\beta + \varepsilon_k \leq \alpha_i|z_k, w_k) & \text{if } 1<i<m \\ P(\alpha_{m-1} < z_k'\beta + \varepsilon_k|z_k, w_k) & \text{if } i=m \end{cases}$$

$$= \begin{cases} \Phi\left(\frac{\alpha_1 - z_k'\beta}{\sigma_k}\right) & \text{if } i=1 \\ \Phi\left(\frac{\alpha_i - z_k'\beta}{\sigma_k}\right) - \Phi\left(\frac{\alpha_{i-1} - z_k'\beta}{\sigma_k}\right) & \text{if } 1<i<m \\ 1-\Phi\left(\frac{\alpha_{m-1} - z_k'\beta}{\sigma_k}\right) & \text{if } i=m \end{cases} \tag{4.33}$$

where $\Phi(.)$ is the normal cumulated distribution function. Hausman et al. (1992) highlight that if we change the partition among the different regions the OP model can be adapted to any multinomial distribution, so that the normality assumption previously considered does not have any particular role when estimating the probabilities of the different states. However, a logistic distribution would have made the conditional heteroskedasticity modeling much more difficult, and this is why it is preferable to use the normal distribution. Given the partition boundaries of the state space Ω^*, a higher conditional mean $z_k'\beta$ means a higher probability of observing a more extreme positive state: even though the labeling of the states is arbitrary, the *ordered* probit model makes use of the natural ordering of the states. Thus, by estimating the partition boundaries α and the coefficients β and γ of the conditional mean and variance, the OP model captures the empirical relation between the unobservable continuous state space Ω^* and the observed discrete state space Ω as a function of the economic variables z_k e w_k (Hausman et al., 1992).

Let c_{ik} be an indicator variable which is equal to 1 if the $k^{-\text{th}}$ observation y_k is within the $i-$state s_i, and zero otherwise. The log-likelihood function for a price change vector $Y = [y_1, y_2, \ldots, y_n]'$, conditionally to a vector of explanatory variables $Z = [z_1, z_2, \ldots, z_n]'$ is equal to:

$$\begin{aligned}
\text{Logl}(Y|Z) = \sum_{k=1}^{n} \Bigg\{ & c_{1k} \cdot \log \Phi \left(\frac{\alpha_1 - z_k' \beta}{\sigma_k} \right) + \\
& \sum_{i=2}^{m-1} c_{ik} \cdot \log \left[\Phi \left(\frac{\alpha_i - z_k' \beta}{\sigma_k} \right) - \Phi \left(\frac{\alpha_{i-1} - z_k' \beta}{\sigma_k} \right) \right] \\
& + c_{mk} \cdot \log \left[1 - \Phi \left(\frac{\alpha_{im-1} - z_k' \beta}{\sigma_k} \right) \right] \Bigg\}. \qquad (4.34)
\end{aligned}$$

As we have seen previously, the conditional variance is heteroskedastic, conditionally to a set of variables w_k; that is $\sigma_k^2 = \sigma_0^2 \left[\exp(\omega_k' \gamma) \right]^2$. Furthermore, to completely identify the OP model, some restrictions on α, β and γ must be set: if we were to double them the likelihood would be unchanged. In fact, only the parameter vector $[\alpha'/\sigma_0, \beta/\sigma_0, \gamma']$ is directly identifiable without any restriction: for the sake of simplicity, it is usually assumed that $\sigma_0^2 = 1$, as in Hautsch and Pohlmeier (2001) and Hausman et al. (1992), even though the latter does not use a multiplicative conditional variance but an arithmetic sum, as we will see in the next section.

The empirical specification of the model

Before we proceed to the empirical applications of the OP model, it is necessary to specify three points: (1) the number of the states m, (2) the explanatory variable z_k, and (3) the specification of the conditional variance.

(1) **Number of the states m**: when you have to choose m, you must consider the fact that extreme regions will hardly have any observations. For this reason, it is useful to observe the price changes' sample histogram to understand which reasonable value m can take.

If we had a situation like the one depicted in Figure 4.1, a reasonable value for m would be 7, where the extreme regions are $s_1 = (-\infty, -3]$e $s_7 = [+3, +\infty)$, while the states from s_2 to s_6 contain the price changes of a single tick. Besides, the symmetry in the price changes' Δp distribution suggests a similar symmetry for the states s_i.

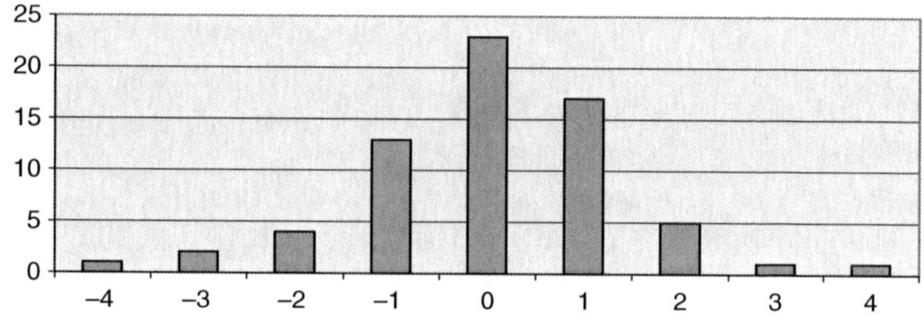

Figure 4.1 A possible distribution for price changes Δp

(2) **Choice of explanatory variables Z'**: the main variables that can be considered within intraday applications are the following ones:

x_k = the time elapsed between the $k-1^{th}$ transaction and the kth (to consider the time effect);
$\Delta bidask$ = the bid–ask spread, if available (to consider the bid–ask bounce);
y_{k-l} = a number of lags (l) of the dependent variable y_k (persistence)
V_{k-l} = a number of lags of the traded volumes; if we deal with stocks, the lagged volume weighted by the stock price, that is the so-called dollar volume, which is defined as the price of the $(k-l)^{-th}$ transaction (in euro or dollars, according to the market) times the number of traded stocks (how the market reacts to bigger volumes).
IND_{k-l} = a number of lags of the market main index returns (how the market influences the single asset price).
IBS_{k-l} = a number of lags of an indicator variable which take the value of 1 if the $(k-l)^{-th}$ transaction price is bigger than the average value between the bid and ask price quoted when the trade took place and the value of -1 if the price is lower than the average value, and 0 otherwise – if available.
$Dummy_{\,i}$ = dummy variables to catch possible day-of-the-week effect.

(3) **Conditional variable specification:** Hausman et al. (1992) use the following equation:

$$\sigma_k^2 = \gamma_0^2 + \gamma_1^2 \Delta x_k + \gamma_2^2 \Delta bidask_{(k-1)} \tag{4.35}$$

where γ_0^2 is set equal to 1, to identify the model's parameters. Hautsch and Pohlmeier (2001) use the following multiplicative specification instead:

$$\sigma_k^2 = \sigma_0^2[\exp(\gamma_1 \log(x_k) + \gamma_2(\log(x_{k-1}) + \gamma_3(\log(x_{k-2}) + \gamma_4(\log(x_{k-3}) + \gamma_5(\log(V_k) + \gamma_6(\log(V_{k-1}) + TREND)]^2 \tag{4.36}$$

where the deterministic intraday trend is modeled with a Fourier series approximation:

$$\text{TREND} = \gamma_7 t_k^* + \sum_{q=1}^{5} \left(\gamma_{c,q} \cos(t_k^* \cdot 2\pi q) + \gamma_{s,q} \sin(t_k^* \cdot 2\pi q)\right) \tag{4.37}$$

where $\gamma_7, \gamma_{c,q}, \gamma_{s,q}$ are the coefficients to be estimated, while $t_k^* \epsilon [0,1]$ is a normalized intraday time trend, which is defined as the number of seconds from market opening until the occurrence of transaction i divided by the length of the trading day. Hautsch and Pohlmeier (2001) assume $\sigma_0^2 = 1$ to completely identify α, β *e* γ; nevertheless, the two authors refer to more interesting selection methods for σ_0^2, such as "minimum distance" estimation or nonlinear restrictions (see Pohlmeier and Gerhard, 2001 for further details).

Diagnostic tests

The first step in verifying the correct specification in a classical OLS model is to examine the residuals' properties: if all variables are included, the residuals should approximate a white noise with no serial correlation left. Unfortunately, we cannot directly estimate the residuals in the OP model because we cannot observe the latent variable y_k^* and the related residuals $y_k^* - z_k'\hat{\beta}$. However, we have an estimate of the distribution of y_k^* conditional to z_k', and a parameter vector estimated by maximum likelihood. From this starting point, we can estimate a conditional distribution of the ε_k, and then build the generalized residuals $\hat{\varepsilon}_k$, following Gourieroux et al. (1987):

$$\hat{\varepsilon}_k = E[\varepsilon_k | y_k, z_k, w_k; \hat{\theta}_{ml}] \tag{4.38}$$

where $\hat{\theta}_{ml}$ are the maximum likelihood estimates of $\hat{\alpha}, \hat{\beta}, \hat{\gamma}$. In our case, if y_k is equal to the j^{-th} state, that is $y_k = s_j$, then the generalized residuals $\hat{\varepsilon}_k$ can be explicitly estimated using the moments of the truncated normal distribution (Hausman et al., 1992):

$$\hat{\varepsilon}_k = E[\varepsilon_k | y_k, z_k, w_k; \hat{\theta}_{ml}] = \hat{\sigma}_k \cdot \frac{\phi(c_2) - \phi(c_1)}{\Phi(c_2) - \Phi(c_1)}, \tag{4.39}$$

where $c_1 = \frac{1}{\hat{\sigma}_k}(\hat{\alpha}_{j-1} - z_k'\hat{\beta})$, $c_2 = \frac{1}{\hat{\sigma}_k}(\hat{\alpha}_j - z_k'\hat{\beta})$, and $\sigma_k^2 = \gamma_0^2 + \gamma_1^2 \Delta x_k + \gamma_2^2 \Delta bidask_{(k-1)}$ (if we follow Hausman et al.,1992), $\sigma_k^2 = \left[\exp(\omega_k'\gamma)\right]^2$ (if we follow Greene, 2000 and Hautsch and Pohlmeier, 2001) and where $\varphi(.)$ is the probability density function of a standard normal, while $\Phi(.)$ is the cumulated distribution function. It is common practice to define $\alpha_0 = -\infty$ and $\alpha_m = +\infty$.

The generalized residuals can be used for different misspecification tests, but they must be used with a certain caution: Gourieroux et al. (1987) show that the autocorrelation of the generalized residuals $\hat{\varepsilon}_k$, in general, is not equal to the theoretical autocorrelation of ε_k. Besides, if the serial correlation is due to the omission of some lags of the endogenous variables y_k, the previous specification tests must be modified. In order to deal with this problem, Gourieroux et al. (1987) built some tests to analyze the serial correlation due to lagged endogenous variables by using the "score statistic." That is, the derivative of the log-likelihood function w.r.t. the autocorrelation parameter, evaluated with the ML estimates under the null hypothesis of no serial correlation. For example, let's consider the following model per y_k^*:

$$y_k^* = \varphi y_{k-1}^* + z_k'\beta + \varepsilon_k, \text{ con } |\phi| < 1 \tag{4.40}$$

In this case, the score statistic $\hat{\xi}_1$ is the derivative of the log-likelihood function w.r.t. ϕ, evaluated with the ML estimates under the null hypothesis $\phi = 0$, that is

$$\hat{\xi}_1 = \left(\sum_{k=2}^{n} \hat{y}_{k-1}\hat{\varepsilon}_k\right)^2 \Bigg/ \sum_{k=2}^{n} \hat{y}_{k-1}^2\hat{\varepsilon}_k^2, \tag{4.41}$$

where $\hat{y}_k = E[y_k^* | y_k, z_k, w_k; \hat{\theta}_{ml}] = z_k'\hat{\beta} + \hat{\varepsilon}_k$. When $\varphi = 0$, $\hat{\xi}_1$ is asymptotically distributed as a χ^2 with one degree of freedom. If we consider the general case and we want to test for the omission of the lagged endogenous variable of order bigger than one, we have:

$$y_k^* = \varphi y_{k-j}^* + z_k'\beta + \varepsilon_k, \text{ con } |\phi| < 1 \tag{4.42}$$

$$\hat{\xi}_j = \left(\sum_{k=j+1}^{n} \hat{y}_{k-j}\hat{\varepsilon}_k\right)^2 \Bigg/ \sum_{k=j+1}^{n} \hat{y}_{k-j}^2\hat{\varepsilon}_k^2 \tag{4.43}$$

that is again asymptotically distributed as a χ^2 with one degree of freedom, under the null hypothesis of $\phi = 0$. Another way to test the possible omission of a lagged endogenous variable is to estimate the sample correlations $\hat{\nu}_j$ of the generalized residuals $\hat{\varepsilon}_k$ with the estimated lagged values $\hat{y}_{k-j}$. Under the null hypothesis of no serial correlation in the residuals ε_k, the theoretical value of this correlation is zero: the sample correlation can thus furnish a measure of the economic impact caused by model misspecification (Hausman et al., 1992).

4.4 An application to futures' markets: Chicago mercantile exchange's S&P 500 and Nasdaq 100

4.4.1 CME data handling

After having examined the theory of ACD and ordered probit modeling, we now present some empirical applications employing intraday futures' data relative to the Standard & Poor 500 and Nasdaq100 stock index futures, quoted at the Chicago Mercantile Exchange (CME). Besides being the most important stock index futures, these two derivatives have the characteristics of being quoted almost 24 hours a day: to be more precise, there is normal "pit" trading from 15.30 to 22.15 CET ("regular trading hour, RTH"), and an electronic session from 22.45 until 15.15 the day after ("Globex"). As the night session usually presents a low number of trades, especially between the closing of American markets and the opening of the Asian one, we analyze here only the data which took place within the daily RTH session. This data has been downloaded from by the CME's web site, www.cme.com, that publishes the "Times and sales" relative to every financial asset quoted during the preceding 24 hours daily. This data is saved as text files and besides the price, they show the hour/minute/second, the traded volumes and other marks relative to the traded derivative (such as cancelled orders) that goes beyond the scope of this chapter and will not be considered.

The analyzed data set runs from April 29, 2002 to June 28, 2002, which covers nine weeks of trading, which took place between 8.30 Chicago local time (9.30 New York local time, 15.30 CET), and 15.00 Chicago local time (16.00 New York local time, 22.00 CET): among the 45 trading days, only the data relative to Monday May 27, 2002 is missing, as the CME was not operative on that day. We grouped the data for every day of the week from Monday to Friday, in order to better estimate the intraday seasonal pattern. Moreover, the first trade which took place every day after 8.30 in the morning (Chicago local time) has been deleted. The CME

Table 4.1 Number of data used divided per day of the week

	SP500	NASDAQ100
Monday (1 day is not present)	21838	9070
Tuesday	25043	10496
Wednesday	25282	11566
Thursday	24560	11010
Friday	23026	9707
Total	**119749**	**51849**

data, unlike the TAQ database by the New York Stock Exchange, does not show the bid–ask quotes relative to every trade. When we observe a duration equal to zero, we have a so-called split-transaction: this means that the bid or sell *market order* was bigger than the first bid–ask level in the market book, and it had to go down to lower market book levels to be executed, thus generating different prices with the same timestamp. Some empirical studies consider these "sub-transactions" separately, and they fix their duration to 1 second. Here, we prefer to follow Grammig and Wellner (2002) and Hautsch and Pohlmeier (2001): if the durations are equal to zero, the sub-transactions are united in a single trade with the same timestamp (hh/mm/ss), the traded volume is equal to the sum of single volumes and the price is the weighted average of the single sub-transactions' prices. After this data-handling process, the amount of data used for the subsequent econometric analysis is detailed below.

4.4.2 ACD modeling: Empirical results

Intraday market patterns

We estimated the intraday market pattern by using the linear splines by Engle (2000): however, unlike Engle, and following Bauwens and Giot (2000), the seasonalities have also been differentiated for every single week day. The final results are reported in Figures 4.2–4.11 (the durations in seconds are reported on the y axis, while the time interval of a single day, that is 23400 seconds, is displayed on the x axis).

As it is possible to see from the previous graphs, the choice to differentiate the seasonalities for a single weekday is surely a proper one. Moreover, splines' coefficients are significant in almost all cases at the 5 percent level (we do not report the result for the sake of space). The common "U-shape" (normal or inverted) for durations and volatility is

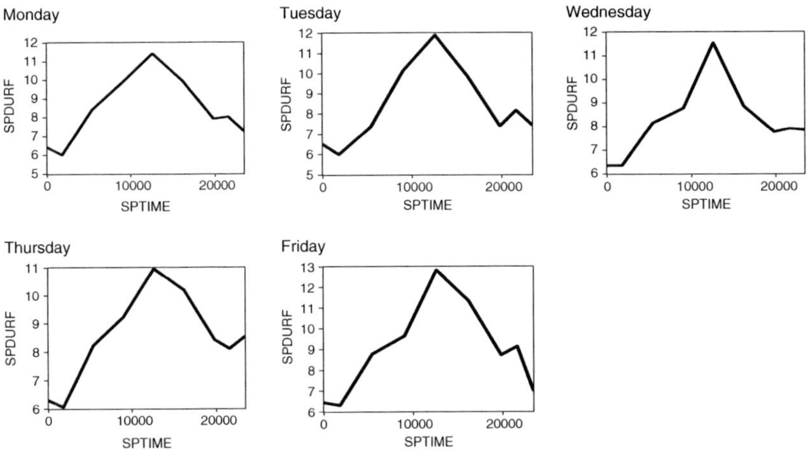

Figure 4.2–4.6 Intraday seasonality SP500 – durations

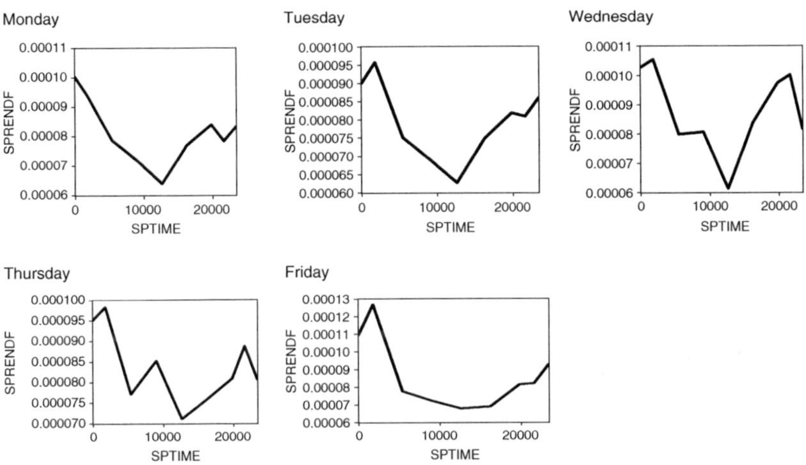

Figure 4.7–4.11 Intraday seasonality SP500 – absolute value returns (Volatility)

also present here: trades are usually very quick and volatility is at its highest value at the opening of the market, while the durations are longer and volatility is at its lowest value during lunchtime. The market close presents quick trades and high volatility once again: however, as opposed to the opening, durations are higher and volatility is slightly lower. This fact confirms the idea that end-of-the-day trades are of a different nature than the ones that take place in the morning, where the former are the result of closing daily positions and the latter are due to the necessity to change portfolio allocations according to news coming out during the night break. As for the day-of-the week-effect, we can observe a lower volatility on Monday afternoon, especially from the lunch break until the closing bell, while Friday morning presents the highest volatility, which is probably due to the closing positions by institutional investors before the weekend. The Nasdaq100 results are similar to the SP500's ones and for sake of space, we do not present them.

Comparison among different ACD models

After we removed the deterministic component using linear splines, we model the correlation left in the normalized duration (4.20) by using the four models presented in paragraph 4.3.1:

(1) Exponential–ACD (EACD).
(2) Weibull–ACD (WACD).
(3) Log–EACD.
(4) Log–WACD.

We used both lagged durations and other trademarks as regressors, such as volumes, when they are greater than 1, and two lagged futures' returns, similarly to Pohlmeier and Hautsch (2001) with the Bund future. As for volumes, we decide to consider only volume greater than 1 since most of the trades regarded only a single contract: this is not a surprise, since SP500 and Nasdaq100 futures are mainly traded by institutional investors and pension funds.

The specification for the expected duration *espdur* with the *simple ACD models* by using the Eviews programming language, both exponential and Weibull, is reported below (the one for the Nasdaq100 is similar, so we do not report it):

(1) EXPONENTIAL /(2) WEIBULL model:

$$\begin{aligned} espdur = {} & cost(1) + alfa1(1) * spduration(-1) + beta1(1) * espdur(-1) \\ & + alfa2(1) * spduration(-2) + beta2(1) * espdur(-2) \\ & + teta1(1) * (spvol > 1) + teta2(1) * abs(spreturn(1)) \\ & + teta3(1) * abs(spreturn(-2)) \end{aligned}$$

For logarithmic ACD models, we used:

(3) EXPONENTIAL model:

$$
\begin{aligned}
espdur = {} & cost(1) + alfa1(1) * (spduration(-1)/exp(espdur(-1))) \\
& + beta1(1) * espdur(-1) + alfa2(1) * (spduration(-2)/ \\
& exp(espdur(-2))) + beta2(1) * espdur(-2) + teta1(1) * (spvol > 1) \\
& + teta2(1) * abs(spreturn(-1)) + teta3(1) * abs(spreturn(-2))
\end{aligned}
$$

4) WEIBULL model:

$$
\begin{aligned}
espdur = {} & cost(1) + alfa1(1) * (spduration(-1) * lam/exp(espdur(-1))) \\
& + beta1(1) * espdur(-1) + alfa2(1) * (spduration(-2) \\
& * lam/exp(espdur(-2))) + beta2(1) * espdur(-2) + teta1(1) \\
& * (spvol > 1) + +teta2(1) * abs(spreturn(-1)) + teta3(1) \\
& * abs(spreturn(-2))
\end{aligned}
$$

where lam=@gamma(1+1/gam(1)) and gam(1) is the estimate of the Weibull parameter γ. This formulation basically reflects an ACD(2,2) model: we opted for this specification because it was the one which had the best empirical results (similarly to Engle and Russell, 1998). The final results are shown in the table below.

The sum of all autoregressive coefficients is less than 1 in every model, which means covariance stationarity and existence of the unconditional mean. All considered models reduce the correlation in the normalized duration, with better results for Weibull logarithmic models (similar results are presented by Engle and Russell, 1998, and Bauwens and Giot, 2000). As for Nasdaq100 data, the results among the models are very close, and even though both the Wald test and the LR test reject the hypothesis of $\gamma = 1$, we need further diagnostic testing to determine which one of the two distributions perform better. As the mean and the standard deviation of the exponential distribution are equal, Engle and Russell (1998) introduce a special Z-statistic to check the correct specification of the residuals distribution:

$$Z = \sqrt{N}\left(\frac{\sigma_{\varepsilon}^2 - 1}{\sqrt{8}}\right) \tag{4.44}$$

where σ_{ε}^2 is the variance of the standardized residuals when we deal with exponential models, while we use the variance of the following

Table 4.2 SP500 ACD models' estimation results

EACD(2,2)	**Coefficient**	**Std. Error**	**z-Statistic**	**Prob.**
COST(1)	0.020313	0.025756	0.788648	0.4303
ALFA1(1)	0.018218	0.004125	4.416818	0.0000
BETA1(1)	0.507759	0.074999	6.770187	0.0000
ALFA2(1)	0.022347	0.004233	5.279689	0.0000
BETA2(1)	0.422662	0.074905	5.642671	0.0000
TETA1(1)	0.049751	0.008636	5.760842	0.0000
TETA2(1)	0.025685	0.005512	4.659931	0.0000
TETA3(1)	−0.026089	0.005579	−4.676487	0.0000
Log likelihood	−118703.3	Akaike info criterion		1.982702
Avg. log lik.	−0.991284	Schwarz criterion		1.983350
Number of Coefs.	8	Hannan–Quinn criterion		1.982897
WACD(2,2)	**Coefficient**	**Std. Error**	**z-Statistic**	**Prob.**
GAM(1)	1.247968	0.002681	465.4655	0.0000
COST(1)	0.026513	0.001664	15.93384	0.0000
ALFA1(1)	0.059019	0.002585	22.82888	0.0000
BETA1(1)	0.540370	0.018966	28.49100	0.0000
ALFA2(1)	−0.024030	0.002659	−9.036271	0.0000
BETA2(1)	0.401573	0.018376	21.85277	0.0000
TETA1(1)	0.010289	0.001556	6.612735	0.0000
TETA2(1)	0.122849	0.003954	31.07282	0.0000
TETA3(1)	−0.127738	0.003852	−33.15843	0.0000
Log likelihood	−113616.0	Akaike info criterion		1.897751
Avg. log lik.	−0.948800	Schwarz criterion		1.898479
Number of Coefs.	9	Hannan–Quinn criter.		1.897970
Log–EACD (2,2)	**Coefficient**	**Std. Error**	**z-Statistic**	**Prob.**
COST(1)	−0.036495	0.011692	−3.121334	0.0018
ALFA1(1)	0.014108	0.004000	3.527073	0.0004
BETA1(1)	0.543728	0.098483	5.521033	0.0000
ALFA2(1)	0.015763	0.003939	4.002136	0.0001
BETA2(1)	0.405556	0.098540	4.115667	0.0000
TETA1(1)	0.037387	0.008598	4.348459	0.0000
TETA2(1)	0.022041	0.005659	3.894538	0.0001
TETA3(1)	−0.022709	0.006071	−3.740522	0.0002
Log likelihood	−118747.2	Akaike info criterion		1.983435
Avg. log lik.	−0.991650	Schwarz criterion		1.984082
Number of Coefs.	8	Hannan-Quinn criter.		1.983630

Continued

Table 4.2 Continued

Log-WACD(2,2)	Coefficient	Std. Error	z-Statistic	Prob.
GAM(1)	1.247617	0.002684	464.8801	0.0000
COST(1)	−0.029107	0.001339	−21.74560	0.0000
ALFA1(1)	0.054047	0.002374	22.76384	0.0000
BETA1(1)	0.482814	0.020598	23.43978	0.0000
ALFA2(1)	−0.019431	0.002442	−7.956889	0.0000
BETA2(1)	0.455358	0.019895	22.88754	0.0000
TETA1(1)	0.011623	0.001696	6.851715	0.0000
TETA2(1)	0.116230	0.003875	29.99455	0.0000
TETA3(1)	−0.124143	0.003817	−32.52790	0.0000
Log likelihood	−113664.0	Akaike info criterion		1.898554
Avg. log lik.	−0.949202	Schwarz criterion		1.899282
Number of Coefs.	9	Hannan-Quinn criter.		1.898773

Table 4.3 SP500 ACD models' residuals' tests

Residuals:	EACD(2,2)	WACD(2,2)	Log–EACD(2,2)	Log–WACD(2,2)
$LB(15)_5\% = 25$	57.911	29.570	146.65	28.576

transformation when we deal with Weibull models:

$$\varepsilon_i^{\gamma} = (\varepsilon_i * \Gamma(1+1/\gamma))^{\gamma} \tag{4.45}$$

which is distributed as an exponential if the Weibull assumption is correct. The Z-statistic is asymptotically distributed as a normal with 5 percent critical value equal to ±1.96. The statistic values for the four models are shown in Table (4.6).

The exponential models are nearer to the 5 percent critical value than the Weibull ones in all cases, and for the Nasdaq100 data the statistic is very close to 1.96 since as we are dealing with a high number N of data, we can certainly say that it fits the data very well. A possible explanation for the different behavior of the two futures can be proposed: the SP500 future, as opposed to the Nasdaq100 future, is composed of both Nyse stocks, which present low volatility and an advanced industrial life cycle, and Nasdaq stocks, which instead show high volatility and a young industrial life cycle. The presence of both of these categories probably causes more noise in the data and a heterogeneity problem, so that it is very difficult to impose a specific distribution to the residuals. Although the Weibull distribution proved to be a good improvement in

Table 4.4 NASDAQ100 ACD models' estimation results

EACD(2,2)	**Coefficient**	**Std. Error**	**z-Statistic**	**Prob.**
COST(1)	0.056714	0.025803	2.198003	0.0279
ALFA1(1)	0.110803	0.007015	15.79476	0.0000
BETA1(1)	0.672378	0.171991	3.909379	0.0001
ALFA2(1)	−0.012069	0.019833	−0.608510	0.5428
BETA2(1)	0.181647	0.142629	1.273566	0.2028
TETA1(1)	0.044101	0.027483	1.604661	0.1086
TETA2(1)	−0.003146	0.007780	−0.404411	0.6859
TETA3(1)	−0.006650	0.006880	−0.966639	0.3337
Log likelihood	−50303.64	Akaike info criterion		1.94077
Avg. log likelihood	−0.970232	Schwarz criterion		1.94214
Number of coefs.	8	Hannan–Quinn criterion		1.94120
WACD(2,2)	**Coefficient**	**Std. Error**	**z-Statistic**	**Prob.**
GAM(1)	1.141792	0.003626	314.9049	0.0000
COST(1)	0.006414	0.001019	6.295759	0.0000
ALFA1(1)	0.092273	0.004146	22.25808	0.0000
BETA1(1)	1.652490	0.029777	55.49641	0.0000
ALFA2(1)	−0.082218	0.003692	−22.26823	0.0000
BETA2(1)	−0.666535	0.027893	−23.89645	0.0000
TETA1(1)	−0.006978	0.001519	−4.592952	0.0000
TETA2(1)	0.000401	0.004200	0.095494	0.9239
TETA3(1)	−0.002486	0.004235	−0.586895	0.5573
Log likelihood	−49454.91	Akaike info criterion		1.90807
Avg. log likelihood.	−0.953862	Schwarz criterion		1.90960
Number of coefs.	9	Hannan–Quinn criterion		1.90855
Log–EACD(2,2)	**Coefficient**	**Std. Error**	**z-Statistic**	**Prob.**
COST(1)	−0.032378	0.020237	−1.599896	0.1096
ALFA1(1)	0.086805	0.005474	15.85878	0.0000
BETA1(1)	1.025186	0.154045	6.655093	0.0000
ALFA2(1)	−0.042512	0.014132	−3.008140	0.0026
BETA2(1)	−0.104960	0.126345	−0.830742	0.4061
TETA1(1)	0.036922	0.028742	1.284613	0.1989
TETA2(1)	−0.020247	0.008699	−2.327442	0.0199
TETA3(1)	0.004366	0.008612	0.506943	0.6122
Log likelihood	−50399.46	Akaike info criterion		1.944470
Avg. log lik.	−0.972081	Schwarz criterion		1.945836

Continued

Table 4.4 Continued

Log–WACD(2,2)	Coefficient	Std. Error	z-Statistic	Prob.
GAM(1)	1.137815	0.003616	314.6226	0.0000
COST(1)	−0.011261	0.001912	−5.889805	0.0000
ALFA1(1)	0.078850	0.004008	19.67264	0.0000
BETA1(1)	1.363993	0.059406	22.96065	0.0000
ALFA2(1)	−0.059118	0.003934	−15.02876	0.0000
BETA2(1)	−0.397115	0.055358	−7.173622	0.0000
TETA1(1)	−0.018547	0.003902	−4.753659	0.0000
TETA2(1)	−0.015076	0.005993	−2.515842	0.0119
TETA3(1)	0.006382	0.006093	1.047448	0.2949
Log likelihood	−49612.45	Akaike info criterion		1.91414
Avg. log likelihood	−0.956901	Schwarz criterion		1.91568
Number of Coefs.	9	Hannan-Quinn criter.		1.91463

Table 4.5 NASDAQ100 ACD models' residuals' tests

Residuals:	EACD(2,2)	WACD(2,2)	Log–EACD(2,2)	Log–WACD(2,2)
$LB(15)_{5\%} = 25$	48.071	**22.766**	**20.676**	**16.847**

Table 4.6 Z-statistic test estimated with ACD models residuals

	EACD(2,2)	WACD(2,2)	Log–EACD(2,2)	Log–WACD(2,2)
SP500	−24.87	35.27	−26.34	35.00
NASDAQ100	−3.06	25.32	−2.86	24.32

duration modeling both in diminishing the serial correlation and achieving a greater log likelihood, the high Z-statistic clearly points out that it must be considered as only a partial approximation of reality. The Nasdaq100 future presents a greater homogeneity among its constituents instead, so that it is easier to assume a specific distribution.

Finally, let us investigate the sign of the explanatory variables: as for SP500 futures, while the positive and negative coefficients for the two lagged future returns highlight the well-known bid–ask bounce, the positive sign of big volumes (Spvol > 1) show an interesting result: bigger traded volumes causes a longer expected duration. If this result is apparently against the main microstructure theories, where greater volume diminishes the expected duration, here we have to take into account the fact that the most trades regard only 1 single contract and the operators are usually only big institutional funds. Since a *single* Bloomberg or

Reuters platform, with the most important news features, costs about \$30000–\$70000 per year, only big players can afford such costs; however, as small- and medium-size traders are *not* present in this market and the common "greater volume–shorter duration" effect is caused by such operators who have access to news with delay, it is easy to realize that when many orders take place at the same time in this market, it takes a while before we see the next trade.

As for Nasdaq100, the autoregressive structure is able to completely model the correlation in the normalized durations, while the other trademarks are not statistically significant: this is not a surprise if we consider that more than 90 percent of trades are 1-contract deals.

Volatility modeling

As we have seen in paragraph 4.3.3, a good model for intraday volatility analysis is the UHF–GARCH proposed by Engle (2000), which can measure price volatility by using single-transaction data and thus considers how the trade timing influences volatility.

The basic form of the UHF–GARCH(1,1) is this one:

$$\frac{r_i}{\sqrt{x_i}} = \delta\ duration + \rho\frac{r_{i-1}}{\sqrt{x_{i-1}}} + e_i + \phi e_{i-1}, \quad \text{[conditional mean equation]} \tag{4.46}$$

$$\text{MODEL A}: \sigma_i^2 = \omega + \alpha e_{i-1}^2 + \beta\sigma_{i-1}^2, \quad \text{[conditional variance equation]} \tag{4.47}$$

while wider specifications include both observed durations and expected ones, as well as a long-run volatility component and traded volumes:

$$\text{MODEL B: } \sigma_i^2 = \omega + \alpha e_{i-1}^2 + \beta\sigma_{i-1}^2 + \gamma x_i^{-1} \tag{4.48}$$

$$\text{MODEL C: } \sigma_i^2 = \omega + \alpha e_{i-1}^2 + \beta\sigma_{i-1}^2 + \gamma_1 x_i^{-1} + \gamma_2\frac{x_i}{\psi_i} + \gamma_3\psi_i^{-1} \tag{4.49}$$

$$\text{MODEL D: } \sigma_i^2 = \omega + \alpha e_{i-1}^2 + \beta\sigma_{i-1}^2 + \gamma_1 x_i^{-1} + \gamma_2\frac{x_i}{\psi_i} + \gamma_3\xi_{i-1} + \gamma_4\psi_i^{-1} + \gamma_5(spvol > 1) \tag{4.50}$$

where ξ_i is the long-run volatility, which is estimated by exponentially smoothing r^2/x with a parameter 0.995 (Engle, 2000):

$$\xi_i = 0.005(r_{i-1}^2/x_{i-1}) + 0.995\xi_{i-1} \tag{4.51}$$

The final results for the SP500 are reported in Tables 4.7–4.8, while for the Nasdaq100 in Tables 4.9–4.10 below.

Table 4.7 SP500 UHF–GARCH models' estimation results (Models A, B, C, D)

Model A	**Coefficient**	**Std. Error**	**z-Statistic**	**Prob.**
SPDURATION	0.001645	0.001307	1.259070	0.2080
AR(1)	−0.202511	0.027240	−7.434433	0.0000
MA(1)	0.301866	0.026557	11.36674	0.0000
		Variance equation		
C	0.004833	0.000463	10.43909	0.0000
ARCH(1)	0.021754	0.000845	25.73806	0.0000
GARCH(1)	0.974877	0.000991	983.4212	0.0000
R-squared	0.012418	Mean dependent var		−0.01224
Adjusted R-sq.	0.012377	S.D. dependent var		1.21220
Sum sq. resid	173774.6	Schwarz criterion		3.12335
Log likelihood	−186972.7	Durbin–Watson stat		1.97447
MODEL B	**Coefficient**	**Std. Error**	**z-Statistic**	**Prob.**
SPDURATION	0.002070	0.001131	1.829721	0.0673
AR(1)	−0.338054	0.042544	−7.945952	0.0000
MA(1)	0.382569	0.041838	9.143962	0.0000
		Variance Equation		
C	−0.016218	0.003048	−5.320075	0.0000
ARCH(1)	0.098539	0.002944	33.46839	0.0000
GARCH(1)	−0.026783	0.005419	−4.942162	0.0000
1/SPDURATION	0.641249	0.004368	146.8205	0.0000
R-squared	0.008025	Mean dep. var		−0.01224
Adjusted R-sq.	0.007975	S.D. dependent var		1.212200
Sum squared resid	174547.6	Schwarz criterion		2.854312
Log likelihood	−170858.1	Durbin-Watson stat		1.866143
Model C	**Coefficient**	**Std. Error**	**z-Statistic**	**Prob.**
SPDURATION	0.000994	0.002757	0.360434	0.7185
AR(1)	−0.388228	0.032371	−11.99312	0.0000
MA(1)	0.448388	0.031392	14.28361	0.0000
		Variance equation		
C	−0.123163	0.013933	−8.839834	0.0000
ARCH(1)	0.024609	0.002878	8.549505	0.0000
GARCH(1)	0.169754	0.006009	28.25108	0.0000
1/SPDURATION	0.331227	0.004304	76.96582	0.0000
SPDURATION/SPEXPDUR	−0.026812	0.000421	−63.72151	0.0000
1/SPEXPDUR	0.410984	0.016059	25.59140	0.0000
R-squared	0.009785	Mean dependent var		−0.01224
Adjusted R-sq.	0.009711	S.D. dependent var		1.21220
S.E. of reg.	1.206300	Akaike info criterion		2.91987
Sum sq. resid	174237.8	Schwarz criterion		2.92067
Log likelihood	−174814.3	Durbin–Watson stat		1.89637

Continued

Table 4.7 Continued

MODEL D	Coefficient	Std. Error	z-Statistic	Prob.
SPDURATION	0.002510	0.002375	1.056762	0.2906
AR(1)	−0.881344	0.022758	−38.72613	0.0000
MA(1)	0.891905	0.021757	40.99357	0.0000
		Variance Equation		
C	−0.234981	0.015941	−14.74100	0.0000
ARCH(1)	0.008682	0.002675	3.246019	0.0012
GARCH(1)	0.089181	0.005333	16.72391	0.0000
1/SPDURATION	0.284048	0.003709	76.57707	0.0000
SPDURATION/ SPEXPDUR	−0.024529	0.000352	−69.76532	0.0000
1/SPEXPDUR	0.290762	0.018881	15.39975	0.0000
LONGVOL(−1)	0.250860	0.006704	37.41899	0.0000
SPVOL>1	0.179032	0.006136	29.17786	0.0000
R-squared	0.002175	Mean dependent var		−0.012249
Adjusted R-sq.	0.002091	S.D. dependent var		1.212200
Sum sq.resid	175577.0	Schwarz criterion		2.895605
Log likelihood	−173307.1	Durbin-Watson stat		1.800906

Table 4.8 SP500 UHF–GARCH models residuals tests

Initial autocorrelation	Residuals	MODEL A	MODEL B	MODEL C	MODEL D
LB(15) = 1615.6	{LB(15)$_{5\%}$ = 25}	115.98	131.55	157.48	401.06

All models are able to diminish the serial correlation present in the returns per unit of time SPRETURN/$\sqrt{SPDURATION} = r_i/\sqrt{x_i}$. However, the last model which considers the long-run volatility component as well is the worst, especially for the SP500 future. This explanatory variable must be considered with great caution. Engle himself highlights that the long-run volatility specification can be improved by optimizing the parameters in equation (4.28).

If we compare the four models, we can clearly see that the introduction of the duration among the explanatory variables of the conditional variance notably improve the log likelihood. The serial correlation in the residuals is similar to the basic UHF–GARCH(1,1), with a slightly worse result for the Nasdaq100 future. Besides, this variable reduces the sum of the GARCH parameters α and β, thus improving the modeling of volatility persistence: this result is similar to the one achieved by Engle (2000), Ghose and Kroner (1995) and Andersen and Bollerslev (1997).

Table 4.9 NASDAQ100 UHF–GARCH models estimation results (Models A, B, C, D)

Model A	**Coefficient**	**Std. Error**	**z-Statistic**	**Prob.**
AR(1)	0.415078	0.032764	12.66874	0.0000
MA(1)	−0.514595	0.030829	−16.69181	0.0000
		Variance equation		
C	0.009147	0.001301	7.030507	0.0000
ARCH(1)	0.017259	0.001224	14.09600	0.0000
GARCH(1)	0.976110	0.001902	513.0951	0.0000
R-squared	0.010399	Mean dependent var		−0.002165
Adjusted R-sq.	0.010323	S.D. dependent var		1.179002
Sum sq. resid	71320.22	Schwarz criterion		3.133263
Log likelihood	−81199.58	Durbin–Watson stat		1.964099
MODEL B	**Coefficient**	**Std. Error**	**z-Statistic**	**Prob.**
AR(1)	0.420843	0.031937	13.17715	0.0000
MA(1)	−0.489002	0.030829	−15.86183	0.0000
		Variance Equation		
C	0.014850	0.002543	5.839832	0.0000
ARCH(1)	0.024899	0.004880	5.101759	0.0000
GARCH(1)	−0.017738	0.005183	−3.422325	0.0006
1/NASDURATION	0.509999	0.002279	223.7784	0.0000
R-squared	0.009608	Mean dependent var		−0.0021
Adjusted R-sq.	0.009513	S.D. dependent var		1.17901
Sum squared resid	71377.19	Schwarz criterion		2.65726
Log likelihood	−68854.44	Durbin-Watson stat		2.02441
Model C	**Coefficient**	**Std. Error**	**z-Statistic**	**Prob.**
AR(1)	0.422356	0.031946	13.22083	0.0000
MA(1)	−0.490382	0.030835	−15.90345	0.0000
		Variance equation		
C	0.042484	0.006599	6.438281	0.0000
ARCH(1)	0.025740	0.004885	5.269156	0.0000
GARCH(1)	−0.018023	0.005224	−3.450299	0.0006
1/NASDURATION	0.507005	0.002844	178.2494	0.0000
NASDURATION/ NASEXPDUR	−0.002104	0.000944	−2.228729	0.0258
1/NASEXPDUR	−0.021175	0.006387	−3.315406	0.0009
R-squared	0.009605	Mean dependent var		−0.002165
Adjusted R-sq.	0.009452	S.D. dependent var		1.179002
Sum squared resid	71377.47	Schwarz criterion		2.657730
Log likelihood	−68850.14	Durbin–Watson stat		2.024664

Continued

Table 4.9 Continued

MODEL D	Coefficient	Std. Error	z-Statistic	Prob.
AR(1)	0.427106	0.031221	13.68004	0.0000
MA(1)	−0.495833	0.030099	−16.47354	0.0000
		Variance Equation		
C	−0.087972	0.008457	−10.40246	0.0000
ARCH(1)	0.019988	0.002135	9.362335	0.0000
GARCH(1)	−0.014275	0.001917	−7.447593	0.0000
1/NASDURATION	0.504070	0.002671	188.6876	0.0000
NASDURATION/ NASEXPDUR	0.000696	0.000812	0.857478	0.3912
LONGVOL(−1)	0.142079	0.006142	23.13348	0.0000
1/NASEXPDUR	−0.081566	0.006780	−12.02972	0.0000
NASVOL>1	−0.041194	0.013004	−3.167823	0.0015
R-squared	0.009668	Mean dependent var		−0.002165
Adjusted R-sq.	0.009496	S.D. dependent var		1.179002
Sum squared resid	71372.92	Schwarz criterion		2.653847
Log likelihood	−68744.06	Durbin-Watson stat		2.023354

Note: The explanatory variable Nasduration, within the conditional mean, was not statistically significant for all four models, so we eliminate it.

Table 4.10 10 NASDAQ100 UHF–GARCH models' residuals' tests

Initial autocorrelation	Residuals	MODEL A	MODEL B	MODEL C	MODEL D
LB(15) = 628.82	$\{LB(15)_{5\%} = 25\}$	114.46	219.15	220.52	227.29

As for the sign of the coefficients, the *conditional mean* shows significant ARMA parameters with alternate signs, reflecting the common bid–ask bounce in the prices; the durations' coefficient is not significant for the Nasdaq100 future. For the SP500, the model with the highest log likelihood presents a significant positive coefficient: this empirical evidence seems to be against the Diamond and Verrecchia (1987) model, which says that no trades mean bad news, so that longer durations should be associated with diminishing prices. This result is reasonable for one simple reason: Diamond and Verrecchia (1987) assume that some market operators cannot short sell: if this can be true for the stock market (such a result is found in Engle, 2000), this does not make any sense for the futures' market where everyone can buy and sell in a completely symmetric fashion. The data simply reflect this characteristic of future markets.

The "conditional variance" equation presents in all models a significant positive sign for the reciprocal of durations, thus supporting the Easley and O'Hara (1992) idea that no trades means no news and volatility fall. As in Engle (2000), observed durations divided by expected durations (which can be considered as a measure of trading surprises) have a negative coefficient, which is significant in almost all cases: the short-term impact is the same as the previous one, that is, longer durations diminish volatility. The trading intensity which is given by the reciprocal of expected duration is positive too, supporting again the idea that more trades cause higher volatility. For the latter coefficient, contrarily to the SP500 future, the Nasdaq100 presents a negative value which is, however, significant only at the 5 percent level. As for traded volumes, the SP500 future presents a high significant positive coefficient, which confirms the idea that bigger volumes bring about higher volatility (Easley and O'Hara, 1992), while Nasdaq100's coefficient is slightly negative; however, the latter result must be viewed with caution as more than 90 percent of trades are 1-contract deals.

4.4.3 Ordered probit modeling: Empirical results

Conditional mean and variance specification

The OP model is a "virtual" regression of a set of latent dependent variables $Y*$, whose conditional mean is a linear function of some observable explanatory variables. Although Y^* is not observable, it is linked to a discreet random variable Y which is observable, and whose values are determined by the particular state of Y^*. The number of states s_j that we considered in our analysis and which constitute the state space Ω of the price changes y_k are:

SP500		**NASDAQ100**	
$\Delta p < -0.4$	1722		
[−0.4, −0.3)	3297	$\Delta p <= -1.75]$	781
[−0.3, −0.2)	29634	(−1.75, −1.25]	730
[−0.2, −0.1)	12701	(−1.25, −0.75]	22663
[−0.1, 0)	12972	(−0.75, 0.75)	3795
[0, 0.1]	12774	[0.75, 1.25)	22208
(0.1, 0.2]	12227	[1.25, 1.75)	714
(0.2, 0.3]	29290	$[\Delta p >= 1.75$	953
(0.3, 0.4]	3060		
$\Delta p > 0.4$	2067		

The conditional mean has been modeled with lagged price changes ("deltaprice"), traded volumes ("vol"), and contemporaneous duration ("dur"), following Hausman et al. (1992) and Hautsch and Pohlmeier (2001). The equations used are reported below:

SP500's conditional mean specification:

$$\begin{aligned}\Delta p^*_{SP500} = &\, beta(1)deltaprice(-1) + beta(2) * deltaprice(-2)\\ &+ beta(3) * deltaprice(-3) + beta(4) * spvol\\ &+ beta(5) * Wednesday + beta(6) * spdur\end{aligned}$$

NASDAQ100's conditional mean specification:

$$\begin{aligned}\Delta p^*_{NASDAQ100} = &\, beta(1) * deltaprice(-1) + beta(2) * deltaprice(-2)\\ &+ beta(3) * deltaprice(-3) + beta(4) * nasvol\\ &+ beta(5) * Wednesday + beta(6) * nasdur\end{aligned}$$

As for the conditional variance, we follow Hautsch and Pohlmeier (2001) and we model the intraday volatility using this specification:

$$\begin{aligned}\sigma_k^2 = &\, \sigma_0^2[\exp(\gamma_1 \log(x_k) + \gamma_2(\log(x_{k-1}) + \gamma_3(\log(x_{k-2}) + \gamma_4(\log(x_{k-3})\\ &+ \gamma_5(\log(V_k) + \gamma_6(\log(V_{k-1}) + TREND + Dum_{MONDAY} + Dum_{FRIDAY})]^2\end{aligned} \tag{4.52}$$

where x is the duration and V are the traded volumes, while Dum_{monday} and Dum_{friday} were the only dummy variables that we find significant to differentiate single days of the week. The seasonal pattern TREND is the Fourier series approximation (4.23),

$$TREND = \gamma_7 t_k^* + \sum_{q=1}^{3} \left(\gamma_{c,q} \cos(t_k^* \cdot 2\pi q) + \gamma_{s,q} \sin(t_k^* \cdot 2\pi q)\right) \tag{4.53}$$

where $\gamma_7, \gamma_{c,q}, \gamma_{s,q}$ are the coefficients to be estimated, $t_k^* \epsilon$ [0, 1] is a normalized intraday time trend, which is defined as the number of seconds from market opening until the occurrence of transaction i divided by the length of the trading day. Expressing the previous equation with Eviews programming language, the conditional variance is as follows:

SP500's conditional variance specification:

$$\begin{aligned}\sigma^2_{SP500} = &\, exp(gam(1) * log(spdur) + gam(2) * log(spdur(-1))\\ &+ gam(3) * log(spdur(-2)) + gam(4) * log(spdur(-3))\\ &+ gam(5) * log(spvol) + gam(6) * log(spvol(-1))\\ &+ gam(7) * sptrend + gam(8) * spcos1 + gam(9) * spcos2\end{aligned}$$

$$+gam(10)*spcos3+gam(11)*spsin1+gam(12)*spsin2$$

$$+gam(13)*spsin3+gam(14)*monday+gam(15)*friday)$$

NASDAQ100's conditional variance specification:

$$\sigma^2_{NASDAQ100} = exp(gam(1)*log(nasdur)+gam(2)*log(nasdur(-1))$$

$$+gam(3)*log(nasdur(-2))+gam(4)*log(nasdur(-3))$$

$$+gam(5)*log(nasvol)+gam(6)*log(nasvol(-1))$$

$$+gam(7)*nastrend+gam(8)*nascos1+gam(9)*nascos2$$

$$+gam(10)*nascos3+gam(11)*nassin1+gam(12)*nassin2$$

$$+gam(13)*nassin3+gam(14)*monday+gam(15)*friday)$$

Estimation results

The final results are reported in the Tables 4.11–4.12. All coefficients are highly significant except for traded volumes [beta(4)] in both the SP500's and Nasdaq100's conditional mean and the contemporaneous duration for Nasdaq100 data, while in the Nasdaq100's conditional variance the first lagged duration [GAM(2)] and some Fourier series coefficients are not significant. Moreover, the fourth region S_4 of the latent variable $\Delta p^*_{NASDAQ100}$ was not significant: we decided, however, to keep it anyway, since its elimination would have caused a large decrease in the log likelihood and a worsening of all diagnostic tests.

As for the coefficients' sign in the *conditional mean* equation, the lagged price changes almost all have a negative sign, again supporting the existence of "bid–ask bounce" effects; simultaneously traded volumes are not significant for both the SP500 and the Nasdaq100, while the contemporaneous duration is significantly positive for the SP500 (while not significant for the Nasdaq100): longer durations usually cause a positive larger price change. This evidence is similar to what we found previously with UHF–GARCH models and against the Diamond and Verrecchia (1987) model, where longer durations should be associated with declining prices. Again, their model does not make any sense here because everyone can buy and sell in a completely symmetric fashion. An interesting result from the previous tables is the significant positive coefficient for the Wednesday dummy variable: this result is only *apparently* surprising. As some anonymous traders pointed out during an informal discussion, Wednesdays are usually positive days for the stock exchanges (especially in the considered period). In predominantly *negative* weeks,

Table 4.11 SP500 ordered probit estimation results

SP500	Coefficient	Std. Error	z-Statistic	Prob.
BETA(1)	0.004439	0.000954	4.651659	0.0000
BETA(2)	−0.004550	0.000976	−4.660623	0.0000
BETA(3)	−0.003646	0.000955	−3.816728	0.0001
BETA(4)	0.000988	0.006896	0.143343	0.8860
BETA(5)	0.016132	0.006431	2.508516	0.0121
BETA(6)	0.002063	0.000346	5.954738	0.0000
GAM(1)	0.046859	0.002630	17.81731	0.0000
GAM(2)	−0.046888	0.002679	−17.50479	0.0000
GAM(3)	−0.011111	0.002586	−4.297303	0.0000
GAM(4)	−0.019279	0.002614	−7.373854	0.0000
GAM(5)	0.198843	0.008236	24.14362	0.0000
GAM(6)	0.309784	0.007777	39.83143	0.0000
GAM(7)	−0.196601	0.017312	−11.35638	0.0000
GAM(8)	0.096722	0.003422	28.26821	0.0000
GAM(9)	0.007639	0.003308	2.309037	0.0209
GAM(10)	0.011790	0.003282	3.592001	0.0003
GAM(11)	−0.066028	0.006429	−10.27075	0.0000
GAM(12)	−0.020968	0.004272	−4.908155	0.0000
GAM(13)	0.026224	0.003817	6.870004	0.0000
GAM(14)	−0.053131	0.006328	−8.396262	0.0000
GAM(15)	0.065369	0.005955	10.97704	0.0000
ALFA(1)	−2.123232	0.028739	−73.88095	0.0000
ALFA(2)	−1.633849	0.022865	−71.45723	0.0000
ALFA(3)	−0.490189	0.010874	−45.08031	0.0000
ALFA(4)	−0.221846	0.009403	−23.59224	0.0000
ALFA(5)	0.031579	0.008988	3.513570	0.0004
ALFA(6)	0.281923	0.009718	29.01165	0.0000
ALFA(7)	0.541903	0.011369	47.66354	0.0000
ALFA(8)	1.679114	0.023722	70.78328	0.0000
ALFA(9)	2.099934	0.028488	73.71356	0.0000
Log likelihood	−232550.4	Akaike info criterion		3.885569
Avg. log likelihood	−1.942534	Schwarz criterion		3.887998
No. of coef.	30	Hannan-Quinn criterion		3.886300

it is usually the day of technical rebound, where those who short sold stocks or sold futures in the first two days of the week cover their positions and realize profits. They thereby prepare themselves for a price fall in the last two trading days. In *positive* weeks, Wednesday gives the "starting sign for the weekend rally" where prices rise from Wednesday till Friday. These traders stressed that this special day is *not* fixed to Wednesday, but can range from Tuesday to Thursday according to the economic and financial news announcements: they did not say, however, which

Table 4.12 NASDAQ100 ordered probit estimation results

NASDAQ100	Coefficient	Std. Error	z-Statistic	Prob.
BETA(1)	−0.096007	0.003611	−26.58375	0.0000
BETA(2)	−0.062066	0.003137	−19.78420	0.0000
BETA(3)	−0.012458	0.002798	−4.451803	0.0000
BETA(4)	−0.068359	0.038918	−1.756502	0.0790
BETA(5)	0.034035	0.013881	2.451830	0.0142
BETA(6)	0.000228	0.000236	0.964131	0.3350
GAM(1)	0.064242	0.004479	14.34304	0.0000
GAM(2)	−0.001290	0.004096	−0.314900	0.7528
GAM(3)	0.010372	0.004073	2.546620	0.0109
GAM(4)	0.009076	0.004112	2.207514	0.0273
GAM(5)	0.289238	0.031007	9.328179	0.0000
GAM(6)	0.680026	0.035743	19.02536	0.0000
GAM(7)	−0.131552	0.033682	−3.905700	0.0001
GAM(8)	0.005325	0.006661	0.799384	0.4241
GAM(9)	−0.002991	0.006151	−0.486305	0.6268
GAM(10)	−0.007812	0.006397	−1.221222	0.2220
GAM(11)	−0.088992	0.012489	−7.125761	0.0000
GAM(12)	−0.033813	0.008290	−4.078589	0.0000
GAM(13)	0.010439	0.007099	1.470407	0.1415
GAM(14)	−0.025550	0.011443	−2.232831	0.0256
GAM(15)	0.024920	0.010991	2.267426	0.0234
ALFA(1)	−2.779756	0.076696	−36.24362	0.0000
ALFA(2)	−2.401710	0.074094	−32.41448	0.0000
ALFA(3)	−0.157096	0.040888	−3.842127	0.0001
ALFA(4)	0.058002	0.040577	1.429439	0.1529
ALFA(5)	2.215708	0.069417	31.91882	0.0000
ALFA(6)	2.534894	0.071994	35.20985	0.0000
Log likelihood	−59350.04	Akaike info criterion		2.291886
Avg. log lik.	−1.145422	Schwarz criterion		2.296501
Num.of Coefs.	27	Hannan-Quinn criter		2.293329

announcements change this day-of-the-week effect from one day to another.

The *conditional variance* presents a positive sign for the contemporaneous duration and negative signs for lagged durations, as previously found by Hausman et al. (1992) with stocks and Hautsch and Pohlmeier (2001) with the Bund Future. The negative sign of the lagged durations shows again that the greater the past trading intensity is (shorter durations), the higher the conditional variance will be, similarly to Easley and O'Hara (1992) and previous ACD results. Both contemporaneous and past volumes show a positive sign. That is, that higher volumes cause higher volatility, thus confirming previous ACD results and Easley and O'Hara's

Table 4.13 Generalized residuals' tests

Generalized residuals correlation	SP500	NASDAQ100
$LB(15)_5\% = 25$	28.14	24.05

Table 4.14 j^{-th} order score statistic tests

Score statistic J^{th} order	**SP500 (p – value)**	**NASDAQ100 (p – value)**
-1	0,71	0,41
-2	0,037	0,23
-3	0,27	0,34
-4	0,06	0,26
-5	0,17	0,50
-10	0,48	0,21

model (1992). The coefficients for the Fourier series approximation are all significant, confirming the presence of strong intraday seasonality, while the two dummy variables highlight a lower volatility for Monday and a higher one for Friday: these results are similar to what we found with the linear splines in paragraph 4.4.2.

As we have seen in paragraph 4.3.4, the main tools for checking the correct specification of the model are the "generalized residuals" (4.39) and the "score statistic" (4.41–4.43), which is asymptotically distributed as a χ^2 with one degree of freedom, under the null hypothesis of $\phi = 0$. The results for both statistics are shown in the following table.

Both models succeed in modeling the data very well, with a slightly worse result for the SP500, probably due to the high number of historical observations (almost 120000), more than double that of Nasdaq100 (52000).

4.5 Conclusion

The aim of this chapter was to introduce the main issues operators or researchers have to consider when analyzing intraday volatility, volumes and spreads. We reviewed ACD and ordered probit models, which take the entire information set into account thanks to single-transaction analysis: the former models are a particular evolution of GARCH models, while the latter models can be considered as a generalization of the linear regression model to the case where the dependent variable is a discrete one. As tick-by-tick data analysis becomes more and more important, we presented an empirical application of ACD and OP models, employing transaction data relative to the Standard & Poor 500 and Nasdaq100 stock index futures, quoted by the Chicago Mercantile Exchange (CME). Both models showed similar results in the *conditional mean*, where they were able to catch bid–ask bounce effects and the symmetry nature of futures' markets, where one can buy and sell without any restriction. The idea that longer durations should be associated with declining prices (because some market operators cannot short sell) must therefore be rejected. The OP model produced the interesting result of a positive mean regularity on Wednesday and we attempted to explain it with the help of some traders. Both models gave similar results for the *conditional variance* too, where they were able to shape intraday market seasonality and highlight differences among days of the week (such as Monday and Friday). Moreover, they gave support to the Easley and O'Hara (1992) model that no trades means no news and volatility fall, while bigger volumes cause higher volatility.

In comparison, even though ACD modeling requires less computational time than OP models, we have to point out that diagnostic tests were quite different in the two cases: while Lyung-box and score-statistic tests on generalized residuals showed that OP models were able to catch the main features of the data with no correlation left, diagnostic tests for ACD models gave much worse results. ACD models can therefore be used as a "first glance" at the data, while OP models can then be employed for more in-depth analysis. Nevertheless, ACD models can still be used as the main tool in the case of illiquid financial assets, where defining the number of states for OP models can be very difficult due to few observations.

References

Admati, A. and Pfleiderer, P. (1988) "A Theory of Intra-Day Patterns: Volume and Price Variability," *Review of Financial Studies*, 1 (1): 3–40.

Andersen, T. and Bollerslev, T. (1997) "Heterogeneous Information Arrivals and Return Volatility Dynamics: Uncovering the Long-Run in High Frequency Returns," *Journal of Finance*, 52 (3): 975–1005.

Andersen, T. and Bollerslev, T. (1998) "Deutsche Mark-Dollar Volatility: Intraday Activity Patterns, Macroeconomic Announcements, and Longer Run Dependencies," *Journal of Finance*, 53 (1): 219–265.

Bauwens, L. and Giot, P. (2000) "The Logarithmic ACD Model: An Application to the Bid/Ask Quote Process of two NYSE Stocks," *Annales d'Economie et de Statistique*, 60: 117–149.

Bauwens, L., Galli, F. and Giot, P. (2008) "The Moments of Log-ACD Models," *Quantitative and. Qualitative Analysis in Social Sciences*, 2 (1): 1–28.

Bollerslev, T. and Melvin (1994) "Bid–Ask Spreads and Volatility in the Foreign Exchange Market: An Empirical Analysis," *Journal of International Economics*, 36 (3–4): 355–372.

Brock, P. and Kleidon (1992) "Periodic Market Closure and Trading Volume," *Journal of Economics Dynamics and Control*, 16 (3–4): 451–489.

Chan, L. and Lakonishok, J. (1995) "The Behaviour of Stock Prices Around Institutional Trades," *Journal of Finance*, 50 (4): 1147–1174.

Demos, F. and Goodhart, C. (1992) "The Interaction Between the Frequency of Market Quotations, Spread and Volatility in the Foreign Exchange Markets," Discussion Paper 152, LSE Financial Markets Group Discussion Paper.

Diamond, D.W. and Verrecchia, R.E. (1987) "Constraints on Short-Selling and Asset Price Adjustment to Private Information," *Journal of Financial Economics*, 18 (2): 277–311.

Easley, D. and O'Hara, M. (1992) "Time and Process of Security Price Adjustment," *The Journal of Finance*, 47 (2): 577–605.

Engle, R.F. (2000) "The Econometrics of Ultra-High-Frequency Data," *Econometrica*, 68 (1): 1–22.

Engle, R. and Russell, J.R. (1995) "Forecasting the Frequency of Changes in Quoted Foreign Exchange Prices with the ACD Model," *Journal of Empirical Finance*, 4 (2–3): 187–212.

Engle, R. and Russell, J.R. (1998) "Autoregressive Conditional Duration: A New Model for Irregularly Spaced Transaction Data," *Econometrica*, 66 (5): 1127–1162.

Fantazzini, D. (2004) *Financial Markets Microstructure and High Frequency Data: Theoretical Issues, Stylized Facts and Econometric Tools*, Digital University Press.

Gallant, R. (1981) "On the Basis in Flexible Functional Form and an Essentially Unbiased Form: The Flexible Fourier Form," *Journal of Econometrics*, 15: 211–245.

Ghose and Kroner (1995) "The Relationship Between GARCH and Symmetric Stable Processes: Finding the Source of Fat Tails in Financial Data," *Journal of Empirical Finance*, 2 (3): 225–251.

Gourieroux, C., Monfort, A., Renault, E. and Trognon, A. (1987) "Generalized Residuals," *Journal of Econometrics*, 34 (1–2): 5–32.

Grammig and Wellner (2002) "Modelling the Interdependence of Volatility and Inter-Transaction Duration Processes," *Journal of Econometrics*, 106 (2): 369–400.

Greene, W.H. (2000) *Econometric Analysis*, Fourth Ed. Prentice Hall.

Gwinlym, O., Buckle, M. and Stephen, T. (1999) Intra-Day Behaviour of Key Market Variables for LIFFE Derivatives, in P. Lequeux (ed.), *Financial Markets Tick-by-tick: Insights in financial Markets Microstructure,* Wiley.

Hausman, J.A., Lo, A.W. and MacKinlay, A.C. (1992) "An Ordered Probit Analysis of Transaction Stock Prices," *Journal of Financial Economics*, 31 (3): 319–379.

Hautsch, N. and Pohlmeier, W. (2001) "Econometric Analysis of Financial Transaction Data: Pitfalls and Opportunities," *Allgemeines Statistisches Archiv*, 86: 5 –30.

Lee, C.M.C., Mucklow, B. and Ready, M.J. (1993) "Spreads, Depths, and the Impact of Earnings Information: An Intra-Day Analysis," *Review of Financial Studies*, 6 (2): 345–374.

McInish, T. and Wood, R. (1990) "A Transaction Data Analysis of the Variability of Common Stocks Returns During 1980–1984," *Journal of Banking and Finance*, 14 (1): 99–112.

Merton, R.C. (1971) "Optimum Consumption and Portfolio Rules in a Continuous-Time Model," *Journal of Economic Theory*, 3 (4): 373–413.

Pohlmeier, W. and Gerhard, F. (2001) "Identifying Intra-Day Volatility," in S. Berninghaus and M. Braulke (eds.), *Beiträge Zur Mikro- und Zur Makroökonomik, Festschrift Zum 65. Geburtstag Von Hans Jürgen Ramser*, Springer.

Sheikh and Ronn (1994) "A Characterization of the Daily and Intra-Day Behaviour of Returns on Options," *Journal of Finance*, 49 (2): 557–580.

Part II

Factor Models and Financial Risk Measures

5
The Consumption-Based Capital Asset-Pricing Model (CCAPM), Habit-Based Consumption and the Equity Premium in an Australian Context

David E. Allen and Lurion Demello

5.1 Introduction

In this chapter, we apply a habit-based consumption model to investigate the determinants of the equity premium in an Australian context. In the derivation of the CCAPM it has been customary to use a utility function displaying CCRA. Mehra and Prescott (1985) challenged the use of such a function. The size of this premium requires unrealistically high coefficients of risk aversion. Constantinides (1990) restated the problem in terms of consumption growth being required to be too smooth, while Weil (1989) raised the issue of the relative size of the risk-free rate. The issue has been reinterpreted in terms of market frictions; see He and Modest (1995) and Heaton and Lucas (1996). It is possible to appeal to a combination of short-sale and borrowing constraints, plus trading costs to weaken the case against the contention that the equity premium is too high. Swan (2002) has also attacked the problem from this angle. Bellamy and Heaney (1997) try to correlate the size of the Australian equity premium with various factors and conclude market volatility is significant, but do not address the issue of whether the premium is too "large."

Other work counters the assumptions of the CCRA model; Epstein and Zin (1989) separate risk aversion and the elasticity of intertemporal substitution by introducing habit, which can permit time-varying risk aversion. Kreps and Porteous (1978) demonstrated this is not integral to CCRA. It can also be argued that agents gain utility from relative but not absolute levels of consumption and that past levels of consumption and related utility affect current levels – contrary to the CCRA assumption of time separability of preferences.

Abel (1990) proposed a model of consumption choice in which consumption preferences are dependent on external consumption patterns. An alternative approach is to model internal agent experiences of prior consumption in the determination of consumption "habit," in the manner of Constantinides (1990) and Sundaresan (1989). We adopt an approach based on Abel's (1990) external model.

This leads to a related issue of how to model the speed with which consumption habits adjust. Hall (1978) adopted a random walk model that implied that consumption would react immediately to shocks to consumption. Campbell and Hamao (1992) used a model with exponential decay, while in this chapter we adopt an autoregressive moving average model with an AR(1) process.

Justifications for the adoption of a habit-based consumption model include viewing it as a form of myopia in which the best prediction of next period's consumption is current consumption. Alternatively, the approach could be viewed as involving "catching up with the Jones's" in which relative consumption is paramount. We adopt a habit-based consumption approach and utilize it to demonstrate whether high relative risk aversion related to the equity premium puzzle in an Australian context can be attributed to preference specification, as opposed to market frictions, noise traders or aggregation problems.

The chapter is divided into six sections: Section 5.2 introduces the research method and models, Section 5.3 discusses the estimation procedures, Section 5.4 introduces the data, Section 5.5 provides the results and Section 5.6 draws some general conclusions.

5.2 The research method and models adopted

We adopt the "habit model" of Campbell and Cochrane (1999) and to generate time-varying expected returns, the model economy adds habit persistence to the standard consumption-based specification. As bad shocks drive consumption down towards the habit level, risk aversion rises, stock prices decline and expected returns rise.

Consumption growth is an i.i.d. lognormal endowment process, where it is assumed that consumption is a random walk with drift.

$$
\begin{aligned}
c_{t+1} &= c_t + g + u_{t+1} \\
\therefore c_{t+1} - c_t &= g + u_{t+1} \\
\therefore \Delta c_{t+1} &= g + u_{t+1} \qquad (5.1)
\end{aligned}
$$

Consequently, consumption growth, g, is constant. The surplus consumption ratio, S_t, is specified as the excess of consumption over the level of habit, X_t.

$$S_t = \frac{C_t - X_t}{C_t} \tag{5.2}$$

Zero surplus habit consumption is the limit at which utility reaches zero. The agent only values the consumption in excess of habit and S_t will approach zero in bad times. The agent will still try to spread utility out across his lifetime and expects consumption to grow. An expectation of future higher consumption means that habit will grow.

Habit is modeled as an AR(1) process. Habit implies persistence, which in turn implies that the surplus consumption ratio should contain a unit root. Ruling out myopia, changes in habit should be close to permanent. Consequently, the log surplus consumption ratio, s_t, is specified as an AR(1) process with φ close to one.

$$S_{t+1} = \phi S_t + \varepsilon_{t+1} \tag{5.3}$$

Hence, a fully informed agent will maintain a constant surplus consumption ratio. If $\phi \neq 1$ then the surplus consumption ratio would revert to zero ($\phi < 1$) or explode to infinity ($\phi > 1$). Under these specifications habit would not exist. Myopia would allow for $\phi < 1$ as long as the reversion is slow enough to be considered realistic. φ controls the persistence of changes in the surplus ratio. It has already been noted that because consumption is a random walk and habit is persistent, φ should be one. However, Hall (1978) finds that changes in stock price have a predictive power in forecasting consumption. This is the main sense by which rational expectations are incorporated. Fama and French (1988) show that a rational investor can use the price dividend ratio to make forecasts about future returns. Although transaction costs rule out price dividend ratios for arbitrage, they will still give an indication of future returns and hence consumption timing. If future consumption can be forecasted, then rational habit should reflect this ability. Consequently, φ is the autocorrelation coefficient from price dividend ratios.

The error terms from (5.1) and (5.2) are not the same: $\varepsilon_{t+1} \neq (c_{t+1} - c_t - g)$. In consequence, the unit root in habit does not imply consumption shocks permanently affect habit on a one-for-one ratio. The two errors are related using a sensitivity function. By including the sensitivity function $\lambda(s_t)$, shocks to consumption can be dampened before they impact upon habit. This controls how the surplus consumption ratio should respond to shocks in the growth rate of consumption,

μ_{t+1}. Campbell and Cochrane specify three criteria for the sensitivity function.

(1) Habit must change so that consumption is never permanently below habit. It would not make sense for habit to be consistently above consumption if consumption was not expected to grow in the future.
(2) Habit must not move for unit with consumption. Perfect correlation would mean that the surplus consumption ratio was constant. This would revoke the characteristics of habit consumption – intertemporal changes in marginal utility and time-varying risk premium.
(3) Habit must be positively correlated with consumption so that habit always increases with rising consumption.

Incorporating these criteria, the sensitivity function is specified as

$$\lambda(s_t) = \left\{ \frac{1}{S}\sqrt{1 - 2(s_t - \bar{s}} - 1, \quad s_t \leq s_{\max} \right\} \tag{5.4}$$

the above is 0 when $s \geq s_{\max}$.

Based on this, the habit model is

$$s_{t+1} = (1-\varphi)\bar{s} + \varphi s_t + \lambda(s_t)\mu_{t+1} \tag{5.5}$$

where $\bar{s}$ is the steady-state surplus consumption ratio or the unconditional expectation of the surplus consumption ratio. Campbell and Cochrane state that the criteria for the sensitivity function imply that in steady state, restriction (5.6) must hold

$$\bar{S} = \sigma\sqrt{\frac{\eta}{1-\phi}}$$

where η is the curvature parameter of the utility function. (5.6)

The utility function is expressed as in (5.7). It is based on the time-separable utility function, but instead agents obtain utility from surplus consumption rather than the level of consumption.

$$U(t) = E_t\left[\sum_{t=0}^{\infty} \delta^j \frac{C_t - X_t)^{1-\eta} - 1}{1-\eta}\right] \tag{5.7}$$

δ - subjective discount factor

η - curvature parameter (note this is not the risk-aversion coefficient)

Substituting the first and second derivatives of utility with respect to consumption into the coefficient of relative risk aversion gives

$$\gamma = \frac{\eta}{S} \tag{5.8}$$

which is time varying if S varies. It has been established that a time-varying risk-aversion coefficient is desirable. Risk aversion increases as S declines. As consumption approaches habit, agents become more risk averse. Intuitively this can explain some of the risk-aversion anomalies since agents are often more prepared to take gambles that decrease discounted future income, rather than equivalent gambles that decrease income today.

We can appeal to the CCAMP to write the unconditional expected return on an asset i, as shown below:

$$E\left[1+R_{i,t}\right] = \frac{1}{E\left[M_t\right]}\left\{1 - Cov\left[(1+R_{i,t}), M_t\right]\right\}$$

This shows that the return on an asset increases as the Arrow–Debreu security price falls, and decreases as the correlation between the return and the Arrow–Debreu security price increases

$$M_{t+1} = \delta \frac{u'(C_{t+1})}{u'(C_t)}$$

and the marginal utility of consumption is

$$u'(C_t) = (C_t - X_t)^{-\eta}$$

$$\therefore u'(C_t) = \left[\frac{C_t}{C_t}(C_t - X_t)\right]^{-\eta}$$

$$\therefore u'(C_t) = [C_t S_t]^{-\eta}$$

$$\therefore u'(C_t) = C_t^{-\eta} S_t^{-\eta}$$

so the Arrow-Debreu price series is

$$\mathrm{M}_{t+1} = \delta\left[\frac{C_{t+1}^{-\eta} S_{t+1}^{-\eta}}{C_t^{-\eta} S_t^{-\eta}}\right]^{-\eta} \tag{5.9}$$

Note that the volatility of the Arrow–Debreu prices now depends on the surplus habit ratio as well as η. This confirms the habit-relative risk-aversion coefficient, which included surplus consumption term S. It is straightforward to derive an expression for the risk-free rate using the required equality of risk-adjusted returns in a CCAPM context as shown below:

$$1 + R_f = \frac{1}{E_t[M_{t+1}]}$$

taking logs and using the property that log (1+x) = x when x is small:

$$\log(1 + R_f) = \log \frac{1}{E_t[M_{t+1}]}$$

$$\therefore R_f = \log {}^{1}\!/_{\delta} \left[\frac{C_t}{C_{t+1}} \frac{S_t}{S_{t+1}} \right]^{-\eta}$$

$$\therefore R_f = -\log \delta - \eta \log \left[\frac{C_{t+1}}{C_t} \right] - \eta \log \left[\frac{S_{t+1}}{S_t} \right]$$

$$\therefore R_f = -\log \delta + \eta g - \eta [s_{t+1} - s_t]$$

Some further substitution using equation (5.5) and manipulation yields:

$$R_f = -\log \delta + \eta g - \eta [(1 - \theta)\bar{s} + \theta s_t + \lambda(s_t)\mu_{t+1} - s_t]$$

$$\therefore R_f = -\log \delta + \eta g - \eta [(1 - \theta)\bar{s} + (\theta - 1)s_t + \lambda(s_t)\mu_{t+1}]$$

$$\therefore R_f = -\log \delta + \eta g - \eta [(1 - \theta)\bar{s} - (1 - \theta)s_t + \lambda(s_t)\mu_{t+1}]$$

$$\therefore R_f = -\log \delta + \eta g - \eta [(1 - \theta)(\bar{s} - s_t) + \lambda(s_t)\mu_{t+1}]$$

$$R_f = -\log \delta + \eta g - \eta (1 - \theta)(s_t - \bar{s}) - \frac{\eta^2 \sigma_g^2}{2} [\lambda(s_t) + 1]^2 \quad (5.10)$$

The third term is like an error-correction term. If describes how the interest rate changes as the surplus consumption rate moves away from the steady-state (mean) consumption ratio. If the surplus consumption ratio is high, then marginal utility today is low. If the agent expects the ratio to return to the steady state then marginal utility today is low. If the agent expects the ratio to return to the steady state then marginal utility will increase in the future. The agent tries to shift consumption into the next period by saving, which lowers the interest rate. It is a form of mean-reversion in marginal utility terms and it is not included in the CRRA equation. The fourth term is a precautionary saving term in a manner similar to the CRRA model, but it includes the sensitivity function as well. Hence, the volatility of the risk can be controlled. The habit specification has also increased the separation of the elasticity of intertemporal substitution from the coefficient of risk aversion, which is a clear advantage over the other models. Rearranging the risk-free equation (5.10) leaves the following expression:

$$\therefore g = \frac{1}{\eta}\log\delta + R_f + \eta(1-\theta)(s_t - \bar{s}) + \frac{\eta^2\sigma_g^2}{2}[\lambda(s_t)+1]^2$$

So the intertemporal substitution is $\varphi = \frac{1}{\eta} = \frac{1}{\gamma\bar{S}}$. Changes in intertemporal substitution do not have to impact on relative risk aversion. They can impact on the surplus habit ratio instead.

5.3 Estimating the model

To test the habit model an estimation of the equity premium was performed. It was expected to compare favorably with actual series if the model could correctly predict returns. First a series of implied habit-based surplus consumption was generated, then the risk-free rate and then finally the equity premium could be forecasted.

To produce a static series of S_t it was assumed that investors are rational and make revisions to the short-run steady-state surplus consumption ratio so that the actual surplus consumption ratio is the steady-state consumption ratio. We are not forecasting habit by first removing the agent's inclination to follow habit because the preference for habit is incorporated by the parameters φ and η. In addition, once the series of steady-state habits was obtained, a one-period-ahead forecast of S_t+1 was produced by reintroducing habit. It was this series that was used to estimate the risk-free rate. The steady-state consumption ratio is given by the previously introduced equation (5.6)

$$\bar{S} = \sigma_g\sqrt{\frac{\eta}{1-\phi}} \tag{5.6}$$

and using the assumption of short-run steady-state revision gives

$$S_t = \sigma_{gt}\sqrt{\frac{\eta}{1-\phi}} \tag{5.11}$$

In the long run the steady-state consumption ratio $\bar{S}$ will still be given by equation (5.6) and this should be the same as the mean of the series S_t generated by the equation above.

The conditional standard deviation of consumption growth was obtained by running a GARCH (p, q) model. φ was estimated by running an ARMA model on price dividend ratios and using the AR(1) coefficient. The curvature parameter η was more difficult to estimate. One method is to follow Campbell and Cochrane and use the Hansen–Jagannathan lower volatility equation shown below:

$$\frac{\sigma_{M_t(\overline{M})}}{\overline{M}} = \frac{E(r_{it} - r_{ft})}{\sigma_{r_{it}-r_{ft}}}$$

where $\overline{\mathsf{M}}$ is the unconditional expectation of the Arrow–Debreu asset.

By taking the unconditional expectation of $\overline{\mathsf{M}}$ there is an assumption that the risk-free interest rate is constant in the long run. Nonetheless, Campbell and Cochrane's method was followed. $\overline{\mathsf{M}}$ can be estimated by using CCAPM identity, if asset prices offer expected returns commensurate with their risk:

$$1 + R_f = \frac{1}{E_t[M_{t+1}]}$$

hence,

$$\overline{M} = \frac{\sum_{t=1}^{n} \frac{1}{1+R_{ft}}}{n}$$

Then by trying different values of η in the habit utility function a series of M_t can be generated until the Hansen–Jagannathan equality holds. We utilize the values from Campbell and Cochrane (1995) that are consistent with the Hansen–Jagannathan lower bound.

5.3.1 The method used to estimate the risk-free rate

Two forecasts of the risk-free rate were made.

(1) Implied risk-free rate

By taking the natural logarithm of S_t an implied risk-free interest rate was generated using Equation (5.12) (shown below). This was compared to the actual risk-free rate.

$$R_f = -\log\delta + \eta g - \eta(1-\theta)(s_t - \overline{s}) - \frac{-\eta^2\sigma_s^2}{2}[\lambda(s_t) + 1]^2 \tag{5.12}$$

The series S_t was generated using all the conditional information. Hence, if the specification of the steady habit is corrected, then the series should generate a risk-free rate that is close to perfectly correlated with the nominal rate.

(2) Static one-period-ahead forecast

The specification of habit equation (5.13) (shown below) was used to make a static forecast of S_{t+1}. Using this forecasted series the risk-free interest rate equation was used again to generate a static forecast of the risk-free rate.

$$s_{t+1} = (1-\varphi)\bar{s} + \varphi s_t + \lambda(s_t)\mu_{t+1} \tag{5.13}$$

5.3.2 The method used to estimate the equity premium

The equity premium was derived using the CCAPM definition of the equity premium shown below:

$$E[R_{i,t} - R_{ft}] = -E[1 + R_{ft}] \times Cov[(1 + R_{i,t}), M_t$$

First the series of Arrow–Debreu prices M_t was generated using the method described in the previous section. Then an ARCH(1,1) model was used to estimate the conditional covariances between risky returns R_t, and the Arrow–Debreu prices M_t. An approximation method was used to estimate the ARCH model. Using the fact that a bivariate ARCH(1) can be specified by equations (5.14) and (5.15), the conditional covariance can be approximated by the static forecasts of the linear equation (5.16) estimated using OLS.

$$\mathrm{var}(R_t|I_{t-1}) = E[(R_t - E[R_t])^2|I_{t-1}] \tag{5.14}$$

$$\mathrm{cov}[(1+R_t)M_t|I_{t-1}] = \omega_0 + \omega_1[(1+R_{t-1}) - E[1+R_{t-1}]] \times (M_{t-1} - E[M_{t-1}]) \tag{5.15}$$

$$\mathrm{cov}[(1+R_t)M_t|I_{t-1}] = \omega_0 + \omega_1(1+R_{t-1})M_{t-1} + \pi_t \tag{5.16}$$

With a conditional covariance series and a forecast of the risk-free rate, it is straightforward to generate an estimated equity premium using the equity premium as defined by the CCAPM previously introduced. Two equity premium series are generated, one from the in-sample period s_t and one from the one-period-ahead forecasts s_{t+1}.

The forecasts of the equity premium and risk-free rate were compared with the observed series. An OLS equation was run on the forecasted and the actual series to determine whether they are the same. If the forecast is accurate then the joint hypothesis $H_0 : \beta_0 = 0, \beta_1 = 1$ should not be rejected in the following regression.

$$y^{actual} = \beta_0 + \beta_1 y^{forecast}$$

5.4 Data

Our study required Australian data for nondurable consumption, equity returns, risk-free asset returns and price dividend ratios. The sample features observations of a quarterly frequency over a 28-year period from January 1973 to June 2002. The data were taken from Datastream International™. The stock market data includes the Australian stock market indicator (with national holidays excluded) quoted in local currency terms. The market index is calculated by Datastream International™ and is a market capitalization weighted index incorporating approximately 80 percent of the market value at any given point in time.

Although a lot of studies in the United States use the Ibbotson Associates data from 1926, there are almost as many using data over shorter time periods, with time periods such as 50, 20 or even 10 years to come up with historical risk premiums. The rationale presented by those who use the shorter periods is that the risk aversion of the average investor is likely to change over time, and that using a shorter time period provides a more updated estimate. This has to be set against the cost associated with using shorter time periods, which leads to greater noise in the risk premium estimate. Damodaran (2002) finds that, given the annual standard deviation in stock prices between 1926 and 1997 of 20 percent, the standard error associated with the risk premium estimate is estimated to be 8.94 percent for 5 years, 6.32 percent for 10 years, 4.00 percent for 25 years and 2.83 percent for a 50-year sample.[1]

The data used in deriving the CRRA, CCAPM and the habit model consists of quarterly observations using Australian data for private household consumption, population, equity returns, risk-free asset returns, dividend yields and price dividend ratios. The sample includes 118 quarterly observations over the period from the 1st Quarter 1973 to the 2nd Quarter 2002. The consumption data set is composed from the sets of NIFC Private Final Consumption Expenditure Food and the NIFC Private Final Consumption Expenditure Other Non Durables (Excluding Oil). It is normalized to a per capita basis using quarterly population statistics. The population includes every age group, including children, prisoners and invalids, who may not be making consumption choice decisions for themselves. This study assumes that population statistics are an adequate proxy for the number of Australians making consumption decisions.

The risk-free rate is represented by the nominal yield on the Australian 90-day Treasury bill. The inflation series is composed from the CPI index that excludes oil. Estimations were run with oil but the results are not good. The nonlinear nature of inflation is not well accounted for in this model. When oil is removed inflation is more stationary in the mean, and the model performs better.

5.5 The results

In this section we present the results of the CRRA, CCAPM and habit models. We also look at the actual and implied risk premium given by our model.

5.5.1 Deriving parameters for the CCAPM and habit models

The AR(1) estimation of the annual price dividend ratio gives a value of φ as 0.996 (0.0308). The estimation was annualized to allow for seasonality. However, neither the Augmented Dickey Fuller or Phillips–Perron tests can reject a unit root, hence the estimate and the standard error are irrelevant. Campbell and Cochrane (1995) used a long-run price dividend ratio and estimate $\varphi = 0.97$ for US stocks. It was this value that was used to estimate S_t.

The consumption growth rate was taken from the mean of the consumption growth series. To estimate a conditional standard deviation σ_{gt} a maximum likelihood GARCH(1,1) is estimated.

Variance Equation for Consumption Growth:

$$\sigma_{gt} = \underset{(0.629)}{-0.0648} \times ARCH(1) + \underset{(0.212)}{0.838} \times GARCH(1)$$

The mean and standard error of the observed risk premium were 0.02022 and 0.1005, respectively. This gave a lower Hansen–Jagannathan bound of 0.22. Using Campbell and Cochrane's estimates, η was estimated to be 2.5. Remember that η is not sensitive to the Hansen–Jagannathan bound, so an approximate estimation should not cause problems with the model. The last parameter to be estimated was the discount rate, δ. Most studies find that a reasonable value of the discount factor is between 0.95 and 0.98. Campbell and Cochrane (1995) used 0.98, while Engsted (1998) chose the lower bound of 0.95. This study takes an intermediary value of 0.97, which was a similar value to the reciprocal of one minus the mean of the risk-free rate (Table 5.1).

Table 5.1 Parameter and brief statistics

Parameter	Quarterly	Annualized
φ	0.98	0.92
Mean return of equity (%)	3.13	12.53
Mean risk-free rate (%)	0.89	3.56
Mean risk premium ($R_i - R_f$) (%)	2.022	8.09
Std error risk premium (%)	9.75	39.0
$\overline{g_t}$ (%)	0.467	1.89
$\overline{\sigma}_{g_t}$ (%)	0.978	7.57
η	2.5	–
δ	0.97	–
Hansen–Jagannathan ratio	0.207	0.207
Covariance g and R	10.10	40.41

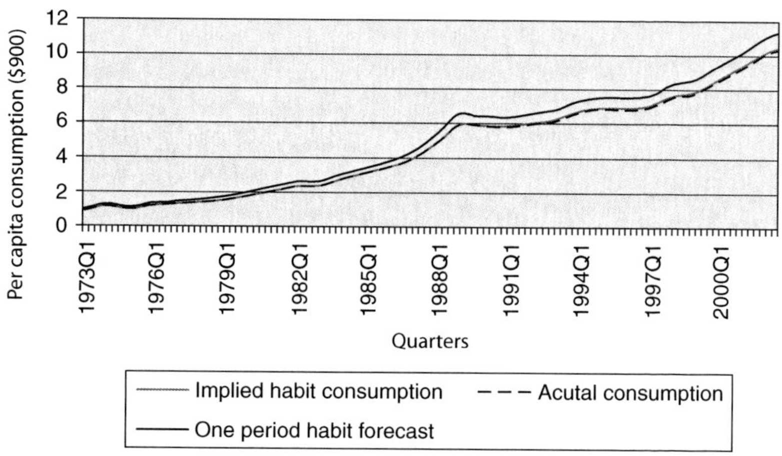

Figure 5.1 Implied habit consumption and actual real consumption per capita

5.5.2 Generating implied habit consumption

Implied habit was derived using the definition introduced earlier, shown below:

$$S_t = \frac{C_t - X_t}{C_t}$$

Using the one-period-ahead forecast of S_{t+1}, a series of implied habit forecasts was made. Figure 5.1 shows implied habit and static forecast habit along with observed consumption. The series are very similar, which is not a surprise as φ is so close to one. Notice that, as expected,

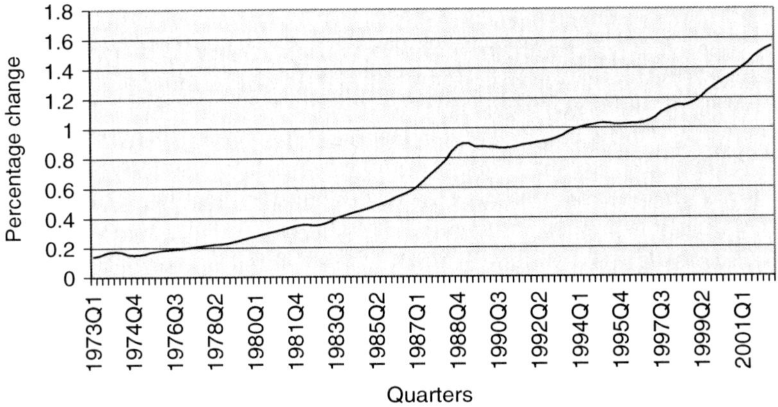

Figure 5.2 The difference between implied habit and actual consumption

the volatility of implied habit (s.e. = 0.298) is slightly greater than the volatility of the forecast habit series (s.e. = 0.297).

The above curves for the three consumption series are very close, thus indicating the smooth consumption patterns observed when we compare actual consumption and the implied or derived consumption series. This clearly addresses the issue of smooth consumption patterns that Mehra and Prescott (1985) referred to in their seminal paper on the equity premium puzzle. An interesting phenomenon is that implied habit and actual consumption are diverging. Figure 5.2 plots the divergence. This means that utility is increasing slowly through time. It also means that either consumption is growing unexpectedly fast or habit is reaching an asymptotic limit. A limit would imply that one-day consumption would rise to such as level that an ultimate habit level is reached. If consumption kept growing after habit leveled out then utility would rapidly increase. An alternative explanation for the divergence between habit and consumption is that the long-run consumption growth rate or the price dividend autocorrelation coefficients were inaccurate.

5.5.3 The risk-free rate

Having made the assumption of a constant risk-free rate, the forecast and actual risk-free series were not expected to be very closely related. Table 5.2 presents the OLS regression for collinearity. Wald tests rejected the hypothesis that either of the forecast series is the same as the actual rate. The F-statistic for the implied risk-free rate rejects the OLS equation altogether. This does not matter because it is only an implied rate, and

Table 5.2 Risk premium results

	Actual risk premium (%)	Implied risk premium (%)	Forecast risk premium (%)
Mean	2.2	−0.89	−0.90
Standard error	9.75	1.20	1.19

Table 5.3 OLS regression for collinearity

	Implied risk-free rate	Static forecast of risk-free rate	Implied risk premium	Static forecast of risk premium
β_0	0.018642 (0.0150)	0.036960 (0.110)	0.0337 (0.00961)	0.0330 (0.00965)
β_1	−0.614316 (0.9412)	−1.824808 (0.689)	1.210 (0.518)	1.240 (0.541)
R^2	0.002851	0.034764	0.036006	0.034764
F-Stat (P-value)	0.426038 (0.5149)	7.014960 (0.00896)	5.416 (0.021338)	5.258 (0.023269)
P-Value H_0: $\beta_0 = 0$ & H_1: $\beta_1 = 1$	0.000000	0.000000	0.000999	0.00134
P-Value H_0: $\beta_1 := 1$	0.086304	0.000041	0.690860	0.658159

the regression could not reject a positive relationship with $\beta_1 = 1$. Of more concern is the static forecast regression. It is significant with a negative β_1 coefficient, implying a negative relationship. Clearly this is an inadequate forecast. Still it is the equity premium, not the risk-free rate, that the model is interested in forecasting. The risk-free rate is generated because it is needed for the premium's estimation.

5.5.4 The equity premium

Table 5.3 shows that the risk premium equation has some predictive power. The F-statistic indicates that the equation for the risk premium has some limited explanatory power. Note that although Wald tests reject the hypothesis that the series are the same, they do not reject the hypothesis that the series are perfectly correlated ($\beta_1 = 1$), although this is not

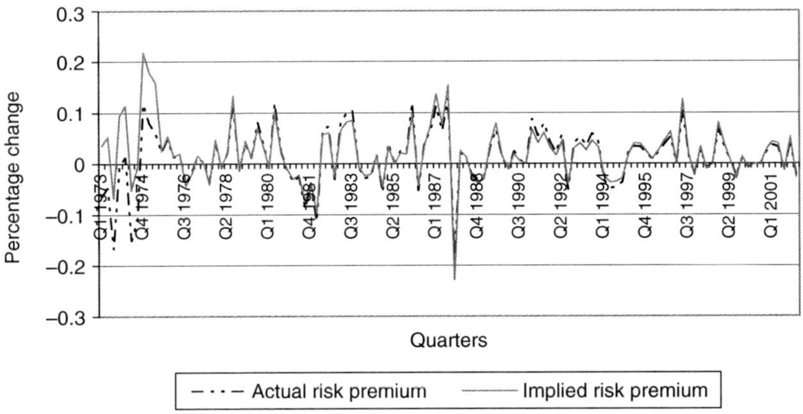

Figure 5.3 Implied and actual risk premium

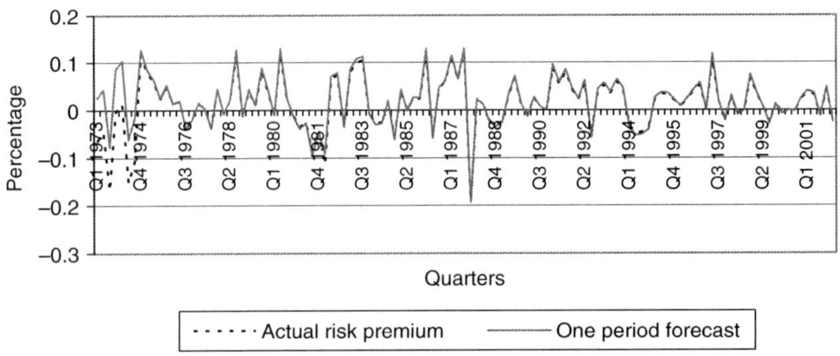

Figure 5.4 One-period forecast and actual risk premium

clear looking at Figures 5.3 and 5.4. It was concluded that this was the case due to the series having significantly different means. As previously mentioned, the expected risk premium is 2.2 percent. The mean risk premiums using recursive utility were −0.89 percent and −0.90 percent (Table 5.2), respectively, which implies the market portfolio is a consumption hedge. However, the standard errors for these means are large, 1.20 percent and 1.19 percent, respectively. Consequently, there is little accuracy in the estimations of the mean risk premium. Nevertheless, the 95 percent confidence interval does not extend to include the actual risk premium of 2.2 percent. Also, the standard errors are substantially less than the standard error of the observed risk premium, 10.1 percent. It appears that the model still cannot account for the large variability in equity returns compared with consumption variability. This was probably due, in part, to the composition of the market portfolio. It is made entirely of equity, from which only a small proportion of the population derive consumption. It may be that the model is predicting the volatility of the true market portfolio – a portfolio that includes broader capital such as property and human capital. Nonetheless, the equity portfolio was used to afford comparisons with Mehra and Prescott (1985) and subsequent papers. One aim of this study was to show that an alternative utility function can help to resolve their puzzle. If the type of portfolio was changed then there would be no basis for comparison.

5.5.5 The coefficient of relative risk aversion

Equation (5.8) is reproduced below and from it a series of the risk-aversion coefficients were generated

$$\gamma_t = {}^{\eta}/\mathrm{S}_t$$

The average surplus consumption ratio, $\overline{\mathrm{S}}$, is 0.154. This implies an average risk-aversion coefficient of 16.23. One of the benefits of the habit model is that it allows for time-varying risk-aversion coefficients and a series is generated. Figure 5.5 shows the time varying γ_t along with de-trended consumption and real GDP. Note that risk aversion increases as output and consumption decline. The derivation of this model requires that the consumption and the risk-aversion coefficient are contemporaneously correlated but the relationship with output may be different. Sengupta (1992) suggests that risk aversion changes before output falls. Business confidence is frequently reported in the media as a weak predictor of business cycles. Future work could test whether the assumption of contemporaneous risk aversion is adequate.

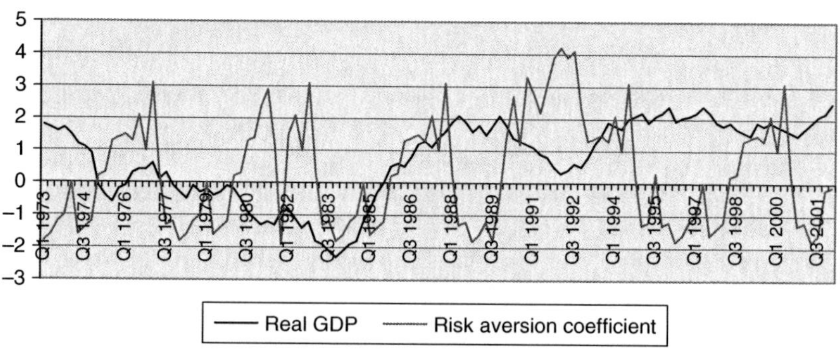

Figure 5.5 Normalized de-trended real GDP and the related risk-aversion coefficient

The time-varying risk-aversion coefficient is negatively but weakly correlated with de-trended real GDP, as shown in Figure 5.5. Note the large increases in risk aversion in 1974, 1975, 1978 and in 1989, corresponding to recessions, OPEC shocks and the senate blocking of supply in 1975. The recession of 1983 does not have a very large risk-aversion coefficient. The only way the model could allow for such an anomaly is if people in the early eighties had foreseen the recession and revised habit before consumption fell. Risk aversion is highest when there are unforeseen consumption shocks. In this sense risk aversion may be able to predict recessions assuming consumption shocks precede output shocks. For curiosity the results for the Granger causality test are tabulated in Table 5.4. Causality is rejected for all lags. Nonetheless, further work may find some causality because it looks like it does exist in Figure 5.4.

5.5.6 Consumption volatility

Table 5.5 summarizes the market volatility results. The standard error for the Arrow–Debreu asset prices is 0.152. The Hansen–Jagannathan lower bound was 0.22. However, this is still an improvement on the CRRA Arrow–Debreu volatility of 0.12. A variance ratio test rejected the hypothesis that the variance of the habit Arrow–Debreu assets were the same as the CRRA volatility or the Hansen–Jagannathan lower bound. The habit model is able to account for more of the variability in equity than the CRRA model. The smooth consumption puzzle is not as severe with the habit model.

Table 5.4 Granger causality test for risk aversion predicting output shocks

	Lag 1	**Lag 2**	**Lag 3**	**Lag 4**	**Lag 8**	**Lag 10**	**Lag 12**
γ_t does not Granger cause rGDP	0.54154	0.27442	0.47044	0.65615	0.94182	0.83427	0.64042

Table 5.5 Volatility of Australian market portfolio

Hansen–Jagannathan lower volatility bound		**0.22**
	CRRA	Habit model
Estimated volatility	0.12	0.152

5.6 Conclusion

We have investigated the habit utility specification of Campbell and Cochrane (1995) an applied it empirically to estimate the Australian equity premium. The results show that habit utility is able to reproduce an equity premium that is comparable to the actual equity premium.

One of the implications is that preferences are not completely rational. If habit is persistent, than fiscal shocks will have persistent effects under certain circumstances. Providing that consumers cannot substitute the increased government consumption for private consumption, total consumption will increase. Once the new consumption level is reached, habit will cause the shock to persist, so that when there is a fiscal contraction, aggregate demand will be maintained. Ricardian equivalence is yet to be empirically proven (Gulley 1994; Vamvoukas 1999), but the results of this study suggest the hypothesis is weak.

If habit is a robust phenomenon, then it has growth policy implications. Our results suggest that utility grows more slowly than the growth rate of consumption. If utility is obtained from surplus consumption then policy should move from emphasizing consumption growth to smoothing consumption shocks. Although this study supports the existence of habit, the results are not clear enough to justify such a policy shift.

Finally, Campbell and Cochrane's model is able to alleviate part of the equity premium puzzle in Australia. The relative risk-aversion coefficient and the estimated volatility of returns are both more acceptable. The habit model still does not completely resolve either of these problems – stock volatility is still too high compared to consumption volatility and the coefficient of risk aversion is unreasonable – however, the habit specification has reduced the discrepancy.

Note

1. These estimates of the standard error are probably understated, because they are based upon the assumption that annual returns are uncorrelated over time. There is substantial empirical evidence that returns are correlated over time, which would make this standard-error estimate much larger.

References

Abel, A. (1990) "Asset Prices under Habit Formation and Catching Up with the Joneses,"*American Economic Review*, 80: 38–42.

Bellamy, D. and Heaney, R. (1997) "An Examination of Variation in the Equity Market Risk Premium," Working paper, Working Paper, Faculty of Business, Australian National University.

Campbell, J.Y. (1999) "Asset Prices, Consumption, and the Business Cycle," in J.B. Taylor and M. Woodforde (eds.), *Handbook of Macroeconomics,* Vols. 1–3, North-Holland.

Campbell, J.Y. and Cochrane, J.H. (1999) "By Force of Habit: A Consumption-Based Explanation of Aggregate Stock Market Behaviour," *Journal of Political Economy,* 107: 205–251.

Constantindes, G.M. (1990) "Habit Formation: A Resolution of the Equity Premium Puzzle," *Journal of Political Economy*, 98: 519–543.

Damodaran, A. (2002) "Estimating Equity Risk Premiums," Working Paper, Stern School of Business, New York.

Engsted, T. (1998) "Evaluating the Consumption-Capital Asset-Pricing Model Using Hansen-Jangannathan Bounds: Evidence from the UK," *International Journal of Finance and Economics*, 3: 291–302.

Epstein, L.G. and Zin, S.E. (1989) "Substitution, Risk-Aversion and the Temporal Behaviour of Asset Returns,"*Journal of Political Economy*, 99: 263–286.

Fama, E.F. and French, K.R. (1988) "Dividend Yields and Expected Stock Returns," *Journal of Financial Economics,* 22 (1): 3–25.

Gulley, O.D. (1994) "An Empirical Test of the Effects of Government Deficits on Money Demand," *Applied Economics*, 26: 239–247.

Hall, R.E. (1978) "Stochastic Implications of the Life Cycle/Permanent Income Hypothesis: Theory and Evidence," *Journal of Political Economy,* 86: 971–987.

Hansen, L.P. and Jagannathan, R. (1991) "Implications of Security Market Data for Models of Dynamic Economies," *Journal of Political Economy*, 99: 225–262.

He, H. and Modest, D.M. (1995) "Market Frictions and Consumption-Based Asset Pricing," *Journal of Political Economy*, 103 (1): 94–117.

Heaton, J.C. and Lucas, D. (1996) "Evaluating The Effects of Incomplete Markets on Risk Sharing and Asset Pricing," *Journal of Political Economy,* 103: 94–117.

Kreps, D.M. and Porteus, E.L. (1978) "Temporal Resolution of Uncertainty and Dynamic Choice Theory," *Econometrica*, Econometric Society, 46 (1): 185–200.

Mehra, R. and Prescott, E. (1985) "The Equity Premium: A Puzzle," *Journal of Monetary Economics*, 15: 145–161.

Sengupta, J. (1992) "Adjustment Costs in Production Frontier Analysis," *Economic Notes,* 21: 316–329.

Sundaresan, S.M. (1989) "Intertemporally Dependent Preferences and the Volatility of Consumption and Wealth," *Review of Financial Studies*, 2: 73–88.

Vamvoukas, G.A. (1999) "The Twin Deficit Phenomenon: Evidence from Greece," *Applied Economics*, 31: 1093–1100.

Weil, P. (1989) "The Equity Premium Puzzle and the Risk-Free Rate Puzzle," *Journal of Monetary Economics,* 24: 401–421.

6

Testing the Lower Partial Moment Asset-Pricing Models in Emerging Markets

Javed Iqbal, Robert D. Brooks and Don U.A. Galagedera

6.1 Introduction

Following Markowitz's (1959) "portfolio optimization theory," Sharpe (1964) and Lintner (1965) developed a generic capital asset-pricing model known as the CAPM that has now become a benchmark asset-pricing model. The CAPM is based on mean and variance of the return distribution and assumes multivariate normality of the joint return distribution of the underlying assets. The normality assumption makes CAPM derivation statistically tractable but an investor's preferences are not necessarily consistent with the mean and variance of return. The CAPM considers beta as the sole measure of systematic risk in a diversified portfolio. The beta is estimated via a market model and is assumed valid under all market conditions. However, several alternative theories based on different perceptions of systematic risk have challenged the dominance of the mean–variance notion of the risk-return relationship. One of the most prominent of these is the asset-pricing theory that recognizes deviation only below a target rate of return as risky. Downside risk measures and the associated asset-pricing models are motivated by economic and statistical considerations – investor psychology is consistent with an asymmetric treatment of the variations in the returns and the empirical return distributions appear to be non-normal.[1]

Harlow and Rao (1989) (henceforth referred to as H&R) developed an asset-pricing model that measures risk based on the deviations of returns from an arbitrary target rate. The asset-pricing model is similar to the

CAPM and can be expressed as:

$$E(R_i) = R_f + \beta_i^{MLPM(\tau)} \left[E(R_m) - R_f \right] \tag{6.1}$$

When $E(R_i)$ and $E(R_m)$ denote the expected returns of asset i and the market m, respectively, then:

$$\beta_i^{MLPM(\tau)} = \frac{E\left[(R_i - R_f) \min(R_m - \tau, 0) \right]}{E\left[\min(R_m - \tau, 0) \right]^2} \tag{6.2}$$

where R_f is the risk-free rate and τ is an arbitrary target rate. In this model, a particular asset contributes to the risk only if the market return is below the target rate τ. We refer to (6.1) as the mean lower partial moment (MLPM) model. Asset-pricing models based on the notion of downside risk are appropriate when asset returns are not symmetrical. Asymmetric asset returns are more pronounced in emerging markets than in developed markets. With identical regulatory environments and taxes, the extra utility of a dollar gain for a developed market investor who has higher initial wealth is lower compared to an emerging market investor with a lower wealth endowment. Conversely, the disutility of a dollar loss in investment is higher for an emerging market investor with lower initial wealth compared to the developed market investor. Hence, downside risk measures may capture risk perceptions better in emerging markets than in developed markets. In addition, with lower liquidity, infrequent trading and volatile political and macroeconomic conditions, the assumptions underlying smooth and symmetric behavior of asset returns are unlikely to be satisfied in emerging markets.

Consistent with this consideration, Bekaert et al. (1998) show that emerging market equities display significant skewness and kurtosis in their returns, while Bekaert and Harvey (1995, 1997) observe that the degree of skewness and kurtosis changes over time. Eftekhari and Satchell (1996) and Claessens et al. (1995) also provide evidence of non-normality of returns in emerging markets. Hwang and Pedersen (2004) linked the applicability of the CAPM and the asymmetry of pricing models to regional and timing effects in emerging markets and found that as the market matures over time the returns tend to be more normal. In addition, Harvey (1995) and Salomons and Grootveld (2003), among others, provide empirical evidence that emerging market returns are more predictable than developed market returns. Conscious of these considerations, Harvey (2001) and Bekaert et al. (1998) argue that the simple benchmark model – the CAPM, does not appropriately describe the empirical relationship between risk and stock returns in emerging markets.

Harvey (2000) and Estrada (2000, 2002) tested various equilibrium- and non-equilibrium-based risk measures and conclude that downside risk measures such as the semi-standard deviation are relevant measures of risk for emerging market equity indices. Estrada (2000) suggests that the downside risk measures are consistent with partially integrated emerging markets. Harvey and Estrada employ the Fama and MacBeth (1973) type of cross-sectional methods in their studies. We contribute to the literature on testing asset-pricing models in a downside framework by proposing multivariate tests that are likely to be more powerful. More specifically, we extend the likelihood ratio test to Wald and GMM tests that are robust to non-normality, heteroskedasticity and serial dependence of returns. The aim is to provide tests that are applicable to the relatively inefficient markets exhibiting extreme return movements and greater volatility than those of relatively stable developed markets.

The "likelihood ratio" test, the "Lagrange multiplier" test and the "Wald" test are generally applied when testing nonlinear parametric hypotheses. Greene (2003: 110) points out that amongst the three asymptotic tests only the Wald test is asymptotically valid under non-normality. Computation of this test requires only the unrestricted parameter estimates for which least squares estimates can be employed. More generally, the GMM-based tests do not require strong distributional assumption regarding normality, heteroskedasticity and serial independence of the residuals. Following this, we formulate robust Wald and GMM tests for the MLPM model of H&R. The GMM test is based on specifying a set of orthogonality conditions between the residuals and market portfolio returns fragmented between upside and downside movements. Black's (1972) "zero-beta" CAPM and the H&R asset-pricing model are particularly relevant for emerging markets since empirical tests for these models do not require specification of a risk-free rate. Due to imperfect money markets in emerging economies a reliable risk-free rate is difficult to obtain.

H&R also investigated nested tests of the CAPM restriction against the MLPM alternative. Under the null hypothesis of the CAPM the betas in up and down markets are equal. In this case, the critical parameter, the target rate, becomes unidentified, while under the alternative of MLPM the target rate is accommodated. This is a nonstandard hypothesis testing problem and the asymptotic Chi-square p-values become no longer valid. The H&R study does not address this issue and uses the asymptotic Chi-square p-values with the target rate as the optimal rate obtained in

MLPM tests. Tests for the nonstandard problems are addressed in the econometric literature.[2] To overcome the said problem, this chapter uses a likelihood ratio test and the robust Wald and GMM tests with the p-values generated from the bootstrap methodology.

We investigate the empirical application of the proposed multivariate tests on the data from the Karachi Stock Market, which is the largest stock exchange in Pakistan.[3] This market has received considerable attention in recent years when in 2002 it was declared as the best performing stock market in the world in terms of the per cent increase in the local market index value. It is interesting to study which of the alternative risk measures and the associated asset-pricing models track the risk-return behavior in this growing but volatile emerging market. Figure 6.1 displays the time series of the KSE-100 index and the continuously compounded monthly return over the sample period in the study. The vertical line separates the two subperiods employed in this chapter. The market is, in general, in a bearish mood in the second subperiod, but occasional sharp downside movements also occur with greater frequency in this period. Iqbal and Brooks (2007a, 2007b) found that unconditional skewness among some other variables significantly affects the stock and portfolio returns in this market. Following this introduction, the plan of

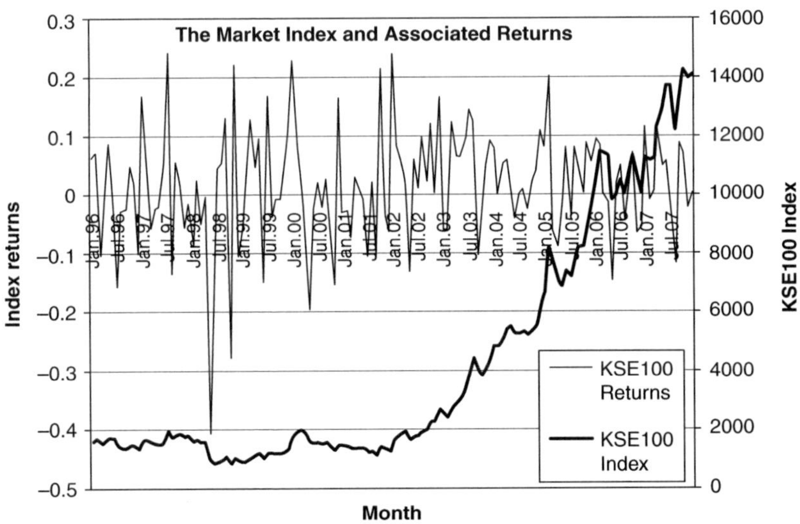

Figure 6.1 The time variation of the Karachi stock exchange −100 index and associated returns

the chapter is as follows: Section 6.2 discusses multivariate tests of the CAPM and the MLPM model. In Section 6.3, robust tests proposed for the MLPM model are discussed. The description of data portfolio construction is given in Section 6.4. Section 6.5 discusses the empirical results and the conclusion is provided in Section 6.6.

6.2 Multivariate tests of the CAPM and the MLPM model

This section describes the existing and the proposed multivariate tests of asset-pricing models.

6.2.1 Tests of the zero-beta CAPM

Assume that the return-generating process is the familiar market model;

$$R_t = \alpha + \beta R_{mt} + \varepsilon_t, \quad t = 1, 2, \ldots, T \tag{6.3}$$

where $R_t = [R_{1t}\ R_{2t} \ldots R_{Nt}]'$ is the $N \times 1$ vector of raw returns on N portfolios, ε_t is the $N \times 1$ vector of disturbances, and α and β are $N \times 1$ vectors of the intercept and slope parameters, respectively, for each of the N time-series regressions. The zero-beta CAPM specifies the following cross-sectional relation:

$$E(R_t) - \gamma I_N = \beta(E(R_{mt}) - \gamma). \tag{6.4}$$

Here, γ is the parameter representing returns on a zero-beta portfolio. Applying expectations on (6.3) yields

$$E(R_t) = \gamma(1 - \beta) + \beta E(R_{mt}). \tag{6.5}$$

The joint restrictions on the parameter imposed by the CAPM are expressed in the following nonlinear hypothesis:

$$H_0 : \alpha_i = \gamma(1 - \beta_i), \quad i = 1, 2, \ldots N. \tag{6.6}$$

This is essentially a nonlinear restriction on the system of the market model equations. Gibbons (1982) provides an iterative estimation and testing of a likelihood ratio test of the null hypothesis where

$$LR = (T - N/2 - 3/2)(\log|\hat{\Sigma} *| - \log|\hat{\Sigma}|) \xrightarrow{d} \chi^2_{N-1}. \tag{6.7}$$

Here, $\hat{\Sigma}^*$ and $\hat{\Sigma}$ are the estimated restricted and unrestricted covariance matrices of the system of the market model (6.3), respectively. The test is derived under the assumption of multivariate normality of the returns. Chou (2000) developed a Wald test that permits the model to be estimated entirely in terms of alphas and betas by expressing the hypothesis as:

$$H_0 : \frac{\alpha_i}{1-\beta_i} = \gamma, \quad i = 1,2,\ldots N. \tag{6.8}$$

The resulting Wald test is

$$W = g(\hat{\theta})' \left[\left(\frac{\partial g}{\partial \theta'} \Big|_{\theta=\hat{\theta}} \right) \hat{\Sigma} \otimes (X'X)^{-1} \left(\frac{\partial g}{\partial \theta'} \Big|_{\theta=\hat{\theta}} \right)' \right]^{-1} g(\hat{\theta}) \xrightarrow{d} \chi^2_{N-1} \tag{6.9}$$

Here, $g(\theta) = [g_1 \ldots g_{N-1}]'$, $g_i = \alpha_i(1-\beta_{i+1}) - \alpha_{i+1}(1-\beta_i), i = 1,2,\ldots N-1, \theta = [\alpha_1\beta_1 \ldots \alpha_N\beta_N]'$ and X is the $T \times 2$ design matrix with a column of 1's and a column of the return on the market portfolio. The partial derivatives $\frac{\partial g}{\partial \theta'}$ are evaluated at the OLS estimates from the unrestricted system. For extension to the GMM case, see Chou (2000). Prompted by return predictability in emerging markets, Iqbal, Brooks and Galagedera (2008) present a version of the GMM test that is more general and allows for the dynamics of the residuals' dependence in addition to heteroskedasticity.

6.2.2 Tests of the MLPM model

The market model (6.3) assumes that beta is valid for all market conditions. An alternative is to allow asymmetry of systematic risk; downside and upside deviations. The downside risk is measured as the deviation below a target rateτ. To investigate asymmetry in systematic risk Bawa et al. (1981) developed a data-generating process called the asymmetric response model (ARM), which is expressed as:

$$R_{it} = \alpha_i + \beta_i^- R_{mt}^- + \beta_i^+ R_{mt}^+ + \delta_i(1-D_t) + \varepsilon_{it} \tag{6.10}$$

where $R_{mt}^- = \begin{cases} R_{mt} & \text{if } R_{mt} < \tau \\ 0 & \text{otherwise} \end{cases}$

$$R_{mt}^+ = \begin{cases} R_{mt} & \text{if } R_{mt} > \tau \\ 0 & \text{otherwise} \end{cases}$$

$$D_t = \begin{cases} 1 & \text{if } R_{mt} < \tau \\ 0 & \text{otherwise} \end{cases}$$

This model, by construction, creates a distinction between downside and upside movement in the market. The downside beta β_i^- captures the co-movement of asset *i* with the market when the market return falls below the target rate of return and β_i^+ measures the co-movement of the asset with the market when the market return is above the target rate. Following H&R, we assume that $\delta_i = \varphi(\beta_i^- - \beta_i^+)$ where $\varphi = E(R_{mt}^+)/P(R_{mt} > \tau) = E(R_{mt}|R_{mt} > \tau)$. The ARM has been employed by Pederson and Hwang (2003) and Eftekari and Satchel (1996), among others, for estimating downside beta in emerging markets. The ARM estimation is facilitated if expressed in a slightly different form, which requires only one new variable D_t to be created.

$$R_{it} = \alpha_i + \beta_i^- D_t R_{mt} + \beta_i^+(1 - D_t)R_{mt} + \delta_i(1 - D_t) + \varepsilon_{it}. \tag{6.11}$$

H&R show that β_i^- is indeed the MLPM beta[4] and derived the following Gibbons' (1982) type restriction for testing the zero-beta version of the lower partial moment model:

$$H_0 : \alpha_i = \gamma(1 - \beta_i^-). \tag{6.12}$$

Assuming multivariate normality of the returns, they tested the restriction as a Bartlett factor corrected likelihood ratio test (6.13) against an unspecified alternative

$$LR = (T - N/2 - 3/2)(\log|\hat{\Sigma}^*| - \log|\hat{\Sigma}|) \xrightarrow{d} \chi^2_{N-1}. \tag{6.13}$$

Here, $\hat{\Sigma}^*$ and $\hat{\Sigma}$ are the estimated restricted and unrestricted residual covariance matrices of the system of ARM(11), respectively.

It is well known that asymptotic tests such as those discussed above have serious size distortions that impede their validity in empirical applications. In this case, the residual bootstrap p-values provide an alternative means of obtaining more reliable decisions. It is well established that if the test statistic is asymptotically pivotal, that is, the null distribution does not rely on unknown parameters, then the magnitude of the error in size of the bootstrap test is only of the order $O(n^{-j/2})$ compared to that of the asymptotic test, which is of the order $O[^{-n(j+1)/2}]$ for $j \geq 1$. All of the three tests have their asymptotic distribution as Chi-square, which depends only on the number of assets under consideration. Therefore, in the empirical applications, only bootstrap p-values are reported.

6.3 Robust testing of the MLPM model

6.3.1 Test of the MLPM model

Assuming that the model disturbances are i.i.d., a normality robust Wald test similar to that in (6.9) can be established for the MLPM model with the following $4N \times 1$ vector of parameters and $N-1$ vector of restrictions:

$$\theta = [\alpha_1 \quad \beta_1^- \quad \beta_1^+ \quad \delta_1 \quad \alpha_2 \quad \beta_2^- \quad \beta_2^+ \quad \delta_2 \ldots \alpha_N \quad \beta_N^- \quad \beta_N^+ \quad \delta_N]' \tag{6.14}$$

$$g_i = \alpha_i(1-\beta_{i+1}^-) - \alpha_{i+1}(1-\beta_i^-), i = 1, 2, \ldots N-1,. \tag{6.15}$$

The $T \times 4$ design matrix X in this case is

$$X = [1 \quad D \circ R_m \quad (1-D) \circ R_m \quad (1-D)]'. \tag{6.16}$$

The partial derivatives $\frac{\partial g}{\partial \theta'}$ (given in equation 6.22) are evaluated at the "seemingly unrelated regression" (SUR) estimates from the unrestricted system. The notation "$\circ$" represents the element-wise product of the vectors. A more robust GMM-based test that is valid under general return distributions, heteroskedasticity and serial dependence of the residuals can be established. If N assets and T time-series observations on each asset are available, the moment conditions' vector on the disturbance of system (6.11) can be defined as:

$$f_T(\theta) = \begin{bmatrix} \varepsilon_{1t}(\alpha_1, \beta_1^-, \beta_1^+, \delta_1) \\ \varepsilon_{1t}(\alpha_1, \beta_1^-, \beta_1^+, \delta_1)(D_t \circ R_{mt}) \\ \varepsilon_{1t}(\alpha_1, \beta_1^-, \beta_1^+, \delta_1)((1-D_t) \circ R_{mt}) \\ \varepsilon_{1t}(\alpha_1, \beta_1^-, \beta_1^+, \delta_1)(1-D_t) \\ \cdot \\ \cdot \\ \cdot \\ \varepsilon_{Nt}(\alpha_N, \beta_N^-, \beta_N^+, \delta_N) \\ \varepsilon_{Nt}(\alpha_N, \beta_N^-, \beta_N^+, \delta_N)(D_t \circ R_{mt}) \\ \varepsilon_{Nt}(\alpha_N, \beta_N^-, \beta_N^+, \delta_N)((1-D)_t \circ R_{mt}) \\ \varepsilon_{Nt}(\alpha_N, \beta_N^-, \beta_N^+, \delta_N)(1-D_t) \end{bmatrix} = \varepsilon_t(\theta) \otimes x_t.$$

The sample moment conditions are defined as $h_T(\theta) = \frac{1}{T}\sum_{t=1}^{T} \varepsilon_t(\theta) \otimes x_t$.

Here $x_t = [1 D_t \circ R_{mt}(1-D_t) \circ R_{mt}(1-D_t)]', \varepsilon_t(\theta) = [\varepsilon_{1t}\varepsilon_{2t} \ldots \varepsilon_{Nt}]'$ and $\varepsilon_{it} = R_{it} - \alpha_i - \beta_i^- D_t R_{mt} - \beta_i^+(1-D_t)R_{mt} - \delta_i(1-D_t)$. The parameter vector is as in (6.14). There are $4N$ moment conditions and $4N$ parameters to be estimated and, therefore, the multivariate system of equations is exactly identified. The GMM parameters (the just-identified system leads to a simple method of moment estimator rather than a generalized method of moment estimator and we continue to use the term GMM following similar treatment of this case in the literature) are estimated by minimizing a quadratic form of the sample moment restriction vector;

$$\hat{\theta}_{GMM} = arg\ min\ h_T(\theta)' U_T h_T(\theta) \tag{6.17}$$

Here U_T is a positive-definite weighting matrix whose elements can be functions of parameters and data. Hansen (1982) shows that the optimal weighting matrix is

$$U_T = S^{-1} = \{Asy\ Var[\sqrt{T} h_T(\theta)]\}^{-1}. \tag{6.18}$$

The asymptotic covariance matrix of the GMM estimator is:

$$V = [\Delta' S^{-1} \Delta]^{-1} \tag{6.19}$$

where $\Delta = P\lim[\frac{\partial}{\partial\theta'} h_T(\theta)]$. In practice "$S$" and "$\Delta$" are unknown but the asymptotic results are valid for some consistent estimator "S_T" and "Δ_T." We estimate Δ_t and S_t matrices as follows:

$$\Delta_T = \frac{1}{T} \sum_{t=1}^{T} I_N \otimes x_t x_t' = I_N \otimes X'X. \tag{6.20}$$

The matrix "S_T" is estimated by the Newey and West (1987) HAC covariance matrix (for details see Ray et al., 1998).

Following the MacKinlay and Richardson (1991) portfolio efficiency testing case the MLPM hypothesis for this exactly identified case can be tested by first estimating the unrestricted system and then computing the test statistic of the market efficiency hypothesis that involves these *unrestricted* estimates. In this case, the GMM estimator is independent of the weighting matrix and is the same as the SUR estimator; however, the covariance matrix must be adjusted to allow for heteroskedasticity and serial correlation. The GMM estimates are asymptotically normally distributed:

$$\sqrt{T}(\theta - \hat{\theta}) \sim N(0, V)$$

Here, V is as defined above. Therefore any nonlinear function g($\hat{\theta}$) of the parameter is also asymptotically normal

$$\sqrt{T}[g(\theta) - g(\hat{\theta})] \sim N\left[0, \left(\frac{\partial g}{\partial \theta'}\right) V \left(\frac{\partial g}{\partial \theta'}\right)'\right].$$

In the test of the MLPM model with $g(\theta) = [g_1 \ldots g_{N-1}]'$ where $g_i = \alpha_i(1 - \beta_{i+1}^-) - \alpha_{i+1}(1 - \beta_i^-), i = 1, 2, \ldots N-1$ the GMM Wald test of the

MLPM restrictions can be formulated as:

$$W = \frac{(T - N - 1)}{\mathrm{T}} g(\hat{\theta})' \left[\left(\frac{\partial g}{\partial \theta'} \Big|_{\theta = \hat{\theta}} \right) \hat{V}_T \left(\frac{\partial g}{\partial \theta'} \Big|_{\theta = \hat{\theta}} \right)' \right]^{-1} g(\hat{\theta}) \xrightarrow{d} \chi^2_{N-1}. \tag{6.21}$$

The test is adjusted by the small sample correction factor as in Jobson and Korkie (1982).

Here the $(N-1) \times 4N$ derivative matrix is

$$\frac{\partial g}{\partial \theta'} =$$

$$\begin{bmatrix} 1-\beta_2^- & \alpha_2 & 0 & 0 & -(1-\beta_1^-) & -\alpha_1 & 0 & 0 & 0 & 0 & . & . & . & . & 0 \\ 0 & 0 & 0 & 0 & 1-\beta_3^- & \alpha_3 & 0 & 0 & -(1-\beta_2^-) & -\alpha_2 & 0 & . & . & . & 0 \\ . & & & & & & & & & & & & & & \\ & . & & & & . & & & & . & & & & & \\ & & . & & & & . & & & & . & & & & \\ 0 & 0 & 0 & . & . & . & & & 0 & 1-\beta_N^- & \alpha_N & 0 & 0 & -(1-\beta_{N-1}^-) & -\alpha_{N-1} \end{bmatrix} \tag{6.22}$$

6.3.2 Test of the CAPM against the MLPM alternative

The asymmetric response model subject to the MLPM restriction is

$$R_{it} = \gamma(1 - \beta_i^-) + \beta_i^- R_{mt}^- + \beta_i^+ R_{mt}^+ + \delta_i(1 - D_t) + \varepsilon_{it}. \tag{6.23}$$

The CAPM can be deducted from this model with the restrictions $\beta_i^- = \beta_i^+$ and $\delta_i = 0$ imposed. H&R test these restrictions as a likelihood ratio test with asymptotic Chi-square critical values.[5] The restricted model is the CAPM, whereas the unrestricted model is the MLPM. They strongly reject the null of CAPM against the MLPM alternative using the target rate found in the MLPM test. It is, however, evident that in the general case testing the null hypothesis of the CAPM is conditional on a specified target rate parameter τ which is not identified under the null hypothesis, while τ appears in the alternative. Therefore, the problem of testing is nonstandard and the asymptotic Chi-square distribution is not valid in this case. Tests for this nonstandard problem are well documented in the econometric literature; see for example, Hansen (1997) for a discussion on the nonstandard problem and a bootstrap method to test the hypothesis of linearity in a threshold autoregressive model. The appropriate test is a likelihood ratio test whose sampling distribution is unknown. However, the p-values can be generated from the bootstrap method as follows:

(1) Estimate the following system of the market model subject to the null hypothesis of zero-beta CAPM using time-series regression by SUR; generate the parameter estimates and form a residual matrix

$$R_{it} = \gamma(1-\beta_i) + \beta_i R_{mt} + \varepsilon_{it} \quad i = 1, 2, ..N. \tag{6.24}$$

(2) Resample T rows of the residual matrix and using the parameter estimates obtained in step (1) above generate the return from the system

$$R^*_{it} = \hat{\gamma}(1-\hat{\beta}_i) + \hat{\beta}_i R_{mt} + \varepsilon^*_{it}. \tag{6.25}$$

(3) Compute the likelihood ratio statistics.
(4) Repeat steps (2) and (3) a large number B of times and compute the p-value of the test as the proportion of cases in which the bootstrap statistic exceeds the test statistics obtained using the real data. Reject the null hypothesis if this p-value is smaller than the level of significance specified.

Although the chapter uses the bootstrap as a method of computing p-values of the nonstandard test the superiority of the bootstrap-based tests over the asymptotic tests in general is well established (see for example MacKinnon, 2002). Keeping in mind the dependencies in the time series of residuals, we have also employed the "sieve bootstrap" of Buhlmann (1997). The results are, however, qualitatively not much different from the i.i.d. case and therefore not reported.

The robust Wald and GMM tests can also be constructed for this case. The $3N+1$ parameter vector is

$$\theta = [\gamma \quad \beta_1^- \quad \beta_1^+ \quad \delta_1 \quad \beta_2^- \quad \beta_2^+ \quad \delta_2 \quad \dots \quad \beta_N^- \quad \beta_N^+ \quad \delta_N]'. \tag{6.26}$$

The $2N \times 1$ vector of null restrictions to be tested is

$$H_0 : g(\theta) = [\beta_1^- \quad -\beta_1^+ \quad \delta_1 \quad \beta_2^- \quad -\beta_2^+ \quad \delta_2 \quad \dots \quad \beta_N^- \quad -\beta_N^+ \quad \delta_N]' = 0.$$

The $(2N \times 3N+1)$ matrix of derivatives simply contains $1, -1$ and zeros and is given by

$$\frac{\partial g}{\partial \theta'} = \begin{bmatrix} 0 & 1 & -1 & 0 & 0 & 0 & 0 & & . & . & 0 \\ 0 & 0 & 0 & 1 & 0 & 0 & 0 & & . & . & 0 \\ 0 & 0 & 0 & 0 & 1 & -1 & 0 & & . & . & 0 \\ & . & & & . & & & . & & & \\ & & . & & & . & & & . & & \\ & & & . & & & . & & & . & \\ 0 & 0 & . & . & . & & & . & . & 0 & 0 & 1 \end{bmatrix}. \tag{6.27}$$

A Wald test can be easily constructed which employs the parameter estimates under the unrestricted alternative model (6.11) and the null hypothesis can be tested using a similar bootstrap procedure as adopted in the likelihood ratio test.

6.4 The data

The tests discussed in Section 6.3 are applied to portfolios formed from a sample of stocks listed in the Karachi Stock Exchange (KSE). The sample period spans 15 years and two months from October 1992 to December 2007. The data consist of monthly closing prices of 231 stocks and the Karachi Stock Exchange 100 index (KSE-100). We consider the KSE-100 as a proxy for the market portfolio. All the available active stocks for which prices have been adjusted for dividend, stock split, merger and other corporate actions were obtained from the DataStream database. The KSE-100 index is a market capitalization weighted index. The index comprises top companies in terms of their market capitalization from each industrial sector classified by the exchange. The rest of the companies are selected on the basis of market capitalization without considering their sector. We use monthly data and compute raw returns assuming continuous compounding. The 30-day repurchase option rate is used as a proxy for the risk-free rate. This was the only interest rate available in the database for the entire sample period considered in the study.

To investigate robustness of the empirical results we consider portfolios based on three different sorting schemes. Some studies, such as Groenewold and Fraser (2001), report that the conclusion of an analysis may be different and even conflicting when different portfolios are employed. H&R use only LPM beta portfolios in their analysis and when testing the CAPM against the MLPM alternative, they use portfolios based on the CAPM and LPM betas. We investigate the robustness of the results in this study to factors such as the size and industry by controlling for them through construction of portfolios based on these characteristics. Three sets of portfolios are constructed on the basis of size, market model beta and industry sorting.

To construct size portfolios all stocks that have a previous three years of price data are ranked into 12 portfolios with respect to market capitalization in ascending order using December 1995 size values. Using this sort, equally weighted portfolios are constructed for all 12 months of 1996. This process is repeated each year up to 2007. Thus, portfolios are balanced each year. The number of stocks in each portfolio is constant (to within one). The stock beta used in construction of beta portfolios is estimated by the market model with Dimson thin-trading adjustment using two forward and two backward adjustments. These market model regressions involve time-series data from October 1992 to December 1995. Twelve equally weighted beta-sorted portfolios are constructed for 1996. This process is repeated for each year. To construct industry portfolios stocks are also classified into 12 industrial sectors. The sector size ranges from 7 in telecommunication, travel and leisure to 33 in other financial institutions. The industry sectors employed are automobile, transport and allied; cement; chemicals and pharmacy; commercial banks; engineering, metal and building material; food, beverages and tobacco; household and personal goods, paper and board; insurance; oil, gas and power; other financial institutions; telecommunication, travel and leisure; and textile and related. The choice of twelve portfolios was considered to handle the curse of dimensionality: not using a large number of portfolios in multivariate testing and avoiding over-aggregation with too few portfolios.

6.5 Results of empirical analysis

6.5.1 Residual diagnostic tests

All residual diagnostics and the asset-pricing tests are performed for the two distinct and equal-length subperiods (January 1996 to August 2001 and September 2001 to December 2007) and for the whole period (January 1996 to December 2007). The objective here is to examine the stability of the risk-return relationship pre- and post-9/11. This is important because volatile political and macroeconomic scenarios in emerging markets are likely to render the return distributions nonstationary.

Table 6.1 reports the Mardia (1970) test of multivariate normality of the residuals of the unrestricted asymmetric response model for the

Table 6.1 Test of multivariate normality of asymmetric response model residuals

	Size portfolios		Industry portfolios		Beta portfolios	
Sample period	**Skewness (P-value)**	**Kurtosis (P-value)**	**Skewness (P-value)**	**Kurtosis (P-value)**	**Skewness (P-value)**	**Kurtosis (P-value)**
Jan 96–Aug 01	64.749	205.387	50.799	192.601	61.077	197.922
	(0.000)	(0.000)	(0.000)	(0.000)	(0.000)	(0.000)
Sep 01–Dec 07	42.468	181.524	52.974	198.152	40.469	181.926
	(0.000)	(0.001)	(0.000)	(0.000)	(0.000)	(0.000)
Jan 96–Dec 07	40.997	222.593	40.818	225.622	44.340	227.278
	(0.000)	(0.000)	(0.000)	(0.000)	(0.000)	(0.000)

Table 6.2 Test of serial independence of asymmetric response model residuals

	Size portfolios			Industry portfolios			Beta portfolios
Sample period	**Lag1**	**Lag2**	**Lag3**	**Lag1**	**Lag2**	**Lag3**	**Lag1**
Jan 96–Aug 01	159.226	303.075	444.091	159.226	303.075	444.091	159.226
	(0.182)	(0.259)	(0.345)	(0.182)	(0.259)	(0.345)	(0.182)
Sep 01–Dec 07	131.576	284.256	443.153	131.576	284.256	443.153	131.576
	(0.762)	(0.551)	(0.344)	(0.762)	(0.551)	(0.344)	(0.762)
Jan 96–Dec 07	154.489	299.541	99.352	154.489	299.541	99.352	154.489
	(0.260)	(0.307)	(0.272)	(0.260)	(0.307)	(0.272)	(0.260)

three sets of portfolios. This test is based on multivariate equivalents of skewness and kurtosis measures. The results are reported for the test based on multivariate skewness and kurtosis measures separately. The tests are performed for the average market return as the target return. Both skewness- and kurtosis-based tests provide overwhelming evidence against normality for all three types of portfolios and for the three sample periods. Table 6.2 reports the Hosking (1980) multivariate portmanteau test of no autocorrelation for up to lag three in the asymmetric response model residuals. The null hypothesis corresponds to the absence of predictability of returns or serial correlation in the residuals. This test is a multivariate generalization of the univariate test of Box and Pierce (1970). Except for the full sample period in the case of beta portfolios, the results do not provide evidence of serial correlation or predictability in the residuals. As the results in this case are mixed it is worthwhile pursuing empirical applications with both robust tests and the usual tests that assume normality.

6.5.2 Multivariate tests of zero-beta CAPM and MLPM models

Table 6.3 presents the results of testing the zero-beta CAPM using three types of multivariate tests. Wald, GMM and LR test results are reported for the three sample periods and across the three sets of portfolios as described in Section 6.4. The results reveal that the LR test rejects the zero-beta CAPM in the post-9/11 subperiod as is evident by the size and industry portfolios and for the full sample period. In the other cases, the CAPM is not rejected. In the case of emerging markets, Iqbal et al. (2008) show that the Wald- and GMM-based tests are generally less powerful relative to the LR test. Hence, the mixed results we observe here may be influenced by the power of the tests as well.

Table 6.4 reports the results of multivariate tests of the MLPM model when the average risk-free rate and average market returns are specified

Table 6.3 Multivariate tests of zero-beta CAPM

Portfolio method	**Size**	**Beta**	**Industry**
Panel A: Jan 96–Aug 01			
Wald	8.295	6.925	13.409
	(0.686)	(0.805)	(0.267)
GMM	9.316	10.582	12.289
	(0.592)	(0.478)	(0.342)
LR	9.299	10.932	14.780
	(0.594)	(0.448)	(0.192)
Panel B: Sep 01–Dec 07			
Wald	10.864	8.695	11.265
	(0.454)	(0.649)	(0.421)
GMM	12.308	9.765	19.213
	(0.341)	(0.551)	(0.057)
LR	21.213	10.557	19.354
	(0.031)	(0.481)	(0.055)
Panel C: Jan 99–Dec 07			
Wald	22.210	8.380	9.955
	(0.023)	(0.678)	(0.534)
GMM	27.832	9.421	12.340
	(0.003)	(0.583)	(0.338)
LR	26.720	11.486	12.715
	(0.005)	(0.403)	(0.313)

Table 6.4 Multivariate tests of lower partial moment CAPM

Panel A: Size portfolios

	Likelihood ratio test		**Wald test**		**GMM test**	
	Risk-free rate	**Average market return**	**Risk-free rate**	**Average market return**	**Risk-free rate**	**Average market return**
Jan 96–Aug 01	6.144	11.219	1.173	2.492	3.209	4.815
	(0.863)	(0.422)	(0.999)	(0.995)	(0.987)	(0.939)
Sep 01–Dec 07	10.086	10.697	2.462	0.426	0.957	1.472
	(0.522)	(0.468)	(0.996)	(0.999)	(0.999)	(0.999)
Jan 96–Dec 07	16.932	15.324	1.941	1.626	4.033	2.403
	(0.109)	(0.168)	(0.998)	(0.999)	(0.968)	(0.996)

Panel B: Beta portfolios

	Likelihood ratio test		**Wald test**		**GMM test**	
	Risk-free rate	**Average market return**	**Risk-free rate**	**Average market return**	**Risk-free rate**	**Average market return**
Jan 96–Aug 01	23.058	26.643	8.099	9.451	9.351	11.350
	(0.017)	(0.052)	(0.704)	(0.580)	(0.589)	(0.414)
Sep 01–Dec 07	18.516	14.505	8.247	3.331	10.408	3.691
	(0.070)	(0.206)	(0.699)	(0.985)	(0.494)	(0.978)
Jan 96–Dec 07	19.260	15.034	8.067	5.798	10.313	6.426
	(0.056)	(0.181)	(0.707)	(0.886)	(0.502)	(0.843)

Panel C: Industry portfolios

	Likelihood ratio test		**Wald test**		**GMM test**	
	Risk-free rate	**Average market return**	**Risk-free rate**	**Average market return**	**Risk-free rate**	**Average market return**
Jan 96–Aug 01	13.907	16.517	11.251	12.308	29.297	30.094
	(0.238)	(0.123)	(0.422)	(0.341)	(0.002)	(0.001)
Sep 01–Dec 07	12.159	12.338	1.242	0.941	2.804	2.801
	(0.351)	(0.338)	(0.999)	(0.999)	(0.993)	(0.993)
Jan 96–Dec 07	19.656	15.640	10.085	4.173	11.003	5.338
	(0.050)	(0.155)	(0.522)	(0.964)	(0.442)	(0.913)

as the target rate. The results remain similar when the observed period-by-period risk-free rate is employed as the target rate as opposed to the average over the sample period. With size portfolios (Panel A) none of the three multivariate tests reject the restriction of the MLPM model in both subperiods and in the full sample period. The LR test in the beta portfolios for the first period rejects the MLPM restrictions when the target rate is specified as average risk-free rate (Panel B). For industry portfolios, the GMM test rejects the MLPM model in the first period. Overall, the results for the zero-beta CAPM and the MLPM model are mixed. It appears that the highly volatile nature of the portfolio returns and the relatively low power of some of the tests considered here, fail to differentiate the two competing models.

Multivariate tests can be sensitive to the specified alternative hypothesis. Intuitively, a test with an unspecified alternative seeks to find evidence against the model in any direction of the sampling distribution while with a specific alternative the test focuses only on the direction of the specified alternative. As the CAPM is nested within the MLPM one can test the CAPM restriction on the more general MLPM model. Table 6.5 reports the results of the CAPM restriction on the MLPM as an alternative through bootstrap tests. The bootstrap tests for the nested

Table 6.5 Multivariate tests of the null hypothesis of the black CAPM against the alternative of the lower partial moment model

Portfolio method	Size	Beta	Industry
Panel A: Jan 96–Aug 01			
Wald	13.376	19.947	26.240
	(0.962)	(0.02)	(0.000)
GMM	41.690	36.916	46.906
	(0.000)	(0.048)	(0.000)
LR	11.751	19.581	26.178
	(0.852)	(0.022)	(0.000)
Panel B: Sep 01–Dec 07			
Wald	19.582	24.103	19.977
	(0.074)	(0.000)	(0.002)
GMM	73.151	62.197	34.460
	(0.000)	(0.000)	(0.038)
LR	25.135	25.108	26.365
	(0.000)	(0.000)	(0.000)
Panel C: Jan 96–Dec 07			
Wald	15.685	21.573	20.111
	(0.042)	(0.028)	(0.002)
GMM	59.913	64.356	52.659
	(0.000)	(0.000)	(0.000)
LR	17.303	23.876	20.173
	(0.000)	(0.006)	(0.000)

tests are computed over 500 simulations. As we argued elsewhere, the asymptotic p-value may not be valid since the likelihood ratio, Wald and GMM tests do not have a known sampling distribution even in large samples. Therefore, the "nuisance parameter problem" makes inference difficult. All three tests reject the CAPM restriction on the MLPM model for industry portfolios. A similar result holds for the size portfolios in the full sample period. In the first subperiod the results with the size portfolio are inconsistent with the other types of portfolios where the Wald and LR tests fail to reject the nested test of the CAPM on the MLPM alternative. Overall, the nested tests provide overwhelming support for the MLPM model.

6.6 Conclusion

This chapter tests and compares the CAPM and the mean lower partial moment (MLPM) asset-pricing model in the context of emerging markets. Considering the stylized facts of emerging market returns the paper extends Harlow and Rao's (1989) likelihood ratio test of the MLPM model to develop robust Wald and GMM tests that allow non-normality and serial dependence in the returns. Also in testing the CAPM against the MLPM alternative, the chapter remedies an econometric problem of testing in the presence of a nuisance parameter with an arbitrary general target rate. Applying the MLPM tests on portfolio data from the Karachi Stock Exchange it is observed that individual zero-beta CAPM and the MLPM tests do not provide unambiguous evidence to distinguish between the two models. However, a more powerful nested test of the CAPM against MLPM alternatives provides overwhelming support for the downside risk model. Thus, it appears that investment appraisal practitioners are likely to benefit if the correct discount rates are derived from the MLPM model. Practitioners of investment allocation and managed funds may also gain a more realistic benchmark return if the expected returns are estimated from the MLPM model. Thus, despite the fact that the market has shown considerable growth during recent years, the possibility of portfolio strategies based on downside risk have the potential to offer a more realistic picture of the riskiness and associated returns for the invested funds in the emerging market under study.

6.7 Acknowledgements

We thank conference participants at the European Conference of Financial Management Association 2007, Far East Meetings of the Econometric

Society 2007 and seminar participants at Monash University for their helpful comments on earlier versions of this chapter.

Notes

1. Non-normality of the asset return distribution is also well studied. As Kan and Zhou (2006) remark "the reason for the wide use of the normality assumption is not because it models financial data well, but due to its tractability that allows interesting economic questions to be asked and answered without substantial technical impediments". Fama (1965), Kon (1984), Affleck-Graves and McDonald (1989), Richardson and Smith (1993) and Dufour, Khalaf and Beaulieu (2003), among others, provide strong evidence against normality of stock returns.
2. For example, Hansen (1996, 1997) discussed the testing problem and provides a bootstrap method to test the hypothesis of linearity in a threshold autoregressive model. Andrews and Ploberger (1994) developed tests for structural breaks for unknown change point-in-time series. Garcia (1998) developed a likelihood ratio test for testing linearity against a Markov switching alternative.
3. Karachi Stock Exchange is the largest of the three stock markets in Pakistan. On April 17, 2006 the market capitalization was US$ 57 billion which is 46 per cent of Pakistan's GDP for the fiscal year 2005–2006 (Ref: Pakistan Economic Survey, 2005–06).
4. Taking expectation on both sides of (6.10):
$$E(R_i) = \alpha_i + \beta_i^- E(R_m^-) + \beta_i^+ E(R_m^+) + \varphi(\beta_i^- - \beta_i^+) P(Rm > \tau)$$
substituting $\varphi = E(R_{mt}^+)/P(R_{mt} > \tau)$ and using the fact that $R^+ + R_m^- = R_m$ it follows that:
$$E(R_i) = \alpha_i + \beta_i^- E(R_m).$$
5. The degrees of freedom employed by H&R Table 4 page 303 are N-2. However, in the testing of the null hypothesis a total of 2N restrictions are imposed, therefore the appropriate number of degrees of freedom with the asymptotic Chi-square is 2N.

References

Affleck-Graves, J. and McDonald, B. (1989) "Non-Normalities and Tests of Asset Pricing Theories," *Journal of Finance,* 44 (4): 889–908.

Andrews, D.W.K and Ploberger, W. (1994) "Optimal Test When Nuisance Parameter is Present only under the Alternative," *Econometrica,* 62 (6): 1383–1414.

Bawa, V., Brown, S. and Klein, R. (1981) "Asymmetric Response Asset Pricing Models: Testable Alternatives to Mean-Variance Mimeo," Warwick Business School, Financial Econometrics Research Centre, Coventry.

Bekaert, G., Erb, C.B., Harvey, C.R. and Viskanta, T.E. (1998) "Distributional Characteristics of Emerging Market Returns and Asset Allocation," *Journal of Portfolio Management,* 24 (2): 102–116.

Bekaert, G. and Harvey, C.R. (1995) "Time-Varying World Market Integration," *Journal of Finance,* 50 (2): 403–444.
Bekaert, G. and Harvey, C.R. (1997) "Emerging Equity Market Volatility," *Journal of Financial Economics,* 43 (1): 29–77.
Black, F. (1972) "Capital Market Equilibrium with Restricted Borrowing," *Journal of Business,* 45 (3): 444–455.
Box, G.E.P. and Pierce, D.A. (1970) "Distribution of Residual Autocorrelations in Autoregressive Integrated Moving Average Time Series Models," *Journal of American Statistical Association,* 65 (332): 1509–1526.
Buhlmann, P. (1997) "Sieve Bootstrap for Time Series," *Bernoulli,* 3 (2): 123–148.
Chou, P.-H. (2000) "Alternative Tests of the Zero-Beta CAPM," *The Journal of Financial Research,* 23 (4): 469–493.
Claessens, S., Dasgupta, S. and Glen, J. (1995) "Return Behaviour in Emerging Stock Markets," *The World Bank Economic Review,* 9 (1): 131–151.
Dufour, J., Khalaf, L. and Beaulieu, M. (2003) "Exact Skewness-Kurtosis Tests for Multivariate Normality and Goodness of Fit in Multivariate Regressions with Application to Asset Pricing Models," *Oxford Bulletin of Economics and Statistics,* 65 (s1): 891–906.
Eftekhari, B. and Satchell, S. (1996) "Non-Normality of Returns in Emerging Markets," *Research in International Business and Finance,* Supplement 1, 267–277.
Estrada, J. (2000) "The Cost of Equity in Emerging Markets: A Downside Risk Approach," *Emerging Market Quarterly,* 4 (3): 19–30.
Estrada, J. (2002) "Systematic Risk in Emerging Markets: The D-CAPM," *Emerging Market Review,* 3 (4): 365–379.
Fama, E.F. (1965) "The Behaviour of Stock Market Prices," *Journal of Business,* 38 (1): 34–105.
Garcia, R. (1998) "Asymptotic Null Distribution of the Likelihood Ratio Test in Markov Switching Models," *International Economic Review,* 39 (3): 763–788.
Gibbons, M.R. (1982) "Multivariate Tests of Financial Models: A New Approach," *Journal of Financial Economics,* 10 (1): 3–27.
Greene, W.G. (2003) *Econometric Analysis,* Upper Saddle River, NJ: Pearson Education.
Groenewold, N. and Fraser, P. (2001) "Tests of Asset-Pricing Models: How Important is the IID-normal Assumption?" *Journal of Empirical Finance,* 8 (4): 427–449.
Hansen, B.E. (1996) "Inference when Nuisance Parameter is not Identified under the Null Hypothesis," *Econometrica,* 64 (2): 413–430.
Hansen, B.E. (1997) "Inference in TAR Models," *Studies in Nonlinear Dynamics and Econometrics,* 2 (1): 1–14.
Hansen, L.P. (1982) "Large Sample Properties of the Generalized Method of Moments," *Econometrica,* 50 (4): 1029–1054.
Harlow, W.V. and Rao, R.K. (1989) "Asset Pricing in a Generalized Mean-Lower Partial Moment Framework: Theory and Evidence," *Journal of Financial and Quantitative Analysis,* 24 (3): 285–311.

Harvey, C.R. (1995) "Predictable Risk and Returns in Emerging Markets," *Review of Financial Studies,* 8 (3): 773–816.

Harvey, C.R. (2000) "The Drivers of Expected Returns in International Markets," *Emerging Markets Quarterly,* 4 (3): 32–49.

Harvey, C.R. (2001) "Asset Pricing in Emerging Markets," Working Paper, Duke University, Durham, NC.

Hosking, J.R.M. (1980) "The Multivariate Portmanteau Statistic," *Journal of American Statistical Association,* 75 (371): 602–608.

Hwang, S. and Pedersen, C. (2004) "Asymmetric Risk Measures when Modelling Emerging Markets Equities: Evidence for Regional and Timing Effects," *Emerging Markets Review,* 5 (1): 109–128.

Iqbal, J. and Brooks, R.D. (2007a) "A Test of CAPM on the Karachi Stock Exchange," *International Journal of Business,* 12 (4): 429–444.

Iqbal, J. and Brooks, R.D. (2007b) "Alternative Beta Risk Estimators and Asset Pricing Tests in Emerging Markets: The Case of Pakistan," *Journal of Multinational Financial Management,* 17 (1): 75–93.

Iqbal, J., Brooks, R.D. and Galagedera, U.A. (2008) "Multivariate Tests of Asset Pricing: Simulation Evidence from an Emerging Market," Working Paper, Department of Econometrics and Business Statistics, Monash University, Victoria, Australia.

Jobson, J. and Korkie, B. (1982) "Potential Performance and Tests of Portfolio Efficiency," *Journal of Financial Economics,* 10 (4): 433–466.

Kan, R. and Zhou, G. (2006) "Modelling Non-Normality using Multivariate t: Implications for Asset Pricing," Working Paper, University of Toronto and Washington University in St Louis.

Kon, S.T. (1984) "Models of Stock Returns – A Comparison," *Journal of Finance,* 39 (1): 147–165.

Lintner, J. (1965) "The Valuation of Risk Assets and the Selection of Risky Investments in Stock Portfolios and Capital Budgets," *Review of Economics and Statistics,* 47 (1): 13–37.

MacKinlay, A.C. and Richardson, M.P. (1991) "Using Generalized Method of Moments to Test Mean-Variance Efficiency," *Journal of Finance,* 46 (2): 511–527.

MacKinnon, J.G. (2002) "Bootstrap Inference in Econometrics," *Canadian Journal of Economics,* 35 (4): 615–645.

Mardia, K.V. (1970) "Measures of Multivariate Skewness and Kurtosis with Applications," *Biometrika,* 57 (3): 519–530.

Markowitz, H.M. (1959) "Portfolio Selection: Efficient Diversification of Investments," Wiley: Yale University Press.

Newey, W.K. and West, K.D. (1987) "A Simple, Positive Semi-definite, Heteroskedasticity and Autocorrelation Consistent Covariance Matrix," *Econometrica,* 55 (3): 703–708.

Pederson, C. and Hwang, S. (2003) "Does Downside Beta Matters in Asset Pricing?" Financial Econometrics Research Centre, Working Paper, Cass Business School.

Ray, S., Ravikumar B. and Savin, E. (1998) "Robust Wald Tests in SUR Systems with Adding up Restrictions: An Algebraic Approach to Proofs of Invariance," Working Paper, Department of Economics, University of Iowa.

Richardson, M. and Smith, T. (1993) "A Test for Multivariate Normality in Stock Returns," *Journal of Business,* 66 (2): 295–321.
Salomons, R. and Grootveld, H. (2003) "The Equity Risk Premium: Emerging vs. Developed Markets," *Emerging Market Review,* 4 (2): 121–144.
Sharpe, W.F. (1964) "Capital Asset Prices: A Theory of Market Equilibrium under Conditions of Risk," *Journal of Finance,* 19 (3): 425–442.

7

Asset Pricing, the Fama–French Factor Model and the Implications of Quantile-Regression Analysis

David E. Allen, Abhay Kumar Singh and Robert Powell

7.1 Introduction

Traditionally, regression-based factor analysis is extensively used in quantitative finance to analyze the performance of the factors in different factor models. These factor models assume that the expected return is linearly dependent on the risk factors and hence "ordinary least squares" (OLS) is widely used to model the risk distribution for these models. When it comes to risk assessment, the parts of the return distributions in which the investor and risk managers are often interested, such as extreme outcomes in the tails, which go beyond the mean values, are not well analyzed by means of OLS.

"Quantile regression" promises to be a more effective tool than OLS when it comes to analyzing the extremes of a distribution, as it captures the behavior of the tails of a distribution more efficiently. In this chapter, we analyze the expected return distribution of 30 stocks of the Dow Jones Industrial average, obtained from the Fama–French three-factor model using quantile-regression techniques.

The chapter is divided into six sections. Following this introductory section we briefly review the Fama–French three-factor model, quantile regression is introduced in Section 7.3, the data and research method follows in Section 7.4, the results are presented in Section 7.5 and a brief conclusion is provided in Section 7.6.

7.2 The Fama–French three-factor model

Volatility is a widely accepted measure of risk and is most commonly quoted in terms of the standard deviation of returns. There is a greater risk involved for an asset whose return fluctuates more dramatically than others. The familiar beta from the CAPM equation is a widely accepted measure of systematic risk and unsystematic risk is captured by the error term of the OLS application of the CAPM. Beta is measured below:

$$\beta_A = \frac{cov(r_A, r_M)}{\sigma_{M^2}} \tag{7.1}$$

where

r_A is the return of the asset
r_M is the return of the market
σ_{M^2} is the variance of the return of the market and
cov(r_A, r_M) is covariance between the return of the market and the return of the asset.

This was a direct development from the work of Jack Treynor (1961, 1962), William Sharpe (1964), John Lintner (1965) and Jan Mossin (1966), who independently proposed "capital asset pricing theory" (CAPM) to quantify the relationship between the beta of an asset and its corresponding return. The CAPM relationship estimation is given in equation (7.2).

$$r_A = r_f + \beta_A(r_M - r_F) + \alpha + e \tag{7.2}$$

where

r_A is the return of the asset
r_M is the return of the market
r_f is the risk-free rate of return
α is the intercept of regression
e is the standard error of regression

Fama and French (1992, 1993) extended the basic CAPM to include size and book-to-market as explanatory factors in explaining the cross-section of stock returns. SMB, which stands for "small minus big," is designed to measure the additional return investors have historically received from investing in stocks of companies with relatively small market capitalization. This is often referred to as the "size premium."

HML, which is short for "high minus low," has been constructed to measure the "value premium" provided to investors for investing in companies with high book-to-market values. The HML factor suggests higher risk exposure for typical "value" stocks (high B/M) versus "growth" stocks (low B/M). On the other hand, the HML factor suggests higher risk exposure for typical "value" stocks (high B/M) versus "growth" stocks (low

B/M). The three-factor Fama–French model is written as:

$$r_A = r_f + \beta_A(r_M - r_F) + s_A SMB + h_A HML + \alpha + e \quad (7.3)$$

where S_A and H_A capture the security's sensitivity to these two additional factors.

7.2.1 Doubts about the model

Black (1993) suggested that the Fama–French results might be the effect of data mining. Kothari et al. (1995) suggest that the use of annual returns provides stronger evidence in favor of the influence of beta. Levhari and Levy (1977) show that beta coefficients estimated with monthly returns are not the same as betas estimated with annual returns. There is an abundance of evidence that stock returns' distributions have fat tails. Knez and Ready (1997) undertook tests of the model after removing extreme observations from their data sets using a "least trimmed squares" technique (LTS). They trimmed one per cent of the extreme returns in their monthly data and found that this greatly reduced the size effect. Horowitz et al. (2000) suggest that the size effect is not robust across different sample periods and argue that it may have disappeared since 1982. In this chapter we follow a lead first suggested by Chan and Lakonishok (1992) and apply robust methods to explore the efficacy of the three-factor model using quantile regressions.

7.3 Quantile regression

Linear regression represents the dependent variable as a linear function of one or more independent variables subject to a random "disturbance" or "error." It estimates the mean value of the dependent variable for given levels of the independent variables. For this type of regression, where we want to understand the central tendency in a data set, OLS is a tried and tested effective method. OLS loses its effectiveness when we try to go beyond the median value or towards the extremes of a data set.

Quantile regression, as introduced in Koenker and Bassett (1978), is an extension of classical least squares estimation of conditional mean models to the estimation of a set of models for conditional quantile functions. The central special case is the median regression estimator that minimizes a sum of absolute errors. The remaining conditional quantile functions are estimated by minimizing an asymmetrically weighted sum of absolute errors. Taken together the set of estimated conditional quantile functions offers a much more complete view of the effect of covariates on the location, scale and shape of the distribution of the response variable.

In linear regression, the regression coefficient represents the change in the response variable produced by a one-unit change in the predictor variable associated with that coefficient. The quantile-regression parameter estimates the change in a specified quantile of the response variable produced by a one-unit change in the predictor variable.

The quantiles, or percentiles or occasionally fractiles, refer to the general case of dividing a data set into parts. Quantile regression seeks to extend these ideas to the estimation of conditional quantile functions – models in which quantiles of the conditional distribution of the response variable are expressed as functions of observed covariates.

In quantile regression, the median estimator minimizes the symmetrically weighted sum of absolute errors (where the weight is equal to 0.5) to estimate the conditional median function. Other conditional quantile functions are estimated by minimizing an asymmetrically weighted sum of absolute errors, where the weights are functions of the quantile of interest. This makes quantile regression robust to the presence of outliers.

We can define the quantiles through a simple alternative expedient as an optimization problem. Just as we can define the sample mean as the solution to the problem of minimizing a sum of squared residuals, we can define the median as the solution to the problem of minimizing a sum of absolute residuals. The symmetry of the piecewise, linear absolute value function implies that the minimization of the sum of absolute residuals must equate the number of positive and negative residuals, thus assuring that there are the same number of observations above and below the median.

The other quantile values can be obtained by minimizing a sum of asymmetrically weighted absolute residuals (giving different weights to positive and negative residuals). Solving

$$\min_{\xi \in \mathcal{R}} \sum \rho_\tau (y_i - \xi) \tag{7.4}$$

where $\rho_\tau(\cdot)$ is the tilted absolute value function as shown in Figure 7.1, this gives the τth sample quantile with its solution. To see that this problem yields the sample quantiles as its solutions, it is only necessary to compute the directional derivative of the objective function with respect to ξ, taken from the left and from the right.

After defining the unconditional quantiles as an optimization problem, it is easy to define conditional quantiles in an analogous fashion. The procedure is similar to ordinary least squares regression. In OLS, if

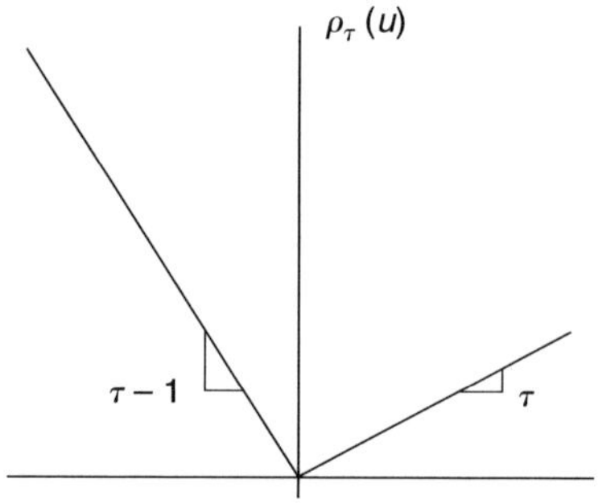

Figure 7.1 Quantile-regression ρ function

we have a random sample, $\{y_1, y_2, \ldots, y_n\}$, we solve

$$\min_{\mu \in \mathcal{R}} \sum_{i=1}^{n} (y_i - \mu)^2 \tag{7.5}$$

and we obtain the sample mean, an estimate of the unconditional population mean, EY. If we now replace the scalar μ by a parametric function $\mu(x, \beta)$ and solve

$$\min_{\mu \in \mathcal{R}^p} \sum_{i=1}^{n} (y_i - \mu(x_i, \beta))^2 \tag{7.6}$$

we obtain an estimate of the conditional expectation function $E(Y|x)$.

The procedure is paralleled in quantile regression. The conditional median function is obtained by simply replacing the scalar ξ in the first equation by the parametric function $\xi(\mathrm{x_t}, \beta)$ and setting τ to $\frac{1}{2}$. Variants of this idea were proposed in the mid-eighteenth century by Boscovich and subsequently investigated by Laplace and Edgeworth, among others (see the discussion in Koenker and Basset, 1985). To obtain estimates of the other conditional quantile functions, we replace absolute values by $\rho_\tau(\cdot)$ and solve

$$\min_{\xi \in \mathcal{R}^p} \sum \rho_\tau(y_i - \xi(x_i, \beta)) \tag{7.7}$$

The resulting minimization problem, when $\xi(x, \beta)$ is formulated as a linear function of parameters, can be solved by linear programming methods.

This technique has been used widely in the past decade in many areas of applied econometrics; applications include investigations of wage structure (Buchinsky and Leslie, 1997), earnings mobility (Eide and Showalter, 1998; Buchinsky and Hahn, 1998) and educational attainment (Eide and Showalter, 1998). Financial applications include Engle and Manganelli (1999) and Morillo (2000) to the problems of "value at risk" and "option pricing," respectively. Barnes and Hughes (2002) applied quantile regression to study CAPM in their work on cross-sections of stock market returns.

7.4 Data and methodology

The study uses daily prices of the 30 Dow Jones Industrial Average Stocks, for a period from January 2002–May 2009, along with the Fama–French factors for the same period, obtained from French's website, to calculate the Fama–French coefficients (www.mba.tuck.dartmouth.edu/pages/faculty/ken.french/data_library.html#International).

Table 7.1 gives the 30 stocks traded at the Dow Jones Industrial Average and used in this study.

The approach here is to study the behavior of the return distribution along the quantiles using quantile regression. The coefficients for all the three factors of the model are calculated both by means of OLS and quantile regressions. While OLS calculates the coefficients along the median (0.50), quantile-regression calculates the values for 0.05, 0.25, 0.50, 0.75 and 0.95 quantiles at 95 percentile confidence levels. We also plot the fitted values using OLS and the two extreme quantile values to examine the behavior of fitted and actual values. The sequence of coefficients along the quantiles is also plotted to show the nonconstant linear relationship between the factors and the return. Both open source statistical software,

Table 7.1 Dow Jones industrial 30 stocks used in the study

3M	Ei Du Pont De Nemours	Kraft Foods
Alcoa	Exxon Mobile	McDonalds
American Express	General Electric	Merck & Co.
AT&T	General Motors	Microsoft
Bank of America	Hewlett-Packard	Pfizer
Boeing	Home Depot	Procter & Gamble
Caterpillar	Intel	United Technologies
Chevron	International Bus.Mchs.	Verizon Communications
Citigroup	Johnson & Johnson	Wal Mart Stores
Coca Cola	JP Morgan Chase & CO.	Walt Disney

GRETL, and STATA is used to calculate the Fama–French coefficients for the OLS and quantile-regression analyses.

7.5 Results: Quantile analysis of Fama–French factors

We have been emphasizing the fact that when it comes to risk assessment, the tail distributions may be more interesting for an investor or risk manager. Here we present the results of an analysis of the three factors, based both on their coefficients as obtained from OLS and quantile regressions,

Table 7.2 Fama–French risk coefficients from OLS

Stock	β	s	h
3M	0.008614	−0.00306	−0.00434
Alcoa	0.012955	0.005359	0.014032
American Express	0.010577	−0.00397	−0.00564
AT&T	0.009078	−0.00364	0.00204
Bank of America	0.009805	−0.00534	0.001711
Boeing	0.011219	−0.00175	−0.0042
Caterpillar	0.01278	0.004763	0.001788
Chevron	0.01319	−0.00306	0.023134
Citigroup	0.010753	−0.00629	−0.00209
Coca Cola	0.007274	−0.00456	−0.00284
Ei Du Pont De Nemours	0.009543	−0.00179	−0.00154
Exxon Mobile	0.013576	−0.00409	0.016094
General Electric	0.008281	−0.00569	−0.00783
General Motors	0.009435	0.002349	0.006133
Hewlett-Packard	0.011637	−0.00377	−0.0123
Home Depot	0.00994	−0.00298	−0.01052
Intel	0.013682	−0.00495	−0.01928
International Bus.Mchs.	0.008343	−0.00474	−0.0105
Johnson & Johnson	0.006264	−0.00811	−0.00738
JP Morgan Chase & Co.	0.013587	−0.00456	0.000826
Kraft Foods	0.004528	−0.00279	−0.00113
McDonalds	0.007624	−0.00072	−0.00257
Merck & Co.	0.009884	−0.00627	−0.004
Microsoft	0.009492	−0.00883	−0.01392
Pfizer	0.010272	−0.00765	−0.00424
Procter & Gamble	0.006126	−0.0038	−0.00562
United Technologies	0.008634	0.002649	0.00037
Verizon Communications	0.009882	−0.00424	−0.00373
Wal Mart Stores	0.007701	−0.00269	−0.00916
Walt Disney	0.008569	−0.00253	−0.004

Table 7.3 Fama–French risk coefficients from quantile regression (0.05)

Stock	β	s	h
3M	0.0087204	−0.005269	−0.005755
Alcoa	0.0118791	0.0058869	0.0236129
American Express	0.0086471	−0.002411	−0.004655
AT&T	0.0117791	−0.005055	0.0126947
Bank of America	0.0071695	−0.007957	0.0019138
Boeing	0.0085358	0.0001884	−0.001396
Caterpillar	0.0122212	0.0068914	0.0133572
Chevron	0.0097339	−0.003475	0.0233514
Citigroup	0.011633	−0.008887	0.0012689
Coca Cola	0.0063103	−0.004425	−0.004786
Ei Du Pont De Nemours	0.0087571	−0.001218	−0.000147
Exxon Mobile	0.0104406	−0.002919	0.0147583
General Electric	0.0104546	−0.008351	−0.011785
General Motors	0.0056712	0.0126481	0.0075143
Hewlett-Packard	0.0149214	−0.00439	−0.01119
Home Depot	0.008633	−0.006773	−0.006451
Intel	0.0149894	−0.002617	−0.018261
International Bus.Mchs.	0.0064724	−0.006006	−0.017403
Johnson & Johnson	0.0069007	−0.011523	−0.01487
JP Morgan Chase & Co.	0.0116703	−0.006588	0.0040308
Kraft Foods	0.0055943	−0.005914	0.0034399
McDonalds	0.0093003	0.0027243	0.0041196
Merck & Co.	0.0130209	−0.007923	−0.007142
Microsoft	0.0066115	−0.006191	−0.023396
Pfizer	0.0065584	−0.006634	−0.0112
Procter & Gamble	0.0058435	−0.006782	−0.006557
United Technologies	0.0093075	0.0031857	−0.006319
Verizon Communications	0.0093486	−0.003566	−0.001303
Wal Mart Stores	0.0065287	0.0004035	−0.001118
Walt Disney	0.0156589	−0.009912	0.001293

to examine whether OLS is able to capture the extreme tail distributions and to explore whether the two techniques provide different insights.

Table 7.2, Table 7.3 and Table 7.4 provide the Fama–French risk coefficients obtained for the stocks for the year 2006, using both OLS and quantile regressions at the 0.05 and 95 quantiles, respectively.

Figure 7.2, Figure 7.3 and Figure 7.4, respectively, provide an example of the values of the individual coefficients of beta s and h across different quantiles plotted against the values obtained from OLS. The plots clearly show that when it comes to boundary values in a distribution, the OLS method becomes inefficient. The plots show that the return on a security

Table 7.4 Fama–French risk coefficients from quantile regression (0.95)

Stock	β	s	H
3M	0.0080196	−0.003683	−0.000769
Alcoa	0.006503	0.009062	0.0070458
American Express	0.0117947	−0.001636	0.0015644
AT&T	0.0094728	−0.004266	−0.013008
Bank of America	0.010973	−0.008827	0.0003039
Boeing	0.0139033	−0.004808	−0.00478
Caterpillar	0.0131213	0.0059623	−0.001055
Chevron	0.0129154	−0.005819	0.0149052
Citigroup	0.0104364	−0.004438	−0.001737
Coca Cola	0.0073888	−0.00249	0.0007961
Ei Du Pont De Nemours	0.0096405	−0.005718	−0.004336
Exxon MOBILE	0.0133279	−0.007701	0.0129131
General Electric	0.007438	−0.006239	−0.00714
General Motors	0.0016224	0.0117895	0.0151127
Hewlett-Packard	0.0146965	−0.008829	−0.019157
Home Depot	0.0073725	0.0017505	−0.019662
Intel	0.0138265	−0.005464	−0.026458
International Bus.Mchs.	0.0082471	−0.00066	−0.012062
Johnson & Johnson	0.0066735	−0.009286	−0.007984
JP Morgan Chase & Co.	0.0164231	−0.005876	0.0065938
Kraft Foods	0.0071095	−0.004679	0.0043544
McDonalds	0.0088204	0.0013117	−0.004949
Merck & Co.	0.0080509	−0.0051	−0.004088
Microsoft	0.0136497	−0.015331	−0.008998
Pfizer	0.0158166	−0.009497	0.0039776
Procter & Gamble	0.0070965	−0.002836	−0.007098
United Technologies	0.0110386	−0.000498	0.0035812
Verizon Communications	0.0111802	−0.005746	−0.011214
Wal Mart Stores	0.0096267	−0.003811	−0.016033
Walt Disney	0.009699	−0.002968	0.0011207

is not linearly dependent in the same way on these factors around the whole distribution. The coefficients are calculated within a 95 percent confidence band, and within this confidence level OLS is unable to capture the distribution of historical returns for the tail distributions. The average relationship between return and beta for Alcoa in Figure 7.2 is 0.018.

In Figure 7.2, which depicts the relationship between the market factor beta and Alcoa, the slope of the relationship changes across the quantiles, moving from a steeper slope to less steep around the median, and then more steep in the tail of the distribution. At the 0.05 quantile the slope is

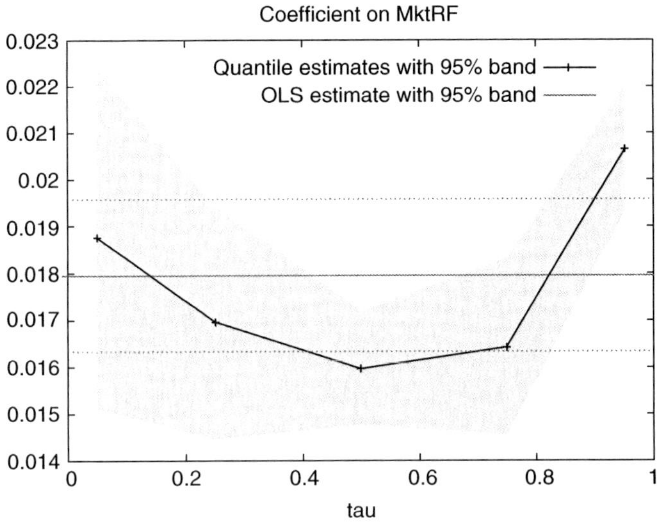

Figure 7.2 Values of beta across quantiles (Alcoa)

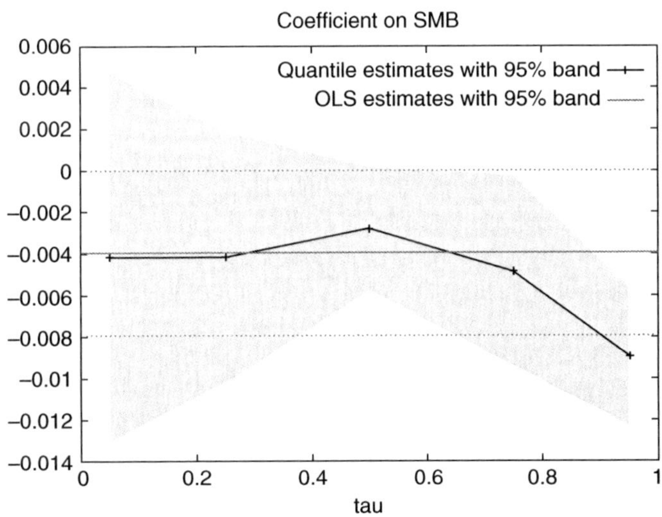

Figure 7.3 Values of s across quantiles (Alcoa)

0.019, but the error band is broad. However, the estimate at the median, which is significantly different from the OLS estimate, is only 0.016, whilst at the 0.95 quantile it is above 0.020 and the error band does not encompass the OLS estimate. Similarly, the coefficient on the size factor *s*

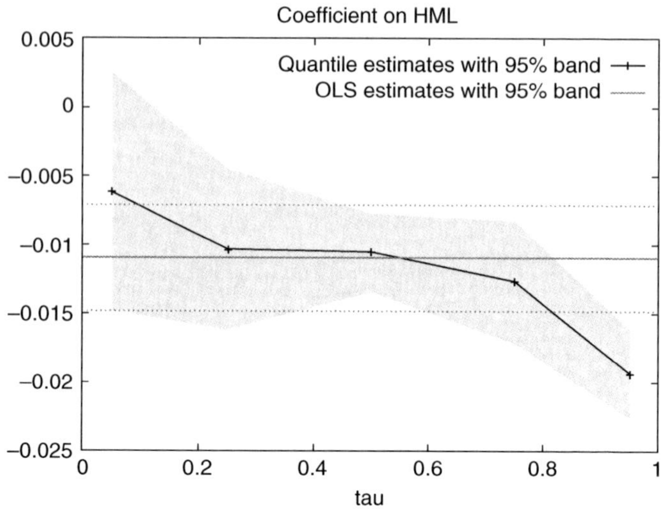

Figure 7.4 Values of h across quantiles (Alcoa)

is insignificantly different from the OLS estimate and relatively constant in the lower quantiles, but then becomes significantly different and more negative in the 0.95 quantile where it approaches −0.02. Finally, the coefficient on book-to-market, whilst having a negative slope, moves from being insignificantly different from OLS to significantly different and more negative as we move up the quantiles.

Another approach to understanding this is to plot the actual and fitted values obtained from both of the regression methods for an actual stock. Figures 7.5, 7.6 and 7.7 plot the fitted and actual values obtained from historical daily returns for a year using OLS, and the 0.05 and 0.95 quantiles, respectively. The plotted values clearly show that OLS is unable to cover the extreme values in the distribution. When it comes to efficient risk assessment, it becomes important for an investor or risk manager to account for the extreme tails of a distribution, which is captured by the quantile-regression fitted values.

Through this analysis we are able to show that quantile regression gives more efficient results when it comes to the boundary values of a distribution.

To further illustrate the additional information garnered by the technique we present some three-dimensional graphs (Figures 7.8–7.10) of how the loadings on the three factors vary from year to year across

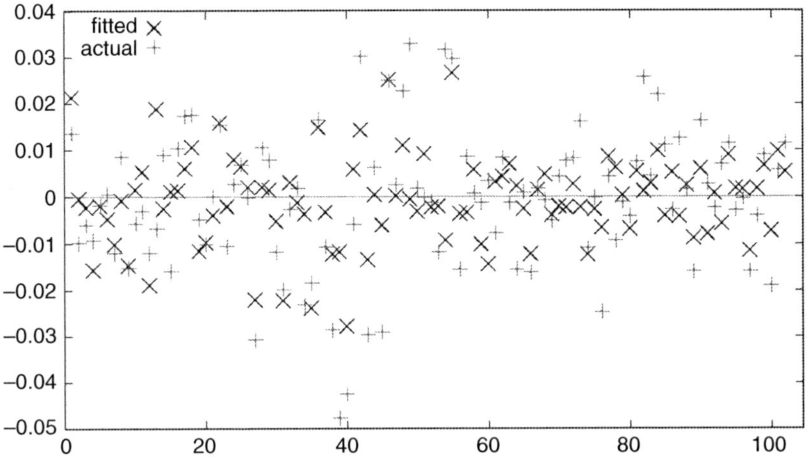

Figure 7.5 Actual Versus Fitted Values of Expected Return for OLS

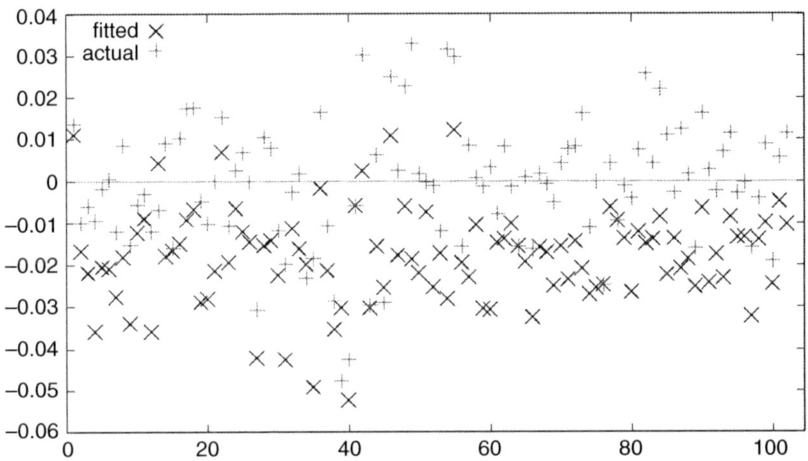

Figure 7.6 Actual Versus Fitted Values of Expected Return for Quantile Regression (0.05)

the quantiles. Standard OLS and asset-pricing techniques simply capture the average; clearly the behavior is much more complex than perusal of the averages would suggest. The results also suggest why simple reliance on standard OLS-based asset-pricing models as benchmarks to capture abnormal returns may produce highly inconsistent results.

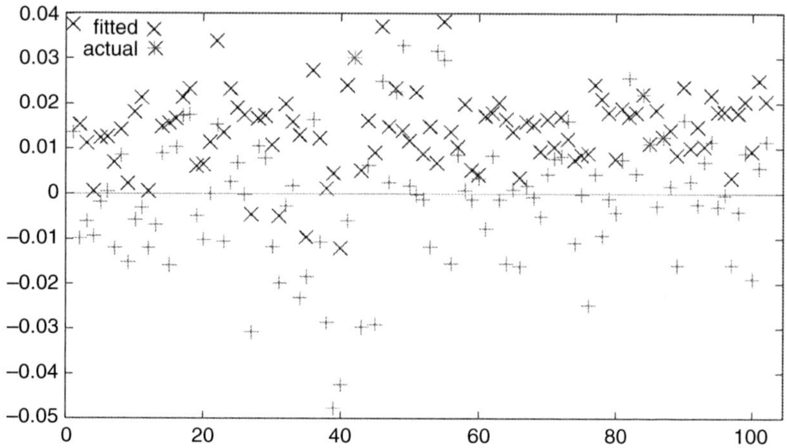

Figure 7.7 Actual Versus Fitted Values of Expected Return for Quantile Regression (0.95)

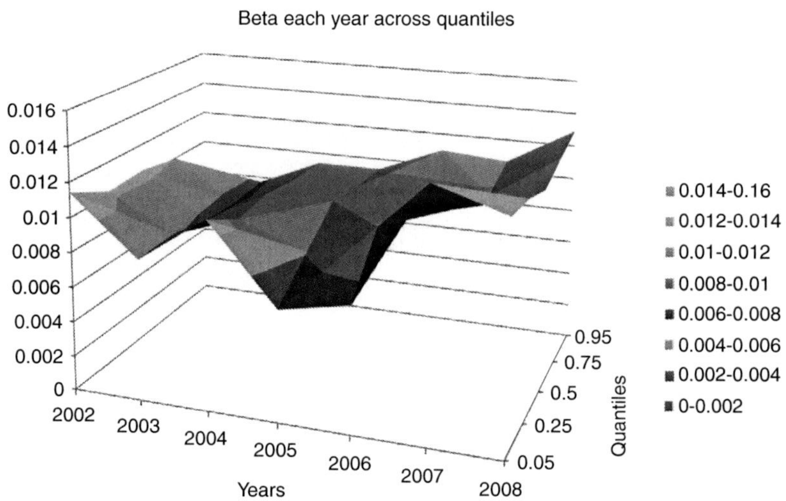

Figure 7.8 Annual beta estimates across the quantiles for Bank of America

The interesting feature of all three figures is that the direction or slope of the coefficients across the quantiles is not consistent and frequently changes slope as we move from the lowest to the highest quantiles. To be consistent with asset-pricing theory and the implications of OLS analysis these estimates should be a constant. This is clearly not the case.

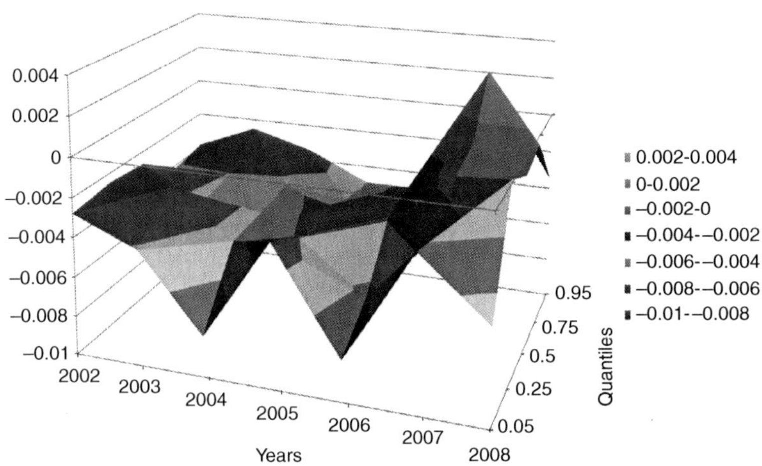

Figure 7.9 Annual estimates of coefficientss (SMB) for Bank of America

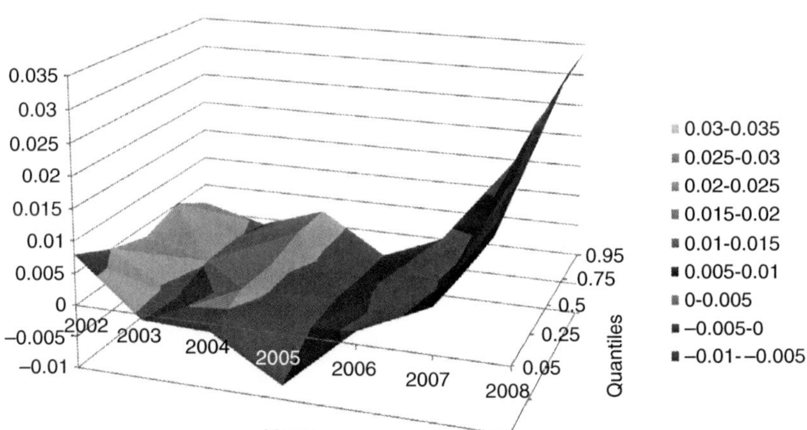

Figure 7.10 Annual estimates of coefficients *h* (HML) for Bank of America

As a further test we examined the equivalence of slopes estimated across different quantiles. We used a bootstrapping technique to test the significances of the differences across the slopes. The results are reported in the appendix. These just provide the results across the whole sample period, for reasons of economy. Over ten percent of the slope estimates

Table 7.5 Two-sample t-test for the fitted lower tail values

Stocks	P-Value (OLS)	P-value (Quantile regression (5%))	Stocks	P-value (OLS)	P-value (Quantile regression (5%))
3M	0.008197	0.186848	HP	0.000010	0.647671
Alcoa	0.000056	0.257715	IBM	0.000013	0.485589
American EX	0.001815	0.801880	Intel	0.005174	0.284515
AT&T	0.000000	0.999886	J&J	0.000020	0.498460
BOA	0.000343	0.757683	JP Morgan	0.002252	0.113751
Boeing	0.000050	0.064725	Kraft Food	0.000000	0.059104
Caterpillar	0.014409	0.286397	McDonalds	0.000000	0.730846
Chevron	0.000081	0.278451	Merk & Co	0.000014	0.085158
Citi Group	0.000578	0.583064	Microsoft	0.011107	0.366676
Coca Cola	0.000004	0.952945	P&G	0.000184	0.053473
Ei Du PONT	0.000349	0.221044	Pfizer	0.008405	0.180927
Exxon	0.000099	0.266374	United Tech	0.000313	0.530723
General Electric	0.000006	0.238482	Verizon	0.000004	0.111493
GM	0.000000	0.023882	Wal Mart	0.000006	0.220995
Home Depot	0.000236	0.229567	Walt Disney	0.000007	0.748839

across quantiles were significantly different at a ten percent level or better across the whole sample period.

7.6 Conclusion

We have explored the relationship between a set of returns of the 30 Dow Jones Index stocks and the three-factor model using factors obtained from Professor Ken French's website for the period 2002 to 2009 and quantile-regression analysis. We report the implications of the assumptions of OLS, as criticized originally by Frances Galton's famous exclamation against his statistical colleagues who: "limited their inquiries to averages and do not seem to revel in more comprehensive views." This appears also to apply in finance in the large literature on testing asset-pricing models. Our results reveal large and sometimes significant differences between returns and these three factors both across quantiles and through time. The picture that results from quantile-regression analysis is far more complex than the assumptions inherent in OLS would lead us to believe.

Appendix 7.1 Bootstrapped tests of the equivalence of slopes for 0.05 and 0.095 quantiles

For sample period 2004–2008

	Rm-Rf	SMB	HML
m3	−0.00018	−0.00041	−0.00028
P > t	0.801	0.751	0.84
ALCOA	0.003963	−0.00257	−0.01131
P > t	**0.002**	**0.31**	**0.001**
American EX	0.000572	0.00221	0.001624
P > t	0.567	0.291	0.501
AT&T	0.000308	−0.00249	−0.001
P > t	0.649	**0.091**	**0.518**
BOA	0.000442	0.001006	0.017042
P > t	0.692	0.631	**0**
Boeing	−0.0007	0.000695	0.001975
P > t	0.384	0.68	0.312
Caterpillar	0.000921	0.002288	−0.00187
P > t	0.355	0.196	0.291
Chevron	0.000376	−0.00285	−0.00256
P > t	0.661	**0.083**	**0.227**
Citi Grp	0.001962	0.001004	0.010286
P > t	0.3	0.812	**0.023**
Coca Cola	−0.00046	0.001428	−9.8E-05
P > t	0.562	0.502	0.969
Ei Du PONT	0.000139	0.001511	−0.00037
P > t	0.849	0.127	0.83
Exxon	−6.3E − 05	−0.00141	−0.00172
P > t	0.921	0.461	0.266
General Electric	−0.00023	−0.00011	0.002797
P > t	0.753	0.955	**0.07**
GM	−0.00114	0.005199	0.003719
P > t	0.658	0.292	0.454
HP	−0.00056	−0.00218	−0.0003
P > t	0.498	0.266	0.861
Home Depot	−1.4E-05	0.001231	0.003014
P > t	0.984	0.506	0.131
Intel	−0.00165	0.00154	0.001875
P > t	**0.069**	0.616	0.443
IBM	−0.00065	0.000105	3.31E-05
P > t	0.251	0.926	0.981
J&J	0.000704	0.000167	−0.00017
P > t	0.462	0.888	0.916
JP MORGAN	−0.00214	0.003513	0.014611

Continued

Appendix 7.1 Continued

	Rm-Rf	**SMB**	**HML**
P > t	0.149	0.155	**0**
Kraft Food	−0.00085	−0.00045	0.000127
P > t	0.385	0.812	0.943
MacD	−0.00095	−0.00112	0.001548
P > t	0.211	0.52	0.339
Merk & Co	0.001212	0.000474	−0.0011
P > t	0.135	0.687	0.56
Microsoft	−6.7E-05	−0.00114	−0.00138
P > t	0.94	0.415	0.491
Pfizer	−0.00094	−0.00151	0.002897
P > t	0.182	0.285	**0.031**
P&G	−2.5E-06	−0.00051	0.00024
P > t	0.997	0.676	0.867
United Tech	0.000871	0.000731	0.000507
P > t	0.191	0.658	0.746
Verizon	−0.0008	0.001036	0.000593
P > t	0.436	0.555	0.722
WalMart	−0.00031	0.00168	0.001433
P > t	0.743	0.379	0.416
Walt Disney	0.000414	0.001964	−0.0017
P > t	0.627	0.224	0.281

Note: Differences significant at .10 percent or better marked in bold.

References

Black, F. (1993) "Beta and Return," *Journal of Portfolio Management*, 20 (1): 8–18.

Barnes, M. and Hughes, T.W. (2002) "A Quantile Regression Analysis of the Cross Section of Stock Market Returns," available online at SSRN: http://ssrn.com/abstract=458522

Buchinsky, M. and Leslie, P. (1997) "Educational Attainment and the Changing U.S. Wage Structure: Some Dynamic Implications," Working Paper no. 97–13, Department of Economics, Brown University.

Buchinsky, M. and Hahn, J. (1998) "An Alternative Estimator for the Censored Quantile Regression Model," *Econometrica*, 66 (3): 653–671.

Chan, L.K.C. and Lakonishok, J. (1992) "Robust Measurement of Beta Risk," *The Journal of Financial and Quantitative Analysis*, 27: 265–282.

Eide, E. and Showalter, M.H. (1998) "The Effect of School Quality on Student Performance: A Quantile Regression Approach," *Economics Letters*, 58 (3): 345–350.

Engle, R.F. and Manganelli, S. (1999) "CAViaR: Conditional Value at Risk by Quantile Regression," NBER Working Paper 7341, National Bureau of Economic Research, Inc.

Fama, E.F. and French, K.R. (1992) "The Cross-Section of Expected Stock Returns," *Journal of Finance*, 47 (2): 427–486.

Fama, E.F. and French, K.R. (1993) "Common Risk Factors in the Returns on Stocks and Bonds, *Journal of Financial Economics*, 33 (1): 3–56.

Horowitz, J.L., Loughran, T. and Savin, N.E. (2000) "Three Analyses of the Firm Size Premium," *Journal of Empirical Finance*, 7: 143–153.

Knez, P.J. and Ready, M.J. (1997) "On the robustness of size and book-to-market in cross-sectional regressions," *Journal of Finance*, 52: 1355–1382.

Koenker, R.W. (2005) *Quantile Regression*, Econometric Society Monograph, Cambridge University Press.

Koenker, R.W and Bassett, G. (1978) "Regression Quantiles," *Econometrica*, Econometric Society, 46 (1): 33–50.

Koenker, R.W. and Bassett, G. (1985) "On Boscovich's Estimator," *Annals of Statistics*, 13 (4): 1625–1628.

Kothari, S.P., Shanken, J. and Sloan, R.G. (1995) "Another Look at the Cross-Section of Expected Returns," *Journal of Finance,* 50 (1): 185–224.

Levhari, D. and Levy, H. (1977) "The Capital Asset Pricing Model and the Investment Horizon," *Review of Economics and Statistics,* 59 (1): 92–104.

Lintner, J. (1965) "The Valuation of Risk Assets and the Selection of Risky Investments in Stock Portfolios and Capital Budgets," *Review of Economics and Statistics*, 47(4): 13–37.

Mossin, J. (1966) "Equilibrium in a Capital Asset Market," *Econometrica*, 34 (4): 768–783.

Morillo, D. (2000) "Income Mobility with Nonparametric Quantiles: A Comparison of the U.S. and Germany," in "Essays in Nonparametric Econometrics," Ph.D. Dissertation, University of Illinois at Urbana-Champaign.

Treynor, J.L. (1961) "Market Value, Time, And Risk," Unpublished manuscript dated 8/8/61, No. 95–209.

Treynor, J.L. (1962) "Toward a Theory of Market value of risky assets," Unpublished manuscript. Subsequently published as Chapter 2 of Korajczyk (1999) *Asset Pricing And Portfolio Performance: Models, Strategy And Performance Metrics*, London: Risk Books.

Sharpe, W.F. (1964) "Capital Asset Prices: A Theory of Market Equilibrium Under Conditions of Risk," *Journal of Finance*, 19 (3): 425–442.

8
The Value of Liquidity and Trading Activity in Forecasting Downside Risk

Lidia Sanchis-Marco and Antonio Rubia

8.1 Introduction

The recent fallout of the sub-prime mortgage and the subsequent international crisis in the financial markets have raised the need of effective risk-control and monitoring systems in the financial sector. The Basel Committee on Banking Supervision has put considerable emphasis on controlling market, credit and operational risk through the implementation of internal models, such as the well-known value-at-risk (VaR). This statistical measure was explicitly introduced by the Basel II Amendment in 1996 for determining capital requirements. Since then, it has become the most common quantitative tool in risk management. The vast literature devoted to downside risk modeling has suggested a number of alternative procedures to forecast VaR accurately, building mainly on the time-series properties of daily returns. However, several empirical studies (e.g. Kuester et al., 2006) show that most of these approaches do not seem to perform successfully in practice, thus underlining the large degree of complexity embedded in the VaR analysis for practical purposes.

In this chapter, we analyze empirically whether one-day VaR forecasts could be enhanced by using market microstructure variables as well as other environmental factors or, in other words, whether the tail of the conditional distribution of returns can be forecast using observable information beyond that conveyed by the return time series. More specifically, we focus on variables that are related to market liquidity and private information, such as bid–ask spread measures as well as volume and trading-related variables. Downside risk metrics, such as the

VaR, are obviously linked to the conditional volatility of the historical returns, from which it is not surprising that this latent process had taken a predominant position in parametric VaR modeling. What it is more surprising, however, is the fact that the existing literature seems to have ignored other effects beyond this variable. For instance, an implicit assumption in all the econometric models analyzed in Kuester et al. (2006) is that returns convey all the information needed for forecasting VaR, whereas there is no economic reason to maintain this particularly restrictive assumption, there exist arguments that support the inclusion of additional variables. Putting aside the vast literature related to liquidity and asset pricing, Jarrow and Protter (2009) have argued, for instance, that execution and illiquidity costs become relevant, if not essential, in a stress scenario. These arguments have motivated the interest in so-called liquidity-corrected VaR models; see Jorion (2007) for an overview. In addition, liquidity and trading-related variables generally characterize the market environment and can reflect the market's sentiment and collective beliefs, thereby conditioning the investor's decision. Consequently, investors may be able to advance large movements in prices not only by analyzing volatility or historical returns, but also by processing other observable information, such as bid–ask spreads and trading-related variables.

Since ultimately this is an empirical question, we analyze the suitability of these variables to predict the conditional tail of daily returns using market data from the US Stock Market in the period January 4, 1988 to December 31, 2002. The most natural way to appraise the potential forecasting ability of a set of instrumental variables in this context is by using the "quantile regression" (QR) methodology developed by Koenker and Bassett (1978). The central idea is to directly model the dynamics of the conditional quantile by specifying a functional form that relates the time-varying dynamics of the (unobservable) conditional VaR process to the predictive variables, building on the CAViaR model by Engle and Manganelli (2004). Since the estimation of these models is not trivial, we adopt the "simulated-annealing" optimization algorithm which, albeit being more computationally intensive, has good properties when the objective function is highly nonlinear and non-differentiable. The analysis on the conditional and unconditional coverage of the one-day VaR forecasts in the standard backtesting analysis (Christoffersen, 1998) suggests that variables such as the effective and relative bid–ask spreads have good predictive power to forecast value-at-risk.

The remainder of the chapter is organized as follows. In Section 8.2 we review the main elements in VaR modeling and describe the most popular parametric models, such as those based on the GARCH and EWMA procedures. This methods will be used together with the "quantile-regression model," described Section 8.3. Section 8.4 is devoted the empirical analysis. Finally, Section 8.5 summarizes and concludes.

8.2 Modeling downside risk: Value-at-risk

Banks, credit institutions, brokerage firms, investment funds and even nonfinancial institutions quantify the risk of the trading positions by computing the VaR measure; see Jorion (2007) for a monographic on the topic. The enormous popularity of this statistical measure is due to its conceptual simplicity. The VaR is an estimation of the percentile of the probability distribution of the market value change for a portfolio under normal market conditions. For instance, suppose that an investor holds a portfolio on stocks for which the VaR for the next day has been estimated to be one million dollars with 99 percent confidence. This means that, under normal circumstances, the investor should expect only a 1 percent chance for his or her portfolio to suffer a daily loss larger than this amount. More formally, and in general terms, given the set of information up to time t, say I_t, we define the h-period-ahead VaR at the $(1-\lambda)$ percent confidence level as (minus) the expected value of the λ-quantile of the conditional distribution of the returns, namely,

$$\begin{aligned} VaR_{\lambda,t+h} &\equiv -\left\{x \in \mathbb{R} : \Pr(r_{t+h} \leq x | I_t) = \lambda\right\} \\ &= -Q_\lambda(r_{t+h}|I_t) \end{aligned} \tag{8.1}$$

where r_t denotes the return at time t. As an example, the Basel Committee suggests the 99 percent confidence level ($\lambda = 0.01$) over a 10-day horizon.

Since the VaR statistic has become the predominant measure in downside risk, the literature devoted to the topic has suggested a large variety of procedures for its estimation. A complete review of this literature is beyond the scope of this chapter. We only discuss briefly the most relevant features in the "VaR–GARCH" and "VaR–RiskMetrics" approaches in this section, since these shall be used in the empirical section together with the "CAViaR."

The distinctive feature of the GARCH and RiskMetrics risk models is that they impose a parametric structure to model volatility to generate h-ahead VaR forecasts, given the empirical distribution of standardized returns or given an explicit assumption that characterizes the conditional distribution of returns (e.g. normality). The GARCH(1,1) model is the most popular approach to model volatility parametrically. It is largely appreciated due to its enormous computational tractability and impressing forecasting accuracy; see, among others, Hansen and Lunde (2005). More specifically, the standard GARCH(1,1) model assumes

$$r_t = E\left(r_t|I_{t-1}\right) + \varepsilon_t; \quad t = 1,\ldots,T$$
$$\varepsilon_t = \sigma_t \eta_t, \quad \eta_t|I_{t-1} \sim iid\ N(0,1) \tag{8.2}$$
$$\sigma_t^2 = \omega + \alpha\varepsilon_{t-1}^2 + \beta\sigma_{t-1}^2, \quad \omega > 0, \alpha, \beta \geq 0$$

where $E\left(r_t|I_{t-1}\right)$ denotes the conditional mean of the (daily) return. Although financial returns are largely known to be non-normally distributed both conditionally and unconditionally, it is convenient to assume conditional normality as this ensures robustness in the parameter estimation (Bollerslev and Woolridge, 1992) and, hence, consistency in the one-day-ahead forecast of the conditional volatility process, namely, $\hat{\sigma}_{T+1|T}^2 = \hat{\omega} + \hat{\alpha}\varepsilon_T^2 + \hat{\beta}\hat{\sigma}_T^2$. Given this forecast, the GARCH–VaR forecast at the $(1-\lambda)$ percent confidence level can readily be obtained as $VaR_{\lambda,T+1} = E\left(r_{T+1}|I_T\right) + \hat{\sigma}_{T+1|T} Q_\lambda\left(\hat{\eta}_t\right)$, where $Q_\lambda\left(\hat{\eta}_t\right)$ denotes the empirical λ-quantile of the standardized returns, $\hat{\eta}_t = \varepsilon_t/\hat{\sigma}_t$, with $\left\{\hat{\sigma}_t\right\}$ being the GARCH in-sample estimates of the volatility process. Note that, by considering the empirical distribution of the standardized returns, we have avoided imposing an a priori belief on the conditional distribution of the returns.

Alternatively, the RiskMetrics approach popularized the "exponential weighting moving average" (EWMA) scheme to estimate the volatility process, setting $\sigma_t^2 = \delta\sigma_{t-1}^2 + (1-\delta)r_{t-1}^2$, where the smoothing parameter $0 < \delta < 1$ is usually set equal to 0.95 for data recorded on a daily basis. RiskMetrics assumes conditional normality, so the one-day EWMA–VaR forecast is $E\left(r_{T+1}|I_T\right) - 1.96\hat{\sigma}_{T+1|T}$ for the 5 percent quantile. Nevertheless, in order to ensure robustness against departures from normality, we shall compute the empirical conditional quantile of the return as in the GARCH model, considering $Q_\lambda\left(\tilde{\eta}_t\right)$from the standardized returns, $\tilde{\eta}_t = \varepsilon_t/\tilde{\sigma}_t$, given the EWMA volatility estimates, $\tilde{\sigma}_t$.

Finally, following standard practices, we shall consider the VaR analysis on the demeaned returns after fitting a simple AR(1) model intended to filter out any predictable component in the mean.

8.3 Modeling VaR: The CAViaR approach

The unconditional λ-quantile of the return time series is the value $Q_\lambda(r_t)$ for which $\Pr\left(r_t \leq Q_\lambda(r_t)\right) = \lambda$. This can be estimated directly from the returns' time series as the corresponding empirical percentile, but the resultant estimation is known to be too inaccurate to be used as a reliable estimation of the VaR. The conditional λ-quantile of r_t is $\Pr\left(r_t \leq Q_{\lambda,t}(r_t)|I_{t-1}\right) = \lambda$, where obviously $Q_{\lambda,t}(r_t) \equiv -VaR_{\lambda,t}$ is the main statistical object of interest in this chapter. Note that the notation used in $Q_{\lambda,t}(r_t)$ emphasizes the conditional nature of the VaR measure.

Following Koenker and Bassett (1978, 1982), the conditional quantile $Q_{\lambda,t}(r_t)$ could be written as a linear function on a set of explanatory variables, say X_t, and a $K \times 1$ vector of (unknown) coefficients β_λ that depends on the λ-quantile, namely, $Q_{\lambda,t}(r_t) = X'_{t-1}\beta_\lambda$. This is equivalent to assume the quantile-regression model $r_t = X'_{t-1}\beta_\lambda + u_{t,\lambda}$, where the distribution of the error term on the right-hand side is left unspecified. More generally, $Q_{\lambda,t}(r_t)$ could be modeled in terms of a possibly nonlinear function of the information set, namely $g(X_{t-1};\beta_\lambda) \equiv -VaR_{\lambda,t}$, from which the relevant parameters can be estimated as:

$$\hat{\beta}_\lambda : \mathop{\mathbf{arg\ min}}_{\beta_\lambda \in \mathbb{R}^k} \left\{ \sum_{r_t \geq g(X_{t-1};\beta_\lambda)} \lambda |r_t - g(X_{t-1};\beta_\lambda)| \right.$$

$$\left. + \sum_{r_t < g(X_{t-1};\beta_\lambda)} (1-\lambda)|r_t - g(X_{t-1};\beta_\lambda)| \right\} \tag{8.3}$$

Engle and Manganelli (2004) proposed this general specification and derived the statistical properties of the resultant estimates (consistency and asymptotic normality) under fairly general regularity conditions. More specifically, they consider a family of models in which the evolution of the quantile over time is seen as a latent autoregressive process which may depend on predetermined values of observable variables, leading to the so-called conditional autoregressive value-at-risk (CAViaR) model. For instance, the so-called symmetric absolute-value (SAV) CAViaR model specifies:

$$VaR_{\lambda,t} = \beta_{\lambda,0} + \beta_{\lambda,1} VaR_{\lambda,t-1} + \beta^*_{\lambda,1} \left|r_{t-1}\right| \tag{8.4}$$

The autoregressive structure ensures that the conditional quantile changes smoothly over time, while the additional variables may be empirically linked by the VaR to observable information. Note that the SAV model includes lagged values of absolute return, that is, the most common nonparametric proxy for the unobservable volatility. Taylor (1999), in a close quantile-regression model, uses the in-sample volatility estimates from a GARCH(1,1) instead of $\left|r_{t-1}\right|$ as the additional explanatory variable. The empirical analysis in Kuester et al. (2006)

shows that this simple model has a good performance in relation to more sophisticated CAViaR-type specifications that involve nonlinear parameterizations. Hence, we shall use the SAV model in the current chapter as a starting point for further specifications. These are discussed below.

8.3.1 Extending the CAViaR model

Several arguments seem to support the suitability of liquidity and trading-related variables to forecast downside risk-measure VaR. The discussion, among others, in Bangia et al. (1998) and Jarrow and Protter (2009), claiming for the relevance of execution and illiquidity costs, justifies the study on bid–ask spreads and volumes. Also, the literature related to market information asymmetry provides additional reasons to consider these variables. Investors must trade in a context of asymmetric information which forces them to make decisions and to reassess the conditional risk of their portfolios under imperfect information. Dupuy (2008) argues that, in this context, asset prices may not only discount risk as measured by the objective probability of occurrence of a bad event, but also the potential biases related to the estimation of this probability under informational asymmetries. If the ambiguity and estimation risk related to imperfect information and market asymmetries is able to generate greater downside risk, the quantile-regression analysis would show a positive relationship between the conditional tail distribution of returns and those variables that are correlated to (or proxy for) the extent of information asymmetry. It is widely accepted that bid–ask spreads include a component that reflects informational asymmetry (e.g. Stoll, 1989), and which are positively correlated to the volatility of returns (see, among others, the theoretical analysis in Admati and Pfleiderer, 1998; Easley et al., 1997 and the empirical analysis in Bollerslev and Melvin, 1994) from which bid–ask spreads may be useful in VaR forecasting. Similarly, Blume et al. (1994) examined the informational role of volume-finding positive correlation between price changes and trading volume (see also Campbell et al., 1993), arguing that large trades or volume may be originated by asymmetric information due to either differential information or differences in opinion. Hence, volume-related variables may also convey useful information for VaR forecasting.

The estimation of the QR models is far from being trivial. In order to keep our models as parsimonious as possible, we analyze the effects of including a single variable in addition to the proxy for volatility. In particular, we consider the series of models

$$VaR_{\lambda,t} = \beta_{\lambda,0} + \beta_{\lambda,1}\, VaR_{\lambda,t-1} + \beta^{*}_{\lambda,1}\left|r_{t-1}\right| + \beta^{*}_{\lambda,2}\left|\log \xi_{t-1}\right| \tag{8.5}$$

where ξ_{t-1} refers to any of the following specific variables:

Trading-related variables

This category includes trading volume measured in thousands of shares (V); number of trades (NTrades); number of sell trades (NS); number of shares sold in thousands (NSS); and traded volume in dollars (TVD).

Liquidity variables

This category includes quoted spread (QS); effective spread (ES); relative quoted spread (RQS); and relative effective spread (RES).

Additionally, we considered other alternative variables which did not yield qualitative changes. For instance, including the unexpected volume (measured as the residuals from an AR(1) model) instead of (the logarithm of) volume did not produce major qualitative changes in the out-of-sample analysis. Additional results are available from the authors upon request.

8.4 Empirical analysis

8.4.1 Data and methodology

We use continuously compounded daily returns from the volume-weighted portfolio in the US market over the period January 4, 1988 to December 31, 2002, totaling 3782 observations. Transactions are averaged over the day to obtain daily liquidity measures; see Chordia et al. (2001).[1] Table 8.1 shows some descriptive information on the return (in levels) and the explanatory variables (in logarithms) used in the analysis. Returns exhibit the stylized features (large excess of kurtosis, mild degree of skewness and autocorrelation), whereas the most salient feature of the predictors is the strong degree of persistence as measured by the first-order autocorrelation. Note that all the predictors are either strictly positive or strictly negative, as indicated by the maximum–minimum range. The cross-correlation between the predictive variables and the absolute value of the return (not reported here due to space restrictions) ranges from 25 percent (RQS) to 40 percent (NSS). All variables are positively correlated.

Following Alexander and Sheedy (2008), we consider a rolling window with the last 2700 observations in the sample to forecast one-day-ahead VaR at the {1 percent, 2.5 percent, 5 percent, 7.5 percent} quantiles. Parameters, volatility and quantiles are re-estimated yielding over a thousand out-of-sample VaR forecasts from (1) the GARCH–VaR and EWMA–VaR models described in Section 8.2, (2) the benchmark SAV

Table 8.1 Descriptive statistics of the variables involved in the analysis

Variable	Mean	Median	Mode	Max.	Min.	Var.	Kurtosis	Skewness	Corr.(1)
Return	0.00	0.01	−6.68	5.54	−6.68	0.98	7.78	−0.20	−0.06
V	7.39	7.21	6.39	9.69	5.51	0.73	1.86	0.36	0.96
NTRADES	6.85	6.69	5.81	8.76	5.06	0.65	1.64	0.30	0.98
NS	6.09	5.94	5.04	8.02	4.24	0.65	1.67	0.29	0.98
NSS	6.51	6.33	5.10	8.80	4.50	0.73	1.86	0.35	0.96
TVD	11.10	11.04	9.13	13.00	9.13	0.76	1.66	0.17	0.96
QS	−1.89	−1.74	−1.59	−1.23	−3.38	0.21	4.79	−1.64	0.99
ES	−2.29	−2.11	−2.13	−1.52	−3.75	0.20	4.48	−1.53	0.99
RQS	−5.39	−5.39	−5.31	−4.82	−6.86	0.20	3.23	−1.02	0.99
RES	−5.96	−5.76	−5.70	−5.17	−7.24	0.20	3.08	−0.96	0.99

Note: See end of Section 8.2 for a description of these. The column Corr(1) shows the first-order autocorrelation.

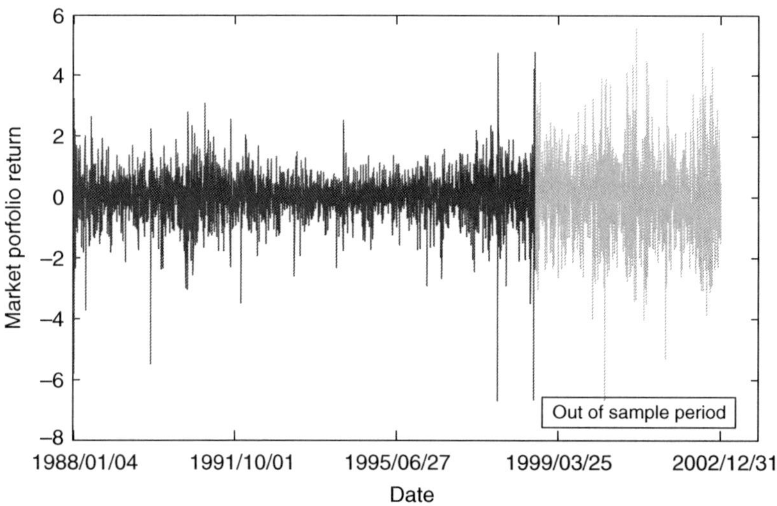

Figure 8.1 Returns of the market portfolio

CAViaR model specified in equation (8.4), and (3) the one-variable extended CAViaR models in (8.5) for any of the variables considered in the analysis. The behavior of the market return in the in- and out-of-sample periods is exhibited in Figure 8.1.

Daily returns are previously demeaned to estimate models by using a simply AR(1) filter; see Hansen and Lunde (2005). The VaR–GARCH model can be estimated by optimizing the "Gaussian maximum likelihood" and does not pose any computational problem. By contrast, the estimation of the CAViaR and the extended CAViaR models are far from being trivial because of the computational complexity of the objective function. This prompted us to use the simulated-annealing (SA) optimization algorithm (see Goffe et al., 1994) as an alternative to the estimation process employed in Engle and Manganelli (2004).

The SA is a local random-search search algorithm which exploits the analogy between the way a metal cools and freezes to obtain a minimum-energy crystalline structure (annealing process) and the search for a minimum in real-valued problems. The main characteristic of this algorithm is that it randomly generates new solutions at any iteration. The search process can accept values that increase the objective function (rather than lower it) with a probability that decreases as the number of iterations increases. The main purpose of this routine is to prevent the search process from becoming trapped in local optima, which additionally provides low sensitivity to the choice of the initial values. Furthermore, because the SA algorithm does not require or deduce derivative information, it avoids the computation problems that may arise with non-differentiable functions. When implementing SA in our empirical analysis, we adopted the strategy of repeating the whole random search process 1000 times more to minimize the possibility of getting convergence to a non-global optimum. The optimization routine in the rolling-window approach was initiated at the solution found in the previous optimization.[2]

8.4.2 Out-of-sample analysis: Mean out-of-sample estimates

First, we discuss the parameter estimates for the simple SAV–CAViaR model. Table 8.2 reports the average values of the parameter estimates over the out-of-sample period. Loosely speaking, the results are consistent with the empirical findings in previous chapters, showing a strongly

Table 8.2 Mean estimates over the out-of-sample period of symmetric absolute-value CAViaR model in equation (8.4)

Model	100λ (%)	$\hat{\beta}_{\lambda,0}$	$\hat{\beta}_{\lambda,1}$	$\hat{\beta}^*_{\lambda,1}$
SAV CAViaR	7.5	0.004	0.966	0.055
	5.0	0.007	0.971	0.051
	2.5	0.022	0.956	0.086
	1.0	0.142	0.842	0.345

persistent VaR process (the slope coefficient $\beta_{\lambda,1}$ ranges from 0.84 to 0.97), and the positive effect of volatility, as captured by the parameter $\beta^*_{\lambda,1}$; see Table 8.2. Not surprisingly, the conditional dynamics of the VaR are less persistent and more influenced by the volatility of the observations when the size of λ decreases: extreme movements are less predictable and driven by the excess of volatility caused by observations that behave statistically as additive outliers.

The analysis on the mean estimates for the extended CAViaR models in (8.5) are reported in Tables 8.3 (volume-related variables) and 8.4 (liquidity variables). The estimated coefficient $\hat{\beta}^*_{\lambda,2}$ is positive in all cases, suggesting a positive dependence between VaR and liquidity and trading-related variables. The inclusion of the additional variables has

Table 8.3 Mean out-of-sample estimates of extended CAViaR models in equation (8.5)

	100λ (%)	$\hat{\beta}_{\lambda,0}$	$\hat{\beta}_{\lambda,1}$	$\hat{\beta}^*_{\lambda,1}$	$\hat{\beta}^*_{\lambda,2}$
Model	**Models with trading activity**				
Model A	7.5	−0.047	0.955	0.056	0.009
log(V)	5.0	−0.055	0.960	0.046	0.011
	2.5	−0.099	0.934	0.076	0.023
	1.0	−0.003	0.822	0.331	0.028
Model B	7.5	−0.047	0.955	0.055	0.010
log(Ntrades)	5.0	−0.034	0.965	0.045	0.008
	2.5	−0.052	0.952	0.058	0.015
	1.0	0.051	0.784	0.399	0.029
Model C	7.5	−0.041	0.954	0.056	0.010
log(NS)	5.0	−0.037	0.962	0.046	0.010
	2.5	−0.079	0.937	0.065	0.025
	1.0	−0.060	0.778	0.382	0.056
Model D	7.5	−0.042	0.954	0.056	0.010
log(NSS)	5.0	−0.041	0.963	0.045	0.010
	2.5	−0.118	0.920	0.084	0.033
	1.0	−0.167	0.775	0.369	0.073
Model E	7.5	−0.074	0.956	0.054	0.008
log(TVD)	5.0	−0.039	0.969	0.044	0.005
	2.5	−0.072	0.956	0.058	0.010
	1.0	0.059	0.789	0.435	0.015

Note: V denotes Volume; Ntrades is the Number of Trades; NS is Number of Sell Trades; NSS Number of Shares Sold in Thousands; TVD stands for Trading Volume in Dollars. All variables are in logarithms.

Table 8.4 Mean out-of-sample estimates of liquidity-extended CAViaR models in equation (8.5)

Model	100λ (%)	$\hat{\beta}_{\lambda,0}$	$\hat{\beta}_{\lambda,1}$	$\hat{\beta}^{*}_{\lambda,1}$	$\hat{\beta}^{*}_{\lambda,2}$
	Models with Market Liquidity				
Model F	7.5	−0.018	0.956	0.061	0.016
|log(QS)|	5.0	−0.018	0.970	0.046	0.017
	2.5	−0.036	0.952	0.068	0.042
	1.0	0.044	0.836	0.349	0.065
Model G	7.5	−0.032	0.954	0.062	0.020
|log(ES)|	5.0	−0.032	0.968	0.046	0.021
	2.5	−0.044	0.955	0.064	0.036
	1.0	0.028	0.844	0.308	0.060
Modelo H	7.5	−0.054	0.959	0.059	0.012
|log(RQS)|	5.0	−0.053	0.971	0.044	0.012
	2.5	−0.115	0.960	0.054	0.027
	1.0	−0.086	0.851	0.300	0.043
Model I	7.5	−0.088	0.954	0.062	0.017
|log(RES)|	5.0	−0.062	0.971	0.043	0.012
	2.5	−0.079	0.963	**0.052**	**0.019**
	1.0	−0.006	0.838	0.348	0.026

Note: QS denotes Quoted Bid–Ask Spread; ES denotes effective spread; RQS is Relative Quoted Spread; RES is Relative Effective Spread. All variables are in logarithms and include in absolute terms in the QR analysis.

large effects on the magnitude of the constant parameter. For most of the predictors the constant is negative, since both the volatility and the explanatory variables include nonzero unconditional effects. In contrast, the inclusion of an additional variable has mild effects on average on the autoregressive VaR coefficients. The sensitivity to volatility $\beta^{*}_{\lambda,1}$ exhibits a more idiosyncratic behavior as a function of the specific quantile and the variable involved. Since the main aim of VaR modeling is predictive, we study whether the inclusion of these variables has a sizeable impact on the VaR forecasts. Even if the in-sample contribution is moderate, the inclusion of new variables may lead to large changes in the forecast's dynamics. This issue is addressed in the next subsection through "backtesting VaR analysis" (see Jorion, 2007).

8.4.3 Out-of-sample analysis: Backtesting VaR models

Following Christoffersen (1998), we define the "exception variable" (also called the "hit variable") for any $t = 1, \ldots, N$ in the out-of-sample space, and for any of the alternative models considered, as a dummy taking value one whenever the actual return exceeds the $VaR_{\lambda,t}$threshold and zero otherwise. The main purpose is to test for the hypothesis of perfect conditional coverage given by

$$E\left[H_{\lambda,t}|I_{t-1}\right]=\lambda \tag{8.6}$$

which implies that the VaR exceptions will approximately occur with the correct conditional and unconditional probability. More specifically, we consider the following sequence of tests:

Unconditional test

The main hypothesis of interest is $H_0 : E\left[H_{\lambda,t}\right] = \lambda$. The most basic assumption is that the risk model provides a correct unconditional coverage. Kupiec (1995) developed a "likelihood ratio" (LR) test defined as:

$$LR_{uc}=2(N-N_\lambda)\left[\log\left(1-\frac{N_\lambda}{T}\right)-\log(1-\lambda)\right]+2N_\lambda\left[\log\frac{N_\lambda}{N}-\log\lambda\right]\sim\chi^2_{(1)} \tag{8.7}$$

where $\chi^2_{(1)}$ stands for a Chi-squared distribution with one degree of freedom, N_λ is the number of exceptions, and N is the total number of out-of-sample observations. Note that N_λ/N is simply the sample mean of $H_{\lambda,t}$, which should be around λ theoretically.

Independence test

VaR forecasts should not exhibit patches or clusters, because the risk of bankruptcy is higher in this case. Christoffersen (1998) proposes the analysis of the first-order serial correlation in the time-series dynamics of $H_{\lambda,t}$ through a binary first-order Markov chain with transition probability matrix

$$\prod=\begin{pmatrix}1-\pi_{01} & \pi_{01}\\ 1-\pi_{11} & \pi_{01}\end{pmatrix},\quad \pi_{ij}=\mathbf{Pr}(H_{\lambda,t}=j|H_{\lambda,t-1}=i) \tag{8.8}$$

For simplicity of notation, we shall denote $H_t=H_{\lambda,t}$ in the sequel, as the dependence of the hit variable on the quantile is already clear. The approximate joint likelihood, conditional on the first observation, is

$$L(\Pi;H_2,H_3,\ldots H_T|H_1)=(1-\pi_{01})^{n_{00}}\pi_{01}^{n_{01}}(1-\pi_{11})^{n_{10}}\pi_{11}^{n_{11}}, \tag{8.9}$$

where n_{ij} represents the number of transitions from state i to state j, that is, $n_{ij} = \sum_{t=2}^{N} I(H_t = i|H_{t-i} = j)$, and the maximum-likelihood estimators under the alternative hypothesis are $\hat{\pi}_{01} = \frac{n_{01}}{n_{00}+n_{01}}$ and $\hat{\pi}_{11} = \frac{n_{11}}{n_{10}+n_{11}}$. Under the null hypothesis of the independence, it follows that

$$L(\pi_0; H_2, \ldots H_T|H_1) = (1-\pi_{01})^{n_{00}+n_{10}} \pi_{01}^{n_{01}+n_{11}}, \tag{8.10}$$

where the parameter π_0 can be estimated as $\hat{\pi}_0 = N_\lambda / N$, the main value in the unconditional coverage test. The LR test for independence is then given by:

$$LR_{ind} = 2\left[LogL(\hat{\Pi}; H_{2,} \ldots, H_T|H_1) - LogL(\hat{\pi}_0; H_{2,} \ldots, H_T|H_1)\right] \sim \chi^2_{(1)}. \tag{8.11}$$

Conditional test

Finally, we can devise a joint test for independence and correct coverage, that is, correct conditional coverage, by combining the previous tests. In particular,

$$LR_{cc} = 2\left[LogL(\hat{\Pi}; H_{2,} \ldots, H_T|H_1) - LogL(\lambda; H_{2,} \ldots, H_T|H_1)\right] \sim \chi^2_{(2)} \tag{8.12}$$

which corresponds to testing that if the sequence of exceptions H_t is independent, and the probabilities to observe a VaR violation in the next period given the set of available information corresponds to the nominal level. Notice that the test is simply $LR_{cc} = LR_{uc} + LR_{ind}$ and that it involves two restrictions, hence the asymptotic convergence to a $\chi^2_{(2)}$ distribution.

8.4.4 Out-of-sample analysis: Main results

Table 8.5 reports the results for the benchmark models (VaR–GARCH, VaR–EWMA and SA–CAViaR) over the out-of-sample period. The mean estimates of the GARCH variance dynamics exhibits the usual empirical features, namely, large persistence and clustering effects, as revealed by the average estimates of the parameters $\hat{\alpha} = 0.1$ and $\hat{\beta} = 0.896$, from which the dynamics of GARCH–VaR forecasts are persistent as well. The overall performance of the VaR–GARCH and the SAV–CAViaR models is very similar in the period analyzed. In general, both models are biased towards yielding overconservative VaR forecasts and, accordingly, the empirical percentage of rejections is higher. This result agrees with previous empirical evidence. The bias is particularly evident as the size of

Table 8.5 Backtesting VaR analysis for the EWMA, GARCH and SAV–CAViaR models

Model	100λ (%)	Viol. (%)	LR_{UC}	*p*-value	LR_{ind}	*p*-value	LR_{cc}	*p*-value	MeanFVaR
VaR–EWMA	7.5	8.9	2.677	0.102	0.670	0.413	3.377	0.185	1.904
	5.0	5.5	0.511	0.475	0.000	0.986	0.521	0.771	2.240
	2.5	1.5	4.777	0.029	0.457	0.499	5.214	0.074	2.977
	1.0	0.5	3.094	0.079	0.050	0.823	3.134	0.209	3.945
VaR–GARCH	7.5	11.3	18.220	0.000	0.289	0.591	18.593	0.000	1.758
	5.0	**7.4**	10.634	**0.001**	0.463	0.496	11.148	**0.004**	2.031
	2.5	2.8	0.356	0.551	0.076	0.784	0.437	0.804	2.683
	1.0	0.9	0.105	0.747	0.164	0.686	0.266	0.875	3.569
SAV–CAViaR	7.5	10.1	8.860	0.003	0.465	0.495	8.739	0.013	1.822
	5.0	**7.4**	10.634	**0.001**	0.507	0.477	11.192	**0.004**	2.041
	2.5	3.2	1.849	0.174	0.000	0.993	1.864	0.394	2.552
	1.0	1.3	0.831	0.362	0.316	0.574	1.153	0.562	3.232

Note: The second column shows the estimation of the sample mean of empirical exceptions. LRUC, LRind and LRcc denote the values of the tests for unconditional coverage, independence and conditional coverage, respectively, whereas the columns labeled as *p*-value show the *p*-values of the respective test statistics. Finally, MeanFVaR denotes the mean of the forecast VaR over the out-of-sample period. Bold letters are used to denote statistical rejection at the 5 percent asymptotic nominal size.

λ tends to increase. As a result, the backtesting analysis strongly rejects the hypothesis of the perfect unconditional coverage hypothesis for both models for $\lambda = \{5$ percent, 7.5 percent$\}$ in this sample.

On the other hand, the VaR–EWMA model produces better results, although it exhibits biases for $\lambda = \{1$ percent, 2.5 percent$\}$ (overestimate the true VaR) and $\lambda = 7.5$ percent (underestimate the true VaR) quantiles. Overall, none of the risk models analyzed is able to pass the backtesting analysis convincingly for the set of quantiles considered.

Next, we analyze the results from the extended CAViaR models. These are shown in Tables 8.6 (volume-related variables) and 8.7 (liquidity variables). The most remarkable finding is that, whereas the standard CAViaR model can be largely biased towards underestimating the true value-at-risk, the inclusion of the volume-related and liquidity variables provides a suitable correction such that most of the departures from the nominal level are eliminated, particularly for the variables in the liquidity group. The improvement in the unconditional properties of the VaR forecast time series is achieved in all the cases without increasing statistically the degree of serial dependence. As a result, all the extended CAViaR models are able to pass the backtesting analysis at any of the usual confidence levels. Note, for instance, that the *p*-values of the decisive LR_{CC} test

Table 8.6 Backtesting VaR analysis for the trading-extended models

Model	100λ (%)	Viol. (%)	LR_{UC}	*p*-value	LR_{ind}	*p*-value	LR_{cc}	*p*-value	MeanFVaR
Models with trading activity									
Model A	7.5	8.1	0.507	0.477	0.064	0.801	0.428	0.808	1.952
log(V)	5.0	5.5	0.511	0.475	0.362	0.547	0.883	0.643	2.208
	2.5	2.2	0.385	0.535	0.945	0.331	1.324	0.516	2.725
	1.0	0.7	1.016	0.314	0.085	0.771	1.094	0.579	3.253
Model B	7.5	8.1	0.507	0.477	0.064	0.801	0.428	0.808	1.947
log(Ntrades)	5.0	6.0	1.984	0.159	0.609	0.435	2.615	0.271	2.158
	2.5	2.3	0.169	0.681	1.037	0.309	1.201	0.549	2.677
	1.0	0.9	0.105	0.747	0.145	0.703	0.248	0.883	3.274
Model C	7.5	8.2	0.687	0.407	0.033	0.855	0.553	0.759	1.945
log(NS)	5.0	5.5	0.511	0.475	0.362	0.547	0.883	0.643	2.183
	2.5	2.0	1.100	0.294	0.776	0.378	1.866	0.393	2.693
	1.0	0.6	1.886	0.170	0.060	0.806	1.939	0.379	3.347
Model D	7.5	8.0	0.353	0.552	0.012	0.914	0.247	0.884	1.954
log(NSS)	5.0	5.6	0.731	0.393	0.282	0.595	1.026	0.599	2.207
	2.5	1.9	1.608	0.205	0.698	0.404	2.294	0.318	2.743
	1.0	0.6	1.886	0.170	0.060	0.806	1.939	0.379	3.459
Model E	7.5	8.3	0.894	0.344	0.013	0.910	0.715	0.699	1.923
log(TVD)	5.0	6.1	2.388	0.122	1.448	0.229	3.859	0.145	2.133
	2.5	2.8	0.356	0.551	0.076	0.784	0.437	0.804	2.621
	1.0	1.2	0.380	0.538	2.449	0.118	2.833	0.243	3.309

Note: The second column shows the estimation of the sample mean of empirical exceptions. LRUC, LRind and LRcc denote the values of the tests for unconditional coverage, independence and conditional coverage, respectively, whereas the columns labeled as *p*-value show the *p*-values of the respective test statistics. Finally, MeanFVaR denotes the mean of the forecast VaR over the out-of-sample period. Bold letters are used to denote statistical rejection at the 5 percent asymptotic nominal size.

statistics are well above the conventional statistical significance levels, particularly for the set of liquidity-extended CAViaR risk models.

As an example, note that the mean value of exception for the CAViaR model for $\lambda = 7.5$ percent is slightly greater than 10 percent, with the GARCH(1,1) closely matching this value. By sharp contrast, the largest mean value for the set of variables analyzed is 8.7 percent, with some variables yielding an even larger bias reduction. For instance, including variables such as effective spread (ES), relative effective spread (RES) or number of shares sold (NSS) leads to an unconditional coverage not greater than 8 percent. Overall, among all the predictors considered, the ES and RES variables in the liquidity group seem to provide the best results in the backtesting analysis.

Finally, Figure 8.2 shows the plots of the one-day forecasts from the standard CAViaR model and the ES-extended CAViaR model for the

Table 8.7 Backtesting VaR analysis for the liquidity-extended model

Model	100λ (%)	Viol. (%)	LR_{UC}	*p*-value	LR_{ind}	*p*-value	LR_{cc}	*p*-value	MeanFVaR
Models with market liquidity									
Model F	7.5	8.6	0.507	0.477	0.064	0.801	0.428	0.808	1.919
|Log(QS)|	5.0	5.3	0.186	0.666	0.554	0.457	0.746	0.689	2.278
	2.5	2.1	0.694	0.405	0.859	0.354	1.544	0.462	2.836
	1.0	1.0	0.000	1.000	0.182	0.670	0.182	0.913	3.531
Model G	7.5	8.0	0.353	0.552	0.104	0.748	0.339	0.844	2.000
|Log(ES)|	5.0	5.0	0.000	1.000	0.924	0.336	0.924	0.630	2.320
	2.5	2.2	0.385	0.535	0.945	0.331	1.324	0.516	2.849
	1.0	0.9	0.105	0.747	0.145	0.703	0.248	0.883	3.446
Model H	7.5	8.6	1.671	0.196	0.095	0.758	1.503	0.472	1.919
|Log(RQS)|	5.0	5.5	0.511	0.475	0.362	0.547	0.883	0.643	2.215
	2.5	2.4	0.042	0.838	1.132	0.287	1.171	0.557	2.717
	1.0	0.7	1.016	0.314	0.085	0.771	1.094	0.579	3.308
Model I	7.5	7.9	0.227	0.634	0.002	0.968	0.136	0.934	1.969
|Log(RES)|	5.0	5.5	0.511	0.475	0.362	0.547	0.883	0.643	2.222
	2.5	2.4	0.042	0.838	1.132	0.287	1.171	0.557	2.669
	1.0	1.0	0.000	1.000	0.182	0.670	0.182	0.913	3.305

Note: See Tables 8.5 and 8.6 for details.

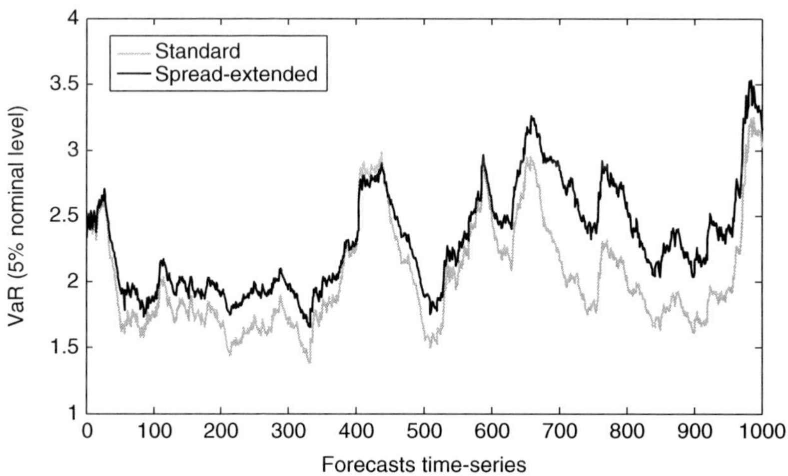

Figure 8.2 Forecasts for the one-day-ahead VaR from the basic SAV and effective spread-extended CAViaR models

5 percent quantile. First, we can observe that the forecasts from the liquidity-extended model tend to be much higher, so the inclusion of liquidity variables tends to generate large changes in the VaR forecasts. Second, and more importantly, the differences in the VaR forecast have the correct sign and, hence, adding liquidity variables reduces significantly the excessive number of exceptions in the baseline SAV–CAViaR model. Similar results arise when analyzing volume-extended models.[3]

8.5 Conclusion

In this chapter we have analyzed the role played by different variables in VaR forecasting by using the quantile-regression methodology proposed by Engle and Manganelli (2004). More specifically, we have analyzed whether market microstructure and trading-related variables have predictive power on the tail distribution of returns. The standard backtesting VaR analysis largely supports the inclusion of these variables. The overall evidence is robust against the inclusion of different measures of liquidity and trading activity as well as for the consideration of different values of the quantile parameter.

Our approach can be related to the so-called liquidity-corrected VaR (LVAR: see Jarrow and Subramanian, 1997; Jorion, 2007), although we provide a different perspective to the problem of forecasting VaR. In particular, while LVAR determines the total VaR as the sum of the "traditional" VaR (as termed in Jorion, 2007: 354) and an additional component related to transaction costs, we use the information conveyed by bid–ask spreads and other variables to forecast the standard VaR itself. The fundamental premise, therefore, is that these variables convey useful information to forecast the tail distribution of conditional returns. The empirical evidence in this chapter strongly supports this hypothesis.

In this chapter, we have considered the value-at-risk measure as the most representative case of a downside risk metric used in practice. Nevertheless, several authors have suggested the use of the so-called expected shortfall (ES), defined as the expected value of the loss of the portfolio at the $(1-\lambda)$ percent confidence level, as a more appropriate measure of risk; see, for instance, Artzner et al. (1999). Taylor (2008) recently proposed a novel procedure in which the ES can be computed using expectiles in a CAViaR-like specification. An interesting question, left for future research, is whether modeling the ES in terms of liquidity and environmental variables may outperform the models that solely consider returns. In view of the empirical evidence discussed in this chapter, this may likely be the case.

Notes

1. Market daily data is available from the CRSP database. We thank Prof. Avanidhar Subrahmanyam for making the remaining data publicly available on his webpage.
2. Optimization is carried out using Matlab R2008a in a PC with processor Intel Core 2, 2.40GHz, and 4.00GB RAM.
3. We do not report these results due to space limitations, but they are available from the authors upon request.

References

Admati, A.R. and Pfleiferer, P. (1988) "A Theory of Intraday Patterns: Volume and Price Variability," *Review of Financial Studies*, 1 (1): 3–40.

Alexander, C. and Sheedy, E. (2008) "Developing a Stress Testing Framework Based on Market Risk Models," *Journal of Banking & Finance*, 32 (10): 2220–2236.

Artzner, P., Dealbaen, F., Eber, J.M. and Heath, D. (1999) "Coherent Measure of Risk," *Mathematical Finance*, 9 (3): 203–228.

Bangia, A., Diebold, F.X., Schuermann, T. and Stroughair, J.D. (1998) "Modeling Liquidity Risk with Implications for Traditional Market Risk Measurement and Management," Working Paper, Wharton School of the University of Pennsylvania, Philadelphia.

Bassett, G.W. and Koenker, R. (1982) "An Empirical Quantile Function for Linear Models with iid Errors." *Journal of the American Statistical Association*, 77 (378): 407–415.

Blume, L., Easly, D. and O'Hara, M. (1994) "Market Statistics and Technical Analysis: The Role of Volume," *Journal of Finance*, 49 (1): 153–181.

Bollerslev, T. and Melvin, M. (1994) "Bid-Ask Spreads and the Volatility in the Foreign Exchange Market," *Journal of International Economics*, 36 (3–4): 355–372.

Bollerslev, T. and Woolridge, J.M. (1992) "Quasi-Maximum Likelihood Estimation and Inference in Dynamic Models with Time-Varying Covariances," *Econometric Reviews*, 11 (2): 143–172.

Campbell, J.Y., Grossman, S.J. and Wang, J. (1993) "Trading Volume and Serial Correlation in Stock Returns," *Quarterly Journal of Economics*, 108 (4): 905–939.

Chordia, T., Roll, R. and Subrahmanyam, A. (2001) "Market Liquidity and Trading Activity," *Journal of Finance*, 56 (2): 501–530.

Christoffersen, P.F. (1998) "Evaluating Interval Forecasts," *International Economic Review*, 39 (4): 841–862.

Dupuy, P. (2008) "Imperfect Information and Contagion in Capital Markets: A Test on Emerging Markets Sovereign Bonds," *Journal of Emerging Market Finance*, 7 (2): 103–140.

Easley, D., Keyfer, N. and O'Hara, M. (1997) "One Day in the Life of a very Common Stock," *Review of Financial Studies*, 10 (3): 805–835.

Engle, R. and Manganelli, S. (2004) "CAViaR: Conditional Autoregressive Value at Risk by Regression Quantiles," *Journal of Business & Economic Statistics*, 22 (4): 367–381.

Goffe, W.L, Ferrier, G.D. and Rogers, J. (1994) "Global Optimization of Statistical Functions with Simulated Annealing," *Journal of Econometrics*, 60 (1–2): 65–99.

Hansen, P.R. and Lunde, A. (2005) "A Forecast Comparison of Volatility Models: Does Anything Beat a GARCH (1,1)?" *Journal of Applied Econometrics*, 20 (7): 873–889.

Jarrow, R. and Protter, P. (2009) "Liquidity Risk and Risk Measure Computation," Forthcoming Review of Futures Markets, Ithaca: Cornell University.

Jarrow, R. and Subramanian, A. (1997) "Mopping up Liquidity," *Risk*, 10 (12): 170–173.

Jorion, P. (2007) *Value at Risk: The New Benchmark for Controlling Market Risk*. Irwin, Chicago: McGraw-Hill.

Koenker, R. and Bassett, G. (1978) "Regression Quantiles," *Econometrica*, 46 (1): 33–50.

Kuester, K., Mittnik, S. and. Paolella, M.S. (2006) "Value-at-Risk Prediction: A Comparison of Alternative Strategies," *Journal of Financial Econometrics*, 4 (1): 53–89.

Kupiec, P. (1995) "Techniques for Verifying the Accuracy of Risk Measurement Models," *The Journal of Derivatives*, 3 (2): 73–84.

Stoll, H.S. (1989) "Inferring the Components of the Bid-Ask Spread: Theory and Empirical Tests," *Journal of Finance*, 44 (1): 115–134.

Taylor, J. (1999) "A Quantile Regression Approach to Estimating the Distribution of Multiperiod Returns." *Journal of Derivatives*, 7(1): 64–78.

Taylor, J. (2008) "Estimating Value at Risk and Expected Shortfall Using Expectiles," *Journal of Financial Econometrics*, 6 (2): 1–22.

9 Portfolio Selection with Time-Varying Value-at-Risk

Erick W. Rengifo and Jeroen V.K. Rombouts

9.1 Introduction

One important venue of portfolio-allocation research started with Markowitz (1952). According to his model, investors maximize their expected return given a risk level measured by the variance. Recently, new risk measures have been proposed with "value-at-risk" (VaR) being one of them. The VaR is defined as the maximum expected loss on an investment over a specified horizon given some confidence level (see Jorion, 1997 for more information).

Campbell et al. (2001) propose a model which allocates financial assets by maximizing the expected return subject to the constraint that the expected maximum loss should meet the VaR limits. Their model is applied in a static context to find optimal weights between stocks and bonds. In this chapter we propose to generalize the work of Campbell et al. (2001), "CHK" hereafter, to a flexible forward-looking dynamic portfolio-selection framework. We propose a dynamic portfolio-selection model that combines assets in order to maximize the portfolio expected return subject to a VaR risk constraint, allowing for future investment recommendations. We determine, from both a statistical and economic point of view, the best daily investment recommendations in terms of percentage to borrow or lend and the optimal weights of the assets in a risky portfolio. For the estimation of the VaR we use ARCH-type models and we investigate the importance of several parametric innovation distributions.[1]

Moreover, following Guermat and Harris (2002) and Jondeau and Rockinger (2003) and, in order to find more accurate VaR forecasts, our approach not only considers time variation in the variance but also allows for evolution of the skewness and kurtosis of the portfolio distributions. The latter is performed by estimating the model parameters by "weighted maximum likelihood" (WML) in an increasing-window setup.

For a data set consisting of two US indices (SP 500 and Russell 2000), we perform out-of-sample forecasts applying our dynamic portfolio-selection model to determine the daily optimal portfolio allocations. We decided to work with two stock indices and not with a bond index in order to capture the asymmetric dependence documented only for stock returns as mentioned by Patton (2004). The dynamic model we propose outperforms the CHK model in terms of failure rates, defined as the number of times the desired confidence level used for the estimation of the VaR is violated and in terms of the dynamic quantile test of Engle and Manganelli (2004) and used to determine the quality of our results. Based on these statistical criteria, the APARCH model gives as good results as the GARCH model. However, if we consider not only the failure rates and the dynamic quantile test but also economic criteria such as the achieved wealth and the risk-adjusted returns, we find that the APARCH model outperforms the GARCH model. Finally, a sensitivity analysis of the distribution innovation shows that the skewed-*t* is preferred to the normal and Student-*t* distributions.

The plan of the chapter is as follows: in Section 9.2 we present the optimal portfolio selection in a VaR framework. In Section 9.3, we describe different model specifications for the estimation of the VaR. Section 9.4 presents two empirical applications using out-of-sample forecasts to determine the optimal investment strategies. We compare the performance of the different models using the failure rates, the dynamic quantile test, the wealth achieved and the risk-adjusted returns as instruments to determine the best model. Section 9.5 evaluates several related aspects of the models and Section 9.6 concludes and provides an outlook for future research.

9.2 Optimal portfolio selection

This section follows Campbell et al. (2001). The portfolio model allocates financial assets by maximizing the expected return subject to a risk constraint, where risk is measured by "value-at-risk" (VaR). The optimal portfolio is such that the maximum expected loss should not exceed the VaR for a chosen investment horizon at a given confidence level. We consider the possibility of borrowing and lending at the market interest rate, considered as given.

Denote by W_t the investor's wealth at time t, b_t the amount of money that he wants to borrow ($b_t > 0$) or lend ($b_t < 0$) at the risk-free rate r_f, according to his desired VaR (VaR_t^*), defined later. Consider n financial assets with prices at time t given by $p_{i,t}$, with $i = 1, \ldots, n$. Define $\Omega_t \equiv [w_t \in R^n : \sum_{i=1}^{n} w_{i,t} = 1]$ as the set of portfolio weights at time t, with well-defined expected rates of return, such that $x_{i,t} = w_{i,t}(W_t + b_t)/p_{i,t}$ is the number of shares of asset i at time t. The budget constraint of the investor is given by:

$$W_t + b_t = \sum_{i=1}^{n} x_{i,t} p_{i,t} = x_t' p_t. \qquad (9.1)$$

The value of the portfolio at $t+1$ is

$$W_{t+1}(w_t) = (W_t + b_t)(1 + R_{t+1}(w_t)) - b_t(1 + r_f), \qquad (9.2)$$

where $R_{t+1}(w_t)$ is the portfolio return at time $t+1$. The VaR of the portfolio is defined as the maximum expected loss over a given investment horizon and for a given confidence level α

$$P_t[W_{t+1}(w_t) \leq W_t - VaR_t^*] \leq 1 - \alpha, \qquad (9.3)$$

where P_t is the probability conditioned on the available information at time t and VaR_t^* is the cut-off return or the investor's desired VaR level. Note that $(1-\alpha)$ is the probability of occurrence. Equation (9.3) represents the second constraint that the investor has to take into account. The portfolio optimization problem can be expressed in terms of the maximization of the expected returns $E_t W_{t+1}(w_t)$, subject to the budget restriction and the VaR constraint:

$$w_t^* \equiv \arg\max_{w_t} (W_t + b_t)(1 + E_t R_{t+1}(w_t)) - b_t(1 + r_f), \qquad (9.4)$$

s.t. (9.1) and (9.3). $E_t W_{t+1}(w_t)$ represents the expected return of the portfolio given the information at time t. The optimization problem may be rewritten in an unconstrained way. To do so, replacing (9.1) in (9.2) and taking expectations yields:

$$E_t W_{t+1}(w_t) = x_t' p_t (E_t R_{t+1}(w_t) - r_f) + W_t(1 + r_f). \qquad (9.5)$$

Equation (9.5) shows that a risk-averse investor wants to invest a fraction of his wealth in risky assets if the expected return of the portfolio is bigger than the risk-free rate. Substituting (9.5) (before taking the E_t) in (9.3) gives:

$$P_t[x_t' p_t(R_{t+1}(w_t) - r_f) + W_t(1+r_f) \leq W_t - VaR_t^*] \leq 1-\alpha, \tag{9.6}$$

such that,

$$P_t\left[R_{t+1}(w_t) \leq r_f - \frac{VaR_t^* + W_t r_f}{x_t' p_t}\right] \leq 1-\alpha, \tag{9.7}$$

defines the quantile $q_t(w_t,\alpha)$ of the distribution of the return of the portfolio at a given confidence level α or probability of occurrence of $(1-\alpha)$. Then, the budget constraint can be expressed as:

$$x_t' p_t = \frac{VaR_t^* + W_t r_f}{r_f - q_t(w_t,\alpha)}. \tag{9.8}$$

Finally, substituting (9.8) in (9.5) and dividing by the initial wealth W_t we obtain:

$$\frac{E_t(W_{t+1}(w_t))}{W_t} = \frac{VaR_t^* + W_t r_f}{W_t r_f - W_t q_t(w_t,\alpha)} E_t(R_{t+1}(w_t) - r_f) = (1+r_f) \tag{9.9}$$

therefore,

$$w_t^* \equiv \arg\max_{w_t} \frac{E_t R_{t+1}(w_t) - r_f}{W_t r_f - W_t q_t(w_t,\alpha)}. \tag{9.10}$$

The two-fund separation theorem applies, that is, the investor's initial wealth and desired VaR (VaR_t^*) do not affect the maximization procedure. As in traditional portfolio theory, investors first allocate the risky assets and second the amount of borrowing and lending. The latter reflects by how much the VaR of the portfolio differs according to the investor's degree of risk aversion measured by the selected VaR level. The amount of money that the investor wants to borrow or lend is found by replacing (9.1) in (9.8):

$$b_t = \frac{VaR_t^* + W_t q_t(w_t^*,\alpha)}{r_f - q_t(w_t^*,\alpha)}. \tag{9.11}$$

In order to solve the optimization problem (9.10) over a large investment horizon T, we partition this in one-period optimizations, that is, if T equals 30 days, we optimize 30 times one-day periods to achieve the desired final horizon.

9.3 Methodology

We observe the following steps in the estimation of the optimal portfolio allocation and its evaluation:

(1) Portfolio construction
In order to implement the model presented in Section 9.2, we form univariate time series of portfolios on which we base the rest of the methodology. In order to do this, we define a grid of weights that satisfy $\Omega_t \equiv [w_t \in R^n : \int_{i=1}^{n} w_{i,t} = 1]$. With these weights we construct different portfolios, one of which should be the optimal one.

(2) Estimation of portfolio returns
A typical model of the portfolio return R_t may be written as follows:

$$R_t = \mu_t + \varepsilon_t, \tag{9.12}$$

where μ_t is the conditional mean and ε_t an error term. In the empirical application we forecast the expected return by the unconditional mean using observations until day $t-1$. We also modeled the expected return by autoregressive processes, but the results were not satisfactory, neither in terms of failure rates nor in terms of wealth evolution. These results are not new, as mentioned for example by Merton (1980) and Fleming et al. (2001), forecasting returns is more difficult than forecasting of variances and covariances.

(3) Estimation of the conditional variance
The error term ε_t in equation (9.12) can be decomposed as $\sigma_t z_t$ where (z_t) is an i.i.d. innovation with mean zero and variance 1. We distinguish three different specifications for the conditional variance σ_t^2:

- The CHK model, similar to the model presented in Section 9.2, where σ_t^2 is estimated as the empirical variance using data until $t-1$. In fact, this can be interpreted as a straightforward dynamic extension of the application presented in Campbell et al. (2001).
- The GARCH(1,1) model of Bollerslev (1986), where

$$\sigma_t^2 = \omega + \alpha \varepsilon_{t-1}^2 + \beta \sigma_{t-1}^2.$$

- The APARCH(1,1) model of Ding et al. (1993), where

$$\sigma_t^\delta = \omega + \alpha_1 (|\varepsilon_{t-1}| - \alpha_n \varepsilon_{t-1})^\delta + \beta_1 \sigma_{t-1}^\delta.$$

with ω, α_1, α_n, β_1 and δ parameters to be estimated. The parameter δ ($\delta > 0$) is the Box–Cox transformation of σ_t. The parameter α_n ($-1 < \alpha_n < 1$), reflects the leverage effect such that a positive (negative) value means that the past negative (positive) shocks have a deeper impact on current conditional volatility than the past positive shocks of the same magnitude. Note that if $\delta = 2$ and $\alpha_n = 0$ we get the GARCH(1,1) model.

With respect to the innovation distribution, several parametric alternatives are available in the literature. In the empirical application, see Section 9.4, we consider the normal, Student-*t* and skewed-*t* distributions. The skewed-*t* distribution was proposed by Hansen (1994) and reparameterized in terms of the mean and the variance by Lambert and Laurent (2001) in such a way that the innovation process has zero mean and unit variance. The skewed-*t* distribution depends on two parameters, one for the thickness of tails (degrees of freedom) and the other for the skewness.

Following Mittnik and Paolella (2000) the parameters of the models are estimated by "weighted maximum likelihood" (WML). We use weights which multiply the log-likelihood contributions of the returns in period t, $t = 1, \ldots, T$. This allows us to give more weight to recent data in order to obtain parameter estimates that reflect the "current" value of the "true" parameter. The weights are defined by:

$$\omega_t = \rho^{T-t}. \tag{9.13}$$

If $\rho < 1$, more weight is given to recent observations than those far in the past. The case $\rho = 1$ corresponds to the usual maximum likelihood estimation. The decay factor ρ is obtained by minimizing the failure rate (defined later in this section) for a given confidence level. Figure 9.1 illustrates the failure rate-ρ relationship for portfolios made of Russell 2000 and S&P 500 indices for an investor using VaR at the 90 percent level. The model used is the GARCH(1,1) with normal innovation distribution. The optimal ρ that minimizes the failure rate is equal to 0.994. We find similar results for other cases. Moreover, the value of the optimal ρ is robust to different innovation distributions. We use WML in an increasing-window set-up, that is, the number of observations of the sample increases through time in order to consider the new information available. The improvement found, in terms of better approximation to the desired confidence levels, by using WML in an increasing-window setup instead of ML is of the order of 10 percent. See also Section 9.5 for more details.

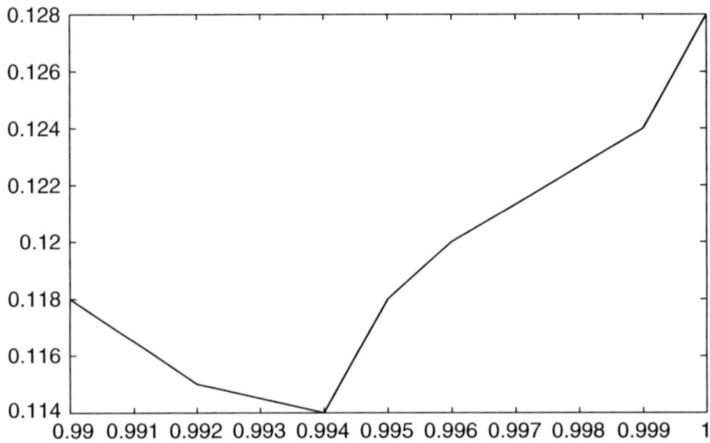

Figure 9.1 Failure rates–ρ relationship
Note: Failure rates (vertical axis) obtained with different ρ-values (horizontal axis) using the geometric weighting scheme for a 1000 out-of-sample period. Portfolios made of Russell 2000 and SP 500 indices for an investor's desired VaR confidence level of $\alpha = 90$ percent. The model used is the GARCH with normal innovation distribution. Out-of-sample period from January 2, 2004 until December 20, 2007 (1000 days).

By using WML in an increasing-window setup, $q_{1-\alpha}$ in (9.14) takes into account the time evolution of the degrees of freedom and asymmetry parameters when we use the skewed-*t* distribution. We do not specify an autoregressive structure for the degrees of freedom and for the asymmetry parameter as in Jondeau and Rockinger (2003), since they find that this approach is subject to serious numerical instabilities.

(4) Estimation of the VaR
The VaR is a quantile of the distribution of the return of a portfolio (see equations [9.3] and [9.7]). In an unconditional setup the VaR of a portfolio may be estimated by the quantile of the empirical distribution at a given confidence level α. In parametric models, such as the ones that we use, the quantiles are functions of the variance of the portfolio return R_t. The $VaR_{t,\alpha}$ (VaR for time t at the confidence level α) is calculated as:

$$VaR_{t,\alpha} = \hat{\mu}_t + \hat{\sigma}_t q_{1-\alpha}, \tag{9.14}$$

where $\hat{\mu}_t$ and $\hat{\sigma}_t$ are the forecasted conditional mean and variance using data until t − 1 and $q_{1-\alpha}$ is the $(1-\alpha)$-th quantile of the innovation distribution.

(5) Determine the optimal risky-portfolio allocation
Once we have determined the VaR for each of the risky portfolios, we use equation (9.10) to find the optimal portfolio weights. These weights correspond to the portfolio that maximizes the expected returns subject to the VaR constraint.

(6) Determine the optimal amount to borrow or lend
As shown in Section 9.2, the two-fund separation theorem applies. Then, in order to determine the amount of money to borrow or lend we simply use equation (9.11).

(7) Evaluate the models
A criterion to evaluate the models is the failure rate:

$$f = \frac{1}{n} \sum_{t=T-n+1}^{T} \mathbf{1}[R_t < -VaR_{t-1,a}], \tag{9.15}$$

where n is the number of out-of-sample days, T is the total number of observations, R_t is the observed return at day t, $VaR_{t-1,\alpha}$ is the threshold value determined at time t − 1 and **1** is the indicator function. A model is correctly specified if the observed return is bigger than the threshold values in 100α per cent of the forecasts. One can perform a likelihood ratio test to compare the failure rate with the desired VaR level, as proposed by Kupiec (1995). We will call this test the Kupiec–LR test in the rest of the chapter.

Another statistical test that we use is the dynamic-quantile test proposed by Engle and Manganelli (2004). According to this test and in order to determine the quality of the results, a property that a VaR measure should have besides respecting the level is that the VaR violations ("hits") should not be serially correlated. This can be tested by defining the following sequence:

$$h_t = \mathbf{1}[R_t < -VaR_{t,\alpha}] - \alpha, \tag{9.16}$$

where the expected value of this sequence is zero. The dynamic-quantile test is computed as an F-test under the null hypothesis that all coefficients, including the intercept, are zero in a regression of the variable h_t on its own past, on current VaR and on any other regressors. In our case, we perform the test using the current VaR and 5 lags of the VaR violations as explanatory variables.

We also evaluate the models by analyzing the wealth evolution generated by the application of the portfolio recommendations of the different models. With this economic criterion, the best model will be the one that reports the highest wealth for similar risk levels. Finally, we evaluate the models by comparing the risk-adjusted returns using equation (9.10), where the expected return is changed by the realized return. With this test we can compare the risk premium adjusted by the risk, measured by the VaR.

9.4 Empirical application

We develop an application of the model presented in the previous sections. We construct 1000 daily out-of-sample portfolio allocations based on conditional variance forecasts of GARCH and APARCH models and compare the results with the ones obtained with the static CHK model. The parameters are estimated using WML in a rolling-window setup. We use the normal, Student-*t* and skewed-*t* distributions in order to investigate the importance of the choice of several innovation densities for different confidence levels. Each of the three models can be combined with the three innovation distributions resulting in nine different specifications. In the applications, we consider an agent's problem of allocating his wealth (set to 1000 US dollars) among two different US indices, Russell 2000 and S&P 500. For the risk-free rate we use the one-year Treasury bill rate in January 2004 (approximately 4.47 percent annual). We have considered only the trading days in which both indices were traded. We define the daily returns as log price differences from the adjusted closing-price series.

To construct the portfolios, according to the first step of Section 9.3, we use a grid of weights of 0.01. Finally, for all the cases the investor's desired VaR_t^* is set to 1 percent of his cumulated wealth at time $t-1$. This assumption makes sense, since we are assuming that the investor is following his investments day-by-day.

With the information until time t, the models' one-day-ahead forecast present the percentage of the cumulated wealth that should be borrowed ($b_t > 0$) or lent ($b_t < 0$) according to the agent's risk aversion expressed by his confidence level α, and the percentage that should be invested in the risky portfolio made of the two indices. The models give the optimal weights of each of the indices in the optimal risky portfolio. We use the real returns obtained with the investment recommendations of the previous day and determine the agent's wealth evolution according to each model's suggestions. Since the parameters of the GARCH and APARCH models change slowly from one day to another, these parameters are reestimated every 10 days to take into account the expanding information and to keep the computation time low. We also reestimate the parameters daily, every 5, 15 and 20 days (results not shown). We find similar results in terms of the parameter estimates. However, in the case of daily and 5-day reestimation, the computational time was about 10-times bigger.

For the estimation of the models we use a Pentium Xeon 2.6 Ghz. The time required for the GARCH and APARCH models is 90 and 120 minutes on average, respectively. Estimating the models with a fixed window requires 60 and 90 minutes on average to run the GARCH and APARCH models, respectively.

In the next section we present the statistical characteristics of the data. Due to space limitations, we introduce two specific examples to show how the models work. Finally, we present the key results for all the models in terms of failure rates, the dynamic-quantile test, the total achieved wealth and the risk-adjusted returns and stress the models' differences.

9.4.1 Description of the data

We use daily data of the S&P 500 composite index (large stocks) and the Russell 2000 index (small stocks). The sample period goes from January 2, 1990 to December 20, 2007 (4531 observations). Descriptive statistics are given in the upper panel of Table 9.1. We see that for all indices skewness and excess kurtosis is present and that the means and standard deviations are similar.

Note that our one-day-ahead forecast horizon corresponds to approximately four years (1000 days). During this period we observe mainly a bull market, except for the last part of 2007, when the indices start a sharp fall. The lower panel of Table 9.1 presents the descriptive statistics corresponding to the out-of-sample period. Note that the volatility in this period for Russell 2000 is higher than the previous one.

9.4.2 A general view of the daily recommendations

We present two examples of model configurations to illustrate our main results. First, we explain the investment decisions based on the CHK model using the normal distribution for portfolios made of Russell 2000–SP 500. The agent's desired VaR confidence level is $\alpha = 90$ percent, that is, a less risk-averse investor. Figure 9.2(a) shows the evolution of the percentage of the total wealth to be borrowed ($b_t > 0$) or lent ($b_t < 0$). In this case the model suggests until day 829 to borrow at the risk-free rate and to invest everything in the risky portfolio. However, after that

Table 9.1 Descriptive statistics

	02/01/1990–20/12/2007 N = 4531	
	SP 500	**Russell 2000**
Mean	0.036	0.039
Standard deviation	0.995	1.079
Skewness	−0.039	−0.244
Kurtosis	3.694	2.663
Minimum	−6.866	−7.256
Maximum	5.733	5.842
	02/01/2004–20/12/2007 N = 1000	
	SP 500	**Russell 2000**
Mean	0.030	0.039
Standard deviation	0.759	1.313
Skewness	−0.272	−0.142
Kurtosis	1.806	0.445
Minimum	−3.473	−3.966
Maximum	2.921	3.973

Note: Descriptive statistics for the daily returns of the corresponding indices. The mean, the standard deviation, the minimum and maximum values are expressed in percent.

day the model recommendation is to change from borrowing to lending. This is a natural response to the negative change in the trend of the indices and to the higher volatility observed in the stock market during the last days of the out-of-sample period (the subprime problem starts to appear in the US market). Figure 9.2(b) presents the evolution of the share of the risky portfolio to be invested in the Russell 2000 index. The model suggests for 807 days investing 70 percent of the wealth (on average) in the Russell 2000 index and the difference in the SP 500 index. After that day, the model recommendations change drastically favoring the investment in SP 500, which increases its portfolio weights to 66 percent, that is, going from 30 percent to almost 50 percent at the end of the out-of-sample period. Again, this responds to the higher volatility of the Russell 2000 compared with the SP 500 during the last days of our out-of-sample period. In summary, the model recommends shifting from the more risky index to the less risky one and from the risky portfolio to the risk-free investment.

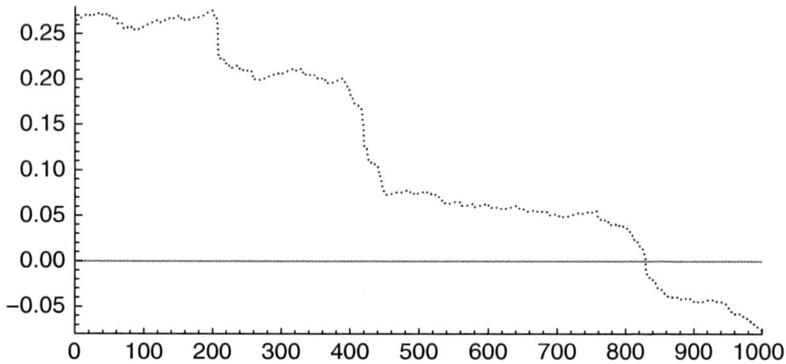

(a) Risk-free weights for portfolios made of Russell 2000 and SP 500 indices for an investor's desired VaR confidence level of $\alpha = 90$ percent

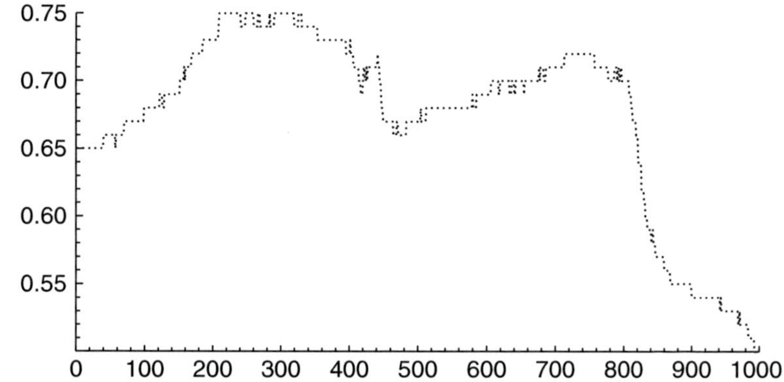

(b) Risky weights of Russell 2000 for an investor's desired VaR confidence level of $\alpha = 90$ percent

Figure 9.2 Weights using CHK model with normal distribution: Out-of-sample period from January 2, 2004 until December 31, 2007 (1000 days).

Figure 9.3 compares the wealth evolution obtained by applying the CHK model suggestions with investments made in either one or the other index. The wealth evolution is higher than the one that could be obtained by investing only in Russell 2000 but lower if investing only in SP 500 during the out-of-sample forecast period. We also include the wealth evolution that an agent can realize when investing everything at the risk-free rate (assumed as constant during the whole forecasted period). More details can be found in Section 9.4.3.

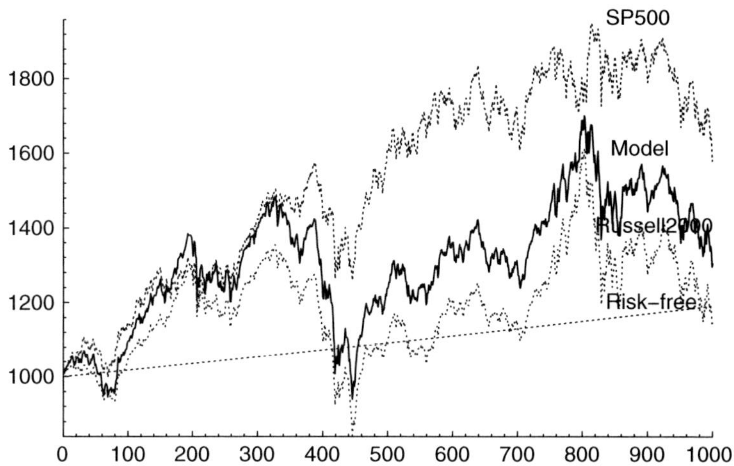

Figure 9.3 Wealth evolution using CHK model
Note: Portfolios made of Russell 2000 and SP 500 indices for an investor's desired VaR confidence level of $\alpha = 90$ percent. Wealth evolution for 1000 out-of-sample forecast using the model recommendations (Model) compared with the wealth evolution obtained by investments made on Russell 2000 or SP 500 alone and with investments done at the risk-free rate. Out-of-sample period from 02/01/2004 until 20/12/2007.

The previous illustration shows how the model recommendations change according to new information coming to the market, allowing the agent to maximize expected return subject to budget and risk constraints in a dynamic way. The next section presents more synthetically the comparison of all models for different distributional assumptions and different confidence levels.

9.4.3 Results

This section presents concisely the results of all the model configurations we used. We compare the three different models explained in Section 9.3: the CHK model in which the variance is estimated simply from the observed past returns and the parametric dynamic model in which the conditional variance is estimated using either the GARCH or the APARCH model. Moreover, we investigate three different distributional assumptions: the normal, the Student-t and the skewed-t. We consider three VaR confidence levels: 90 percent, 95 percent and 99 percent, corresponding to increasing risk aversion and show how these levels affect the results. The parameters are estimated using WML in a rolling-window setup.

From the optimization procedure presented in Section 9.2, see equation (9.10), we determine the weights of the risky portfolio and, considering the agent's desired risk expressed by the desired VaR (VaR_t^*), the amount to borrow or lend; see equation (9.11). With this information at time t the investment strategy for day $t+1$ is set: percentage of wealth to borrow or lend and percentage to be invested in the risky portfolio. In order to evaluate the models we consider the wealth evolution of the initial invested amount, the risk-adjusted returns, the failure rate of the returns obtained by applying the strategies with respect to the desired VaR level and the dynamic-quantile test. A model is good when the wealth and adjusted return are high, when the failure rate is respected and when the VaR violations are not serially correlated.

We expect that the forecasted VaRs by the different models be less than or equal to the threshold values. We present the Kupiec–LR test for the portfolios made of Russell 2000–SP 500 (Table 9.2), for the probabilities of

Table 9.2 Results for portfolios made of Russell 2000 – SP 500

		Normal			**Student-*t***			**Skewed-*t***		
1 − α	**Model**	**FR**	**p**	**r**	**FR**	**p**	**r**	**FR**	**p**	**r**
0.10	**CHK**	**0.177**	0.000	6.9	**0.200**	0.000	6.8	**0.188**	0.000	6.8
	GARCH	**0.114**	0.148	7.9	**0.130**	0.002	7.8	0.117	0.080	7.7
	APARCH	0.126	0.008	12.2	0.129	0.003	13.0	0.118	0.064	9.5
0.05	**CHK**	0.127	0.000	6.7	**0.135**	0.000	6.8	**0.120**	0.000	6.7
	GARCH	**0.071**	0.004	7.3	**0.074**	0.001	7.3	0.060	0.159	7.1
	APARCH	**0.083**	0.000	10.6	0.081	0.000	11.0	0.062	0.093	8.2
0.01	**CHK**	**0.068**	0.000	6.3	**0.048**	0.000	6.2	**0.032**	0.000	6.0
	GARCH	**0.029**	0.000	6.6	0.021	0.002	6.7	0.011	0.754	6.4
	APARCH	0.030	0.000	8.9	0.027	0.000	8.5	0.012	0.538	7.0

Notes: **FR** are the empirical tail probabilities for the out-of-sample forecast for portfolios made of linear combinations of Russell 2000 and SP 500 indices. The Kupiec–LR test is used to determine the specification of the models. The null hypothesis is that the model is correctly specified, that is, that the failure rate is equal to the probability of occurrence $1-\alpha$. **p** is the *p*-value for this test. **r** is the annualized rate of return in (%). Bold numbers refer to the results that do not satisfy the dynamic-quantile test at the 5 percent confidence level, in terms of their *p*-values of the F-test under the null hypothesis that all coefficients, including the intercept, are zero in a regression of the variable h_t on its own past and on current VaR. The risk-free interest rate is 4.47 percent annual. The results are obtained using WML with $\rho = 0.994$.

occurrence of $1-\alpha=10$ percent (upper panel), 5 percent (middle panel) and 1 percent (lower panel). Several failure rates are significantly different from their nominal levels when we do out-of-sample forecasts. For in-sample forecasts (results not presented) we found p-values as high as those presented by Giot and Laurent (2004), for example. This is understandable since the information set, on which we condition, contains only past observations so that the failure rates tend to be significantly different from their nominal levels. However, these failure rates are not completely out of scope of the desired confidence level (see, for example, Mittnik and Paolella, 2000 for similar results).

Moreover, we estimate the dynamic-quantile test proposed by Engle and Manganelli (2004) in order to determine the quality of our results. With this test, we evaluate the property that any VaR measure should have besides respecting the level: the VaR violations (h_t) should not be serially correlated. We perform the test using the current VaR and 5 lags of the VaR violations as explanatory variables. The results (shown in the tables) suggest that most of the static results present serially correlated VaR violations. The GARCH outputs present mixed results, and for almost all the results of the APARCH model this test is satisfied, meaning that in this case the VaR violations are not serially correlated.

Table 9.2 presents the failure rates, the p-values for the Kupiec–LR ratio test and the annualized rate of returns for portfolios made of Russell 2000 and SP 500. In general, we observe that the dynamic model performs considerably better than its CHK counterpart for any VaR confidence level α. In terms of the distributional assumption we see that in the case of the probability of occurrence of $1-\alpha=10$ percent the normal distribution performs better than the Student-t even for low degrees of freedom (7 on average). This happens because the two densities cross each other at more or less that confidence level. See Guermat and Harris (2002) for similar results. Looking at lower probabilities of occurrence (higher confidence levels), one remarks that the skewed-t distribution performs better than the other two distributions. This is due to the fact that the skewed-t distribution allows not only for fatter tails but it can also capture the asymmetry present in the long and short sides of the market. This result is consistent with the findings of Mittnik and Paolella (2000), Giot and Laurent (2003) and Giot and Laurent (2004), who used single indices, stocks, exchange rates or a portfolio with unique weights.

With respect to the conditional variance models, we observe that for all the confidence levels, the APARCH model performs almost as good as the GARCH model. However, considering that an agent wants to maximize his expected return subject to a risk constraint, we look for good results for portfolio optimization (in terms of the final wealth achieved, presented in Table 9.2 in terms of the annualized returns), respecting the desired VaR confidence level (measured by the failure rate). We can appreciate the following facts: first, the annualized rate of return obtained by the static model is not only lower than those attained by the dynamic models but also, as pointed out before, has a higher risk. Second, even though we cannot select a best model between the APARCH and GARCH models in terms of failure rates, we can see that for almost the same level of risk the APARCH model investment recommendations allow the agent to get the highest annualized rate of return. Therefore, we infer that the APARCH model outperforms the GARCH model. Thus, if an investor is less risk averse ($1 - \alpha = 10$ percent) he could have earned an annualized rate of return of 9.5 percent, two times bigger than simple investing at the risk-free rate.

Finally, we compute the evolution of the risk-adjusted returns. On average, 90 percent of the time the risk-adjusted returns obtained by the APARCH model outperform the ones obtained using the GARCH model. With this test, we can confirm that indeed the APARCH model outperforms the GARCH model.

9.5 Evaluation

9.5.1 Risk-free interest rate sensitivity

We have used as a risk-free interest rate the one-year Treasury bill rate in January 2004 (approximately 4.47 percent annual) as an approximation for the average risk-free rate during the whole out-of-sample period (January 2004 to December 2007). In order to analyze the sensitivity of our results to changes of the risk-free rate, we develop four scenarios based on increments (+1 percent and +4 percent) or decrements (−1 percent and −4 percent) with respect to the benchmark.

The results show that neither the borrowing/lending nor the risky portfolio weights are strongly affected by either of these scenarios. This is due to the fact that we are working with daily optimizations, and that those interest rates (at a daily frequency) are low. For example, 4.47 percent annual equals 0.01749 percent daily (based on 250 days).

9.5.2 Time-varying Kurtosis and asymmetry

As in Guermat and Harris (2002), our framework allows for time-varying degrees of freedom parameters, related to the kurtosis, when working with either the Student-*t* or the skewed-*t* distributions. Moreover, when the skewed-*t* distribution is used we allow for time-varying asymmetry parameters. Figure 9.4 presents the pattern of the degrees of freedom and asymmetry parameter of the skewed-t distribution estimated using the APARCH model. Similar to Jondeau and Rockinger (2003), we find time dependence of the asymmetry parameter but we also remark that the degrees of freedom parameter is time varying.

We also test the significance of the asymmetry parameter and of the asymmetry and degrees of freedom parameters, for the Student-t and skewed-t, respectively. We find that they are highly significant.

9.5.3 Weighted maximum likelihood vs. maximum likelihood

We study the effect of using weighted maximum likelihood (WML) instead of maximum likelihood (ML). Note that when $\rho = 1$ WML is equal to ML. Table 9.3 presents a comparison of failure rates for portfolios made of Russell 2000–SP 500. Both dynamic models improve their failure rates by using WML in a rolling-window setup instead of ML. In terms of the p-values (not presented) it turns out that when ML is used almost none of the failure rates were significant at any level. Thus, using WML helps to satisfy the investor's desired level of risk.

9.5.4 Rolling window of fixed size

We analyze the effect of using a rolling window of fixed size. The idea behind this procedure is that we assume that information until n days in the past conveys some useful information for the prices, meanwhile the rest of the information does not. We use a rolling window of fixed size of $n = 1000$ days for performing the out-of-sample forecasts. The results presented in Table 9.4 show that the gains in better model specification are nil: the failure rates are worse and the final wealth achieved is almost the same. The computational time decreases (about 30 percent less).

9.5.5 VaR subadditivity problem

According to Artzner et al. (1999), Frey and McNeil (2002) and Szegö (2002), a coherent risk measure satisfies the following axioms: translation invariance, subadditivity, positive homogeneity and monotonicity. They show that VaR satisfies all but one of the requirements to be considered as a coherent risk measure: the subadditivity property. Subadditivity means that "a merger does not create extra risk," that is, that diversification must reduce risk. Moreover, the VaR is not convex with respect to portfolio rebalancing no matter what the assumption made on the return distribution. Following Consigli (2002), we do not discuss the limits of the VaR and instead we try to generate more accurate VaR estimates considering the asymmetry and kurtosis of the financial data.

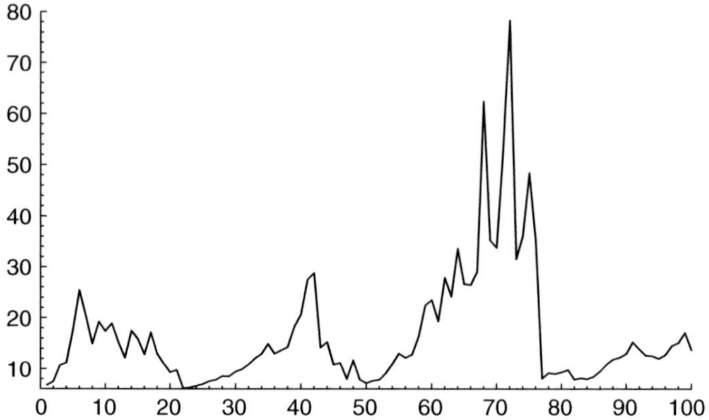

(a) Degrees of freedom

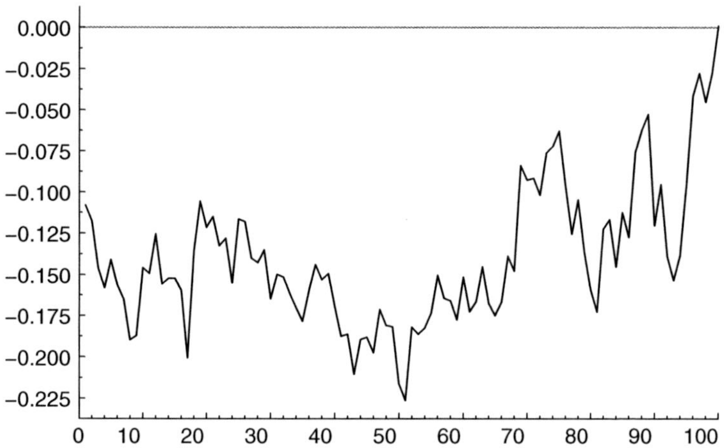

(b) Asymmetry parameter

Figure 9.4 Time-varying degrees of freedom and asymmetry parameters
(a) Degrees of freedom
(b) Asymmetry parameter
Note: Time-varying degrees of freedom and asymmetry for the skewed-*t* innovation distribution estimated using the APARCH model. The parameters are estimated every 10 days during the out-of-sample forecast. The figure corresponds to a portfolio made only of RUSSELL 2000.

Table 9.3 Comparison of failure rates

		Normal		Student-*t*		Skewed-*t*	
$1-\alpha$	Model	ML	WML	ML	WML	ML	WML
0.10	CHK	0.177	0.177	0.200	0.200	0.188	0.188
	GARCH	0.128	0.114	0.153	0.130	0.139	0.117
	APARCH	0.132	0.126	0.149	0.129	0.126	0.118
0.05	CHK	0.127	0.127	0.135	0.135	0.120	0.120
	GARCH	0.085	0.071	0.094	0.074	0.069	0.060
	APARCH	0.085	0.083	0.086	0.081	0.068	0.062
0.01	CHK	0.068	0.068	0.048	0.048	0.032	0.032
	GARCH	0.037	0.029	0.026	0.021	0.011	0.011
	APARCH	0.040	0.030	0.030	0.027	0.014	0.012

Note: Comparison of empirical tail probabilities for the out-of-sample forecast for portfolios made of linear combinations of Russell 2000 and SP 500 using the ML procedure ($\rho = 1$) with WML with $\rho = 0.994$.

Table 9.4 Results for portfolios made of Russell 2000 – SP 500, using ML with rolling window of fixed size

		Normal			Student-*t*			Skewed-*t*		
$1-\alpha$	Model	FR	p	r	FR	p	r	FR	p	r
0.10	CHK	**0.177**	0.000	6.9	**0.200**	0.000	6.8	**0.188**	0.000	6.8
	GARCH	**0.133**	0.001	7.0	**0.148**	0.000	6.4	0.129	0.003	6.8
	APARCH	0.141	0.000	13.6	0.145	0.000	14.3	0.130	0.002	9.9
0.05	CHK	0.127	0.000	6.7	**0.135**	0.000	6.8	**0.120**	0.000	6.7
	GARCH	**0.081**	0.000	6.6	**0.088**	0.000	6.5	0.069	0.009	6.5
	APARCH	**0.085**	0.000	12.1	0.087	0.000	11.8	0.067	0.019	8.6
0.01	CHK	**0.068**	0.000	6.3	**0.048**	0.000	6.2	**0.032**	0.000	6.0
	GARCH	**0.039**	0.000	6.2	0.028	0.000	5.9	0.012	0.538	5.7
	APARCH	0.045	0.000	10.0	0.031	0.000	9.5	0.016	0.079	7.5

Notes: **FR** are the empirical tail probabilities for the out-of-sample forecast for portfolios made of linear combinations of Russell 2000 and SP 500 using a rolling window of fixed size of 1000 days. The Kupiec–LR test is used to determine the specification of the models. The null hypothesis is that the model is correctly specified, that is, that the failure rate is equal to the probability of occurrence $1-\alpha$. **p** is the *p*-value for this test. **r** is the annualized rate of return in (%). Bold numbers refer to the results that do not satisfy the dynamic-quantile test at the 5 percent confidence level, in terms of their *p*-values of the F-test under the null hypothesis that all coefficients, including the intercept, are zero in a regression of the variable h_t on its own past and on current VaR. The risk-free interest rate is 4.47 percent annual. The results are obtained using WML with $\rho = 0.994$.

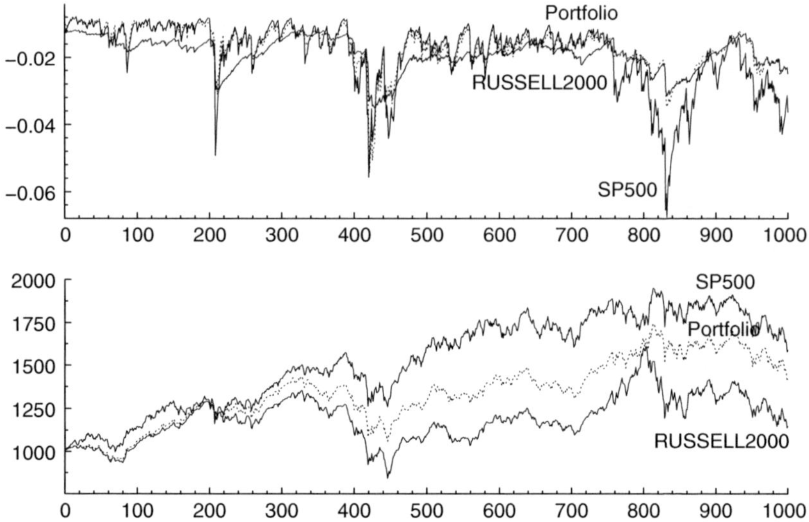

Figure 9.5 Compared VaR and wealth evolution: Russell 2000 – SP 500
Note: VaR evolution for a confidence level of $\alpha = 95$ percent (above) and wealth evolution (below) for SP 500, Russell 2000 and for the optimal portfolios using a GARCH model with skewed-*t* innovation distribution. Out-of-sample period goes from January 2, 2004 until December 20, 2007.

Figure 9.5 presents the VaR and wealth evolution for an investor whose desired confidence level is 95 percent for portfolios made of Russell 2000 and SP 500, the model used is GARCH and the innovation distribution is the skewed-*t*. The optimal portfolio VaRs are consistently smaller that the VaRs of the individual series. This is the case for all the models in our empirical application, implying that by combining the two indices optimally we are reducing the risk. Moreover, the portfolio model not only allows us to decrease risk but also to obtain portfolio returns between the returns of the individual indices.

9.6 Conclusions and future work

The dynamic portfolio-selection model we propose performs well out-of-sample statistically in terms of failure rates, defined as the number of times the desired confidence level used for the estimation of the VaR is violated and in terms of the dynamic-quantile test, used to determine the quality of our results. Based on the failure-rate test, the APARCH model gives as good results as the GARCH model. However, if we consider not only the failure-rate test but also the dynamic-quantile test, the wealth achieved and the risk-adjusted returns, we find that the APARCH model outperforms the GARCH model. A sensitivity analysis of the distribution of the innovations shows that in general the skewed-t is preferred to the normal and Student-t distributions. Estimating the model parameters by weighted maximum likelihood in an increasing-window setup allows us to account for a changing time pattern of the degrees of freedom and asymmetry parameters of the innovation distribution and to improve the forecasting results in the statistical and economical sense: smaller failure rates, larger final wealth and risk-adjusted returns.

There are a number of directions for further research along the lines presented here. A potential extension could use the dynamic model to study the optimal time of portfolio rebalancing, as day-to-day portfolio rebalancing may be neither practicable nor economically viable. A more ambitious extension is to work in a multivariate setting, where a group of different financial instruments are used to maximize the expected return subject to a risk constraint. Another interesting extension of the model is to investigate its intra-daily properties. This extension could be of special interest for traders who face the market second-by-second during the trading hours in the financial markets.

Notes

The authors would like to thank Walid Ben Omrane, Luc Bauwens, Pierre Giot, Sébastien Laurent, Bruce Lehmann, Samuel Mongrut, Olivier Scaillet and Léopold Simar for helpful discussions and suggestions. The usual disclaimers apply. This research was partially carried out while both authors were at the Center for Operations Research and Econometrics (CORE), at the Université Catholique de Louvain, and we wish to extend particular thanks to Luc Bauwens and members of CORE for providing a great research environment. The usual disclaimers apply.

Corresponding author. Economics Department, Fordham University, 441 East Fordham Road, Bronx, NY 10458–9993, USA. Tel (+1) 718 817 4061, Fax (+1) 718 817 3518, e-mail: rengifomina@fordham.edu.

1. The VaR is estimated by computing the quantiles from parametric distributions or by nonparametric procedures such as empirical quantiles or smoothing techniques. See Gourieroux, Laurent and Scaillet (2000) for an example of the latter techniques.

References

Artzner, P., Delbaen, F., Eber, J. and Heath, D. (1999) "Coherent Measures of Risk," *Mathematical Finance*, 9 (3): 203–228.

Bollerslev, T. (1986) "Generalized Autoregressive Conditional Heteroskedasticity," *Journal of Econometrics*, 52 (4): 5–59.

Campbell, R., Huisman, R. and Koedijk, K. (2001) "Optimal Portfolio Selection in a Value-at-Risk Framework," *Journal of Banking and Finance*, 25 (9): 1789–1804.

Consigli, G. (2002) "Tail Estimation and Mean-VaR Portfolio Selection in Markets Subject to Financial Inestability," *Journal of Banking and Finance*, 26 (7): 1355–1382.

Ding, Z., Granger, C. and Engle, R. (1993) "A Long Memory Property of Stock Market Returns and a New Model," *Journal of Empirical Finance*, 1 (1): 83–106.

Engle, R. and Manganelli, S. (2004) "CAViaR: Conditional Autoregressive Value at Risk by Regression Quantile," *Journal of Business and Economic Statistics*, 22 (4): 367–381.

Fleming, J., Kirby, C. and Ostdiek, B. (2001) "The Economic Value of Volatility Timing," *Journal of Finance*, 56 (1): 329–352.

Frey, R. and McNeil, A. (2002) "VaR and Expected Shorfall in Portfolios of Dependent Credit Risks: Conceptual and Practical Insights," *Journal of Banking and Finance*, 26 (7): 1317–1334.

Giot, P. and Laurent, S. (2003) "Value-at-Risk for Long and Short Trading Positions," *Journal of Applied Econometrics*, 18 (6): 641–663.

Giot, P. and Laurent, S. (2004) "Modelling Daily Value-at-Risk Using Realized Volatility and ARCH Type Models," *Journal of Empirical Finance*, 11 (3): 379–398.

Gourieroux, C., Laurent, J. and Scaillet, O. (2000) "Sensitivity Analysis of Values at Risk," *Journal of Empirical Finance*, 7 (3–4): 225–245.

Guermat, C. and Harris, D. (2002) "Forecasting Value at Risk Allowing for Time Variation in the Variance and Kurtosis of Portfolio Returns," *International Journal of Forecasting*, 18 (3): 409–419.

Hansen, B. (1994) "Autoregressive Conditional Density Estimation," *International Economic Review*, 35 (3): 705–730.

Jondeau, E. and Rockinger, M. (2003) "Conditional Volatility, Skewness, and Kurtosis: Existence, Persistence, and Comovements," *Journal of Economic Dynamics and Control*, 27 (10): 1699–1737.

Jorion, P. (1997) *Value-at-Risk: The New Benchmark for Controlling Market Risk*. New York: McGraw-Hill.

Kupiec, P. (1995) "Techniques for Verifying the Accuracy of Risk Measurement Models," *The Journal of Derivatives*, 3 (2): 174–184.

Lambert, P. and Laurent, S. (2001) "Modelling Financial Time Series using GARCH-type Models with a Skewed Student Distribution for the Innovations," Working Paper 0125, Institut de Statistique, Université Catholique de Louvain, Louvain-la-Neuve, Belgium.

Markowitz, H.M. (1952) "Portfolio Selection," *Journal of Finance*, 7 (1): 77–91.

Merton, R. (1980) "On Estimating the Expected Return on the Market: An Exploratory Investigation," *Journal of Financial Economics*, 8 (4): 323–361.

Mittnik, S. and Paolella, M. (2000) "Conditional Density and Value-at-Risk Prediction of Asian Currency Exchange Rates," *Journal of Forecasting*, 19 (4): 313–333.

Patton, A. (2004) "On the Out-of-sample Importance of Skewness and Asymmetric Dependence for Asset Allocation," *Journal of Financial Econometrics*, 2 (1): 130–168.

Szegö, G. (2002) "Measures of Risk," *Journal of Banking and Finance*, 26 (7): 1253–1272.

10
A Risk and Forecasting Analysis of West Texas Intermediate Prices

David E. Allen and Abhay Kumar Singh

10.1 Introduction

As one of the biggest traded commodities, the behavior of crude oil prices has enormous significance and impacts the different parts of the world economy including government, private enterprises and investors among others. Therefore, there are increasing demands for a better characterization and prediction of crude oil prices. The four major benchmarks in the world of international oil trading today are: (1) West Texas Intermediate (WTI), the reference crude for the USA, (2) Brent, the reference crude oil for the North Sea, (3) Dubai, the benchmark crude oil for the Middle East and Far East, and (4) Tapis, the benchmark crude oil for the Asia–Pacific region. West Texas Intermediate (WTI) is the major benchmark of crude oil prices in the Australian market.

Various time-series modeling techniques including ARMA, ARIMA, ARCH, GARCH etc. have been used in oil-price and volatility prediction in the past. In addition, some advanced learning algorithms including neural networks, genetic algorithms, machine learning etc. are frequently tested. "Support-vector machines" (SVMs) are a new generation of learning systems based on recent advances in statistical learning theory. The "Vapnik–Chervonenkis theory" (also known as VC theory) was developed from 1960–1990 by Vladimir Vapnik and Alexey Chervonenkis. The concept of the support-vector machine was developed by Vapnik (1995) and his colleagues. The theory is a form of computational learning theory which attempts to explain the learning process from a statistical point of view. Established on the unique theory of the structural risk-minimization principle to estimate a function by minimizing an upper bound of the generalization error, SVM is resistant to the over-fitting problem and can model nonlinear relations in an efficient and stable way. Furthermore, SVM is trained as a convex optimization problem resulting in a global solution that in many cases yields unique solutions. Originally, SVMs were developed for classification tasks (Burges, 1998). With the introduction of Vapnik's ε -insensitive loss function, SVMs have been extended to solve nonlinear regression and time-series prediction problems; and they exhibit excellent performance (Huang et al., 2005; Muller et al., 1997).

The widely used risk standard, "value-at-risk" (VaR), reduces the risk associated with any kind of asset to just a number (an amount in terms of a currency). One of the objectives of this study is to employ a new value-at-risk methods' approach proposed by Engle and Manganelli (2004) to the forecasting of oil-price risk. Previous work in oil-price risk measurement has employed various other techniques including the ARMA historical simulation approach (Cabedo and Moya, 2003), ARCH-based volatility measures (Kuper, 2002) and other VaR-based risk-measuring techniques (Sauter and Awerbuch, 2002).

In this study we employ CAViaR, the value-at-risk modeling technique that uses quantile regression, to forecast WTI value-at-risk, which has not been used in its original state to predict value-at-risk for oil prices. We also show the applicability of "support-vector regression" for oil-price prediction and compare it with ARIMA modeling.

The rest of the chapter is divided into 6 sections; the following section gives the background and introduces quantile regression, the CAViaR model, ARIMA and support-vector machine regression. Section 10.3 presents the data and methodology used in the study. Section 10.4 discusses the results of the CAViaR implementation on WTI oil prices followed by Section 10.5 which compares the forecasting results obtained from ARIMA and support-vector regression techniques. Section 10.6 provides the conclusion.

10.2 Background

10.2.1 CAViaR and quantile regression

The problem in estimating VaR is that it is a particular quantile of potential future portfolio values, conditioned on current available information. However, portfolio returns and risk change over time, so a time-varying forecasting procedure is required. Essentially this involves forecasting a value each period that will be exceeded with a probability of $(1-\theta)$ by the current portfolio value. In this case $\theta \in (0,1)$ are representative of the confidence level attached to the VaR.

Engle and Manganelli (2004) used the robust technique of quantile regression and proposed another method for calculation of value-at-risk, which they termed "conditional autoregressive value-at-risk by regression quantiles," or CAViaR. CAViaR uses quantile regressions and instead of modeling the whole return distribution for calculation of VaR, it models the required quantiles of the return distribution directly. To predict the value-at-risk by modeling the lower quantiles, the model uses a conditional autoregressive specification, inspired by the fact that the distribution of volatilities over time is autocorrelated, hence the model. In their CAViaR paper, Engle and Manganelli (2004) propose four different specification processes for the calculation of value-at-risk: an "adaptive" model, a "symmetric absolute value" model, an "asymmetric slope" model and an "indirect GARCH" model. We follow suit and test the relative suitability of all the four models on our Australian sample data set in the calculation of VaR.

The first model, an adaptive model, is a smoothed version of a step function (for finite G), and is given by

$$f_t(\beta_1) = f_{t-1}(\beta_1) + \beta_1\{[1+\exp(G[y_{t-1} - f_{t-1}(\beta_1)])]^{-1} - \theta\}, \qquad (10.1)$$

where G is some positive finite number. Engle and Manganelli suggest that the adaptive model incorporates the following rule: "whenever VaR is exceeded, you should immediately increase it, but in circumstances where you do not exceed it, you should decrease it very slightly." This strategy serves to reduce the probability of sequences of hits whilst also making it improbable that there will never be hits. The structure of this model means it learns little from returns that are either close to the VaR or are extremely positive, when G is large. It increases the VaR by the same amount regardless of whether the returns exceed the VaR by a small margin or a large margin. This model has a unit coefficient on the lagged VaR.

A second model that features symmetric absolute values is set out below:

$$f_t(\beta) = \beta_1 + \beta_2 f_{t-1}(\beta) + \beta_3 |y_{t-1}| \qquad (10.2)$$

A third has an asymmetric slope:

$$f_t(\beta) = \beta_1 + \beta_2 f_{t-1}(\beta) + \beta_3 (y_{t-1})^+ + \beta_4 (y_{t-1})^- \qquad (10.3)$$

where, notation $(x)+ = max(x,0)$, $(x)^- = -min(x,0)$.

Whilst the fourth is an indirect GARCH(1,1):

$$f_t(\beta) = (\beta_1 + \beta_2 f_{t-1}^2(\beta) + \beta_3 y_{t-1}^2)^{1/2} \tag{10.4}$$

Engle and Manganelli point out that both the first and third models respond symmetrically to past returns, whereas the second is more flexible in the sense of permitting different responses to positive and negative. Furthermore, all three models are mean-reverting given the coefficient on the lagged VaR is not constrained to be 1.

Engle and Manganelli (2004) state that "the indirect GARCH model would be correctly specified if the underlying data were truly a GARCH(1, 1) with an independent and identically distributed (i.i.d.) error distribution. The symmetric absolute value and asymmetric slope quantile specifications would be correctly specified by a GARCH process in which the standard deviation, rather than the variance, is modeled either symmetrically or asymmetrically with i.i.d. errors." Earlier versions of this type of model were developed by Taylor (1986) and Schwert (1988), whilst Engle (2002) did further analysis of it. A merit of the CAViaR specification, as suggested by Engle and Manganelli (2004), is that it is more general than these GARCH models.

The VaR results from the four methods are tested using a dynamic-quantile test, as proposed by Engle and Manganelli (2004). We will omit further details of the methods for the sake of brevity, as further insights can be obtained from their original paper.

Quantile regression

CAViaR uses quantile regression for estimation of its parameters. Quantile regression was first introduced by Koenker and Bassett (1978). Koenker and Bassett showed how to extend the notion of a sample quantile to a linear regression model.

Quantile regression, as introduced in Koenker and Bassett (1978), is an extension of classical least squares estimation of conditional mean models to the estimation of a group of models for conditional quantile functions. The central special case is the median regression estimator that minimizes a sum of absolute errors. The remaining conditional quantile functions are estimated by minimizing an asymmetrically weighted sum of absolute errors. Taken together the set of estimated conditional quantile functions offers a much more complete view of the effect of covariates on the location, scale and shape of the distribution of the response variable.

In linear regression, the regression coefficient represents the change in the response variable produced by a one-unit change in the predictor variable associated with that coefficient. The quantile-regression parameter estimates the change in a specified quantile of the response variable produced by a one-unit change in the predictor variable.

The quantiles or percentiles, or occasionally fractiles, refer to the general case of dividing a data set into parts. Quantile regression seeks to extend these ideas to the estimation of conditional quantile functions – models in which quantiles of the conditional distribution of the response variable are expressed as functions of observed covariates.

In quantile regression, the median estimator minimizes the symmetrically weighted sum of absolute errors (where the weight is equal to 0.5) to estimate the conditional median function – other conditional quantile functions are estimated by minimizing an asymmetrically weighted sum of absolute errors, where the weights are functions of the quantile of interest. This makes quantile regression robust to the presence of outliers.

In summary, consider a series of observations $y_1, \ldots y_T$ generated by the following model

$$y_t = \mathbf{x'}_\mathbf{t}\boldsymbol{\beta}^0 + \varepsilon_{\theta t}, \quad Quant_\theta(\varepsilon_{\theta t} | \mathbf{x_t}) = 0, \tag{10.5}$$

where $\mathbf{x_t}$ is a p-vector of regressors and $Quant_\theta(\varepsilon_{\theta t} | \mathbf{x_t})$ is the θ-quantile of $\varepsilon_{\theta t}$ conditional on $\mathbf{x_t}$. Let $f_t(\boldsymbol{\beta}) \equiv \mathbf{x}_t\boldsymbol{\beta}$. Then the θth regression quantile is defined as any $\hat{\boldsymbol{\beta}}$ that solves:

$$\min_\beta \frac{1}{T}\sum_{t=1}^{T}[\theta - \mathbf{I}(y_t < f_t(\boldsymbol{\beta}))]\,[y_t - f_t(\boldsymbol{\beta})] \tag{10.6}$$

We will not discuss further the mathematical details of the regression technique – please refer to Koenker's (2005) monograph for a comprehensive discussion.

10.2.2 Autoregressive Integrated Moving Average (ARIMA)

Forecasting is the process of estimation in unknown situations from the historical data. For example, forecasting weather, stock index values, commodity prices etc. Time-series forecasting provides a method to forecast future price levels using the historical price series of the commodities in question; here oil. In statistics, ARIMA models, sometimes called Box–Jenkins models after the iterative Box–Jenkins methodology usually used to estimate them, are typically applied to time-series data for forecasting.

Given a time series of data $X_{t-1}, X_{t-2}, \ldots X_2, X_1$, the ARIMA model is a tool for understanding and, perhaps, predicting future values in this series. The model consists of three parts, an autoregressive (AR) part, a moving-average (MA) part and the differencing part. The model is usually then referred to as the ARIMA(p, d, q) model where p is the order of the autoregressive part, d is the order of differencing and q is the order of the moving-average part.

If $d = 0$, the model becomes ARMA, which is a linear stationary model. ARIMA (i.e. $d > 0$) is a linear nonstationary model. If the underlying time series is nonstationary, taking the difference of the series with itself d times makes it stationary, and then ARMA is applied onto the differenced series.

The ARIMA(p, d, g) model is given by:

$$\varphi \nabla^d X_t = \theta \epsilon_t \tag{10.7}$$

where the AR part is

$$\varphi = 1 - \sum_{i=1}^{p} \varphi_i L^i$$

and the MA part is

$$\theta = 1 + \sum_{j=1}^{q} \theta_j L^j$$

And the I (difference) part is

$$\nabla = (1 - L^1)$$

Here L is a lag operator, that is, $L^i X_t = X_{t-i}$. φ_i and θ_j are the model parameters which need to be found before applying the model for forecasting. ε_t is a white-noise process with zero mean and variance σ^2.

φ_i are the parameters of the autoregressive part of the model, θ_j are the parameters of the moving-average part and the ε_t are error terms. The error terms ε_t are generally assumed to be independent, identically distributed variables sampled from a normal distribution with zero mean.

10.2.3 Support-Vector Machine (SVM) and Support-Vector Regression (SVR)

SVM and SVR are a set of related supervised learning methods used for classification and regression, respectively. They belong to a family of generalized linear classifiers. A special property of SVMs is that they simultaneously minimize the empirical classification error and maximize the geometric margin; hence they are also known as maximum margin classifiers. SVMs follow the "structured risk-management" (SRM) principle.

Linear separating functions, however, generalized with an error-minimization rate are not suitable for real-world applications. The idea of the "support-vector machine" (SVM) is to map the input vectors into a *feature space* with a higher number of dimensions, and to find an optimal separating hyperplane in the feature space. For example, points in a two-dimensional space $(x_1, x_2) \in R^2$ may be mapped into the 5-dimensional plane$(x_1, x_2, x_1x_2, x_1^2, x_2^2) \in R^5$; a separating hyperplane in this larger space will correspond to a conic separator in R^2 (see Figure 10.1).

A kernel is used to construct a mapping into high-dimensional feature space by the use of reproducing kernels. The idea of the kernel function is to enable operations to be performed in the input space rather than the potentially high-dimensional feature space. Hence, the inner product does not need to be evaluated in the feature space. This provides a way of addressing the curse of dimensionality. However, the computation is still critically dependent upon the number of training patterns and to provide a good data distribution for a high-dimensional problem will generally require a large training set.

The kernel function $K\langle .,. \rangle$ is a convolution of the canonical inner product in the feature space. Common kernels for use in an SVM are the following:

(1) **Dot product**: $K(x, y) = x.y$; in this case no mapping is performed, and only the optimal separating hyperplane is calculated.
(2) **Polynomial functions**: $K(x, y) = (x.y+1)^d$, where the *degree d* is given.

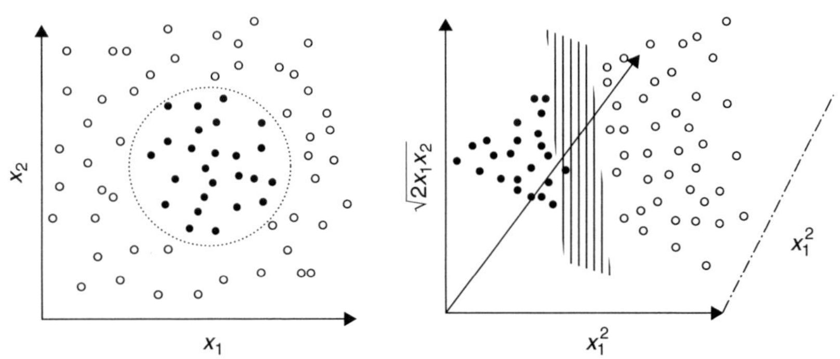

Figure 10.1 Separating the hyperplane in a higher dimension

(3) **Radial-basis functions** (RBFs): $K(x,y) = e^{-\gamma\|x-y\|^2}$ with parameter γ.
(4) **Sigmoid (or neural) kernel**: $K(x,y) = \tanh\,(ax.y + b)$ with parameters a and b.
(5) **ANOVA kernel:** $K(x,y) = (\sum_{i=1}^{n} e^{-\gamma(x_i - y_i)})^d$, with parameters γ and d.

Due to prior work with an emphasis on "radial-basis functions"' kernels, it is used in the current study for prediction.

SVM for regression

The basic idea Suppose we are given training data $\{(x_1,y_1),\ldots,(x_l,y_l)\} \subset X \times R$ where X denotes the space of input patterns (e.g. $X = R^d$). In $\varepsilon - SV$ regression, our goal is to find a function $f(x)$ such that it has at most ε deviation from the actually obtained targets y_i for all the training data and at the same time is as flat as possible. In other words, we do not care about errors as long as they are less than ε, but will not accept any deviation larger than this. We begin by describing the case of linear functions f taking the form

$$f(x) = \langle w, x\rangle + b \text{ with } w \in X, b \in R \tag{10.1}$$

where $\langle .,. \rangle$ denotes the dot product in X. "Flatness" in this case (10.1) means that one seeks a small lw. One way to ensure this is to minimize the norm, that is, $||w||^2 = \langle w, w\rangle$. We can write this problem as a convex optimization problem:

$$\text{Minimize } \frac{1}{2}||w||^2$$

$$\text{Subject to } \begin{cases} y_i - \langle w, x_i\rangle - b \le \varepsilon \\ \langle w, x_i\rangle + b - y_i \le \varepsilon \end{cases} \tag{10.2}$$

Here, the assumption is that such a function f actually exists that approximates all pairs $(x_{i,}y_i)$ with ε precision, or in other words, a convex optimization problem is really possible. Sometimes, however, this may not be the case or we also may want to allow for some errors. This can be achieved via introducing slack variables ξ_i, ξ_i^* to cope with the otherwise infeasible constraints of the optimization problem. Vapnik provided the following formulation:

$$\text{Minimize } \frac{1}{2}\|w\|^2 + C\sum_{i=1}^{\ell}(\xi_i + \xi_i^*)$$

$$\text{Subject to } \begin{cases} y_i - \langle w, x_i \rangle - b \le \varepsilon + \xi_i \\ \langle w, x_i \rangle + b - y_i \le \varepsilon + \xi_i^* \\ \xi_i, \xi_i^* \ge 0 \end{cases} \quad (10.3)$$

The constant $C > 0$ determines the trade-off between the flatness of f and the degree to which deviations larger than ε are tolerated. This corresponds to dealing with a so-called ε-sensitive loss function $|\xi|_\varepsilon$ described by

$$|\xi|_\varepsilon := \begin{cases} 0 & \textit{if } |\xi| \le \varepsilon \\ |\xi| - \varepsilon & \textit{otherwise} \end{cases} \quad (10.4)$$

It turns out that in most cases the optimization problem can be solved more easily in its "dual formulation." The dual formulation provides the key for extending the SVM to nonlinear functions.

The dual problem Now the Lagrange function is constructed from the objective function and the corresponding constraints. It can be shown that this function has a saddle point with respect to the primal and dual variables at the solution.

$$\begin{aligned} L := \frac{1}{2}||w||^2 + C\sum_{i=1}^{\ell}(\xi_i + \xi_i^*) - \sum_{i=1}^{\ell}(\eta_i\xi_i + \eta_i^*\xi_i^*) \\ - \sum_{i=1}^{\ell}\alpha_i(\varepsilon + \xi_i - y_i + \langle w, x_i \rangle + b) \\ - \sum_{i=1}^{\ell}\alpha_i^*(\varepsilon + \xi_i^* + y_i - \langle w, x_i \rangle - b) \end{aligned} \quad (10.5)$$

Here L is the Lagrangian and $\eta_i, \eta_i^*, \alpha_i, \alpha_i^*$ are Lagrange multipliers. Hence, the dual variables in (10.5) have to satisfy positive constraints

$$\alpha_i^{(*)}, \eta_i^{(*)} \ge 0 \quad (10.6)$$

Note that by $\alpha_i^{(*)}$, we refer to α_i and α_i^*.

The Saddle point condition: partial derivatives L with respect to primal variables (w, b, ξ_i, ξ_i^*) have to vanish for optimality.

$$\partial_b L = \sum_{i=1}^{\ell} (\alpha_i^* - \alpha_i) = 0 \tag{10.7}$$

$$\partial_w L = w - \sum_{i=1}^{\ell} (\alpha_i - \alpha_i^*) x_i = 0 \tag{10.8}$$

$$\partial_{\xi_i^{(*)}} L = C - \alpha_i^{(*)} - \eta_i^{(*)} = 0 \tag{10.9}$$

The dual optimization problem reduces to

$$maximize \begin{cases} -\frac{1}{2} \sum_{i,j=1}^{\ell} (\alpha_i - \alpha_i^*)(\alpha_j - \alpha_j^*) \langle x_i, x_j \rangle \\ -\varepsilon \sum_{i=1}^{\ell} (\alpha_i + \alpha_i^*) + \sum_{i=1}^{\ell} y_i (\alpha_i - \alpha_i^*) \end{cases} \tag{10.10}$$

$$subject\ to \sum_{i=1}^{\ell} (\alpha_i - \alpha_i^*) = 0 \ and\ \alpha_i - \alpha_i^* \in [0, C]$$

In deriving (10.10), we already eliminated the dual variables η_i, η_i^* through condition (10.9) which can be reformulated as $\eta_i^{(*)} = C - \alpha_i^{(*)}$.

Equation (10.8) can be rewritten as follows:

$$w = \sum_{i=1}^{\ell} (\alpha_i - \alpha_i^*) x_i, \ thus\ f(x) = \sum_{i=1}^{\ell} (\alpha_i - \alpha_i^*) \langle x_i, x \rangle + b \tag{10.11}$$

This is support-vector expansion, that is, w can be completely described by a linear combination of the training patterns x_i. In a sense, the complexity of a function's representation by SVs is independent of the dimensionality of the input space X and depends only on the number of SVs.

10.3 Data and methodology

The current work analyses both the risk of oil prices and then attempts to forecast them. The data used is a 15-year sample taken from October 21, 1994–October 10, 2009 of daily closing spot prices of WTI. We use the new model developed by Engle and Manganelli (2004), CAViaR, which uses quantile regression, and employ it as a means to model the value-at-risk of the WTI oil-price return series. ARIMA and support-vector regression techniques are also utilized and compared for the purposes of forecasting of oil prices. We make use of percentage daily returns calculated in logarithms, which also makes the time-series stationary for forecasting methods.

10.3.1 Risk analysis

We apply the four CAViaR methods to WTI spot-price data. We use three window sizes to estimate the model: (1) 3000 daily observations with 2500 in-sample observations and 500 out-of-sample observations, (2) 2000 daily observations with 1600 in-sample observations and 400 out-of-sample observations, and (3) 1000 daily observations with 700 in-sample observations and 300 out-of-sample observations. We estimate 1 percent CAViaR using the model – the obvious choice of 1 percent for VaR comes from the current industry standards.

Engle and Manganelli (2004) discuss the appropriate specifications for testing these time-series models based on quantile regressions. They derive both in-sample tests and out-of-sample tests. These essentially feature measuring the proportion of hits of the limiting VaR and having them equal to the target fraction with no correlation with their own lagged values, no autocorrelation in the hits and the correct fraction of exceptions. They explain that the in-sample test, or DQ test, is a specification test for the particular CAViaR process under study and it can be very useful for model-selection purposes. They suggest the parallel DQ out-of-sample tests could be used by regulators to check that the VaR estimates submitted by a financial institution satisfy some basic model-specification requirements such as unbiasedness, independent hits and independence of the quantile estimates. We utilize their tests and Matlab code in this chapter. (We are thankful to Simone Manganelli for making available his MATLAB code for the exercise.)

10.3.2 Forecasting

We analyze two different forecasting techniques, ARIMA and support-vector regression to forecast the oil prices. The logarithm percentage daily returns are used for forecasting as it makes the time-series stationary, which is nonstationary otherwise. The time series is tested for presence of unit roots using the "augmented Dickey–Fuller" (ADF) test.

We use the last 1000 observations in the data set for prediction purposes with 990 observations for building the model (in both ARIMA and SVR) and 10 for testing purposes. The two models are compared based on the errors of prediction given by the root mean square error and mean error. The lower the error the better the prediction technique is.

GRETL, an open-source software package is used for the ARIMA analysis. The ARIMA model is identified based on the significance of coefficients based on the *t*-statistics. WEKA java-based machine-learning software, which uses LIBSVM wrapper class is used for support-vector regression prediction.

SVR forecasting involves the following steps:

(1) Data sampling. We use WTI daily spot-price data for this research.
(2) Data preprocessing. The collected oil-price data may need to be transformed into certain appropriate ranges for the network learning by logarithmic transformation, difference or other methods. Here a logarithmic return series is used. Then the data should be divided into in-sample data and out-of-sample data. We use the first 990 observations (in-sample) for training the SVR model and the other 10 observations (out-of-sample) for testing the built model.
(3) Training and learning. The SVM architecture and parameters are determined in this step by the training results. There are no criteria in deciding the parameters other than by a trial-and-error basis. In this investigation, the RBF kernel is used because the RBF kernel tends to give good performance under general smoothness assumptions. Consequently, it is especially useful if no additional knowledge of the data is available. Finally, a satisfactory SVM-based model for oil-price forecasting is reached.
(4) The parameters of SVR are tuned using the trial-and-error method. The parameters are tuned based on the error received from the forecasting results. We use the last 2 days' returns as predictor variables.
(5) Future price forecasting.

Both the methods are used to forecast the next 10-day's returns and then are analyzed based on the root mean square error received.

10.4 Analysis of results

10.4.1 CAViaR risk results

Table 10.1 gives the results obtained by using 1000 time-series returns of WTI spot prices, with 700 in-sample and 300 out-of-sample observations. DQ test results show that while the value-at-risk is significant for the in-sample period for the symmetric absolute value (SAV), asymmetric slope (AS), and adaptive model, it is insignificant for the indirect GARCH model. On the other hand, the indirect GARCH model gives

Table 10.1 Estimates for four CAViaR specifications with 1000 return series

	SAV	AS	Indirect GARCH	ADAPTIVE
Beta1	2.8165	2.3795	0.3201	−0.0878
Std Errors	1.94	2.0784	0.607	0.1393
p-Values	0.0733	0.1261	0.299	0.2641
Beta2	0.32	0.3957	0.9444	0
Std Errors	0.4209	0.4483	0.0297	0
p-Values	0.2235	0.1888	0	0
Beta3	0.3354	0.2994	0.2795	0
Std Errors	0.1465	0.1572	0.2836	0
p-Values	0.011	0.0284	0.1621	0
Beta4	0	0.2576	0	0
Std Errors	0	0.1668	0	0
p-Values	0	0.0613	0	0
RQ	35.6822	35.1623	35.9985	37.4356
Hits in-sample (%)	0.7143	1.1429	0.8571	0.7143
Hits out-of-sample (%)	8	7.6667	0.6667	42
DQ In-sample (p-value)	0.9995	0.9915	0.0051	0.9996
DQ Out-of-sample (p-value)	0	0	0.9985	0

significant out-of-sample results when the rest of the models fail. Refer also to Figure 10.2.

Table 10.2 gives the results from the last 2000 return series from the experiments' sample data with 1600 in-sample and 400 out-of-sample observations. The results here change with sample size – it is evident from the DQ test results that now all the four models are significant for in-sample results. The out-of-sample results show that none of the models are significant. This shows that the results from the caviar model do change with sample size. (See Figure 10.3.)

Finally, Table 10.3 gives the results when we increase the sample size further by 1000 observations. Here, the in-sample size is 2500 and the out-of-sample size is 500, which matches the out-of-sample size used in the original study by Engle and Manganelli (2004). The oil-price CAViaR predictions show here that the first three models are efficient for both in-sample and out-of-sample observations while, with this sample size, the adaptive model fails to give significant results.

The results here show that with an increase in in-sample size the first three models become more relevant than the adaptive model. (See Figure 10.4.)

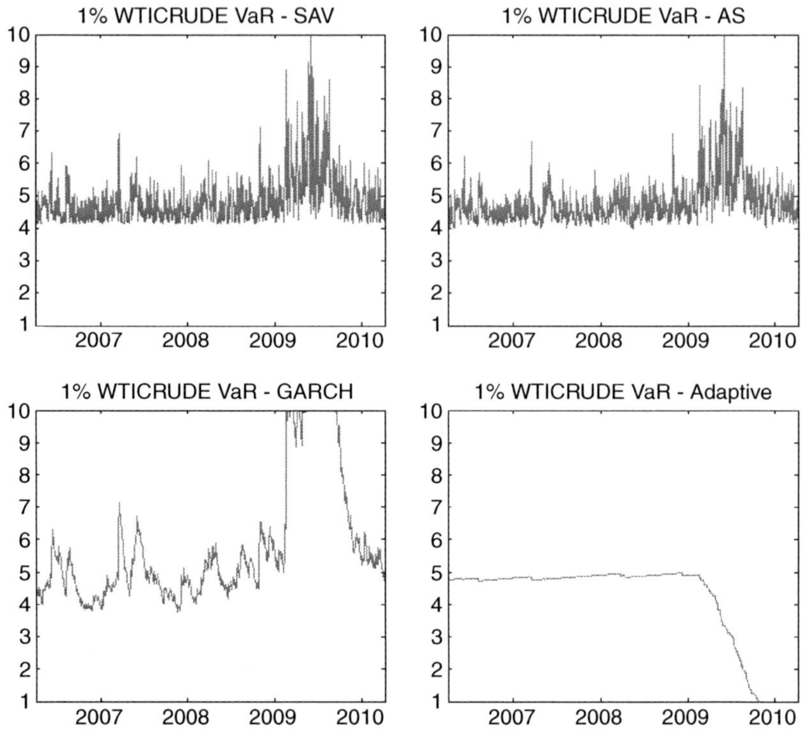

Figure 10.2 Estimated 1 % CAViaR graph for sample 1

10.4.2 Forecasting result analysis

For oil-price prediction using ARIMA and SVR we use the last 1000 WTI logarithmic return series. The series itself is not stationary and gives a unit root when tested with an augmented Dickey–Fuller (ADF) test with a constant. The return series is use, which is useful as it makes the sample time-series stationary and hence it can be used for prediction.

ARIMA forecasting result analysis

Based on the significance of factor coefficients, ARIMA(2,0,2), ARIMA(3,0,2) and ARIMA(2,0,3) models are identified. No differencing of the series is needed as we are using the return series which is stationary. We will forecast the time series using all the three models identified and will choose the one having minimum "root mean square error" (RMSE).

Table 10.4 gives the error obtained from forecasting using the three ARIMA models. ARIMA(3,0,2) gives the minimum error and hence it is

Table 10.2 Estimates for four CAViaR specifications with 2000 return series

	SAV	AS	Indirect GARCH	ADAPTIVE
Beta1	6.3503	7.139	0.0622	0.3498
Std Errors	1.7954	1.8129	0.252	0.2684
p-Values	0.0002	0	0.4025	0.0962
Beta2	−0.3402	−0.4942	0.9816	0
Std Errors	0.3565	0.3403	0.0101	0
p-Values	0.17	0.0732	0	0
Beta3	0.3621	0.341	0.1055	0
Std Errors	0.0846	0.115	0.0908	0
p-Values	0	0.0015	0.1228	0
Beta4	0	0.2654	0	0
Std Errors	0	0.1048	0	0
p-Values	0	0.0057	0	0
RQ	102.1509	102.1364	102.7917	104.9777
Hits in-sample (%)	0.9375	1	1.0625	0.75
Hits out-of-sample (%)	7	7.25	1.75	3.75
DQ In-sample (p-value)	0.9793	0.9759	0.4681	0.1265
DQ Out-of-sample (p-value)	0	0	0.0002	0

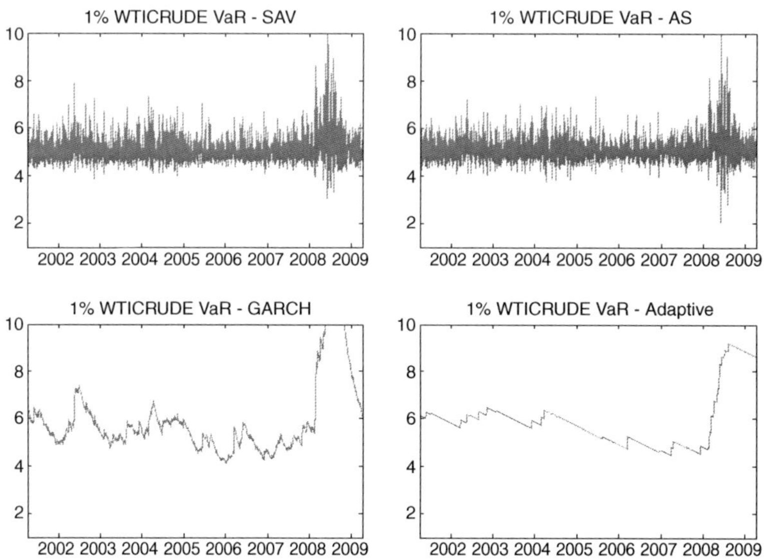

Figure 10.3 Estimated 1 % CAViaR graph for sample 2

Table 10.3 Estimates for four caviar specifications with 3000 return series

	SAV	AS	Indirect GARCH	ADAPTIVE
Beta1	1.5846	1.1258	6.914	0.5981
Std Errors	1.0244	0.6523	5.9457	0.2411
p-Values	0.0609	0.0422	0.1224	0.0065
Beta2	0.6348	0.6622	0.6611	0
Std Errors	0.1976	0.1226	0.1721	0
p-Values	0.0007	0	0.0001	0
Beta3	0.5567	0.6642	1.3579	0
Std Errors	0.1602	0.1161	1.5042	0
p-Values	0.0003	0	0.1833	0
Beta4	0	0.5028	0	0
Std Errors	0	0.1283	0	0
p-Values	0	0	0	0
RQ	212.4748	212.3826	213.6665	220.4636
Hits in-sample (%)	1.08	1.04	1.04	0.72
Hits out-of-sample (%)	1	0.8	0.8	2.2
DQ In-sample (p-value)	0.9044	0.9361	0.9184	0.0493
DQ Out-of-sample (p-value)	0.9943	0.9955	0.9798	0

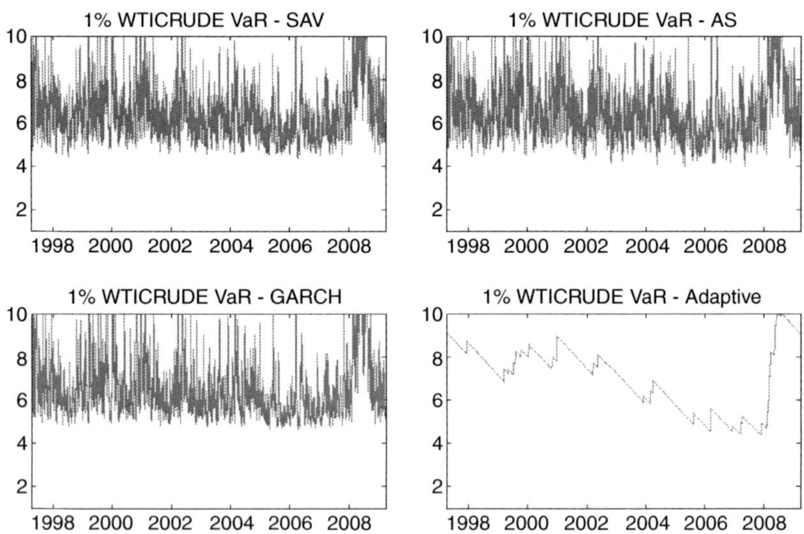

Figure 10.4 Estimated 1 % CAViaR graph for sample 3

Table 10.4 Errors for ARIMA models

Model	Root mean square error
ARIMA(2,0,2)	1.5653
ARIMA(3,0,2)	1.5427
ARIMA(2,0,3)	1.557

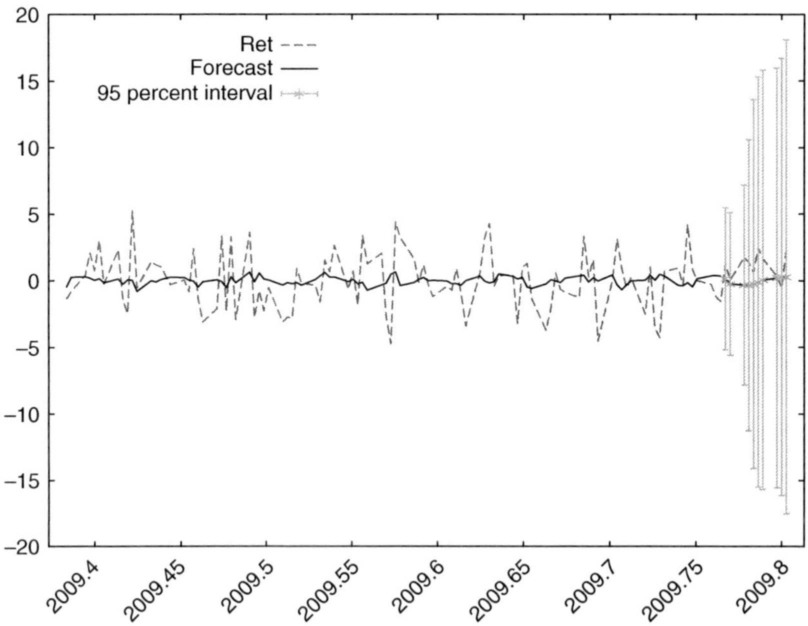

Figure 10.5 Graph for actual and forecasted return series

used for the prediction of the remaining 10 observations after building the model on the first 990 observations.

Figure 10.5 shows the forecasting results using the ARIMA(3,0,2) model. The forecast here is a conditional mean forecast as the technique uses the "ordinary least squares" (OLS) regression method.

Table 10.5 gives the rest of the prediction statistics for the model.

Support-vector regression-based forecasting

The main issue in time-series forecasting using SVR is the tuning of parameters. Though more computationally intensive methods like grid

Table 10.5 Prediction statistics for ARIMA model

Mean error	1.1701
Mean squared error	2.3799
Root mean squared error	1.5427
Mean absolute error	1.3319
Mean percentage error	170.35
Mean absolute percentage error	140.15
Theil's U	1.2044
Bias proportion, UM	0.57532
Regression proportion, UR	0.0452
Disturbance proportion, UD	0.37948

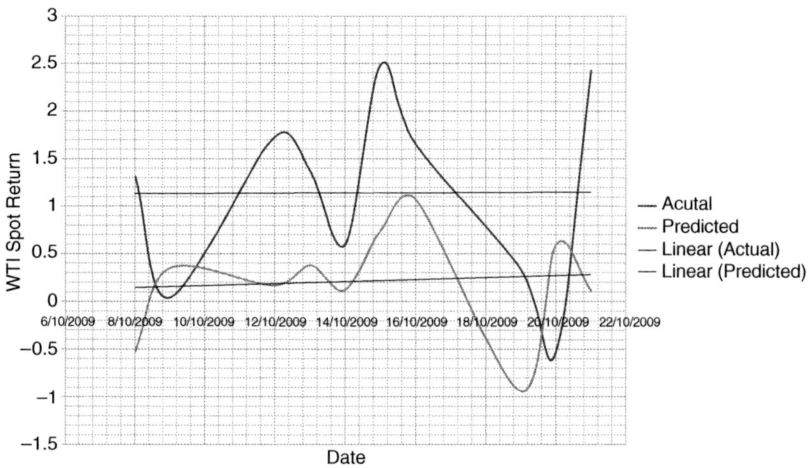

Figure 10.6 Graph for actual and predicted returns obtained from SVR

search are available, we decided to use a trial-and-error approach for tuning the parameters to save computational time and complexity. We tune the first parameter C, the cost using the module "CV ParameterSelection." The parameter is tested between $1000 < C < 2000$ with 10 steps; this gives an efficient value of 1500. Finally we tune the other two parameters, gamma γ and epsilon ϵ using trial-and-error. The final values used for the parameters after trial-and-error optimization (based on minimum RMSE) are, C = 1500, gamma = 0.333 and epsilon = 0.0001. The choice of lagged predictor variables here is the last two days' returns. This choice can be further tested by widening the window size.

Table 10.6 SVR forecasting statistics

Correlation coefficient	0.2062
Root mean squared error	1.3658
Mean absolute error	1.2194
Relative absolute error	97.7989 %
Root relative squared error	91.8446 %
Total number of instances	10

Figure 10.6 shows the graph for actual and predicted out-of-sample values. This shows that even if the values are not so efficiently predicted they follow the trend better than the trend followed by the ARIMA model. Table 10.6 gives the prediction test statistics; the value of RMSE clearly indicates the efficiency of SVR over the ARIMA model. The current model is tuned with a trial-and-error approach, which is more likely to reduce the error when tuned using more computationally intensive search algorithms.

10.5 Conclusion

In this work, we applied a new quantile-regression approach to modelling VaR ("value-at-risk"); CAViaR on WTI spot-price returns. The analysis shows that the proposed VaR risk-modeling technique though efficient, is dependent on the sample size. There is further scope for improving the technique and testing via other sample sizes, thus facilitating a comparative analysis. This research also focused on the prediction of WTI price levels and presented a comparative analysis of two methods, ARIMA, a widely used method based on lag and momentum effects and support-vector regression, a more efficient machine-learning approach. The results obtained clearly indicate that SVR is more efficient in predicting the future price levels. The current work can be extended by using more sophisticated optimization routines for tuning the parameters of SVR and also by changing the frequency of data used.

This research work also made use of open-source software platforms for the forecasting analysis, which are highly capable for financial econometrics and machine-learning projects and can be further used by researchers and practitioners to analyze market scenarios and financial time series.

References

Abramson, B. and Finizza, A. (1995) "Probabilistic Forecasts from Probabilistic Models: A Case Study in the Oil Market," *International Journal of Forecasting*, 11 (1): 63–72.

Allen, D.E. and Singh, A.K. (2010) "Caviar and The Australia Stock Markets: An Appetiser," Working Paper Series, School of Finance, Economics and Accounting, Edith Cowan University, Perth, Australia.

Allen, D.E., McAleer, M. and Scarth, M. (2008) "Realised Volatility Uncertainty," Working Paper, 0807, School of Finance, Economics and Accounting, Edith Cowan University, Perth, Australia.

Burges, C.J.C. (1998) "A Tutorial on Support Vector Machines for Pattern Recognition," *Data Mining and Knowledge Discovery*, 2 (2): 121–167.

Cabedo, J.D. and Moya, I. (2003) "Estimating Oil Price Value-at-Risk using the Historical Simulation Approach," *Energy Economics*, 25 (3): 239–253.

Engle, R.F. (2002) "New Frontiers in ARCH Models," *Journal of Applied Economitrics*: 425–446.

Engle, R.F. and Manganelli, S. (2004) "CAViaR: Conditional Autoregressive Value at Risk by Regression Quantiles," *Journal of Business & Economics Statistics*, 22 (4): 367–381.

Huang, W., Nakamori, Y. and Wang, S.Y. (2005) "Forecasting Stock Market Movement Direction with Support Vector Machine," *Computers & Operations Research*, 32 (10): 2513–2522.

Koenker, R.W. (2005) *Quantile Regression*, Econometric Society Monograph, Cambridge University Press.

Koenker, R.W. and Bassett, G. (1978) "Regression Quantiles, Econometrica," *Economic Society*, 46 (1): 33–50.

Muller, K.R., Smola, J.A. and Scholkopf, B. (1997) "Prediction Lime Series with Support Vector Machines," Proceedings of In|ternational Conference on Artificial Neural Networks. Lausanne: 999–1004.

Nelson, Y., Stoner, S.G., Gcmis, H. and Nix, D. (1994) "Results of Delphi VIII Survey of Oil Price Forecasts," *Energy Report*, California Energy Commission.

Panas, E. and Ninni, V. (2000) "Are Oil Markets Chaotic? A Non-Linear Dynamic Analysis," *Energy Economics*, 22 (5): 549–568.

Sauter, R. and Awerbuch, S. (2002) "Oil Price Volatility and Economic Activity: A Survey and Literature Review," IEA Research Paper, International Energy Agency, Paris.

Schwert, G.W. (1988) "Business Cycles, Financial Crises and Stock Volatility," University of Rochester, Business, Papers 88–06.

Taylor, S. (1986) *Modelling Financial Time Series*, New York: Wiley.

Vapnik, V.N. (1995) *The Nature of Statistical Learning Theory*, New York: Springer.

Index